AND THE HILLS SHOUTED FOR JOY

The Day Israel Was Born

by

Bernard Postal and Henry W. Levy

DAVID McKAY COMPANY, Inc.

New York

To Marge and Mildred

Without whose sympathetic understanding
and
cooperation this book would not
have been possible

SECOND PRINTING, FEBRUARY 1973

LIBRARY OF CONGRESS CATALOG CARD NUMBER: 72-86963
MANUFACTURED IN THE UNITED STATES OF AMERICA

15 באפת 1948.

AND THE HILLS
SHOUTED FOR JOY

FOREWORD

THE PROLOGUE to the epochal drama of Israel's Declaration of Statehood was played out on a world stage during the first thirteen days of
May, 1948. It was a fortnight fraught with international intrigue, subtle
diplomatic threats, wild rumors, dire warnings of invasion, bloodshed,
stunning military surprises, jittery indecision, and firm resolve.

The Jews in Palestine were dug in, determined to go ahead with the
Declaration regardless of military risks and the inevitable world political
repercussions. After thirty years of Mandatory rule Great Britain was
completing her evacuation of the Holy Land, leaving the country in chaos,
hoping that in the end she would be asked to stay on. Because of differences between the State Department and President Harry S Truman,
United States policy vacillated and was at times incomprehensible. The
Russians, with their anti-British stand, were enigmatic as always but a
source of great hope to the Jews. The Arabs of Palestine tightened their
noose around Jerusalem and its environs, retreated in disarray elsewhere
in the country, and banked on the military might of the Arab states to
thwart Jewish statehood and the orders of the United Nations. At the
United Nations the endless torrent of talk and doubletalk continued to
confuse matters while delaying compromises were being hatched behind
closed doors. American Jewry, in the van of the political struggle for the
Jewish state, frantically stepped up its battle for American support of the
Zionist cause.

Newspapers throughout the world that went to press on the night of
May 13, as Britain's thirty-year Mandate over Palestine drew to a close,
reflected in their news and editorial columns the indecisions, doubts, con-
troversies, and threats that confronted the thirty-seven-man National

Council of the Jews of Palestine as it completed plans to meet on Friday, May 14, in the Tel Aviv Museum to proclaim a Jewish state. Despite secrecy about the place, and no final approval of the text of the proposed Proclamation until the last minute, there was a widespread feeling that a Jewish state was on the verge of being proclaimed.

The *Palestine Post* of Friday, May 14, reveals both the uncertainties of the day and of the future in these front-page headlines: "BRITAIN PLEADS FOR ARAB-JEWISH COMPROMISE AS MANDATE IS GIVEN UP"—"U.S. STILL SEEKS TO POSTPONE PARTITION" —"AGENCY REJECTS U.S. RESOLUTION"—"KFAR ETZION EVACUATED BY ITS DEFENDERS"—"JAFFA SIGNS SURREN-DER TERMS"—"MANDATE WOUND UP TODAY"—"SIR ALAN TAKES LEAVE OF PALESTINE"—"VACUUM MUST BE FILLED"—"TRUSTEE PLAN APPROVED."

The final last-minute brief bulletin was headlined "JEWISH STATE BEGINS TODAY."

This was the background for the air of expectancy that pervaded Jewish communities throughout the world as the sun rose on Friday, May 14, 1948. It was to be a day of tense, suspenseful, heroic, and fast-moving but uncertain drama. It was a day Jews had dreamed of each time they gave voice to the age-old prayer, "Next Year in Jerusalem."

It was 1878 years since the Jews had had a state of their own. It was just a little over half a century since Dr. Theodor Herzl, founder of modern political Zionism, had prophetically written in his diary a few days after the first World Zionist Congress had met in 1897: "At Basle, I founded the Jewish State. If I said it today, it would be greeted with laughter, but in five years, perhaps, and certainly in fifty, everybody will see it."

It was just a little more than thirty years after the foundation for the Jewish State had been laid with the promulgation of the Balfour Declaration in 1917. In this document Great Britain had pledged that it would "view with favor the establishment in Palestine of a national home for the Jewish people," the first recognition by a major power of the Zionist concept.

It was not quite twenty-six years since the League of Nations Mandate for Palestine had made Great Britain responsible for "placing the country under such political, administrative and economic conditions as will secure the establishment of the Jewish national home."

And it was less than six months since November 29, 1947, when the General Assembly of the United Nations had adopted the resolution approving the majority report of the United Nations Special Committee on Palestine (UNSCOP) that called for the termination of the Mandate and the partition of Palestine into sovereign Jewish and Arab states.

It was the day Israel was born.

A NOTE ON SOURCES,
AND ACKNOWLEDGMENTS

DURING THE FIVE YEARS of research for this book, we read thousands of pages of documents, records, minutes, letters, diaries, and reports (public and confidential), interviewed or corresponded with more than eight hundred individuals—Jews and non-Jews—in Israel, the United States, Canada, Europe, and South Africa, pored through nearly two hundred books, and examined scores of newspaper files here and abroad.

Nevertheless, this book could not have been written without the immeasurable volume of helpfulness freely and cheerfully given by an immense number of people. Among them were some of the leading participants as well as minor actors in the drama this book recreates, newspapermen who covered some aspect of this story, government officials, diplomats, Zionist leaders of all countries and parties, rabbis, communal leaders, social workers, archivists, librarians, and a host of others.

A remarkable number of these people gave us far more than we had anticipated, often opening new lines of inquiry and leading us to unsuspected sources of information. The elementary facts about the day Israel was born were fairly well known, but in our search for the stories and people behind the headlines we found enthusiastic helpers.

Some contributed flashes of insight. Some provided illuminating anecdotes. Some gave us personal recollections. Some came up with invaluable sidelights and footnotes. Some even became voluntary researchers and a number translated material from the Hebrew. Some patiently tracked down the answers to troubling questions, while others checked the veracity of reported incidents. Collectively, this small army of colleagues—

friends and strangers alike—enabled us to piece together what really happened on the day Israel was born.

The names of many of those to whom we are so greatly indebted for so much are here recorded. To them and to the larger number whose names it has not been possible to list, we say, *"Todah rabah"*—"Thanks a million"—for their assistance, which, whatever its dimension, contributed in some way toward the making of this book. There are a few, however, whom we must single out because of their major contributions.

Of the Israelis, we are particularly grateful to Julian Meltzer, veteran journalist and author, who for the past twenty-four years has been associated with the Weizmann Institute and who is now Executive Vice-Chairman of Yad Chaim Weizmann and Director of its Archives and Managing Editor of the Letters and Papers. His incomparable familiarity with sources, his tireless checking to confirm or refute what we had otherwise uncovered, and his first-hand knowledge of people, places, and events were always at our disposal. His generosity of time and effort, including a reading of our manuscript, saved us from many errors of omission and commission and his many suggestions and advice were of inestimable value.

Among other Israelis on whom we leaned were the late Leo Heiman, the late Ben Oyserman, Eliezer Whartman, and, of course, Zeev Sharef, the Secretary of the provisional government, whose book *Three Days* was a basic reference. Leo Heiman is responsible for many of the personal recollections developed in interviews with Israelis. Before he was tragically killed while covering the Six-Day War as a newsreel cameraman, Ben Oyserman shared with us many sidelights of the last days of the Mandate. A few years ago, in collaboration with Justin Turner of Los Angeles, Whartman interviewed a large number of the actual signers of the Proclamation.

To Mr. Turner and Mr. Whartman we are deeply appreciative for permission to peruse this material. Other Americans were equally helpful. The late Dr. Joseph B. Schechtman, Zionist leader as well as author, editor, and historian, made available to us much documentary material that he had assembled for his various projects. Mrs. Sylvia Landress, Director of the Zionist Archives and Library in New York, with her encyclopedic memory and her knowledge of the whereabouts and sources of Zionist history, was a veritable goldmine of information; her helpfulness surpassed any call of duty. Henry Montor and Rusty Jarcho were our first-hand sources for the material on the "Sonneborn Institute."

We are indebted to former Secretary of Defense Clark Clifford, who served as an advisor to President Truman, for opening his personal files to us; and to Dr. Emanuel Neumann, dean of American Zionists, who for many years was a member of the Jewish Agency Executive and the most intimate associate of the late Rabbi Abba Hillel Silver. Dr. Nahum Goldmann, for many years President of the World Zionist Organization, and Meyer W. Weisgal, intimate friend and biographer of Dr. Chaim Weizmann, favored us with invaluable personal and unpublished recollections. Judge Samuel Rosenman, David Ginsburg, Harry Zinder, Dr. Josef Cohn, Mrs. Ernest Peiser, Mrs. Herman Rosenberg, and Paul Rosenberg helped us uncover little-known aspects of the story that we set out to tell.

We are indebted as well to many of the members of the staffs of the Israel Embassy in Washington, the Israel Consulate in New York, and Information Officers of the government of Israel, in Jerusalem and Tel Aviv, for their cooperation and helpfulness. We owe thanks also to the Information Offices of the United Nations in New York, to the Harry S Truman Library in Independence, Missouri and the Library of the American Jewish Committee. The files of the *New York Times,* the New York *Herald Tribune,* the Jewish Telegraphic Agency, and the *Jerusalem Post* were a constant help.

We want to express our gratitude to James O'Shea Wade, Vice-President and Editorial Director of the David McKay Co., for his patience and many helpful suggestions; and to Rachel Whitebook, who did the final editing of the manuscript.

In the preparation of our illustrations and the reproduction of photographs from sometimes very poor copies we were favored with the dedicated assistance of Heinz Weissenstein of Whitestone Studios in New York.

No authors can happily prepare a manuscript for publication without the assistance and cooperation of secretarial help. We have been fortunate in and very thankful for that given us by Henrietta Levick, Charlotte Marchuck, and Martha Amlauer.

Among other Americans who have given us help in one way or another are: Elie Abel, Dr. Selig Adler, Harry Alderman, American Veterans of Israel, Moshe Avital, Jacques Back, Ruby Barnett, Judge Harry Batshaw, Judge David L. Bazelon, Elihu Bergman, Ted Berkman, Victor Bernstein, Victor Bienstock, Kenneth Bilby, Maurice Bisgyer, Julius Bisno, Eugene Bloch, Sam Bloch, Albert W. Bloom, Rabbi Eugene B. Borowitz, Maurice Boukstein, The Boston Public Library, Josephy Brainin, Mrs. Barnett R. Brickner, British Information Services, Philip C. Brooks.

And Rabbi Samuel M. Burstein, Joseph Cummins, Clifton Daniel, Carter Davidson, Benjamin E. De Ray, Irving Dickman, William S. Dix, John Donovan, Dr. Abraham G. Duker, Ben Dunkelman, Julius C. C. Edelstein, Ben Epstein, Moses Eskolsky, Rabbi Leon I. Feuer, Bernard Figler, Monroe Fine, Dr. Louis Finkelstein, Jack Fishbein, Mendel Fisher, Arnold Forster, Farnsworth Fowle, Gerold Frank, Joseph N. Frank, M. Z. Frank, Mrs. Felix N. Frankfurter, Leo Frisch, Judy Gable, Ben Gallob, Dr. Abraham P. Gannes, Rabbi Irving Ganz, Lionel Gelber.

And Rabbi Roland B. Gittelsohn, Bert Gold, Miss Hannah Goldberg, Capt. Harold J. Goldfarb, Ralph Goldman, Paul Gould, A. J. Granoff, Dr. Solomon Grayzel, Harold Greenberg, Dr. Simon Greenberg, Hank Greenspun, Johnathan Grober, Reuben Gross, Philip S. Gutride, Nahum Guttman, Dr. William Haber, Rose Halprin, Thomas J. Hamilton, Isadore Hamlin, Ralph Hamovich, Rabbi Abraham L. Hartstein, Sam Hartstein, Saul Hayes, Yehuda Hellman, Louis Heren, Judith Herschkopf, Rabbi Nathan Hershfield, Gertrude Hirschler, Minna Hoffenstein, Arthur D. Holtzman, David Horowitz, Julian N. Jablin, Monte Jacobs, Rabbi Robert P. Jacobs, Rabbi Alfred Jospe, Samuel Kadison, Rabbi Benjamin M. Kahn, Rabbi Harry Kaplan, Dr. Louis L. Kaplan, Bernard S. Karmatz, Murray Kass, Herbert Katski.

And I. L. Kenen, Rabbi Abraham J. Klausner, Rabbi Bert A. Klein, Rabbi Edward E. Klein, Rabbi Simcha Kling, Hillel Kook, Louis Kraft, Mrs. Siegfried Kramarsky, Gen. Melvin L. Krulewitch, Philip D. Lagerquist, Morris Laub, Hal Lehrman, Rabbi Arthur J. Lelyveld, Dr. Emil Lehman, Harry Levin, William Levine, Rabbi Albert L. Lewis, Dr. David Lieber, Rabbi Oscar M. Lifshutz, Rabbi Eugene J. Lipman, Eleazar Lipsky, Ralph L. Lowenstein, Jesse Lurie, John Luter, Frank Mankiewicz, Daniel Mann, Harold Manson, Dr. Jacob R. Marcus, Dr. Sidney Marks, Joseph Meyerhoff, James McGunigal, Rabbi Elihu Michelson.

And Rabbi Israel Miller, Jacques Minkus, Robert R. Nathan, Dr. Allan Nevins, David S. Noyes, Paul O'Dwyer, Dr. Raphael Patai, Rabbi Albert Plotkin, Col. S. J. Pomrenze, Zelda Popkin, Joseph M. Proskauer, Sid Rabinovich, Freda Ramm, Irving G. Rhodes, Mrs. Adolph C. Robison, David Rome, Alan H. Rose, Adolph Rosenberg, Sidney Rosenfeld, Clare Salkind, Maurice Samuel, Rachel Schechtman, Daniel Schorr, Dr. Joseph J. Schwartz, Leo Schwarz, Clarence Seid, Leo Shapiro, Monroe Sheinberg, Robert Shosteck, Rabbi Daniel Jeremy Silver, Mrs. Rose Singer, Leonard Slater, Philip Slomovitz.

And Boris Smolar, Rudolf G. Sonneborn, Moshe Starkman, Miss Hannah Stein, Harry Steinberg, Meyer Steinglass, Henry B. Stern, Morris

Strauss, Irving Spiegel, Marie Syrkin, Harry N. Tarlin, Frieda Taub, Judd Teller, Esther Togman, Jacques Torczyner, Harry S Truman, Mrs. Justin G. Turner, Rabbi Herbert Weiner, Dr. Harold Weisberg, Joseph G. Weisberg, Eugene Weissbluth, Dr. Emil Weitz, Arthur Weyne, Rabbi Gershon Winer, Mary Wisotsky, Mrs. Marjorie Wyler, Richard Yaffe, Rebecca Zapinsky, S. J. Zacks, Nathan Ziprin, and Murray Zuckoff.

From Israel we received cooperation from the following: Dr. Benjamin Akzin, Carl Alpert, Dr. A. Alsberg, Dr. M. Altbauer, David L. Andor, Tuvia Arazi, Moshe Aumann, Molly Bar-David, Judith Beilin, Dr. Alex Bein, David Ben-Gurion, Zvi Berinson, Werner Braun, Moshe Brilliant, Simcha Dinitz, Arieh Dissentchik, Ya'acov Dori, Fay Doron.

And Abba Eban, Shulamith Eisner, Elihu Elath, Simon Eliav, Walter Eytan, A. Frenkel, Rabbi Israel Goldstein, Moshe Goodman, Paul Gould, Moshe Gurary, David HaCohen, Adina Haran, Avraham Harman, Lucien Harris, Dr. M. Hesky, Lt. Col. Elchanan Ishai, Shelomo Kaddar, Matiyahu Kalir, Eli Kaminer, A. Kaplan, Jon Kimche.

And Teddy Kollek, Joseph Kopilov, Dan Leon, Yitzhuk Leor, Meyer Levin, Arthur Lourie, Jonathan Magnes, U. Mane, Miss Violet Menachem, Dr. Meron Medzini, Shulamit Nardi, Hugh Orgel, Erika Oyserman, Gabriel Padon, Moshe Pearlman, Lionel Peytan, Olga Rachmilevitch, Aharon Remez, David Rivlin, Gershon Rivlin, Shabtai Rozenne, Viscount Edwin Samuel, Ashev Schwartz, Haim Schachter, Shlomo Shafir, Eiga Shapiro, Israel Shapiro, President Zalman Shazar, Sigla Stern, Paula Van Gelder, Chaim Vinitsky, Weizmann National Memorial, Geoffrey Wigoder, Raphael Rothstein, Dr. Emanuel Rackman, L. F. Rushbrook-Williams.

Among those from other parts of the world to whom we are indebted are the late Dr. Konrad Adenauer, Melvin Durden, Samuel Goldsmith, Lionel Hodes, Institute of Contemporary History, Dr. S. Levenberg, Dr. George J. Liban, Joseph I. Linton, *London Jewish Chronicle,* Dr. Judah J. Slotki, P. Vainik.

We wish to acknowledge our thanks to those who, in the broadest sense, have been our collaborators. However, we must absolve all of our many friends and helpers for such errors as we may have made, or such judgments as we have reached. There were many cases when we had to choose between two points of view or, in some instances, varying reports on the same subject made by the same people at different times. When in doubt on major matters, we have generally presented the varying opinions that we uncovered. For the most part we leaned toward the acceptance of immediate first-hand recollections, rather than on viewpoints or opinions later developed.

With this in mind, as Israel prepares to celebrate its twenty-fifth anniversary, we give you *And the Hills Shouted for Joy: The Day Israel Was Born.*

HENRY W. LEVY and BERNARD POSTAL

CONTENTS

"For ye shall go out with joy, and be led forth with peace; the mountains and the hills shall break forth before you into singing, and all the trees of the field shall clap their hands."
—ISAIAH LV:12.

Part One

THE BRITISH ERA

chapter

∘ ∘ ∘ ∘ ∘ ∘ ∘ ∘ ∘ ∘ ∘ ∘ ∘ 1 ∘ ∘ ∘ ∘ ∘ ∘ ∘ ∘ ∘ ∘ ∘ ∘ ∘

THE BRITISH
LEAVE JERUSALEM

BRITISH RULE in Palestine ended symbolically where it had begun—in Jerusalem, an ancient city long sacred to three great religions. As the sun came over the storied hills of the city, at 5:05 A.M. on Friday, May 14, 1948, less than nineteen hours remained before the legal termination of the Palestine Mandate that twenty-six years earlier had been awarded to Great Britain by the League of Nations.

No trumpets heralded Britain's last day of power in the Holy Land as she prepared to surrender the responsibility assumed with imperial confidence in 1918, when Gen. Edmund H. H. Allenby's legions ended Turkey's four-hundred-year rule of the Middle East. No thunderbolts lit up the skies as portents of the rebirth of the ancient nation that would replace the British before another sunrise.

Only the occasional pop of sniper fire and the thud of Arab mortar shells being lobbed into the Jewish quarter of the Old City and into the laboriously built New City punctuated the final hours of one epoch and the dawn of the new. The odor of cordite filled the air. Tree branches stripped of foliage by shell blasts stretched skyward as if pleading for the preservation of the city of peace, which had been under siege for so many weeks.

May 14 gave promise of being hot and muggy. A tense but artificial calm pervaded the city. Every darkened wall and corner hid armed men, Jews and Arabs. They were waiting for the signal that the British had left before beginning a frantic scramble to occupy strategic buildings and key strong points, possession of which would determine the fate of the New City.

The symbol of British authority was the High Commissioner for Palestine. An appointee of the Colonial Office in London, General Sir Alan Gordon Cunningham also had the unenviable responsibility of carrying out orders of the Foreign Office and the War Office. Until the High Commissioner actually vacated his official residence at Government House in Jerusalem, no one could say for sure that the British would really leave.

Britain's decision to leave Palestine had first been announced to the United Nations on September 26, 1947, by Arthur Creech-Jones, the Colonial Secretary. A Foreign Office spokesman ominously predicted that chaos and bloodshed were bound to follow. This was twenty-five days after the publication on September 1 of the report of the United Nations Special Committee on Palestine (UNSCOP). Termination of the British Mandate, the partition of Palestine into sovereign Jewish and Arab states by September, 1949, and the internationalization of Jerusalem were the key recommendations of the majority report UNSCOP submitted to the United Nations General Assembly.

With the United Nations still debating the report, the High Commissioner for Palestine offered a little doubletalk at a press conference at Government House on October 8 after his return from London. "I think it is essential that the people of this country should realize that withdrawal is really meant," he said. "It is essential that they should see what the effect of it will mean." He warned that it was "physically possible for Britain to go, leaving nothing to replace her in Palestine," but only at "the expense of misery, distress, and chaos."

A few days later, at separate meetings, General Cunningham expressed to both David Ben-Gurion and a spokesman for the Arab Higher Committee his surprise that neither Jews nor Arabs were taking seriously the British announcement of imminent withdrawal. At the end of October, Sir Henry Gurney, chief secretary of the Palestine government, confided to a Jewish friend that the British were prepared to stay if the Jews asked for their help. But to get that help, they would have to abandon plans for a Jewish state and agree to some form of continued British control.

By November 29, 1947, when the United Nations adopted the UNSCOP majority report, the British had managed to convince everyone that their departure would lead to chaos, and they proceeded to do their best to make it so. Jewish and Arab suspicions that the British were not serious about leaving were strengthened by the deliberate policy of chaos encouraged by His Majesty's Government between December, 1947, and May, 1948.

On December 4 London told the world that she would surrender the Mandate over Palestine at midnight, May 15, 1948. Evacuation of all British forces from the country was promised by August 15. The High Commissioner for Palestine made an official announcement of the impending withdrawal to Jewish representatives in Jerusalem three days later, on December 7. He stated that the government wanted to evacuate as soon as possible and desired the departure to be as smooth, quiet, and rapid as possible. "You already know," he said, "that the Army intends to leave by August 1, and if possible sooner."

On the basis of these statements the Jews of Palestine had decided as early as March, 1948, to proclaim a Jewish state on May 16 in that portion of Palestine assigned to them by the United Nations.

On May 12, the last official communiqué from the office of the chief secretary of the Palestine government revealed that the British departure was being advanced by twenty-four hours. Bulletin No. 156 announced that the Mandate would lapse after midnight May 14, but that the High Commissioner would leave Jerusalem on the morning of that day. The announcement also said that on or before the expiration of the Mandate all British forces would be transferred to Haifa from Jerusalem and elsewhere in Palestine. Final evacuation from Haifa was scheduled for June 30. Between the moment the Mandate expired and the complete pullout Gen. G. H. A. Macmillan, Commander of the British forces in Palestine, would assume powers equivalent to those vested in the commander of troops on occupied foreign territory in order to protect his lines of withdrawal and communications.

Suspicious of this new timetable, the Jewish shadow government in Tel Aviv hastily revised its own schedule. Instead of waiting to proclaim Jewish independence on May 16, as they had been planning to do for months, they decided to act eight hours before the Mandate would expire, at 4 P.M. on May 14.

Two considerations dictated this choice of time. One was the determination to have a legal Jewish government in existence when the Mandate ended in order to avoid a vacuum in authority. The other was the desire not to launch the Jewish state by desecrating the Jewish Sabbath. If independence was proclaimed after the Mandate terminated at midnight, May 14, it would have been Saturday, May 15.

The exact hour and details of the High Commissioner's departure

from Jerusalem were given to local and foreign newsmen at a final briefing by Richard Stubbs, government press officer, at the Public Information office in the David Building on the morning of May 13. Ben Oyserman, British Paramount News cameraman—who would be killed while
covering the Six-Day War of 1967—was told to be at Government
House early on May 14 because a seat had been reserved for him on the
plane that would take the High Commissioner to Haifa. Oyserman would
be the only outsider aboard.

When the sun climbed over the Mount of Olives and Mount Scopus
on May 14, Harry Levin, nighttime announcer for "The Voice of the Defender," the Haganah's secret radio station in Jerusalem, a senior officer at
the Jewish National Fund office, and free-lance correspondent for a British newspaper, left his microphone and wrote in his diary: "For the moment time hangs suspended. Any minute it may break into violent action.
Soon I shall go to the roof opposite. Perhaps from there I can see the
High Commissioner leave." Levin possessed one of the few pairs of binoculars that had not been turned in when the Haganah ordered the surrender of every object of any conceivable military use.

The foreign press corps and local Jewish and Arab newspapermen on
their way to cover the ceremonial departure of His Majesty's representative in Palestine were watching when at 6:51 A.M. two British Army
sergeants climbed to the roof of the King David Hotel, headquarters of
the Palestine military authorities. Slowly they lowered the Union Jack.
Waiting to hand up the Red Cross banner was Jacques Reynier, International Red Cross representative.

The barbed-wire fences enclosing the British security zones were still
up. Behind them, soldiers and civilian officials in the cantonment huts
with corrugated iron roofs were emptying makeshift laundry lines, hastily
packing and tossing trunks, valises, and cartons into waiting trucks.

Early in 1948 the British command had created fortified buffers between Jewish and Arab quarters by pulling its troops and the remaining
civilian officials into three enclaves in the heart of the New City. Each
compound was surrounded by fences taller than a man. They were protected by concrete guard posts, wire entanglements, sandbags, patrolling
tanks, and tank traps. Heavily armed sentries guarded every entrance to
the three zones, which had become virtually self-imposed British ghettos.
No one moved in or out without a careful check of credentials.

Best known of the three security zones was "Bevingrad," so called by
the Jews in ironic reference to the hated British Foreign Secretary, Ernest
Bevin. Inside "Bevingrad" were the main headquarters of the British
Criminal Investigation Police, which had directed the searches for secret

Jewish arms caches; also the Municipal Building, the Supreme Court, the General Post Office, the Bank Leumi, the Generali Building, and the Russian Compound, which included the Russian Cathedral.

En route to Government House from his apartment on Jaffa Road, Oyserman encountered raggedly dressed youths with guns slung over their shoulders and older citizens carrying spades. They were heading home from the nightwatch or from a stint of digging trenches. Going the other way, he saw lines of thirteen- and fourteen-year-olds marching toward the southern outskirts of the city to help build defensive emplacements.

The red-bereted British trooper, who recognized Oyserman as he approached the heavily guarded British security zone, checked the cameraman's press card only casually. He raised the barrier with a good-natured warning to "keep your head near the wall; you'll get your block shot off otherwise." On the other side, Oyserman met the Agence-France Presse correspondent who the day before had promised him a lift to Government House. As he left the British security zones and drove through the Arab areas beyond, Oyserman paled at the sight of heavily armed Arab guards.

At Allenby Barracks on the Bethlehem Road, Oyserman, weighted down with a heavy cartridge belt in which the compartment intended for bullets was crammed with films and accessories, photographed scores of British tanks lined up along the road, ready for departure. There were also Bren carriers and army trucks, with soldiers already seated and anxious to go, waiting only the order for the withdrawal to begin. At the gateway to Government House, Oyserman and the French correspondent were challenged and then passed through by the sentry who said, "Great day, gentlemen. Hope you make it in time. Thank God we're getting out of here. Couldn't stand another day of it."

Government House perched on the crest of a gray hilltop of the Talpiot Ridge overlooking the Bethlehem Road on the southern rim of the city. The imposing square white stone building, surrounded by well-kept gardens and trees, was almost palatial in its dimensions and appointments. The thirty-two-acre compound had been completed in March, 1931, when British domination of the Middle East was unchallenged. From this commanding and strategically located eminence the High Commissioner had a matchless view of the gray-walled Old City looking toward the Mount of Olives, on which the first Government House had been located. (After 1948 Government House became UN headquarters in a no-man's land between Israel and Jordan. Jordanian troops attacked the compound during the Six-Day War, but they were driven out and it is now in Israel territory.)

Jews generally referred to the hill as Abu-Tor, the name of the Arab village that hugged the foot of the hill along the Bethlehem Road. Abu-Tor ("Father of the Ox" in Arabic) was the nickname of one of the favorite lieutenants of Saladin, who captured Jerusalem from the Crusaders in the twelfth century. The Arabs called the hill Mount Mokkabar.

The site of Government House has long been known in Christian tradition as "the Hill of Evil Counsel," so named because the residence of Joseph Caiaphas, high priest of the Jews at the time of Jesus' death, is supposed to have been somewhere on this hill. Caiaphas became the villain of the New Testament account of the crucifixion.

Later, when the Jews bitterly protested and resisted the orders that emanated from Government House, they often recalled the bitter observation of the British author John Marlowe that "the spirit of this hill seems to have brooded over the British adventure in Palestine. At the beginning, the attempt to use Zionism as an instrument of British counsel was prompted by evil counsel. At the end, the attempt to use Arab nationalism as an instrument of British policy was equally prompted by evil counsel."

The Union Jack was still flying over Government House when Oyserman arrived shortly after 7 A.M. A BBC radio team had already set up its equipment in the driveway. More than a score of foreign correspondents and other newsmen, together with several photographers, were on hand to witness and record the final descent of the British flag.

At the head of a long line of cars parked in the driveway stood the High Commissioner's black Rolls-Royce. At the entrance there was much coming and going. High-ranking officers mingled with civilian officials, laughing and joking. On the parade ground an honor guard of fifty men of the Highland Light Infantry stood at ease. In front of them was a solitary bagpiper. Off to the side a small military band waited.

Precisely at 8 A.M. a tall, erect but tired-looking officer in the full-dress uniform of a British general came through the covered portico of Government House, flanked by a small entourage of officers and civilians. This was sixty-one-year-old General Sir Alan Gordon Cunningham, seventh and last British High Commissioner for Palestine. He had occupied this political and military hotspot since the end of World War II, after a distinguished career with the British Eighth Army.

As he passed through the honor guard the drums beat a tattoo and the bagpiper skirled the mournful "Highland Lament." Then the Union Jack began its slow descent as all stood at attention, watching the beginning of the British withdrawal and the last hours of British rule in the Holy Land. Sir Alan's face was white and drawn as he saluted the flag. He was obviously overwhelmed by emotion. Retreat is always distasteful to a military man, but on this hot May morning Sir Alan had been given the unenviable duty of winding up a historic failure, the result of policies he and his predecessors had carried out on the orders of politicians in London.

After reviewing the guard of Highlanders and shaking hands with the civilian officials, he never looked back to see the Red Cross emblem climbing the flagstaff of Government House. As he walked briskly to his bulletproof limousine, the Highlanders dipped their flags to the ground and the band began playing "God Save the King."

It was 8:15 A.M., Oyserman recalled, when the High Commissioner's Rolls-Royce pulled away from the grounds of Government House, trailed by a line of other official cars. At Allenby Barracks it was joined by a convoy of 250 tanks, gun carriers, and Army trucks filled with the remnants of rear-echelon forces. The bulk of the British Army units around Jerusalem had pulled out before May 1.

The convoy formed two columns. One threaded its way from the Bethlehem Road along the tortuous narrow streets overlooking the Old City, down into the military zone, where additional units fell into line. Moving slowly into the New City and through the Sheikh Jarrah quarter, near the American Colony and St. George's Anglican Cathedral areas, it headed northward toward Ramallah. There it swung southwest to the Latrun Monastery crossroads toward the main highway from Jerusalem to Jaffa. This first column then took the coastal road through Ramleh and Lod to Hadera and Haifa. A second column of similar size and makeup moved southward through Bethlehem. It made its way past the ruins of the Etzion bloc of Jewish settlements, which only hours before had surrendered to the Arab Legion, through Hebron and across the desert to Rafa and the Palestine-Egyptian frontier.

As if from nowhere the residents of Jerusalem came from all corners of the city to witness the unbelievable—the withdrawal of His Majesty's Forces. Paced by the High Commissioner's car, the northbound convoy bypassed the King David Hotel and the towered YMCA as it wound its way up and down St. Paul's Road, a narrow and steep street still in Jewish hands leading from the old central business district past monasteries and ancient walls toward the Damascus Gate. Both sides of the street were lined with silent people watching the procession as it departed, unhonored and unsung. Many of the British forces sympathized with the Jews and admired their courage. Quite a number of them stayed on to fight with the Israelis, some because they had Jewish wives or Jewish girlfriends, others because they had fallen in love with the country or because their religious convictions swayed them to side with the people of the Bible. A handful of Tommies deserted the convoy as it passed through the Jewish quarters and then tried to join the Jewish forces. Three are known to have been accepted by an Irgun unit. One stole a tank from the convoy and handed it over to the Irgun. Others less daring contented themselves with throwing packs of food and candy and cigarettes to Jews along the evacuation route.

Heavily armed Arab legionnaires stood atop the Old City walls as the convoy lumbered through the Damascus Gate. It was completely transformed. Gone were the donkeys, camels, and Arab vendors. In their places were large forces of Arabs, many armed, among them villagers from the surrounding Arab settlements. Filling the square, they stared silently at the spectacle of British withdrawal. They had expected this to be the signal for their onslaught on the Jewish-held quarters. As the tail of the convoy rounded a bend—bypassing Mount Scopus and the Hebrew University, a Jewish island in an Arab sea—the Arabs surged into the road.

In the heart of Jewish Jerusalem crowds also watched silently as the convoy moved along King George V Avenue, named for the monarch whose Foreign Secretary had issued the Balfour Declaration. They were finally convinced that the British were going. Soon the convoy passed the last Jewish outposts, the settlements of Ataroth and Neve Yaacov, both completely encircled by Arab forces. Its defenders, many of them boys, viewed the convoy as the end of one era, the beginning of a new one. They had little chance to withstand the coming Arab attack and were under orders to vacate. By nightfall they would be heading over the hills to the more protected Jewish sections of the city.

Three Spitfires, circling over the convoy, were seen shortly after 8:30 A.M. by the residents of Romema, a Jewish suburb of Jerusalem on the road to Tel Aviv. For weeks the people of Romema had been under siege, spending their nights in makeshift shelters and coming out in the daylight to prepare food under Arab sniper fire in smokeless cookers made of pipe and twigs. Mrs. Borya Cymberg and her two school-age daughters had passed some of the time choosing a name for the baby expected by a woman next door. Borya Cymberg, an engineer who spent his nights on Haganah duty, returned a little before 9 A.M. with news of the British pullout, as his wife was mopping the floor of their apartment with the morning's dishwater.

At the entrance to Romema stood a monument commemorating the British conquest of Jerusalem in 1917. The stone memorial bears this inscription: "Near this spot the Holy City surrendered to the 60th London Division, December, 1917. Erected by their comrades to those officers, NCOs, and men who fell in the fighting for Jerusalem."

The lead cars left the northbound convoy at Kalandia Airport, a tiny airstrip (it was greatly expanded from 1949 to 1967 during the Jordanian occupation of the Old City, and now it has been enlarged as the Jerusalem Airport), where two military planes were revving up. A score of reporters was already waiting, most of them having come by Arab taxis and private cars. Oyserman brought up the rear of the convoy in an Arab taxi that he shared with the BBC radio crew. Not a single representative of the Arab or Jewish communities was there to bid Cunningham farewell. They had also ignored the ceremonies at Government House.

At the edge of the airfield the cars stopped. Cunningham stepped out of his limousine, exchanged a few words and handshakes with the British officials who had accompanied him from Government House, and then quickly boarded a Royal Air Force DC-3 at the controls of which was the commander of the Royal Air Force units in Palestine. Oyserman was so busy filming the departure that he was almost left behind. Only a last-minute rush enabled him to reach the top steps of the gangway and squeeze through the closing hatch.

General Cunningham seated himself next to a window on the left of the plane, which was facing due north. Oyserman sat down right behind him. Not a word was exchanged in the plane as it taxied and took off for Haifa. Sir Alan kept looking out of the window and was heard to murmur, "How can they divide this land?" No one knew what was really on his mind as he left the Holy City and England's sacred trust. And to this day he has publicly declined to talk about the evacuation.

c h a p t e r

o o o o o o o o o o o o $\boxed{2}$ o o o o o o o o o o o

DEPARTURE FROM HAIFA

IT WAS 9:02 A.M. by the watch of a waiting newspaperman when the
RAF plane rolled to a stop at Haifa's seaside airstrip on May 14 after the
short hop from Jerusalem. The first to deplane was General Cunningham.
He saluted the select fifty-man company of Palestine police assigned to
guard and welcome him and then strode briskly to a waiting car. Before
getting in, he shook hands and chatted briefly with Shabtai Levi, the Jewish Mayor of Haifa, and his Arab deputy, Haj Taher Karaman. This was
Cunningham's only face-to-face farewell with Jewish and Arab leaders.
Ten minutes later he was on his way to Haifa port for the last official act
of British dominion over Palestine.

Almost at the same moment, forty-four miles to the south in Tel Aviv,
four of the men who had helped hasten the High Commissioner's exodus
were poring over a typewritten Hebrew document in an inconspicuous
house on Keren Kayemet Boulevard. It was the final draft of the Israel
Declaration of Independence, revised the night before by the owner of the
house, David Ben-Gurion. Checking it with him for the last time, before
its scheduled adoption later that afternoon, were Rabbi Yehuda Leib Ha
Cohen Fishman (Maimon), Moshe Shertok (Sharett),* and Aharon Zisling. All four would be among its signers.

---

* After the birth of the state many Israelis Hebraized their names. Golda Myerson
became Golda Meir, Moshe Shertok became Moshe Sharett, Rabbi Fishman became Maimon, etc. As this book deals largely with the pre-state era, we have generally used the original names and given the new name in parenthesis—e.g., Moshe
Shertok (Sharett). The principal exception to this is in references to later events
with which the new name is definitely associated.

From the airport, which had just been handed over to Haganah by the British, Cunningham was driven swiftly to Haifa Harbor in a convoy, protected front and rear by armored cars and motorcycles carrying armed men. Bren-gun teams manned rooftops along the way, which lay mainly through the abandoned Arab quarters. The residents had fled a few weeks earlier when the Jews captured the city. Along the almost deserted streets every corner was patrolled by British troopers. Neither cheers nor jeers was heard.

From the harbor gates to the docks the convoy moved between lines of Tiger and Sherman tanks, their turret guns ready for action. At dockside spit-and-polish lines of Grenadier Guards and Royal Marines in blue stood waiting. On hand to greet Cunningham was Gen. G. H. A. Macmillan. The two generals reviewed the troops and stood at attention as the band of Irish Grenadier Guards struck up "God Save the King."

Off to the side some three hundred Jews—burly stevedores, employees from nearby offices and factories, and hooky-playing children—looked on in silence. They knew what had happened so many times on that same dock after the British White Paper of 1939 had nailed down the escape hatches from Hitler Europe. For thousands of Jews who had tried desperately to reach Palestine in an odyssey of unseaworthy vessels the Haifa dock had been a tantalizing glimpse of the forbidden shores of the Promised Land.

Intercepted by British naval patrols in Palestinian waters, the refugee ships had been towed into Haifa Harbor, where their unhappy, often emaciated passengers were dumped on the dock before being herded into prison ships and hauled off to detention camps on Cyprus. On the very dock from which Cunningham was getting ready to leave crowds of weeping relatives and friends, pressing against military barriers at the port, had seen their kinsmen turned back. One of those illegal ships, the *Af Al Pi* ("In Spite Of"), is still perched on a low cliff at the southern entrance of the harbor as a permanent memorial to the saga of the immigrant ships.

At 10:15 A.M. Cunningham shook hands with the commanders of the guards of honor and walked slowly toward the steps of the dock. Before starting down, he turned and ceremoniously saluted the Union Jack flying from the Port Authority building. Standing with his back to the water, Cunningham almost fell into the harbor. Only the quick action of a nearby officer, who caught him by the arm, saved him.

"Good going-away weather," the General said, as he was piped aboard a Royal Navy launch by a bagpiper skirling the melancholy, strangely inappropriate strains of "The Minstrel Boy." As the launch pulled away amid the slap of hands on rifle butts, the hollow explosions and puffs of smoke from a salute fired by a destroyer drifted into shore. This time a lookout on the destroyer had made sure it was Cunningham on his way —an hour earlier the same destroyer firing a twenty-one-gun salute had mistakenly taken another launch, carrying a group of reporters, for the one that was to ferry Cunningham.

The launch headed for the aircraft carrier HMS *Ocean*, flagship of Vice-Admiral Sir Thomas Trowbridge, commander of the flotilla sent to escort Cunningham from Palestine. He remained aboard HMS *Ocean* as Admiral Trowbridge's guest until a little after 10 P.M. Then another launch took him to the 5450-ton cruiser, HMS *Euryalus,* which had been riding at anchor all day in Haifa Bay.

At 11:30 P.M. Capt. Cecil Campbell received a message on the *Euryalus* that it was time to sail for Malta. A few minutes later the little fleet began moving out of Haifa Bay, HMS *Ocean* leading the way, followed by the *Euryalus* and a screen of destroyers and frigates. At the edge of Palestinian waters the flotilla's searchlights were trained on the flagship on whose flight deck stood a naval guard of honor. As HMS *Euryalus* moved slowly past HMS *Ocean,* Cunningham took the last salute and watched his flag unfurled from the cruiser's masthead. A band played "Auld Lang Syne" and "God Save the King" as the cruiser steamed out to sea under a cone of white light from the searchlights of her destroyer escorts.

At exactly midnight HMS *Euryalus* passed the three-mile limit of Palestinian waters and a single flare shot up from the Royal Navy headquarters atop Mount Carmel. It arched slowly and then fell flaming among the tall dark cypresses on the mountain slopes, a portent that the British Mandate over Palestine was dead and a beacon welcoming the birth of the State of Israel.

After HMS *Euryalus* had disappeared over the Mediterranean horizon, British authority in Palestine was confined to a tiny enclave in Haifa port and the military and naval encampments on Mount Carmel. The only representative of civilian British rule was C. H. A. Marriott, who became British Consul-General in Haifa in the early hours of May 15. On orders from London, which still did not want to recognize the new provisional Israel government officially, he addressed messages by wire and mail "to the Jewish authorities at Tel Aviv." All were returned unopened. This nonrecognition was in line with the tradition of Great Britain's often unrealistic, indecisive, and blundering policy in dealing with the Jewish community in Palestine.

In preparation for their leaving the British were under orders to destroy all equipment they could not load aboard the evacuation fleet that clogged Haifa Harbor. In the afternoon, at about the time that the Israel Declaration of Independence was being proclaimed in Tel Aviv, three Sherman tanks were scheduled to be pushed off the peak of Mount Carmel into a ravine 870 feet below. But agents of Rehesh, Haganah's secret arms-procurement section, had picked out the best-looking tank and boldly bribed its driver and the officer in charge to turn it over to them. Pinhas Vasa, former Rehesh chief, saw the officer sign a document saying that the three tanks had been destroyed in his presence. Only two ended up in the ravine, while the third was loaded on a Haganah truck at dusk and driven toward Athlit Junction, which had already been occupied by Jewish troops. By dawn on May 15 the first tank to be acquired by the Jewish state had reached Haganah's ordnance base outside Tel Aviv.

To avoid possible clashes with Jews, the British had imposed a 6 P.M. curfew on May 14 for their troops and police in Haifa. But Jews and British appeared to be unusually friendly. Some Haganah men surrounded British privates and insisted on being photographed with them. The celebrating in Haifa started immediately after midnight. Once the Israeli flag was raised over the British district commissioner's office in solemn ceremonies, the city took on a carnival atmosphere. The market square was packed with a singing and dancing crowd of nearly 8000. A band and several companies of Haganah soldiers paraded. At street corners uniformed soldiers hawked subscriptions for Israel's first war loan. Loudspeakers blared mobilization orders as truckloads of men rode off to battle the invading Arab armies.

The last British forces left Palestine on June 30 in nine troop ships that sailed from Haifa. Moving down from the top of Mount Carmel, 5000 men came through Hadar Carmel to the business area in the lower town and thence to the docks. They were protected by Royal Marine commandos with orders to shoot to kill if they met interference. Yigal Sonenshine, later an Israeli paratrooper, remembers himself as a five-and-a-half-year-old boy standing near his father's store on the Kingsway (now called Ha-Atzmaut—Independence Avenue), watching the Army trucks unload red-bereted soldiers who raced up the gangplanks of the waiting transports. Some of them were assigned to bunks in the same steel cages on the decks of a ship named *Ocean Vigour* in which illegal Jewish immigrants had been transported to Cyprus. The evacuation fleet was escorted by an aircraft carrier, a cruiser, and four destroyers, all with guns unlimbered for action, while a squadron of Spitfires patrolled the sky. Every half hour depth charges were exploded in the harbor to discourage saboteurs from attaching limpet mines to the ships' hulls.

As the troop transports hoisted anchor the Union Jack was swiftly hauled down for the last time in Palestine. Since May 15 it had been flying beside the blue and white Israeli flag from the flagpole on the roof of the Haifa Port Authority building.

The Union Jack had been unfurled to the Palestine skies under vastly different circumstances in 1917, when Britain was conquering the Holy Land. The British War Cabinet had asked Gen. Edmund H. H. Allenby to give Jerusalem to the Allies as a Christmas present. He was two weeks ahead of schedule when the Turks surrendered Jerusalem on December 9, putting the Holy City in Christian hands for the first time in seven hundred years.

Two days later—on the second day of Hanukkah—Allenby dismounted from his horse outside the city walls, and at the head of a troop of cavalry walked bareheaded and solemn through the Jaffa Gate to accept the key to Jerusalem. A cheering, tearful, joyous crowd watched as dignitaries of all faiths extended an official welcome to the city's deliverer. After acknowledging the multilingual greeting, Allenby read a brief proclamation that promised freedom of religion to all inhabitants under the British flag.

Although tidings of the Balfour Declaration had created jubilation in the Jewish community, Allenby's singular failure to mention it in his address was a shock. His ominous silence, and the subsequent hostility of his military regime, turned out to be the first indication of Britain's backing away from the promise of 1917. The retreat commenced with the separation of Transjordan in 1921, gained momentum with the series of white papers that hacked away at the letter and spirit of the Mandate, and assumed major proportions during and after World War II.

THE PLAN FOR EVACUATION

"Operation Deluge" was the code name the British gave their plan for liquidating the Mandate and evacuating Palestine. The Jews called it "Operation Chaos" because it was devised to create confusion and prevent an orderly transfer of power. Even pro-British observers could find no justification other than "mischievous incompetence" and "embittered cussedness" for the chaotic liquidation policy that hindered the Jews and aided the Arabs.

Active steps toward evacuation began in December, 1947, when the first troops and military equipment were moved out to Cyprus, Malta, and Egypt, followed by the departure of several RAF squadrons. Early in January 700 dependents of civilian officials left for Cyprus after the heads of all government departments were instructed to wind up their work and be ready to go on a month's notice. Half the government agencies were virtually immobilized by February 1. As one public service after another shut down government offices were moved from the center of Jerusalem to makeshift quarters in the cantonment of tin-roofed huts in the British security zones.

On February 22 the British Treasury announced that Palestine had been removed from the sterling bloc and that its balances in London of £100 million (Palestine) were blocked. This left Palestine Jews, with savings in government bonds and postal savings certificates, with their assets frozen in London. When the Mandatory's tax-collecting machinery ground to a halt, Jews and Arabs stopped paying taxes. The government's assets, which had reached over £11 million in the quarter ending December, 1947, shrank rapidly. Nevertheless, it made a last-minute grant to the Moslem religious funds administered by the Arab Higher Committee. Using taxes paid by the Jews, the last government budget charged £2 million for the maintenance of the Cyprus camps housing Jewish deportees from Palestine.

Sale of through tickets to neighboring countries was halted by the Palestine Railways on February 26, after which internal travel by rail was also discontinued. In March all British shipping lines were ordered to avoid any Palestine port. New or renewed licenses for the import of goods to Palestine, including newspapers, books, building materials, and agricultural machinery, were denied.

Families of British civilian employees of the Palestine government were told to leave by mid-March unless they were prepared to sail on uncomfortable military transports. As a result many officials quit ahead of schedule, preferring to accompany their wives and children aboard fruit vessels plying between Haifa and England.

Among those who left was Edwin Samuel, son of the first High Commissioner, who had served in the Palestine government since 1917, when he arrived as a young artillery subaltern with General Allenby's forces. In the closing years of the Mandate he had to walk a tightrope to remain loyal to His Majesty's Government while retaining the confidence of the Jewish community. Before he left his last post as director of broadcasting, he received a high British decoration. At almost the same time he was being consulted by the Jewish Agency on the administrative structure of the projected Jewish state.

As the British officials disappeared their Jewish and Arab deputies

who took over became increasingly suspicious of each other. Daily, on arriving at their offices, they searched each other for weapons. Jews in the
civil service had been instructed by the Jewish Agency to show up for
work daily despite the disintegration around them. Almost all of them
were secretly members of Haganah who took orders from the shadow
Jewish government. Later they came over en masse to the Jewish state.

In some government departments officials acted independently, as
their consciences dictated, once their superiors had gone. One Jewish department chief, who had transferred his loyalty to the Jewish Agency, obtained two truckloads of blank stationery from the government printing
office. The supply lasted the Israel government nearly a year. Amid the
confusion the Jewish Agency acquired a valuable collection of maps from
the government Lands Department and a prized album of aerial photographs from the Survey Department. In the government forestry office the
Jewish director packed up the entire contents of his office and moved
them into a warehouse; then he drew out official funds from Barclay's
Bank and redeposited them in the names of three senior Jewish officials.

As part of the planned disintegration of the government the remaining civilian and military officials were ordered to burn files and archives
and transfer as much military stores and equipment as possible to the
Arab Legion. The British considered the Legion part of their forces and
used them as replacements for the withdrawing British garrisons. Some
British officers took advantage of this situation to make private deals with
Arabs and Jews, giving rise to a lucrative black market.

S. H. Shaw, consulting geologist to the Palestine government, had received specially firm instructions "to burn all geological data in your possession forthwith." He was warned "under no circumstances" to permit
"the contents of your files to fall into the hands of the Jews." A non-Jew,
Shaw had become close friends with Jewish colleagues in the geology department of the Lands Department and he knew the worth of his records.
On receipt of his orders he wrote a brief note and sent it by messenger to
a friend. Within hours the message was in the hands of Haganah. Then
Shaw made a bonfire in his office of a large pile of worthless papers from
his wastebasket. The ashes were still hot when a Haganah unit burst into
the building, raced for Shaw's office, and shot off the locks on his files.
The contents, carried off in canvas bags, later proved to be of inestimable
value to the Jewish state, particularly in connection with the Negev. Shaw
was dismissed from the British civil service and for years thereafter was
unable to get a job anywhere in England.

The last British civilian officials left Jaffa on April 15. The Jerusalem municipality, controlled by the High Commissioner, ceased to exist on April 26, when Robert Graves, the last British mayor, sailed for home. After Arab members of the city council had followed other Arab notables out of the country, the six remaining Jewish councilors organized a rump council. The British staff of the chief secretary of the Palestine government, huddled for months in their self-imposed ghettos, started packing on April 15. By the end of April all British civilian officials had been withdrawn from Jerusalem, except for 2000 police and 20 senior officials. The Jerusalem military court shut down on April 20 and its civilian employees received termination notices. Civilian judicial processes were also suspended. Even convicted prisoners, Jews and Arabs, were free to leave prisons when the government withdrew all guards. Press and radio censorship, in effect since 1936, came to an end shortly after army headquarters was shifted from Jerusalem to Haifa. Nearly 4000 troops had sailed from Haifa in the first week of March and a similar number left four weeks later.

The British-owned oil refineries in Haifa, Palestine's sole fuel source, closed down in mid-April. Company tankers began removing existing stocks to Tripoli and Beirut. The flow from the pipeline at Kirkuk, in Iraq, was diverted to Amman. Lydda Airport, the only one with facilities for landing the four-engine overseas craft used by BOAC and TWA, ceased operations April 25.

One of the meanest acts of the dying Mandatory authority was its suspension of mail and telegraph service. The postmaster general ordered the closing of rural postal agencies on April 14 and of those in the towns on April 30. The main post offices in Haifa, Jerusalem, Jaffa, and Tel Aviv were given until May 5 to discontinue internal and air mail service. That same day Palestine was expelled from the International Postal Union. Discontinuance of mail service was justified by the government on the curious ground that it had received no communication from the UN implementation commission guaranteeing its acceptance of responsibility for the maintenance of postal services.

Bent on frustrating partition, the British not only shredded the entire fabric of Palestine's civilian administration but defied the United Nations request to do nothing "to prevent, obstruct or delay the implementation by the Commission of the measures recommended by the General Assembly." The partition resolution had asked the United Kingdom to coordinate its evacuation plans with those of a five-member UN commission appointed to take over the government of Palestine progressively as the British withdrew. Until two weeks before the Mandate lapsed the commission was refused admittance to Palestine. Karl Lisicky of Czechoslovakia, chairman of the commission, dubbed its members "the five lonely pilgrims" because they never did get to Palestine. The commission's secretary, Ralph Bunche, later won the Nobel Peace Prize for bringing about the Arab-Jewish armistice agreements. The General Assembly's last-minute creation on May 14 of a mediator for Palestine relieved the commission of "the further exercise" of the responsibilities the British had never given it a chance to undertake.

The most the commission could do was to send an advance party headed by Pablo Azacarate, Ambassador to England of the former Spanish Republic. The UN emissaries included an Indian economist, a Norwegian colonel, a Greek lawyer, and two women secretaries. Housed in an unventilated basement opposite British military headquarters in Jerusalem, they were completely ignored by the Palestine government. Confined largely to the restricted military zones, the UN delegation was forbidden to fix boundaries, form armed militias, or set up interim governments in the areas earmarked for the Jewish and Arab states. They were refused the loan of officials from the Mandatory government's staff and facilities for traveling around the country. Most of their time was spent scrounging for food in hungry Jerusalem while the two secretaries occupied themselves with keeping their quarters clean.

Even before the delegation arrived on February 22, the British had ignored the United Nations recommendation that a seaport for immigration be put at the Jews' disposal by February 1. Instead, the Palestine authorities tightened the blockade of the Palestine coast, relentlessly pursued searches for and seizures of Jewish arms, blocked the movement of arms and ammunition into besieged Jerusalem, and forbade the Jews to build fortifications. The auction of Palestine government lands around Haifa Harbor without consulting the UN delegation was another instance of British hostility to the United Nations policy.

On April 10, 1948, the commission reported to the General Assembly that "the lack of cooperation from the Mandatory Power" was one of the reasons "which have made it impossible . . . to implement the Assembly resolution." Other factors cited were "the armed hostility of both Palestinian and non-Palestinian Arab elements . . . the disintegrating security situation in Palestine," and the failure of the Security Council to furnish the commission "with the necessary armed assistance."

British roadblocks to partition paralleled a changing attitude toward it by the United States and a growing reluctance by the United Nations to implement its own decision. A major defect in the partition resolution had been the failure to provide for any means of enforcing partition should force become necessary. All the General Assembly had done was to ask the Security Council "to term as a threat to the peace, breach of the peace or act of aggression . . . any attempt to alter by force the settlement envisaged by this resolution."

As the situation in Palestine worsened the United States delegation at Lake Success began looking for ways to postpone if not to circumvent partition. Warren Austin, head of the American delegation, maintained before the Security Council on February 24, 1948, that the United Nations Charter "does not empower" the Security Council "to enforce a political settlement, whether it is pursuant to a recommendation of the General Assembly or of the Security Council itself."

The pro-Arab American oil lobby and its allies in the State Department and American military leadership, worried over Russian ambitions in the Middle East, pressed hard for a reversal of the US position on Palestine. Concerned with protecting the Middle East oil supplies, and encouraged by the British, both groups persuaded the State Department that continued US support of partition would throw the Arabs into the arms of the Russians.

On March 19 the US tossed a bombshell by announcing that it wanted action on partition suspended and the General Assembly recalled to consider the establishment of a temporary United Nations trusteeship over Palestine. Meanwhile, the US proposed, the British should be "induced to retain the Mandate." Only five days earlier the US and the USSR had voted together in the Security Council for a resolution committing it to "do everything it can under the Charter to give effect" to the Assembly's partition resolution.

The British eagerly supported the trusteeship scheme, which they had originally advanced. They knew that if the Security Council agreed, this would undermine the legal basis of partition and destroy the legal status of the Jewish state-to-be. This in turn would open the way for a military settlement to be imposed by the invading Arab armies and negotiated through the good offices of the British government.

To the very end the British fought to achieve a pro-Arab solution to Palestine in order to remove the principal obstacle to friendship with the Arab states. London had blundered in accepting exaggerated estimates of Arab military strength and parallel miscalculations of the Jews' resources. The chaotic withdrawal policy turned out to be an equally fatal error. Had Britain maintained an orderly central government until May 15, there might have been a going concern that the UN could have taken over under some form of trusteeship. The existence of such a UN regime would have made it difficult for the Jews to set up a provisional government of their own.

Belated realization of this was behind the frantic maneuvers of the Americans and the British in the United Nations to impose some kind of interim administration. Intentionally or not, Britain's policy of planned chaos in Palestine and her refusal to cooperate with the UN commission turned out to be the Jews' secret weapon. The Jews took advantage of the disorganization to make partition a fact. The Arabs could not exploit the administrative collapse because they were unable to destroy the Jews militarily, as everyone had confidently expected they would. If the Arabs had accepted partition in 1947, Israel would have been a tiny geographical monstrosity. The UN resolution had given the Jews 55 percent of Palestine (UNSCOP had recommended 62 percent), but as a result of the war of independence and the ensuing armistice agreements, Israel was left with 80 percent of the land. No wonder that after 1948 the Arabs were eager to return to the prewar status, as they would be again in 1956 after the Suez campaign and again in 1967 following the Six-Day War.

BEGINNINGS OF PLANNING FOR A STATE

Faced with the implacable hostility of the British, the hesitancy of the UN, and the shifting attitude of the US, the Jewish Agency had concluded in mid-March that partition would be carried out only by the Jews and that the Jewish state would have to be set up and defended by the Jews alone.

On March 23 a joint meeting of the Jewish Agency Executive and the Va'ad L'umi (Jewish National Council in Palestine) vowed to oppose any proposal to prevent or postpone the establishment of the Jewish state. Trusteeship in any form was categorically rejected. The moment the Mandate terminated, they declared, a provisional Jewish government would begin to function in cooperation with whatever representatives of the UN were in Palestine.

In the United Nations, Rabbi Abba Hillel Silver and Moshe Shertok proclaimed the Jewish Agency's determination to implement partition with or without the UN's help. They informed the Political and Security Committee that if the UN was unable to carry out its own recommendations, the Jewish community in Palestine would "take all necessary measures which the situation will call for" if it "is confronted with the threat of annihilation."

This tough talk belied the crisis facing the Jewish leadership in Palestine. The Arabs still had the upper hand in the undeclared war because the Jews hesitated to take the offensive. They hoarded their armor and kept their general military weakness a secret. The strategy was to impress the UN with Jewish stability as a political force while holding off the Arab guerrillas until May 15, when a legal Jewish army could take the field.

At this point the Zionists cast the die for independence by moving boldly on two fronts simultaneously: at Lake Success and in Washington they redoubled the pressure to defeat trusteeship; in Palestine they embarked on offensive action aimed at breaking the siege of Jerusalem. This dual objective led to the adoption of a preliminary declaration of independence on April 12, 1948, at a meeting in Tel Aviv of the Zionist General Council and a statement by Ben-Gurion that the Jewish state already existed.

The declaration was followed by the election of a thirty-seven-man National Council drawn from the members of the Jewish Agency-Zionist Executive living in Palestine, the executive of the Jewish National Council, and from other Jewish groups not represented in these two bodies. From the thirty-seven, a smaller group of thirteen, known as the National Administration, with Ben-Gurion as Chairman, was chosen to function as a provisional government answerable to the National Council. Ideological differences between pro- and anti-partitionists were brushed aside in light of the growing danger to the Yishuv (Jewish Palestine). Even the extreme Left-wingers and ultra-Orthodox Agudat Israel on the right were drawn into a Jewish united front.

Establishment of the National Council and the National Administration were among the last steps in the process of building the organizational machinery of statehood. While Haganah moved to fill the power vacuum created by the gradual withdrawal of British military units, the Jewish Agency neutralized the administrative void by erecting a parallel civilian structure to replace the collapsing Palestine government. The skeleton already existed in the schools, hospitals, and other public services the Agency had long maintained as a state within a state.

On January 12, 1948, an Agency spokesman told the press in Jerusalem that "the entire plan for the structure of the Jewish state, from the preparation of ministries down to the number of Hebrew and Arabic typewriters needed, will be ready by the end of this month." A week later the chairman of the Jewish National Service Census Board announced that 72 percent of young men aged seventeen to twenty-five had registered for "national service." The rest were otherwise occupied, he explained—that is, they were serving in the underground Haganah forces. On February 27 the Jewish Agency banned foreign travel for all Jews between sixteen and forty "who are liable for national service."

On February 17 the Hebrew press published for the first time a Jewish Agency advertisement that read: "Candidates required to undergo a course of training as officers of the police force of the Jewish State. Command of either Hebrew or Arabic is essential." At the end of February the Histadrut (Jewish Labor Federation) made public a comprehensive plan for social-security legislation in the future Jewish state.

Filed away against the day of Jewish independence was a complete blueprint for a Foreign Office and Foreign Service of the Jewish state. It had been completed in February by Walter Eytan, principal of the Jewish Agency's Public Service College, and his students. Founded in 1946 to train cadets for public service in Palestine, the college had been nicknamed "the School for Diplomats" because its ultimate purpose had been guessed.

The day the British postal services were suspended the Agency ordered all Jewish postal employees to remain at their posts. They were told that the "Hebrew Post" would commence full operation after the cessation of the Mandate. They were instructed to continue every possible mail service in the interim. A circular letter announced that the stamps of the Keren Kayemet L'Israel (Jewish National Fund) and the Kofer Hayishuv (Community Tax) and provisional postmarks of the National Administration would be ready for use in the settlements and villages on May 1 and in the towns and cities on May 6.

Sheets of JNF stamps were sent to the main post offices in Haifa and Tel Aviv where they were overprinted with rubber stamps by officials using different colored inking pads. The use of schoolchildren and volunteers over military age in the emergency postal service resulted in a variety of errors in the overprints.

The stamps used in Haifa and Tel Aviv could not be delivered to beleaguered Jerusalem, so the local JNF office provided stocks of the latest issue of its propaganda stamps. They depicted the map of Israel with the boundaries as approved by the UN. These stamps were still on sale in Jerusalem as late as June 20, 1948. Similar improvisations prevailed in other areas. In isolated Nahariya the town council issued its own stamp and sent mail by boats from a makeshift jetty to Haifa.

Haganah, which had organized a private postal service at the end of 1947, used its own stamps until its merger into the Israel Army at the end of May, 1948. Haganah mail bore cachets of the chief of staff in Haifa and of the town commanders in Tel Aviv, Jerusalem, Safad, and the

Negev. The French Consulate in Jerusalem issued separate stamps on April 30 to enable the French community to contact families abroad. They were first put on sale on May 5 in the form of ordinary French stamps overprinted with "Jerusalem Post Aerienne 10 FRs."

When the British and Arab officials abandoned the government post office in Jerusalem, a corps of Jewish postmen suddenly appeared in the building on May 9 to maintain service. People risked sniper fire to buy the new JNF stamps. Three branch offices were also opened in Jerusalem from which mail was sent to Tel Aviv via secret road and Piper Cub. One of the few accomplishments of the UN implementation commission was an agreement it concluded at Lake Success on May 6 with H. R. Gratz, President of the Haifa Chamber of Shipping, to resume interrupted air mail service to and from Palestine. But the pact needed the approval of the International Postal Union.

The records and files from the offices of the dying Mandatory government became prime objectives of the shadow Jewish government as fighting divided Jerusalem into Arab and Jewish sectors. The task of salvaging these records was handed to a shy middle-aged employee of the Jewish Agency, Mrs. Hannah Eventov. As one government office after another was abandoned, Mrs. Eventov directed a unit of volunteers that stole into no-man's land and came back with tons of government archives.

One of her most dramatic exploits was the rescue of the invaluable 10,000-volume legal library of the Palestine Supreme Court. The books were in danger of being destroyed during the closing days of the British regime because a Haganah unit that had occupied the building was using the fat volumes in lieu of sandbags. After talking the Haganah commander into giving up his literary barricade, Mrs. Eventov organized a brigade of volunteer "porters" led by two lawyers, Shabtai Rozenne and Haim Cohn. Rozenne later became legal adviser to the Israel Foreign Ministry and Cohn served as attorney general. Under the command of the two lawyers the labor detail lugged the volumes from the courthouse in the Russian Compound and moved them by truck to safety in Motza. A special food allotment was arranged for the workers who preferred extra rations to cash payment. The entire operation took six days. Today the books are part of the library of the Israel Supreme Court, which is housed in the same building from which they were snatched. And Haim Cohn is a Justice of the Supreme Court.

Before an Arab Legion detachment was posted to guard the Palestine Broadcasting Authority's station on Jerusalem's Queen Melisande Street in December, 1947, Jewish employees had "salvaged" a trio of grand pianos,

8000 records of classical and Israeli music, 6000 sheets of music, and a truckload of technical equipment. The British had not yet left when Jewish engineers began testing clandestine transmitters on an improvised radio station. First it was hidden in the house of Rabbi Simcha Assaf, later a Supreme Court Justice, who gave Talmud lessons on the air. Then it was moved to the Bet Hechalutzot of the American Women's League for Israel and later to the Rehaviah Café.

The change of locations was necessary to circumvent British search parties. In its first location the station, known as "Kol Hamagen," the Voice of Haganah, was on the sixth floor of an apartment house that had no electricity. Power was obtained by running a house-to-house cable from a nearby hospital, with the line camouflaged as a clothesline on which wash was regularly hung. Besides broadcast notices in Hebrew, Arabic, and English of meetings, news, and regulations promulgated by the Jewish Agency, the station never missed carrying a weekly concert by a small orchestra. The musicians played by the light of kerosene lamps to save current for the transmitter.

While the Jews in Palestine were systematically doing what the UN said should be done, a last-ditch political battle erupted at the United Nations to postpone Jewish statehood. By persuasion, the intervention of prominent Jewish personalities, and thinly veiled threats the State Department tried to pressure the Jewish Agency into accepting UN trusteeship. State Department officials cautioned Agency leaders in New York and at Lake Success that unless they accepted, they risked economic sanctions, exposure of Haganah's illicit arms purchases, a ban on tax exemption for contributions to Zionist campaigns, and a freeze on funds sent to Palestine. Dr. Judah L. Magnes, President of the Hebrew University and long an advocate of binationalism, held press conferences in New York and Washington to rally support for trusteeship. He was promptly repudiated by the University's senate in a resolution declaring that he spoke only for himself and his Ihud Society, and that his political views in no way represented those of the University or its academic staff. Dean Rusk, then director of the State Department Office for UN Affairs, tried desperately to win leading American Jews to support a proposed new round-table conference of Arabs and Jews on Rhodes or Cyprus.

Moshe Shertok reported these developments to a meeting of the Agency's American section on May 3. Shertok and Dr. Nahum Goldmann were inclined to accept Rusk's proposal, but a majority—Dr. Abba Hillel Silver, Dr. Emanuel Neumann, Mrs. Rose Halprin, and Rabbi Wolf Gold—turned it down. After informing Rusk on May 4 of the Agency's rejection,

Shertok met with Secretary of State George C. Marshall and heard his plea for a temporary delay in proclaiming independence. By the time Shertok returned to Tel Aviv on May 12 he was less inclined to accept an agreement with the US in order to avert the imminent Arab invasion. He had become convinced that the pressure for postponement reflected chiefly the attitude of a small group in the State Department eager to retrieve its own lost position. By then Chaim Weizmann already knew that at the proper time President Truman would stand by his promises on partition and would recognize a Jewish state once it was proclaimed. The presumption is that Shertok also knew and so advised his colleagues poised for independence in Tel Aviv.

Just thirty-one hours and thirty-one minutes before independence was voted in Tel Aviv, Dr. Philip K. Jessup of the US delegation submitted a new resolution in the UN Political and Security Committee, calling upon the Jews and Arabs to take no political action while "the Palestine problem" was under consideration. For all of the effect it had on Tel Aviv, the twelfth-hour debate in the UN might have been a metaphysical disputation.

On the last day of "Operation Deluge" virtually all British forces had moved out of Palestine and the entire machinery of the Palestine government had broken down. Half an hour after the High Commissioner left Government House in Jerusalem on the morning of May 14 the last British civilian personnel boarded planes for Haifa. When the Jerusalem garrison was evacuated soon after, the only British forces left were in the Haifa port enclave where the Palestine Mandate expired with the departure of General Cunningham.

The last hours of the Mandate found the Jews confident they could wrest political independence and territorial integrity for the first state of their own in 1878 years (since 70 B.C.E.) to which the UN had given them a universal title but without universal support. The Palestine Arabs were completely demoralized and many of them looked across the Jordan to Emir Abdullah to save them from utter defeat. The British, who had assumed the international title deed to Palestine with imperial assurance in 1922, left behind a country in chaos, ravaged by war, and virtually cut off from the rest of the world.

chapter

∘ ∘ ∘ ∘ ∘ ∘ ∘ ∘ ∘ ∘ ∘ ∘ ∘ ∘ |3| ∘ ∘ ∘ ∘ ∘ ∘ ∘ ∘ ∘ ∘ ∘ ∘ ∘ ∘

EVENTS LEADING TO THE
BALFOUR DECLARATION

THE HIGH COMMISSIONER'S DEPARTURE from Jerusalem completed England's repudiation of a unilateral promise made in 1917 and
the abandonment of an international trust she accepted in 1922.

The promise was freely and openly given in the Balfour Declaration.
It committed His Majesty's Government to "view with favor the establishment in Palestine of a national home for the Jewish people" and "to
use their best endeavors to facilitate the achievement of this object." The
trust, which gave international sanction to the Balfour Declaration, was
the League of Nations Mandate for Palestine, awarded to Great Britain
on July 24, 1922.

The Balfour Declaration and the Mandate, the basis for thirty-one
years of British rule in Palestine, became the legal cornerstones of the
claim to Jewish statehood. This was set forth in the fifth paragraph of the
Israeli Declaration of Independence that was taking final shape on May
14 as High Commissioner Cunningham began his leavetaking.

Although the British government had promised to be both its midwife
and godfather, the new state went through birth pangs without England's
blessing or help and in the face of her stubborn opposition. Having failed
to abort what she had once pledged to "facilitate" and to "secure," Britain
was getting out of Palestine "amid chaos, carnage, and confusion."

Britain acquired dominion over Palestine as part of the spoils of war.
To retain it, she needed a moral case. Control of Palestine—as a buffer
on the eastern flank of the Suez Canal and as a key element in the defense

network in the Near East that controlled the routes to India—had always been a major objective of British imperial strategy. The Balfour Declaration, issued during World War I when the British conquest of the Holy Land over the Turks appeared to be near, enabled England to move into Palestine with a good conscience.

This, however, could be done "only by making room for the original owners," as Barbara Tuchman pointed out in *Bible and Sword,* thus putting Britain, "to her own dismay, in the role of accoucheur to a new state." The Allied Supreme Council in 1920 agreed to give the Palestine Mandate to Britain and incorporated the Balfour Declaration into the peace treaty with Turkey. An accomplished fact had won international recognition. What one British statesman called "the most important international obligation ever entrusted to a single nation" had become a sacred trust of the British government.

The Balfour Declaration was never read in the House of Commons, published as a state paper, or announced from the steps of 10 Downing Street. It was a three-sentence letter of only a hundred and sixteen words addressed to a private citizen. Thirty-one words of the sixty-seven-word second sentence formed the historic promise to "view with favor the establishment in Palestine of a national home for the Jewish people" and "to facilitate the achievement of this object."

This was the promissory note to the Promised Land which set in motion the train of events that would be climaxed thirty-one years later by the British withdrawal from Palestine and the establishment of an independent Jewish state in a small segment of the Palestine of 1917.

Typewritten on the stationery of the Foreign Office, the Balfour Declaration bore the signature of Arthur James Balfour, Secretary for Foreign Affairs. It was addressed to Lionel Walter Rothschild, the second Lord Rothschild, who became a Zionist after his first meeting with Dr. Chaim Weizmann. The first Lord Rothschild had raised the money with which Prime Minister Benjamin Disraeli acquired control of the Suez Canal. The second Lord Rothschild had broken with the family tradition of banking by becoming a naturalist, world-renowned for his collections of birds and insects and as the author of hundreds of scientific papers. Although he sat in the House of Lords for eleven years, he never once spoke there, perhaps because he suffered from a curious speech impediment that caused him to speak either in a choked whisper or a loud bellow. He was a crack shot and liked to drive a zebra-drawn carriage through Piccadilly, but the Balfour Declaration was his sole emergence into the political limelight. His French cousin, Baron Edmond de Rothschild, had been the

supporter of the pre-Zionist Jewish settlements in Palestine in the 1880s
and 1890s.

A copy of Balfour's letter (the original is in the British Museum, to
which Lord Rothschild gave it before he died) was given to Dr. Weizmann, President of the English Zionist Federation, on November 2. He
was advised that the official text was being handed to Lord Rothschild. In
the opening sentence of the letter Balfour said he was conveying on behalf of the British government "the following declaration of sympathy
with Jewish Zionist aspirations which has been submitted to and approved by the Cabinet." In the last sentence Balfour asked Rothschild to
"bring this declaration to the knowledge of the Zionist Federation."
Weizmann's letter of acknowledgment, dated November 4, said it was
received "with affectionate acknowledgment and gratitude," and referred
to the declaration as "the glad tidings." Weizmann made no reference to a
Jewish state, but spoke of the "reestablishment of a self-governing and
prosperous Jewish nationality in Palestine."

What appeared to be bureaucratic clumsiness was in fact prearranged.
As the middleman between the Zionists and the British government,
Rothschild had forwarded to Balfour on July 18 the draft of the kind of
statement the Zionists wanted. Balfour had officially asked for it in June
at a meeting with Weizmann and Rothschild. His request reflected rising
sentiment in the highest government quarters for some pro-Zionist pronouncement. Since early in 1917, Dr. Weizmann, Dr. Nahum Sokolow,
and their associates in the Zionist movement had engaged in frequent but
unofficial exchanges with Cabinet members and lower-echelon officials of
the Foreign and War Offices.

These conversations had encouraged the Zionists to begin preparing a
specific formulation. Several tentative drafts were discussed with government spokesmen. One of the earliest had been shown to Sir Mark Sykes,
Secretary of the War Cabinet, on February 7. This version, which asked
that "Palestine be recognized as the Jewish national home," was the first
use of the phrase "Jewish national home."

Its author was Dr. Sokolow, chairman of a Zionist drafting committee
that had been at work since the end of 1916. Weizmann was also a member of this group, though he still lacked the Zionist authority of Sokolow.
They worked together smoothly, however. Weizmann's connections with
the War Cabinet helped move the Zionist proposal in its various stages
into official channels on an informal basis. Because Weizmann was abroad
on a Zionist mission from the end of June until July 22, he had no part
in phrasing the draft that went to Balfour.

The Sokolow "formula" contained these forty-six words: "His Majesty's Government accepts the principle that Palestine should be reconstituted as the national home of the Jewish people. His Majesty's Government will use its best endeavors to secure the achievement of this object and will discuss the necessary methods and means with the Zionist Organization."

In an accompanying note Rothschild wrote, "At last I am able to send you the formula you asked me for. If His Majesty's Government will send me a message on the lines of the formula, if they and you approve it, I will hand it on to the Zionist Federation."

Practical reasons dictated the decision to communicate the Zionist draft privately via Rothschild rather than by way of a formal presentation from the English Zionist Federation to the British government. They also determined the choice of Rothschild as the prospective recipient of the Balfour Declaration. Although Weizmann was President of the Zionist Federation and had gained access to influential people in the government because of his scientific contributions to the war effort, he was still junior to Sokolow, the ranking representative of the World Zionist Organization in London. Moreover, Sokolow was a foreigner who spoke for a movement whose nominal headquarters were still in Berlin, the enemy capital. By using Rothschild, a strong Zionist, as the go-between, these embarrassments would be avoided while simultaneously linking any government statement to the best-known name in the Jewish world.

While Balfour had invited the Zionists to prepare a formula, neither he nor Prime Minister David Lloyd George had given them any precise promises. The closest they had come to a commitment was a go-ahead to spread the word among world Jewry that some form of British control in Palestine would be the best guarantee of fulfilling Jewish aspirations there.

Rothschild's letter and the questions of policy it raised first came before the War Cabinet on September 3. Balfour, who was not a part of this inner group but was often invited to its sessions, had already let it be known that the original draft was acceptable to him with minor word changes. What the War Cabinet actually considered, however, was a redraft by Lord Milner, the number-two man in the government. He had eliminated the concept of "reconstituting" Palestine as the national home for the Jewish people, substituting "establishment of a home for the Jewish people" in Palestine. His revision further diluted the Zionist formula by replacing "Palestine as the national home for the Jewish people" with "a home for the Jewish people in Palestine." That this went beyond semantics would become evident when England began diluting the Balfour Declaration by later interpretations.

The Secretary of State for India, Edwin Montagu, who was then the only Jew of ministerial rank in the government, although not in the War Cabinet, was called in to give his views. A militant anti-Zionist, he protested so violently that even Milner's amended draft would seriously prejudice the position of Jews everywhere that action was deferred. The matter did not come up again until October 4.

Meanwhile, US Supreme Court Justice Louis D. Brandeis, who had talked to Woodrow Wilson at the request of Weizmann, cabled Wilson's agreement with the original text submitted to Balfour. On October 3 Weizmann and Rothschild wired the War Cabinet an urgent request for speed in issuing the declaration to counteract "the demoralizing influence which the enemy press is endeavoring to exercise by holding out vague promises to the Jews." The following day the War Cabinet returned to the question. Once again Montagu sought to block it. Balfour silenced him by citing "the great efforts" being made by Germany "to capture the sympathy of the Zionist movement." He also referred to a sympathetic statement by France, relayed by the Zionists, and to Brandeis's report of Wilson's friendly attitude.

Leopold Amery, a member of the Cabinet secretariat, was then instructed by Lord Milner to revise the latter's own draft. Amery inserted language aimed at placating the anti-Zionists in the British Jewish community, substituted "the Jewish race" for "the Jewish people," and restored the adjective "national" in "national home."

On October 6 the War Cabinet sent the Milner-Amery version to eight leading British Jews, four Zionists and four anti-Zionists. They were told that preliminary consideration was being given to drawing up a formula setting forth the government's attitude toward the Zionist movement in general and to the future of Palestine. In view of the conflicting opinions in the Jewish community, the Cabinet sought the recipients' reactions in writing within a week. One of the recipients was Dr. Joseph Hertz, the American-educated Chief Rabbi of the British Empire. When the messenger from the Cabinet called at the Rabbi's residence, he was informed that Dr. Hertz was at the synagogue. It was the eighth day of Sukkot, the Festival of Tabernacles. Unauthorized to leave the momentous document, the messenger returned that night, only to learn that the Rabbi was again in synagogue. It was now the eve of Simhat Torah. This time he left the letter, and Dr. Hertz later became one of the leading advocates of the Balfour Declaration.

By October 31 the War Cabinet was on the verge of giving final approval to the Declaration, but the exact language was still troublesome. At the last moment Amery took all the suggested changes and put them together hurriedly in one last draft, scribbled on the back of a discarded memo. In this final form "the Jewish people" displaced "the Jewish race," and a few other words were altered. As finally agreed to by Lloyd George, Balfour, Milner, Lord Curzon, and Gen. Jan Christiaan Smuts, what has come to be known as the Balfour Declaration, but which Balfour didn't write, differed little from the October 4 Milner-Amery text. Amery, who later became Colonial Secretary, was speaking as one of the authors of the Balfour Declaration when he said of Britain's withdrawal from Palestine on May 14, 1948, that "we decamp ignominiously amid carnage and confusion."

The Declaration was not made public, however, until November 9. Weizmann had reported it confidentially to the inner circle of the Zionist Federation on November 5. He and Sokolow were acclaimed for having "brought about this momentous achievement toward the realization of the national aspirations of the Jewish people."

C. P. Scott, editor of the influential *Manchester Guardian,* whose fortuitous meeting with Weizmann three years before had paved the way for his government contacts, got wind of the Declaration on November 7. He wanted to publish it on November 8. Leopold Greenberg, editor of the *London Jewish Chronicle,* learned of it from Weizmann on November 2, a Friday, after that week's *Chronicle* had appeared. Greenberg persuaded a reluctant Weizmann, but amenable government authorities, to hold up publication for a week so that the *Chronicle* would not be scooped before its next issue, to be published on November 9. By then the Balfour Declaration had been overshadowed in the world's headlines by an even more momentous event, the November 7 Bolshevik takeover in Russia.

HERZL'S ROLE

In the Balfour Declaration the Zionists achieved a settlement charter they had been trying to pry out of Turkey for twenty years. The goal had been set by the first World Zionist Congress at Basle: "Zionism seeks to secure for the Jewish people a publicly recognized, legally secured home in Palestine." This public recognition was achieved in the Balfour Declaration, a precursor and a pillar upon which the legal foundation of the State of Israel was eventually built. For the first time since Roman legions had erased the last vestige of Jewish independence nearly nineteen hundred years earlier, a great power had publicly pledged itself to restore the Jewish people to its homeland.

This was not a wholly new moral or political concern of the British people and government. Christian writers and preachers in the seventeenth century had advocated English sponsorship of a Jewish return to the Holy Land as the key to the messianic age. The readmission of the Jews to England by Oliver Cromwell in 1656 was said to have been prompted in part by a widespread religious belief that their absence was delaying the coming of the messiah. An "Anglican Israel" restored to Palestine under the protection of Protestant England had been envisaged in 1840 by Lord Shaftesbury, a social and religious reformer, as hastening the second coming of Jesus. Anglo-French rivalry in the Levant in the 1840s had led Foreign Secretary Lord Palmerston to press the Turks to permit Jewish settlement in Palestine. He instructed British envoys in the Near East to encourage Jews in the Sultan's dominions to look to Great Britain for protection.

George Eliot's pro-Zionist novel, *Daniel Deronda,* won wide approbation in the 1870s. Laurence Oliphant, an English mystic, anticipated the first modern wave of Jewish colonization by his efforts to win Turkish support for a Jewish settlement near the Dead Sea in 1879.

Despite this sympathetic moral and political climate, Dr. Theodor Herzl turned first to Germany in seeking political backing for the rebirth of the Jewish state he had blueprinted in his famous pamphlet of that name. The Vienna journalist neither founded nor invented Zionism— he didn't even give it its name, which had been coined some years before by Nathan Birnbaum. Brought up in an assimilationist background, Herzl was completely ignorant of the place of Zion in Jewish prayers, liturgy, and way of life. He knew nothing of the historic impact of the hope of return on Jewish thought and literature. He was even unaware that others had advanced similar ideas of a Jewish restoration before him, had written books about it, had organized in support of it, and had even started to implement it in a modest way. Even more surprising is the fact that in its first edition, published in German in Vienna in 1895, "The Jewish State" ("Judenstaat") made no commitment to Palestine as the site of the Jewish state or to Hebrew as its language. Any available territory —Argentina was mentioned together with Palestine—favored by Jewish opinion would be acceptable.

It is ironic that an earlier version of "The Jewish State" had been a memorandum entitled "Speech to the Rothschilds" which Herzl had vainly sought to present to Lord Rothschild, whose son was to receive the Balfour Declaration twenty years later.

Herzl's unique contribution was the conversion of a millennial dream into a political movement through which Zionism embarked on the final road to Jewish statehood. Herzl died thinking himself a failure because he had been unable to secure a charter to Palestine. But two decades later the Balfour Declaration became that charter.

The award to Great Britain of the Mandate for Palestine constituted the "international guarantee" for which Herzl had beseeched the courts of Europe, a guarantee that became a reality in 1947, when the United Nations General Assembly voted to create a Jewish state in part of Palestine.

Herzl's earliest political approaches were to Kaiser Wilhelm II as a way of reaching the Sultan of Turkey. The moment seemed propitious since Germany was trying to persuade the Turks on the idea of a Berlin-to-Baghdad railway.

The Kaiser received Herzl twice. At their first meeting in Constantinople on October 19, 1898, Herzl urged the Kaiser to persuade the Sultan to agree to the establishment of a Jewish chartered company that would launch Jewish colonization in Palestine under the wing of Germany. At first intrigued with the idea of Hohenzollern sponsorship of a Jewish Palestine, the Kaiser broached the matter to the Sultan. A few weeks later, on November 2, the Kaiser met Herzl again, in Jerusalem, exactly nineteen years before the Balfour Declaration. When Herzl found that his courting of the Kaiser was futile, he tried a direct approach to the Sultan, who granted Herzl audiences in 1901 and 1902. Both proved fruitless.

Herzl had previously shifted his attention to England by convening the fourth Zionist Congress in London in the summer of 1900. In a remarkably prophetic utterance, he said to the opening session, "England, free England, England looking over all the seas, will understand our aspirations. From here the Zionist idea will take its flight further and higher, of that we are sure." Six weeks after the London congress adjourned, all Parliamentary candidates in the 1900 election received a circular signed by Joseph Cowen. One of Herzl's earliest supporters and one of the owners of the *London Jewish Chronicle,* Cowen would have a part in the events leading up to the Balfour Declaration.

Made with Herzl's knowledge and consent, Cowen's circular said, with considerable exaggeration, "the question of Zionism is now agitating the minds of the masses of the Jewish voters in the United Kingdom." In what today must be viewed as an incredible and naïve political action, the circular on behalf of the English Zionist Federation appealed to the candidates "whenever the same may be necessary, to use your influence to secure the sympathetic consideration of Her Majesty's [Queen Victoria's] Government to the Zionist movement and its government offices in favor of Zionist aspirations whenever the same may be required with those governments who have interests in Palestine and Syria."

The circular baldly invited its recipients to let Cowen know if they viewed "our movement with sympathy." If they did, he would "be glad to advise our friends in the constituency you seek to represent to give all the support to your candidature of which they are capable." Favorable replies came from 143 candidates, 41 of whom were elected. Among those introduced to Zionism through the circular were men who were to be influential in the issuance of the Balfour Declaration—two future Prime Ministers, Arthur James Balfour and David Lloyd George, and Joseph Chamberlain, the incumbent Colonial Secretary.

Finding the front door to Palestine barred, Herzl began to consider temporary staging areas in such adjacent British colonies as Cyprus and El Arish in the Sinai Peninsula. In 1902 Leopold Greenberg arranged for Herzl to meet Chamberlain. Cyprus was out of the question but Chamberlain saw possibilities in El Arish, both on humanitarian grounds and as "a useful instrument for extending British influence in Palestine proper when the time came for the inevitable dismemberment of the Ottoman Empire."

Chamberlain made it possible for Herzl to see Lord Lansdowne, the Foreign Secretary, who referred the El Arish proposal to the British officials in Cairo. Their coolness, as well as Turkish opposition, put an end to the scheme but not to British interest. When Chamberlain returned from a visit to Africa in 1903, he suggested to Herzl the possibility of an autonomous Jewish colony in the East Africa Protectorate under the British flag. Herzl's diary said Chamberlain mentioned Uganda, but he really meant what is now Kenya.

At first Herzl was cool to Africa, seeing it as a diversion of the Zionist objective, but when Chamberlain asked the Zionists to submit specific proposals for an East African project, Herzl displayed interest. Leopold Greenberg engaged a firm of solicitors, one of whose members was Lloyd George, to draft a definite plan. Chamberlain referred it to Lansdowne, who on August 14, 1903, wrote Greenberg a letter indicating that the scheme was being seriously considered by the Foreign Office.

The letter raised a violent storm of opposition when it was read to the sixth Zionist Congress on August 26, 1903. With the horror of the Kishinev pogroms of April, 1903, still fresh in his consciousness, Herzl urged acceptance of East Africa as a temporary solution for the sufferings of the

Jews in the Russian Empire. Herzl was ready to compromise on Palestine and willing to accept East Africa as a halfway station. Two weeks before the Lansdowne communication was made public Herzl had gone to Russia for two meetings with Count von Plehve, Czarist Minister of the Interior. Although von Plehve was the instigator of the Kishinev atrocity, Herzl had sought his aid in promoting Jewish colonization.

The Zionist Congress delegates hailed the British offer as a significant recognition of the Zionist movement by a great power. But they also felt that acceptance would destroy the movement by diverting it from its goal. The bitter opposition led by the Russian delegates, among them the twenty-nine-year-old Chaim Weizmann, rocked the hall with cries of "suicide," "criminal," and "treachery." The nay-sayers mustered 185 delegates out of some 500 voting. The minority walked out, threatening the movement with a split. Final action was deferred to 1905, when the seventh Zionist Congress overwhelmingly rejected Africa as well as all Zionist activity outside Palestine. In the interim a Zionist commission had examined the East African site and reported unfavorably. Simultaneously, strong opposition from the British settlers in Kenya made pursuit of the scheme academic.

In turning down Kenya, the Zionists left the door open to further negotiations with the British government. Satisfied with the recognition the offer had implied, the Congress expressed the hope that "the Zionist Organization may be accorded the further good offices of the British Government, where available, in any matter it may undertake in accordance with the Basle Program." These "good offices" would be "accorded" in the Balfour Declaration by two men intimately concerned with the Kenya scheme: David Lloyd George, author of the proposed East Africa charter submitted by the Zionists, and Arthur James Balfour, the Prime Minister whose government made the offer.

Only weeks before Chamberlain had talked to Herzl about El Arish, Herzl had testified before the Royal Commission on Alien Immigration, which was seeking to curb Jewish immigration from Eastern Europe. In 1905 the Balfour government put the Aliens Act through Parliament while emphatically disclaiming and denouncing any anti-Semitic implications in the legislation. Years later Balfour felt that in the Balfour Declaration he had made amends.

The Kenya debate led to Balfour's first meeting with Weizmann. Charles Dreyfus, Chairman of the Manchester Conservative Party and President of the Manchester Zionist Society, brought them together in January, 1906, at Balfour's election headquarters in Manchester. Balfour was then contesting a Parliamentary seat in the eastern division of

Manchester. Dreyfus, Weizmann's employer at the Clayton Aniline Works, was an advocate of the Kenya scheme, and he hoped Balfour could persuade Weizmann that he had been wrong in opposing it. During their conversation, Balfour told Weizmann that he, Balfour, had once met Cosima Wagner and that he had previously shared her anti-Semitic views. The year after his meeting with Balfour, Weizmann made his first visit to Palestine.

Between the collapse of the East African project and the Balkan Wars of 1912–13 the Zionists had no further formal contacts with the British government. Yet they managed to incur the mistrust of the Great Powers.

France began to suspect the Zionists of working for Germany because so many of their leaders were Germans or Austrians, and because the World Zionist headquarters were in Berlin and Zionist Congress proceedings were conducted in German. British circles in Constantinople voiced fears that the Zionists were a German fifth column in the Ottoman Empire.

Similarly, they lost support of the Germans and the Turks. Knowing of the political efforts of Herzl and Weizmann in England, the Germans were very wary; and after the Young Turk revolution of 1909 toppled the Sultan, Turkish hostility to any kind of Jewish settlement became so strong that it ended all talk of a charter to Palestine.

After 1908 Zionist spokesmen began downgrading Herzl's plan of securing political legal title to all or part of Palestine. Sokolow, General Secretary of the World Zionist Organization, declared in 1908 that there was no truth in the allegation that Zionism aimed at establishing an independent Jewish state in Palestine. Max Nordau, the movement's orator, said at the ninth Congress in 1909 that "We respectfully deposit the charter idea in the archives of modern political Zionism and speak of it no more."

David Wolffsohn, Herzl's successor as President of the World Zionist Organization, gave a pledge of unreserved Zionist loyalty to the Ottoman Empire in 1909. In 1911 he asserted that the Zionists wanted a homeland, not a Jewish state, while Nordau denounced as "infamous traducers" those who claimed the Zionists "wanted to worm their way into Turkey in order to seize Palestine." Otto Warburg, Chairman of the Zionist Executive, renewed the pledge of loyalty to Turkey at the 1913 Congress.

Even Weizmann, who a year later would take the diplomatic road that led to the Balfour Declaration, told the 1913 Congress that there was little or nothing to be expected from the Great Powers. He had created a stir at the 1907 Congress by his insistence that a charter would be meaningless unless the Jews had meanwhile established themselves by their own hands in Palestine. "The charter is to be aimed at," he said, "but only as a result of our own endeavors in Palestine. If the governments give us a charter today, it will be a scrap of paper. Not so if we work in Palestine; then it will be written and indissolubly cemented in our blood."

BEGINNINGS OF COLONIZATION

Having reached an impasse in its effort to win a charter to Palestine, the Zionist Organization began to shift from primary emphasis on political work to practical colonization and the promotion of Jewish culture. Colonization under Zionist Organization auspices did not actually begin until 1908. Before that European settlers had come largely as individualists. The first wave began in the late 1870s and early 1880s under the leadership of the Chovevei Zion (Lovers of Zion) societies in Russia. They derived their inspiration from the tracts of such early Zionist philosophers as Moses Hess and Leo Pinsker and their impetus from the intolerable conditions of Jewish life under Czarist persecution.

These pioneers founded the first Jewish farm villages at Rishon le Zion (First in Zion), Petach Tikvah (Gateway of Hope), Zichron Yaacov (Memory of Jacob), Rosh Pina, and Gedera. From the Hebrew initials of the Biblical phrase "Beit Yaacov lechu venelecha"—"O House of Jacob, come ye and let us go"—they took the name BILU. With the help of Baron Edmond de Rothschild of Paris, who sent experts to teach wine-production to these early pioneers, and the agricultural school opened at Mikveh Israel by the Alliance Israélite Universelle, the settlements survived. By 1900 there were seventeen such villages.

The World Zionist Organization had discouraged the second wave of immigration which began in 1904 and gained headway in 1905 after the collapse of the first Russian Revolution. Among the idealistic 1904–05 immigrants, who were imbued with a desire to build a homeland by Jewish self-labor and who created the first collective settlements known as kibbutzim, were many of the founding fathers of the State of Israel. One of these was a young laborer in the orange groves of Petach Tikvah named David Green, who as David Ben-Gurion would complete what Herzl had started.

The change in Zionist tactics did not alter Turkish hostility to Jewish immigration. Those who managed to trickle in did so because of the venality of Turkish officials. They avoided expulsion because the Russian consuls protected them.

When the future of the Turkish Empire again appeared on the agenda of the major European powers with the outbreak of the Balkan Wars in

1912, a new opportunity arose for making a fresh Zionist approach to the British government. Among the first to urge this on the Zionist Executive was Chaim Weizmann. Not yet in a position of leadership, he was refused permission to raise the matter with influential people. Sokolow, who went to London in 1914 to make soundings, made no impression on the Foreign Office.

The Russian-born Weizmann, who had arrived in England a few days after Herzl's death in 1904, was then teaching chemistry at the University of Manchester. He was also experimenting with a fermentation process for producing acetone from starch. In a letter to his teacher, written in 1885 when he was eleven years old, Weizmann had predicted that England alone of the nations might help the Jews return to their ancient land.

Weizmann had not yet won a commanding place in the Zionist movement. He had first made his mark at the 1903 Zionist Congress when he joined in opposing Herzl's stand on the East Africa project. On the eve of World War I he was serving as one of the two English members of the World Zionist Actions Committee and as a vice-president of the English Zionist Federation. But he had no authority to speak for Zionism.

A chance meeting in the fall of 1914 with C. P. Scott, editor of the *Manchester Guardian,* proved decisive. In his conversations with Scott, Weizmann emphasized that Zionist aspirations in Palestine paralleled British strategic and political interests in the Middle East. Scott was won over by Weizmann's argument that Palestine under the Union Jack would provide "an effective barrier . . . separating the Suez Canal . . . from the Black Sea and any hostility which may come from that side . . . and we would have a country."

Scott not only pressed this viewpoint on key figures in the Cabinet of Prime Minister Herbert Asquith, he also brought Weizmann together with Herbert Samuel, the first consciously nonassimilative Jew to sit in a British Cabinet. Through Samuel, Weizmann met Lloyd George, then Chancellor of the Exchequer but soon to become Minister of Munitions. A few days after Britain declared war on Turkey on November 5, 1914, Samuel had handed Lloyd George and Sir Edward Grey, the Foreign Secretary, a remarkable note that coincided with Weizmann's views. That was a month before Weizmann first met Samuel.

Now that dismemberment of the Turkish domains had become one of England's war aims, Samuel suggested there might arise the opportunity for the restoration in Palestine of a Jewish state. Grey and Lloyd George indicated sympathy with Samuel's reasoning that British influence ought to play a major role in the creation of a Jewish state because of Palestine's proximity to Egypt. In January and February of 1915 Samuel expanded his ideas into a formal memorandum that became the first paper on Zionism circulated to the entire Cabinet. This time he did not mention a Jewish state but plumped for a British protectorate in Palestine in which Jewish self-government would follow when the Jewish population had become a majority. Weizmann was pushing the same thought in his first meetings with Lloyd George and Balfour when Scott again entered the picture.

Britain was then facing a desperate shortage of acetone, a key component in the manufacture of cordite, the explosive used in making gunpowder. It was Scott who informed Lloyd George about "a very remarkable professor of chemistry at Manchester" who happened to be experimenting with artificial acetone. In his Manchester laboratory Weizmann was trying to make artificial rubber. To do this, he had to create butyl alcohol, which was in critically short supply because of the depletion of England's forests. Weizmann's research had produced a fermentation process that yielded thirty quarts of acetone for every sixty quarts of butyl alcohol.

Scott's tip brought Weizmann to London in September, 1915, as chemical adviser to the Ministry of Munitions. The following year Weizmann's research came under the wing of the British Admiralty, then headed by Winston Churchill, whose successor was Balfour. In a few weeks Churchill would become Foreign Secretary in Lloyd George's coalition Cabinet and by then Weizmann's process would be credited with breaking a munitions bottleneck at a crucial point in the war.

WEIZMANN'S FIRST GREAT ACHIEVEMENT

The story that Weizmann asked for and received the Balfour Declaration as a reward for his chemical formula is pure myth. Lloyd George's version of the Balfour Declaration, in his memoirs, drew a picture of a top-hatted diplomat handing a document to a white-coated scientist in exchange for a flask of acetone. It is true that Weizmann's scientific endeavors and their contribution to the war effort opened important doors to him and brought him into close contact with government ministers whose respect and confidence he won. Lloyd George's own statement in 1925 that "acetone converted me to Zionism" meant that acetone had introduced him to Weizmann, whose chemical wizardry gave him the stature and prestige to make his Zionist advocacy and diplomacy effective. Weizmann himself said that Lloyd George's "narrative makes it appear that the Balfour Declaration was a reward given me by the Government for my services to England. I almost wish that it had been as simple as that and that I had never known the heartbreaks, the drudgery and the uncertainties which preceded the Declaration. But history does not deal in Aladdin's lamps."

The British government had, of course, not been blind to the practical imperial and political advantages of a foothold in Palestine even before Zionist diplomacy hitched them to the rising sentiment for doing "something for the Jews." In 1917 the convergence of British interest and Jewish destiny gave birth to the Balfour Declaration just as the conjunction of world events and Jewish tragedy paved the way for the last ten years of Anglo-Jewish conflict in Palestine that led to the birth of Israel.

In the Sykes-Picot agreement of May, 1916, France and Britain had carved up Turkey's Arab domains in the Near East into French and British zones. All of Syria and some of its hinterland were assigned to France, long a British rival in that part of the world. Most of Arabia was designated a British sphere of influence. Not yet an identifiable geographical entity but still part of southern Syria, Palestine was specifically excluded. France had laid claim to Greater Syria, including Palestine, if the Turkish Empire were partitioned, but the secret Sykes-Picot understanding left Palestine subject to "a special regime" to be determined by France, Great Britain, and Russia.

The treaty paved the way for an Anglo-French effort to detach the Arabs from the Turks in exchange for a promise to lay the foundations of a postwar Arab state or confederation of Arab states under the joint suzerainty of England and France. Simultaneously, England was offering Sherif Hussein, the Arab ruler of the Bedouin principality of Hejaz, an independent Arab nation after the war if he would lead his Bedouin tribes in revolt against Turkey. The bribe was offered in a series of ten letters between Sir Henry MacMahon, British High Commissioner in Egypt, and Hussein in the fall of 1915 and the first months of 1916. The MacMahon letters did not mention Palestine, which the British later insisted was excluded from the bargain. The correspondence spoke of a Pan-Arab state within some kind of protectorate system to be run by Britain, but no boundaries were specified. Though never embodied in any treaty, the proposals were described as "declarations of policy" on behalf of the British government.

The Zionists were, of course, unaware of these behind-the-scenes arrangements that developed into "the revolt in the desert" under the leadership of Col. T. E. Lawrence. Neither did they know that their aspirations were being supported by British military and political strategists as furthering the British position in the Middle East. The situation was thus ripe for merging British imperial concerns with Zionist hopes into some kind of concrete political pronouncement.

All through 1916 and the first half of 1917 Weizmann, Sokolow, and other Zionist leaders had been involved in a series of backstage conversations, meetings, and exchanges with highly placed people in the government. These talks involved neither negotiations nor agreements but constituted mutual probings. Not until Lloyd George succeeded Asquith as Prime Minister in December, 1916, and named Balfour as Foreign Secretary were the Zionists encouraged to begin putting their proposals into writing. In the drafting of a Zionist formula many highly placed officials were consulted, including Sir Mark Sykes, who as co-negotiator of the Sykes-Picot agreement knew all about Britain's eagerness to replace the Turks in Palestine. The military decision to invade Palestine in the spring of 1917 pushed the Zionist question closer to the political forefront. Once the Turks were swept out of Palestine and Jerusalem was captured, Britain had to decide what to do with the Holy Land when it fell into her hands. Before that Britain needed a moral underpinning for what was to be an imperial acquisition. Timing and language became the determining factors once the War Cabinet had agreed in principle to some kind of statement. The phrasing had to satisfy the Zionists, avoid offending the Arabs, placate the anti-Zionists among influential British Jews, and be acceptable to world public opinion.

General Allenby's advance through the Holy Land determined the timing. On October 31 he captured Beersheba and swept north along the Mediterranean coast toward Jaffa. That same day the War Cabinet ratified the Balfour Declaration.

As the War Cabinet watched Balfour sign the declaration on November 2 at 10 Downing Street, Weizmann, like an expectant father, was waiting in an outer room. He was still hoping to be asked for his views to counteract the anti-Zionist position taken by Edwin Montagu. A copy of the document was brought to Weizmann by Sir Mark Sykes. If he had known any Hebrew, he might have said, *"Mazel Tov."* Instead he exclaimed, "Dr. Weizmann, it's a boy!"

At first reading Weizmann didn't like his progeny. It was not what he had expected. The draft approved by Balfour had been substantially whittled down. Moreover, by introducing a caveat against prejudicing "the civil and religious rights of the non-Jewish population," the Declaration imputed possible oppressive intentions to the Jews. Both of these amendments, Weizmann feared, would become crippling limitations.

Nevertheless, he understood that something of a miracle had been achieved. The Balfour Declaration was the first public acknowledgment by a Great Power of the Jewish connection with Palestine as well as an undertaking by that government to help restore the Jewish people to its homeland. For the first time a sovereign government had entered into a pact with a people scattered over the face of the earth to return them to a land largely occupied by another people. Weizmann had in effect obtained recognition for himself and his associates as a kind of government-in-exile, negotiating for Jewish settlement in a land over which Britain still had no jurisdiction.

The Balfour Declaration, representing three years of painstaking proselytizing among the British ruling class by Weizmann, was no small advance for Zionism, nor was it easily achieved. Man by man, Weizmann had converted a unique group in the British government—imperialists like Curzon and Milner, the Bible-reading Lloyd George, the agnostic Balfour, and the Boer hero Smuts—into Gentile Zionists. In the process, from 1914 to 1917 he conducted 2000 personal interviews and conversations with statesmen, politicians, and public-opinion-makers and wrote over 1000 letters.

Weizmann broke the historic news first to his wife, in a telephone call from the office of Philip A. Kerr, secretary to Prime Minister Lloyd George. Then he went back to his laboratory off Oxford Street.

A massive-domed tall figure, with magnetic eyes, a black mustache, and small Vandyke, Weizmann was equally at home in the scientist's white coat and the diplomat's frock coat. Suave and multilingual, he was a shrewd negotiator who seldom got excited.

When Weizmann began pressing for a reconstituted national home for the Jewish people in Palestine, there was no such country, the "Jewish people" was not a recognized juridical entity, and the meaning of a "national home" was known to no one. In 1917 Palestine was the southern district of Syria, a province of the crumbling Ottoman Empire with which England was engaged in a frustratingly unsuccessful war. Palestine had changed hands fourteen times in the thirteen centuries since it was first conquered by the Arabs in 637 C.E. In all that time it was never an independent country but was ruled as a province of some foreign power. Palestine had at various times been a Jewish state. Conquerers had wiped out Jewish sovereignty and decimated the Jewish population, but the link between the Jewish people and land of Israel remained unbroken over twenty centuries of continuous Jewish life on the soil of Palestine.

At the time of the Balfour Declaration there were 80,000 Jews in Palestine. The Jewish community consisted of two dozen struggling farm villages, the still raw town of Tel Aviv, a few Jewish quarters in Jerusalem, the old settlements of pietists in Safed and Hebron, a sparse school network, the nucleus of a Jewish armed forces in the Hashomer watchmen, and a language spoken mainly by schoolchildren. The world Zionist movement, of which Weizmann was not yet the elected leader, had only 130,000 members, and there was little sign of any mass support for it, even in Eastern Europe.

THE BALFOUR DECLARATION PAVES THE WAY FOR A BRITISH MANDATE

Although Weizmann had brought off what was later described as the greatest act of diplomatic statesmanship of World War I, the absence of any agreed-upon interpretation of the Balfour Declaration's ambiguous language would bedevil the Jews and British for three decades. In 1917, however, the Zionists and the British shied away from probing too deeply into its meaning. Both sought to avoid public mention of the term "Jewish state."

The equivocal phrasing of the Declaration has been attributed to a compromise in the War Cabinet. The hardheaded imperialists who were impressed by Weizmann's shrewd appeals to imperial self-interest did not see themselves as making Britain responsible for the establishment of a Jewish national home. All they were ready to promise was England's best endeavors to facilitate such an establishment. The intellectuals, Left-wing liberals, and ambitious politicians who had been moved by Weizmann's impassioned pleas to conscience supported a future Jewish state and accepted the language of the Declaration as leaving the way open to such a development.

A "national home" was a new concept in international law. It was not clear whether the national home was to be the vehicle for the creation of a Jewish state or an end in itself. If the latter was meant, at what stage could the national home be considered established? No one was sure what the Declaration promised to "facilitate." Did the commitment to safeguard the rights of the non-Jewish population contradict the promise to the Jews?

Some Zionists saw the Declaration "foreshadowing a Jewish Palestine." A Zionist manifesto to the Jewish people, whose signers included Weizmann and Sokolow, was glossed over with vague allusions to the realization of "the aspirations of 1897." Herzl had dreamed of a Jewish state but the Basle Program of 1897 did not go that far. The term "national home" had been invented by Max Nordau, on whose advice it was made the goal of the Basle Platform, rather than Herzl's "Judenstaat" ("Jewish State"). Nordau later confessed that he had done his best to persuade the claimants of the Jewish state that "we might find a circumlocution that would express all we meant, but would say it in a way so as to avoid provoking the Turkish rulers of the coveted land." Nordau suggested "Heimstaat" as a synonym for "Jewish state." He conceded it was equivocal "but we all understood what it meant. To us it signified 'Judenstaat' then and it signifies the same now."

In May, 1917, Weizmann had warned it was not "safe statesmanship" to say that the Zionists wanted the immediate creation of a Jewish state. States, he cautioned, "must be built up slowly, gradually, systematically, and patiently." He never repudiated that idea. In 1918 Sokolow branded as "wholly fallacious" any idea that the aim of Zionism was an independent Jewish state. At the Versailles Peace Conference in 1919 US Secretary of State Robert Lansing asked Weizmann how he defined "a Jewish national home." Weizmann replied, "to build up something in Palestine which will be as Jewish as England is English."

Sir Mark Sykes had advised the War Cabinet that in asking for a national home, the Jews were not seeking a Jewish republic. Sir Harold Nicolson, Sykes's assistant, said that Balfour never expected that Zionism would entail the creation of a sovereign nation. At best he saw it as heading toward "a gentle sanctuary, in which the despised Jews of Eastern Europe would find peace and religion." Sir William Ormsby-Gore, another member of the 1917 Cabinet secretariat, asserted twenty years later that Balfour regarded the Declaration as "the beginning of a policy" whose end would be Jewish statehood.

After examining the secret minutes of the 1917 War Cabinet, the Peel Commission came to a different conclusion in its report on the causes of the 1936–37 Arab uprising in Palestine. When the final draft of the Declaration was on the agenda, Balfour assured his colleagues that no early establishment of a Jewish state was contemplated. This, he explained, "was a matter of gradual development in accordance with the ordinary laws of political evolution."

Lloyd George, in his testimony before the Peel Commission in 1937, said that in 1917 his government was indeed thinking of an ultimate

Jewish commonwealth. Balfour's assistant, Lord Robert Cecil, told a Jewish rally in 1918 that the Declaration marked the rebirth of a nation. A year later Gen. Jan Christiaan Smuts, who was a member of the War Cabinet, predicted "a great Jewish state rising" in Palestine "in generations to come." Winston Churchill spoke or wrote in similar terms before the administration of Palestine came under his jurisdiction as Colonial Secretary.

The British and world press took for granted that the Balfour Declaration pointed toward a state for the Jews under the aegis of Britain, if not at once, then within a generation. The Jewish press acclaimed the Declaration as the next thing to the coming of the messiah. World Jewry reacted with exultation and unprecedented excitement. When Herbert Samuel pronounced the traditional Hebrew prayer, "Next Year in Jerusalem," at a mass meeting of thanksgiving in the London Opera House on December 2, he reflected the universal Jewish sentiment.

The tremendous enthusiasm aroused among Jews throughout the world by the Balfour Declaration was most poignant in Eastern Europe. In Odessa 150,000 Jews filled the streets in a daylong celebration. On November 6 Ha'Am, a Hebrew newspaper in Moscow, headlined its festive issue "ERETZ ISRAEL FOR THE PEOPLE OF ISRAEL."

In New York, Ben-Gurion discussed the Declaration in a series of three articles in Der Yiddisher Kampfer, organ of the Poale Zion (Labor Zionists). Writing a few days after the publication of the Declaration, Ben-Gurion agreed that it was "a miracle," but denied that England has "restored our land to us. . . . It is not in England's power to return our land to us. . . . It will not be ours even with their consent, and even if all the nations of the world agree to it. No people can establish title to a land except through its own toil, creative effort, and settlement." On November 26 his second article warned "we must establish a Jewish majority in Eretz Israel within the next twenty years." In his third article he conceded that the Declaration had achieved a major Zionist aspiration, but that there remained the more serious and difficult task "to link the revival of the Homeland with the personal fate of the wide masses of Jewry." What he meant, he said, was aliyah, ("the building of the land by the Hebrew people").

The Arabs were not unhappy about the Balfour Declaration after a British emissary had assured Sherif Hussein that "a national home" did not mean a Jewish state in Palestine. In later years the British government would insist that in 1917 it had been in no position to say that a Jewish state would or should come into being in Palestine at England's volition. It was, of course, aware that it could happen. The Zionists, on the other hand, felt that despite its clumsy language, the terms of the Balfour Declaration did not preclude an eventual Jewish state. The British then shared the Jewish belief that Palestine could be transformed peacefully from a largely Moslem Arabic-speaking territory to a Hebrew-speaking land. Neither the British nor the Zionists took Arab nationalism too seriously in 1917.

The "diplomatic egg dance" engaged in over the meaning of the Balfour Declaration had its parallel in the conflicting versions of why it was issued at all. It was seen simultaneously as a master stroke of political warfare, as a rare act of justice to a persecuted people, and as a characteristic British move toward territorial aggrandizement.

In his memoirs Lloyd George claimed that Weizmann and his associates had promised to rally worldwide Jewish sentiment to the Allies in exchange for their promise to back a Jewish national home in Palestine. The Zionists' pro-British propaganda in the United States in 1916, when the Balfour Declaration was under discussion, helped change the attitude of many American Jews. Large numbers of them were pro-German because they were anti-Russian, and they remained so until the United States entered the war in April, 1917.

The Central Powers had also become aware of the importance of Jewish sympathy, especially in those areas of Eastern Europe occupied by German and Austrian forces. Weizmann had tipped off Balfour to a German scheme to set up a Zionist-chartered company in Palestine. It was to have limited autonomy but freedom to further Jewish immigration. The Turks reluctantly agreed but took violent exception to a related plan for mobilizing a force of Polish-Jewish volunteers to fight with the Turks in Palestine.

Before the Germans could move, millions of copies of the Balfour Declaration were dropped by air on Jewish towns in Poland, Lithuania, and Galicia. Some British military strategists naïvely believed that a pro-Zionist proclamation by Russia's ally would help rally Jewish support for the tottering Kerensky government. This, they reasoned, might enable the regime that had overthrown the Czar to hold off the threatening Bolsheviks and keep Russia in the war on the Allied side. The Jewish masses in the former Czarist empire, however, were already overwhelmingly Zionist in sympathy, if not yet in affiliation.

That the Balfour Declaration was simply a clever piece of war propaganda is also unlikely since it was a unilateral pronouncement of the British government. Something of such gravity would not have been merely propaganda because it involved delicate relations with France, Italy, the

Vatican, and, before November 7, with Russia. Neither France, Italy, nor Russia was consulted before the Balfour Declaration was made public. The endorsement of France and Italy was communicated not to the British government but to the Zionists. The French approved it in a communiqué dated February 9, 1918, in which Foreign Minister Pichon summarized a conversation with Sokolow. Italy extended its blessing in a letter the Italian Ambassador in London addressed to the Zionists on May 9, 1918, on instructions from the Italian Foreign Office.

Since the United States was not at war with Turkey, Washington could take no public action involving disposition of Turkish territory. But the British sought the views of Woodrow Wilson, although his closest adviser, Col. Edward House, and Secretary of State Lansing were both suspected of being anti-Semitic. Wilson's first reaction was in response to an inquiry from the British Cabinet. A cable from House said that the President felt the time was not ripe for anything beyond a vague statement of sympathy involving no commitment. Subsequently, Justice Louis D. Brandeis advised Weizmann that Wilson and his closest advisers were in full sympathy with the Zionist draft submitted to Balfour.

When Balfour cabled to the White House the text of the Milner-Amery version being considered in London, Wilson let a week go by without an answer. On October 13 he wrote to House: "I find in my pocket the memorandum you gave me about the Zionist movement. I am afraid I did not say to you that I concurred in the formula suggested by the other side. I do, and would be obliged if you would let them know it." Another cable explained why Wilson was stalling on any public identification with the Declaration: "Colonel House put formula before President who approves of it but asks that no mention of his approval shall be made when His Majesty's Government makes formula public as he has arranged that American Jews shall then ask him for his approval, which he will give publicly here."

Lansing had warned Wilson against yielding to Zionist pressure for a public endorsement. He finally gave the Declaration oblique support in a Rosh Hashanah message dated August 31, 1918, addressed to Rabbi Stephen S. Wise. Actually, Wilson had no part in the Declaration—he simply let it happen.

Officially, the United States did not endorse the Balfour Declaration until two months after the Mandate for Palestine had been awarded to England. On June 30, 1922, the Balfour Declaration was approved in a joint resolution of both Houses of Congress. The resolution, signed by President Warren G. Harding on September 22, expressed a moral inter-

est but emphasized that it "commits us to no foreign obligations or entanglements." The United States consented to the British Mandate for Palestine in the Anglo-American Convention of 1924. This document, which
incorporated the Balfour Declaration, safeguarded American commercial
interests in Palestine, including oil exploration rights.

Leonard Stein, the historian of the Balfour Declaration, concedes that
when it was issued, it had a strictly practical purpose related to the war
situation, but he rejects the notion that it was an eleventh-hour political
warfare scheme. "Behind it lay a long story," he wrote, "of links forged
between Great Britain and the Zionists by their early pre-war contacts,
instinctive sympathy with Zionist aspirations shown by leading British
statesmen from the moment Turkey entered the war; the impression made
by Weizmann and Samuel in their sustained effort to convince the British
Government that the Zionists were a powerful force in Jewry and that
Jewish goodwill was an intangible asset worth acquiring; the response of
some imaginative minds to the suggestion that a large scale Jewish settlement in Palestine might have a stabilizing influence in an area where important British interests were at stake."

THE REALITIES OF THE DECLARATION

Any illusions that the Balfour Declaration was a clear title to a Jewish
Palestine faded even before the Mandate certified British control of the
country. An international Zionist Commission that arrived in Palestine
in April, 1918, to blueprint the Jewish national home was stunned to find
that the Declaration had been suppressed by the Occupied Enemy Territory Administration.

This military regime, which ruled Palestine during the first three years
of British occupation, was honeycombed with officials openly hostile to
the Jews. In defiance of orders from London, OETA gave the Arabs the
impression that Balfour's promise was nothing but propaganda that would
be forgotten as soon as convenient.

As head of the Zionist commission sent by the Foreign Office, Weizmann was received politely but coolly by Gen. Edmund Allenby, British
commander-in-chief. Warm letters of introduction from Balfour and Lloyd
George made little impression on the conqueror of the Holy Land. "Nothing can be done at present," he advised Weizmann at their first meeting,
held while the guns were still booming in Palestine. "We have to be extremely careful not to hurt the susceptibilities of the population."

Traveling around Palestine with Allenby, Weizmann visited the hill near Rehovot, where he later built his home and the Sieff Research Institute (which later became the Weizmann Institute). As Allenby looked out over the dry, barren, eroded landscape, he said, "Here is your Promised Land, but I don't know what you will ever be able to make of it." Neither Allenby nor anyone else in his right mind could have foreseen that in little more than fifty years a former Prime Minister of Great Britain, Harold Macmillan, would say in all seriousness, "the future for Britain is more like that of Israel."

Allenby was not anti-Zionist but his undisguised skepticism of the practicality of a Jewish homeland emboldened his own staff and that of OETA to downgrade the Balfour Declaration. Few of them had even seen it—it was not published in Palestine until 1920. But many of them had copies of the spurious Protocols of the Elders of Zion, circulated by former members of the British Military Mission to Russia. The few Jews with whom OETA had dealings were mostly Russian-born and thus suspect because of mounting hostility to the Bolsheviks.

The depleted Jewish community, many of whose leaders had been deported by the Turks or who had fled to Egypt, were at first bewildered by the animosity of those they had acclaimed as deliverers. Shock quickly turned to resentment as OETA made it plain that whatever the politicians in London had said or done, things were different in Palestine.

OETA's contempt for the Jews resulted as much from the incompetence of its personnel as from bigotry. Except for a small nucleus of professional soldiers, OETA was manned largely by carpetbaggers washed up in Palestine by the tides of war. Ronald Storrs, military governor of Jerusalem from 1917 to 1920, who has often been accused of being anti-Zionist if not anti-Semitic, listed the kind of people that staffed OETA: "a cashier from a bank in Rangoon, an actor-manager, two assistants from the Cook Travel Agency, a picture dealer, an Army coach, a clown, a land valuer, a bo'sun from the Niger, a Glasgow distiller, an organist, an Alexandria cotton broker, a taxi driver, two schoolmasters and a missionary."

Lacking clear-cut authority or functions, the Zionist Commission met with ill-concealed resistance from OETA. Responsible for maintaining order, the military and OETA saw a threat to security in the Commission's experts who came to survey the land's natural resources. Tension and clashes between OETA and the Zionist Commission not only thwarted the latter's plans for swift implementation of the Balfour Declaration, but fanned latent Arab suspicions of Jewish intentions as well.

Balfour's orders not to permit Arab agitation to interfere with the decision to create a Jewish national home were deliberately flouted by the military chiefs in Palestine. Their warnings that the Zionist Commission saw itself as the forerunner of a Jewish government found an echo in Arab fears. These were heightened by the dedication on July 24, 1918, of a symbolic cornerstone of the Hebrew University on the crest of Mount Scopus where the Roman General Titus had directed the siege of Jerusalem in 70 C.E.

The Arabs were unmoved by Weizmann's earlier assurances that Zionist development "would not and must not be to the detriment of any of the great communities already established in the country, but must, on the contrary, be to their advantage." In June, 1918, Weizmann reached an amicable understanding with Emir Feisal at the Arab commander's desert encampment at Aqaba. In the presence of Col. T. E. Lawrence, Weizmann assured Feisal that the Jews planned no government of their own in Palestine. Feisal accepted Weizmann's explanation that the goal was colonization and development of the country under British protection, "with all consideration for legitimate vested interests."

The two leaders met again in London and on January 3, 1919, a few days before the opening of the Versailles Peace Conference, and signed a mutual assistance pact. It committed the Arabs to back a Jewish Palestine unencumbered by any Arab claim. "The fullest guarantees" were specifically given for "carrying into effect the Balfour Declaration" and for "all necessary measures to encourage and stimulate the immigration of Jews into Palestine on a large scale." The Zionist Organization undertook to "use its best efforts to assist the Arab state" in developing its natural resources and economic potential. Both parties agreed to act "in complete accord" at the Peace Conference.

Feisal, who with his father, Sherif Hussein, had raised the banner of Arab revolt against the Turks, reaffirmed the agreement on March 3. In a letter to Felix Frankfurter, an adviser to the American delegation at Versailles, Feisal approved the Zionist proposals to the Peace Conference as "moderate and proper" and promised to support them. Weizmann had defined the Zionist goal in his address to the Council of Ten at Versailles as a Palestine that would be as Jewish as England is English but with explicit recognition of the rights of the non-Jewish population.

Feisal had wished the Jews "a hearty welcome home," adding, "There is room in Syria, including Palestine, for both of us." In a handwritten Arabic appendix to the pact, Feisal had made his promises dependent on complete fulfillment of Arab demands on France and England. The rest of the document, written in English, had been drafted by Colonel Lawrence.

The hero of the revolt in the desert believed the Jews would be of great help to the Arabs and that the Arab world had much to gain from a Jewish homeland in Palestine.

Feisal counted on the agreement with the Zionists to persuade the French to yield their claims to Syria, where Feisal had been installed as king of an Arab state. In welcoming the Jews back, he had in mind at most a Jewish province in a Greater Syria. An Arab congress in Damascus in July, 1919, repudiated Feisal's promises to Weizmann and opposed Jewish immigration in any part of Syria, including Palestine. The following year Feisal was kicked out of Syria by the French. The British solaced him with the throne of Iraq, but his father, Hussein, was subsequently driven out of Mecca and the Hejaz by Ibn Saud. With the collapse of the dream of Arab unity under the leadership of Hussein's family, the agreement with the Jews became a dead letter.

It was only then that Feisal's successors and supporters in the British government "discovered" that the Balfour Declaration conflicted with a prior promise to the Arabs. The forgotten MacMahon letters were suddenly uncovered to minimize the Balfour Declaration.

BRITAIN RETREATS

The increasingly anti-Zionist military administration in Palestine had meanwhile gone from opposition to the Zionist Commission to attacks on the Balfour Declaration itself. In 1919 and 1920 the OETA chiefs had demanded the abolition of the Commission, charging that it considered itself the government of Palestine. In December, 1918, the Commission had formulated an "outline for the provisional government of Palestine." It called for proclaiming the country as "the Jewish homeland in whose affairs the Jewish people as a whole shall have the determining voice." The Jewish flag was to be the national emblem and the name of the country was to be changed from Palestine to Eretz Israel.

In May, 1919, Gen. Arthur W. Money, head of the military administration, secretly asked the Foreign Office to drop the Balfour Declaration. He even warned that if Britain wanted the Mandate, she would have to make an authoritative pronouncement that the Zionist program would not be enforced in opposition to the wishes of the majority. Balfour rejected Money's caution that the Balfour Declaration was inimical to public security and advised him that nothing in Zionist plans involved displacing the Arabs. He also brushed off the report of Woodrow Wilson's King-

Crane Commission that the people of Palestine were overwhelmingly opposed to Zionist aspirations. But the authorities in Jerusalem continued to
be defiant, withholding publication of Balfour's telegram that Britain intended to become the Mandatory power and that the Balfour Declaration
was to be carried into effect. Money ordered all tax forms and receipts
printed in English and Arabic only and ignored complaints that military
officials addressed Jewish delegations in Arabic.

Gen. Louis Bols, Money's successor, was publicly rebuked for his anti-
Zionist policies by Justice Louis D. Brandeis, when the Justice went to
Palestine in 1919 on the invitation of the Zionist Commission. Brandeis
was so outraged by what he found that he demanded that every OETA
decision receive the prior consent of the Zionist Commission.

To Bols fell the embarrassing duty of giving the first public reading in
Palestine of the Balfour Declaration. It was part of his report, in May,
1920, to the leaders of the Moslem, Jewish, and Christian communities, of
the decisions of the Allied Supreme Council at San Remo. In April the
Great Powers had agreed to give the Mandate to England and to write
the Balfour Declaration into the future peace treaty with Turkey.

Bols made it plain that the British intended to govern Palestine. "In
no sense," he warned, "will a minority be allowed to control the majority
of the population when the time arrives for any form of representative
government." The decision, he said "has at last been given and henceforth
there must be an end to political strife and unrest."

"Unrest" was Bols's euphemism for the spreading Arab incitement
that erupted into violence in March and April, 1920, after having been
left unchecked for more than a year by the authorities. There was a feeling
in some Jewish quarters that the military administration would not mind
"a little pogrom" just to prove to London that the Balfour Declaration
could not be implemented and that the Arabs would not hesitate to use
force to punctuate their demands.

It began on March 1 with the murder in an ambush at Tel Hai of
Capt. Joseph Trumpeldor, the Jewish community's first hero, and seven
other defenders of four exposed upper Galilee villages. On the eve of the
Moslem festival of Nebi Moussa, which coincided with Easter and Passover, every British battalion in Palestine received a circular from OETA
which began as follows: "As the government had to pursue in Palestine a
policy unpopular with the majority of the population, trouble may be expected to arise. . . ." The last week in March all Jewish policemen in the
walled Old City of Jerusalem were relieved of duty.

On April 4 an Arab mob, shouting *"El dowleh ma'ana"*—"The government is with us"—attacked unarmed Jewish worshipers in the Jew-

ish quarter of the Old City. The city was "stiff with troops," and five Jews were killed and 211 injured in the three days of rioting. Two companies of the Jewish self-defense unit, Haganah, tried to come to the rescue but were barred by rifle-wielding Tommies at the Jaffa and Damascus Gates. In the New City outside the walls, guarded by Jewish patrols, not a single Jew was harmed.

Three days later the military arrested nineteen members of the defense group, including their commander, Vladimir Jabotinsky. The former chief political officer of the Zionist Commission, he had warned the military that their toleration of Arab agitation would lead to violence. A secret court-martial sentenced Jabotinsky to fifteen years' penal servitude. The other eighteen were given three years at hard labor. All were convicted for illegal possession of arms. Several Arabs were also imprisoned, among them Haj Amin el Husseini, the principal Arab agitator. His sentence was identical with that given Jabotinsky.

The military had an old score to settle with Jabotinsky. He had been irritating them since 1915, when he and Trumpeldor had organized the Zion Mule Corps in Egypt. A widely known Russian journalist and Zionist orator and propagandist, Jabotinsky was en route to North Africa to cover the Moslem side of the war with Turkey when he turned up in Alexandria in December, 1914. There he found a motley throng of distraught and quarreling Jewish refugees from Palestine, most of whom were Russian subjects. They had either been expelled by the Turks as potential enemies or had hastily fled of their own accord when Turkey entered World War I in November.

One of the latter was Trumpeldor, a one-armed veteran of the Russo-Japanese War. The only Jewish officer in the Czar's army, he had been wounded at the siege of Port Arthur and spent a year in a Japanese prison camp. There he became a passionate Zionist as well as a pacifist, socialist, and vegetarian. In 1911 he settled at Degania, the first kibbutz, where he taught the colonists how to shoot and ride. The sharp-tongued and hotheaded Jabotinsky, who wrote poetry in four languages and prose in eight, had for two stormy years directed the Zionist press bureau in Constantinople.

THE JEWISH LEGION

Jabotinsky and Trumpeldor shared the conviction that a Jewish military force under British command would influence the future of Palestine by helping to liberate it. From the ranks of the bedraggled Alexandria refugees, few of whom had ever handled a gun, they signed up six hundred recruits. All were pledged to "join a Jewish Legion and to propose to England to make use of it in Palestine." In Russian, Hebrew, Yiddish, and Ladino they put their names to a seven-line resolution scrawled in Hebrew on a page torn from a schoolboy's notebook.

The idea of a Jewish army to regain Palestine was not new. It had first been advanced in 1160 by David Alroy, a false messiah, and again in 1524 by David Reubeni, another would-be Jewish redeemer. When Napoleon landed in Alexandria in 1798, he offered land in Palestine as an inducement to Jews to join his armies. Herzl, too, had spoken of the need for a Jewish military force.

The offer of a Jewish Legion ready to join the British Army for service in Palestine astonished Gen. John G. Maxwell, commander of the British forces in Egypt. He knew of no immediate or future plans for an offensive in Palestine but he was aware that regulations barred the enlistment of foreign nationals. All he could suggest was that the volunteers form an auxiliary detachment for mule transport to be employed on some other sector of the Turkish front.

Repelled by the name "Mule Corps" and scorning to send a Jewish unit to any front but Palestine, Jabotinsky bowed out of the adventure. Trumpeldor, however, felt that any Turkish front led to Zion, and became second-in-command to Lt. Col. J. H. Patterson, an Irish Protestant, when a battalion of 562 men was officially organized as the Zion Mule Corps.

Wearing the Star of David as their emblem, and lustily singing "Tipperary" in Russian and Yiddish accents, the Zion muleteers sailed for the Gallipoli Peninsula in February, 1915. Driving mules loaded with ammunition from supply dumps to the front lines was their lowly but hazardous assignment. In the disastrous 1915 campaign that failed to dislodge the Turks from the Dardanelles, they suffered heavy casualties. Evacuated and disbanded in May, 1916, the survivors became the nucleus of the Jewish Legion.

To the Turks, the Zionist Mule Corps was a Zionist declaration of war for which the Jews of Palestine suffered heavily. Jemal Pasha, Turkish Governor of Palestine, arrested and imprisoned hundreds of Jews and had thousands more deported or forced into exile. Retaliation against the Jews of Palestine became more widespread at the end of 1915, when the Turks got wind of NILI, a clandestine Jewish intelligence network working for the British behind the Turkish lines in Palestine and Egypt.

One of those jailed as an enemy of the Sultan was twenty-eight-year-old David Green, a staff member of *Ha'Achdut* (Unity), a Hebrew weekly

magazine edited by Isaac Shimshelevitz as the mouthpiece of the Labor
Zionists. In his first article Green signed himself "Ben-Gurion," which in
Hebrew means "Young Lion." As a farm laborer at Sejera, Ben-Gurion
had been one of the organizers of Hashomer (The Watchmen), a secret
society of armed guards founded in 1907 to protect Jewish villages
against raiding Bedouins. Its principal organizer was Shimshelevitz, who,
as Itzhaak Ben Zvi, would become the second President of the Jewish
state.

Ben Zvi and Ben-Gurion, known as "the twins," went off to Constantinople in 1913 to study at the Ottoman University School of Law and to
dream of what they would do for Palestine Jewry when they became
members of the Turkish Parliament. They were joined by Moshe Shertok,
a boy of nineteen, just out of the Herzliah High School in Tel Aviv, who
would later make his mark as Moshe Sharett, Israel's first Foreign Minister.

All three returned to Jerusalem a few weeks before Turkey entered
the war. Shertok became a captain in the Turkish Army, serving until
1918. Ben-Gurion and Ben Zvi appeared in Alexandria while the Zion
Mule Corps was being trained, but neither joined it. They left instead for
the United States, where they spent two years recruiting settlers for Palestine and propagandizing for Labor Zionism among the Yiddish-speaking
trade unionists.

While the secret negotiations that would lead to the Balfour Declaration were being pressed in 1915 and 1916, Jabotinsky became the most
detested man in the London Jewish community because of his lonely fight
for a Jewish Legion. Most British Jews scoffed at the idea as quixotic or
denounced it as dangerous. Zionist officialdom, for the most part, shied
away from it. The Russian Zionists were hostile because it would have allied them with Czarism. The Americans were still split over the war. The
British War Secretary, Lord Kitchener, wanted "no fancy regiments" and
opposed an offensive in Palestine.

Jabotinsky initially tried to persuade the Russian Jews in London's
East End to volunteer for the British Army. As aliens they were exempt
from conscription but the country was rumbling with complaints about
Jewish slackers. Recruiting rallies in Whitechapel were broken up by
mobs of anti-Zionist socialists and anarchists, and Jabotinsky himself was
often stoned and pummeled. The remnant of the lowly Zion Mule Corps,
once rejected by Jabotinsky, turned the tide.

When 120 veterans of the demobilized Jewish muleteers, headed by
Captain Trumpeldor, arrived in London at the end of 1916, every one of

them reenlisted. All were posted to the same outfit, the 20th County of London. Jabotinsky promptly joined them, as a private, in January, 1917. From his barracks he began negotiating with Prime Minister Lloyd George and the War Office. The flow of communications between Private Jabotinsky and the War Office became a battalion joke. Whenever an orderly arrived with a brown envelope, Jabotinsky's sergeant cracked, "I suppose it is another telegram for Mr. Jug-o'-Whiskey," which is how the name sounded to some of the Cockney soldiers. Jabotinsky was a teetotaler but the nickname stuck and followed him to Palestine.

The brown envelopes contained encouraging news. One communication advised Private Jabotinsky that his memorandum of January 24, 1917, to the Prime Minister had been carefully read. Leopold Amery, who would soon be busy formulating the final text of the Balfour Declaration, sent word that the War Cabinet was interested. Another message from Amery said that Jabotinsky's plan for a Jewish force had been referred to the War Office. On a sunny April morning Jabotinsky, a private in pince-nez, and Trumpeldor, a captain with one empty sleeve, presented themselves at the War Office. Amery had made an appointment for them with Lord Derby, Secretary of War. After his first astonishment at the lowly rank of his callers, who had been vouched for by higher authorities, Derby listened politely but made no promises.

In July, Britain and the Kerensky government reached an agreement giving Russian citizens in England the choice of enlisting in the British Army or returning to Russia for military service there. On August 23, just seventy-one days before the Balfour Declaration, the War Cabinet approved the formation of two regiments of Jewish volunteers; Jabotinsky was commissioned a lieutenant and made chief recruiter. Trumpeldor had already left for Russia, where he hoped to mobilize an army of Jews who would invade Palestine by way of the Caucasus. Two years later he returned to Palestine, alone, the Bolshevik Revolution having drawn the iron curtain, before the phrase was coined, between the Jewish masses of Russia and their brethren in Palestine.

The first of the two authorized regiments was the 38th Royal Fusiliers. Its nucleus was the Zion Mule Corps veterans, with their own Colonel Patterson in command, and filled out by Yiddish-speaking tailors, pressers, and shopkeepers recruited in Whitechapel. The Tommies dubbed them the "Jewsiliers." On February 5, 1918, they sailed for Egypt after having marched in full battle dress through the City of London as a band of the Coldstream Guards played "Hatikvah." Jabotinsky, the Zionist Garibaldi, carried the blue and white flag with the Star of David and the Hebrew motto "If I forget thee, O Jerusalem, may my right hand forget her cunning."

A second Jewish regiment, the 39th Royal Fusiliers, was organized from volunteers in the United States and Canada. Among the chief recruiters were Ben-Gurion and Ben Zvi who counted on the enlistees staying in Palestine. The "twins" had found themselves on the wrong continent when the Balfour Declaration and the British capture of Jerusalem created wild excitement in the Jewish world. Both enlisted in April, 1918, and landed in Egypt in August. In a few weeks Ben-Gurion was a corporal. Eager to get on with the building of the land, however, he lost his stripes when he went AWOL from a camp near Tel Aviv to call on Weizmann at the Jerusalem headquarters of the Zionist Commission. It was the first meeting of the two men whose lifework was bound up with creating the State of Israel.

Ben-Gurion's outfit included Jacob Epstein, the sculptor, and Gershon Agronsky, a future mayor of Jerusalem. The commander was Col. Eleazar Margolin, a native of Palestine, who had grown up in Australia. He was the first Jew to lead an official Jewish military force into action on Palestinian soil since the days of Simon Bar Kochba.

Once the British invaded Palestine, they were swamped with Jewish volunteers demanding the right to help complete the conquest. Allenby and Bols opposed enlisting Palestinian Jews and only reluctantly permitted the formation of the 40th Royal Fusiliers. It was organized by Eliahu Golomb, later chief of the underground Jewish militia that became Haganah, and commanded by Col. F. D. Samuel, an English Jew.

When the fighting ended in Palestine in October, 1918, the three regiments, known collectively as "The Judeans," numbered over 5000 men. In their ranks were many future officers of Haganah and builders of the Jewish state. Official dispatches cited their gallantry during the conquest of southern Palestine and the Jordan Valley, but not a word of their heroism was permitted to be published in the Palestine or Egyptian newspapers. By early 1919 the Judeans constituted about one-sixth of the British army of occupation in Palestine.

Threats of Arab violence made the existence of the Jewish regiments crucial to the defense of the Jewish community. Jabotinsky saw the Jewish Legion as the core of a permanent Jewish militia of a future Jewish government. The British wanted the Legion demobilized as quickly as possible and did everything they could to compel its liquidation. For more than a year the Jewish troops languished in idleness at an Egyptian camp. At the end of 1919 the force had dwindled to 400 men. Discharges were being accepted as soon as offered because of the violent Jew-baiting by British officers. They treated the Jewish soldiers like foreigners and potential troublemakers whose chief they mocked as "Mr. Jug-o'-Whiskey." Two companies of Americans and Canadians, who made up more than half of the Jewish Legion, mutinied in protest against open discrimination. Jabotinsky defended them at a court-martial.

The cockiness and militancy that were to make him Zionism's stormy petrel for twenty years reached a climax with a sensational letter he addressed to General Allenby. "Anti-Semitism," he charged, "is permeating the whole administration and military atmosphere" in Palestine. The efforts of the Jewish Legion, he wrote, were "breaking into pieces under the intolerable burden of disappointment, despair, and broken pledges."

Jabotinsky became a marked man with his warning to Allenby that "the common opinion is that you are the enemy of Zionism in general and of the Jewish Legion in particular." Adding that he still wanted to believe "that this is not true" and conceding that perhaps things were happening without Allenby's knowledge, he ended the incredible letter by requesting a personal interview "as the last attempt to stop a process which threatens to impair forever Anglo-Jewish friendship throughout the world."

On August 9, 1919, General Headquarters at Cairo ordered Lieutenant Jabotinsky forcibly demobilized. Things had changed since Private Jabotinsky was invited to confer with the Secretary of War, although London had sent him a decoration for his war services.

Once the Judeans were demobilized early in 1920, the Zionist Commission grudgingly consented to Jabotinsky's proposal for a permanent Jewish defense organization. The Labor Zionists held out for a secret militia patterned on the Hashomer, but Jabotinsky's insistence that the unit be public won a bare majority. Once again he became the chief recruiter.

The core around which he built was a small underground force established by Zionist teen-agers in February, 1920. It was called "Haganah" ("Defense"). Guns obtained from an Armenian smuggler were cached in Jabotinsky's apartment and in the residence of his aide, Jeremiah Halperin. Demobilized officers from the Jewish Legion drilled the recruits in night hikes and grenade-throwing. Training was entirely in the open. Jerusalem's military governor, Ronald Storrs, was kept informed. A few days before the festival of Nebi Moussa members of Haganah staged maneuvers on the slope of the Mount of Olives, where OETA had its headquarters. It was this force that tried to defend the Jews of the Old City during the pogrom of April 4–6.

A JEWISH HIGH COMMISSIONER

Ten weeks after the savage reprisals against the Jewish defenders of the Old City, the generals and the entire military regime in Palestine were replaced. Installed in their stead was a civilian administration headed by an English Jew, Herbert Samuel, who had first raised the banner of Zionism inside the British Cabinet in 1914. He was appointed High Commissioner as well as commander-in-chief. It was a calculated move to calm the worldwide storm of protest raised by the harsh sentences meted out to the Haganah men and their commander.

The Arabs swore Samuel would not live four days after he landed. But the Jews hailed him as a new Nehemiah when he disembarked from a British destroyer at Haifa on June 30, 1920. Resplendent in white uniform and gold braid, Samuel reached Jerusalem by armored train. Tanks and cavalry escorted him from the Jerusalem railway station to a huge stone house on the Mount of Olives. The massive building, from which OETA's anti-Zionist policies had emanated since 1917, now became the official residence of a Jewish governor. Government House was its new name. Until the British occupied it as military headquarters it had been a rest home for German Christian pilgrims. Erected before World War I by Kaiser Wilhelm I and named in honor of his consort, Augusta Victoria, it loomed over the Old City from a high wooded ridge between Mount Scopus and the Mount of Olives, within sight of the Garden of Gethsemane.

In that house in 1921 Winston Churchill wrote an early draft of a White Paper that would be the first major whittling-down of the Balfour Declaration. In that house in 1925 Lord Balfour was a guest when he came to dedicate the Hebrew University. In that house Samuel's only son, Edwin, was married and his two grandsons were circumcised. (Edwin Samuel went to Palestine as a liaison officer with the Zionist Commission and then served in the British Mandatory government until ordered out of the country in 1948 with other British subjects.) In that house High Commissioner Samuel officially took over the administration of Palestine from General Bols, the last commander of OETA.

As a parting gag, Bols asked Samuel to give him a receipt for the Holy Land. Two documents were drawn up. One, handing over Palestine, was signed by Bols and ceremoniously given to Samuel. The other, a receipt for "one Palestine, complete and in good order," was signed by Samuel and with equal pomp presented to Bols. Because he knew how the Jewish community felt about OETA, Samuel insisted on adding the letters

"E & O E" (errors and omissions excepted). In England these initials were usually appended to bank invoices for goods sold to absolve the signer from responsibility for any omissions and errors subsequently discovered. Years later the Samuel document was sold at auction in New York for $5000. It is now in the Israel Archives, together with Bols's receipt to Samuel.

Samuel arrived with a sense of messianic mission and the Jews greeted him as a messianic ruler. They addressed him as *"Hanassi"*—among other meanings, "The Prince"—the precise Hebrew title later adopted for the President of Israel. The Oriental Jews wrote Hebrew psalms in his praise. For weeks Jerusalem was placarded with Arab proclamations that Samuel was marked for assassination, but he pointedly ignored the threats.

On the first Saturday after his arrival the Governor walked the two miles from the Mount of Olives to the Old City, whose narrow, winding alleys were lined with weeping and cheering Jews. Overwhelmed with joy at greeting a fellow Jew who represented His Majesty, the King of England, the Sabbath throng followed him to the ancient Hurva Synagogue, later to be destroyed by the Arab Legion in the siege of Jerusalem in 1948. In this historic building Samuel read in Hebrew the weekly prophetic portion from Isaiah: "Comfort ye, comfort ye, my people." The people of Jerusalem that day were "almost faint with happiness," Ronald Storrs wrote, "moving as if in the glory and freshness of a dream come true." At a reception Samuel gave for his staff a few days after being installed at Government House, one of them blurted, "And there I was at Government House, and there was the Union Jack flying as large as life, and a bloody Jew sitting under it."

Amnesty for Jabotinsky and his fellow Haganah prisoners was one of Samuel's first actions, and similar clemency was extended to the Arab rapists and arsonists of the 1920 pogrom. He reached an amicable agreement on immigration with the Zionist Commission and established Hebrew as one of Palestine's official languages. He even found an ingenious way of giving recognition in official documents and on postage stamps to Eretz Israel as the traditional Jewish name of the country. But his deliberate policy of trying to treat Jews and Arabs alike won him friends in neither community, and the passionate expectation aroused among Jews by Samuel's appointment quickly evaporated.

In a futile attempt to appease Arab extremists, he committed what turned out to be a fatal blunder for which the Palestine government and the Jewish community would pay in violence and bloodshed. Samuel shocked the Jews by pardoning Haj Amin el Husseini, instigator of the 1920 Arab disturbances, who had been condemned in absentia to fifteen years' imprisonment after he fled to Transjordan. Samuel named him President of the Supreme Moslem Council and Mufti of Jerusalem, to succeed his half-brother. Given control of the Moslem religious courts and $500,000 in annual charity funds, the Mufti would use them henceforth, until his second flight from Palestine in 1938, to inflame the Arab populace against the Jews and the government.

Samuel had proposed a mixed Arab-Jewish militia to avert civil disorder, but the idea was abandoned in the face of a new eruption of Arab violence in Jaffa on May 1, 1921. Martial law was imposed to quell the weeklong outbreak that claimed ninety lives and injured four hundred. While a Royal Commission was still investigating, Samuel capitulated to Arab threats.

In a speech that sounded to Jewish ears like a complete negation of the basic concept of the Balfour Declaration, Samuel announced the temporary suspension of Jewish immigration. He assured the Arabs that the Balfour Declaration gave the Jews no special privileges and no right to a share in the government. Arab worries over a Jewish invasion were groundless, he said, because the government had no policy that would permit Jews to displace the Arab population. Moreover, he added, there would be definite limits on the number of Jews admitted.

By 1921 there was still no sign of any mass movement of Jews to the Promised Land. The Soviets had already banned immigration and outlawed Zionism, and the gates to the United States were still open to Jewish masses in Eastern Europe. Only 1806 Jews had arrived in Palestine in 1919 and 8000 had come in 1920. For the next three years the annual average would barely top 8100.

The Arabs accepted Samuel's surrender as a signal that violence could force the government's hand, a tactic they would consistently employ in trying to slow down or halt Jewish immigration and land purchases. The Jews regarded Samuel's actions as a serious setback, coupling them with the upsurge of anti-Zionist opinion in England. The British public's war-weariness and the angry debate over whether Britain should accept the Palestine Mandate had fueled agitation for the swift liquidation of all British commitments in the Middle East.

As early as 1919, when the Foreign Office began to consider the terms of the Mandate, there were already signs that the government was backing away from any actual or implied commitment either to a Jewish state or to a Jewish commonwealth. Lord Curzon, Balfour's successor as Foreign

Secretary, had supported the Balfour Declaration in the War Cabinet, but had become cautious in the face of a revolt against the Mandate by die-hards in his own Conservative Party. He firmly opposed Zionist pressure for inserting into the Mandate some reference to the eventual establishment of a Jewish commonwealth. Such a move, he warned, would jeopardize Britain's acceptance of the Mandate.

The Zionists also wanted a phrase in the Mandate's preamble to recognize "the historical right of the Jews to Palestine." Curzon flatly refused to accept this language formulated by his own secretary and by Benjamin V. Cohen, an American who was one of Weizmann's advisers. "If you word it like that," Curzon said, "I can see Weizmann coming to me every other day and saying he had a right to do this, that, or the other in Palestine. I won't have it." The way it finally read was "historical connection," words suggested by Balfour. Irked by Curzon's rejection of draft after draft, Weizmann ruefully observed that "the temperature has dropped in this office since your predecessor left."

An Arab delegation, armed with complaints against the Jews and High Commissioner Samuel, spearheaded the attack on the Mandate even before its text had been completed. Anti-Zionists in Parliament, backed by the Northcliffe and Beaverbrook newspapers, echoed the Arab line: the Jews were riding roughshod over the Arabs at the expense of the British taxpayer; Zionists' plans were both dangerous and utterly impractical; Jewish immigrants were the advance agents of Bolshevism; the Balfour Declaration should be repealed and Britain should leave Palestine. The previously unpublished 1915 MacMahon correspondence with Sherif Hussein was suddenly revealed in order to give support to the Arab claim that the Balfour Declaration violated a prior promise to them. Subsequently, however, in a letter to the editor of *The Times* of London in 1937, MacMahon himself denied that the area of Palestine had been included in the pledge to the Arab emirs.

The Haycraft Commission's report on the causes of the 1921 riots refuted allegations of Jewish Bolsheviks in Palestine but nevertheless gave the charges wide currency. Foes of the Mandate seized on the Commission's implication that Arab bitterness over Zionist ambitions to dominate Palestine was the root of the trouble and that immediate safeguards were required to dispel Arab fears.

A motion to reject the Mandate was overwhelmingly approved in the House of Lords in June, 1922. The vote was tantamount to saying the Balfour Declaration should be nullified. When Weizmann worriedly called on Balfour to learn the significance of the upper house's action, Balfour's bland reply was, "What does it matter if a few foolish lords passed such a motion?" He himself had spoken eloquently against the motion in his first appearance in the House.

Although an identical motion was decisively turned back in the House of Commons, the foes of the Mandate wrung from the same government that had issued the Balfour Declaration a sweeping reinterpretation that greatly diluted the original commitment. On the eve of the formal submission of the Mandate for League of Nations ratification, the disintegrating Lloyd George coalition published a White Paper dated June 22, 1922, in which it sought to reassure the Arabs and their friends without entirely repudiating the promise to the Jews.

That pledge had already been whittled down by the first partition of Palestine in 1921. In a scheme devised by War Secretary Winston Churchill and Col. T. E. Lawrence, four-fifths of the 45,000 square miles of Palestine proper were lopped off from the area supposedly assigned to the Jewish national home. Everything east of the Jordan River was assigned to the new emirate or principality of Transjordan, within whose borders Jews were forbidden to buy land. On the throne of the new desert realm the British set the Emir Abdullah, whose brother, the Emir Feisal, had signed a short-lived pact of friendship with Weizmann in 1919, when the Zionist leader traveled to Transjordan for the purpose.

The 1922 statement of policy is also linked with the name of Winston Churchill, who was then head of the Colonial Office, to which the administration of Palestine had been transferred. Much of it, however, had been drafted by Herbert Samuel, who had requested an official definition of the Jewish national home and a clarification of the Balfour Declaration.

The White Paper explained that the terms of the Balfour Declaration "do not contemplate that Palestine as a whole should be converted into a Jewish national home." All that was intended was that such a home "should be founded in Palestine." This involved nothing more than "the further development of the existing Jewish community with the assistance of Jews in other parts of the world." It did not mean "the imposition of a Jewish nationality upon the inhabitants of Palestine as a whole."

To silence talk of an immediate Jewish state, the statement disavowed "unauthorized statements" implying that the Balfour Declaration had in mind the creation of "a wholly Jewish Palestine." The government warned that it "regards any such expectation as impracticable and has no such aim in view." Churchill spelled out the new policy more precisely in the House of Commons on June 27, when he said, "Again and again it has been stated that the intention from the beginning has been to make a national home for the Jews, but every provision has been made to prevent it from becoming in any sense a Jewish state or a state under Jewish domination."

Within these limitations the White Paper affirmed that the Balfour Declaration remained the bedrock of the government's Palestine policy. The Jews were in Palestine "as of right and not on sufferance," but further Jewish immigration "will not exceed the economic capacity of the country to absorb new arrivals."

The Arabs remained unmoved by the guarantee against Jewish domination and by the introduction of the principle of regulated Jewish immigration. The Mufti rejected the entire White Paper because it recognized some Jewish rights in Palestine. The Zionists reluctantly accepted the new policy even though it ended hope of a quick buildup of a Jewish majority. They had been privately warned that Britain might forget the Mandate if they protested too loudly.

When the Mandate came up for action in the Council of the League of Nations on Saturday morning, July 24, 1922, neither the Zionists nor the British delegation was at all certain of the outcome. Ratification required unanimity. Spain, whose representative was the chairman, had been wavering under the pressure of the Vatican, which opposed the Mandate. British protests had strengthened the Arabs' position. At the last moment the Spanish delegate agreed to support the Mandate, having been reminded by the Zionists that it was Spain's chance to repay an old debt to the Jews. When Lord Balfour moved for ratification, the Mandate was adopted unanimously.

The Mandate made Great Britain responsible for placing Palestine "under such political, administrative and economic conditions as will secure the establishment of the Jewish national home." This carried with it a commitment to "putting into effect" the Balfour Declaration, which was made part of the Mandate's preamble. England's unilateral promise of 1917, which could have been repudiated or permitted to lapse, had become part of an international treaty. In acquiring the international title deed to Palestine, Britain assumed "the most important international obligation ever entrusted to a single nation."

This obligation required her to facilitate Jewish immigration "under suitable conditions"; to encourage close settlement of Jews on the land, including state and waste lands not required for public purposes; to protect the rights of all inhabitants of the country, regardless of race and religion. The Mandate became effective September 29, 1923, two months after the Treaty of Lausanne in which Turkey surrendered all claim to Arab Asia.

The primary purpose of the Mandate was to make a reality out of a concept unprecedented in international law—the establishment of the Jewish national home. The nature of this home and when it would be considered as having come into being were ignored in the Mandate. It was equally silent on whether the national home was to be the vehicle for the creation of a Jewish state or whether the home was to be an end in itself. Nevertheless, the Mandate authorized the setting up of a Jewish administration and political apparatus that would become the mainspring of the first government of the Jewish state.

Article IV provided for "an appropriate Jewish agency" empowered to advise and cooperate with the Palestine government on all matters affecting the establishment of the Jewish national home. The Mandate specifically recognized the World Zionist Organization "as such agency" and gave it the right to enlist the cooperation of all Jews willing to help build the national home.

THE BEGINNINGS OF JEWISH SELF-GOVERNMENT

The Jewish community in Palestine (Yishuv) dealt with domestic problems of health, education, and religion through an elected National Council (Va'ad L'umi), but when it came to the national home the Zionist Organization was the international representative and spokesman of Jews everywhere. Thus the Zionist Executive, elected by the biennial World Zionist Congresses, became responsible for directing immigration, colonization, and economic planning in the homeland and for fending off repeated attempts to breach the Mandate.

The two financial instruments of Zionism were the Jewish National Fund, founded in 1901, and the Keren Hayesod, established in 1920. The former acquired land as Jewish national property on which communal and collective settlements were established. The latter raised the funds for immigration, colonization, and agricultural development. In the United States the two funds were joined together as the United Palestine Appeal, which later, in partnership with the Joint Distribution Committee (JDC), became the United Jewish Appeal.

The national home made steady progress during the uneasy Arab-Jewish peace of the Mandate's first years. By 1929 the Jewish population had trebled, to 162,000, largely as a result of 100,000 postwar immigrants. The number of Arabs had meanwhile doubled to 800,000. The 50 agricultural colonies of 1919, with their 12,000 inhabitants, had grown to 120 villages with 40,000 Jews spotted in a pattern of settlement that would shape the future map of Israel. Draining of swamps and marshes, afforestation, intensified agriculture, and the beginning of light industry had begun to change the face of the land. Tel Aviv had become the country's metropolis while new Jewish agricultural and residential suburbs had given Jerusalem a modern look.

The Arabs saw this growth as confirming their worst fears. When in 1925 Lord Balfour paid his only visit to Palestine, to dedicate the Hebrew University, the Arab community denounced him as an enemy. His arrival was observed as a day of mourning and by a twenty-four-hour strike proclaimed in black-bordered newspapers and wall posters. Government House was stacked high with hundreds of Arab telegrams protesting against the Jewish national home, but they were never shown to Balfour. Except in the Jewish quarter, he passed through silent streets in the Old City of Jerusalem. Fearing an attempt on his life, the Palestine government kept him away from the Mosque of Omar. When the seventy-seven-year-old statesman, scarlet-robed as the Chancellor of Cambridge University, rose to speak on Mount Scopus, he was flanked by General Allenby, Dr. Weizmann, and High Commissioner Samuel, all guarded by armed Tommies.

Only in Tel Aviv and on the Jewish farm settlements did Balfour's visit provoke intense enthusiasm and excitement. Children garlanded him with wreaths of flowers, rabbis sang his praises in special prayers, scores of babies born during and after his visit were named Balfour.

The rebuilding Balfour witnessed had commenced with the arrival of the first *chalutzim* ("pioneers"), hardy and idealistic young people committed to personal and physical rejuvenation through labor on the soil of Eretz Israel. Trained for self-defense and agriculture in camps and model colonies in Poland, they were the products of the Hechalutz movement, launched in Russia in the summer of 1917 by Captain Trumpeldor. Most of the 37,000 *chalutzim* who came to Palestine between 1919 and 1924 were militant socialists and Zionist zealots. Under the leadership of the earlier generation of Labor Zionists led by Ben-Gurion and Ben Zvi, the *chalutzim* became the builders of the kibbutzim, cooperative institutions, Haganah, and Histadrut, the trade union movement.

A second wave of immigration to Palestine in 1925 brought 35,000 refugees from anti-Semitism and economic upheaval in Poland after the United States had closed its doors to immigration. Mostly artisans and small shopkeepers, they were unprepared for the hardships of an underdeveloped country.

An economic collapse in 1927 not only created serious unemployment and dried up immigration for almost two years; it also provoked bitter conflict between anti-labor employers and Histadrut, the rising General Confederation of Jewish Labor that had been organized in 1920 with Ben-Gurion as general secretary. Controversy in Palestine was part of the political struggle that rocked the Zionist movement from 1920 to 1929. The clash of principles and personalities reflecting the rising pressures that would explode into the birth of Israel hinged on three issues: how to deal with the Mandatory Power and the Arabs, the character and temper of the national Home's development, and the need to mobilize wider Jewish support.

Delegates in 1921 to the first postwar World Zionist Congress were so dazzled by the messianic vision of the Balfour Declaration that many came prepared with lists of portfolios for the Jewish state's Cabinet. They were stunned and angered by Weizmann's sober warning that they first had to show they could make barren soil fertile, drain swamps, move masses across a continent, and lay the foundations for a sound economy.

The first rift appeared when the Brandeis wing of American Zionists failed to commit the movement to end all political efforts for the homeland in favor of all-out concentration on economic upbuilding. Backed by Ben-Gurion and his Labor Zionists, Weizmann insisted that both had to be pursued simultaneously. Far more challenging to Weizmann's policies was Vladimir Jabotinsky, the hero of the Jewish Legion who had a mass following in Eastern and Central Europe.

Jabotinsky's reiterated demands for a more aggressive political offensive against Britain, and his repeated calls for a Jewish state on both sides of the Jordan, brought him into conflict with Weizmann and the Zionist establishment. His ceaseless advocacy of a permanent publicly recognized Jewish Legion to defend the homeland won him the enmity of the Labor Zionists, who held out for an underground force as the only answer to the Yishuv's security.

Jabotinsky was the first contributor to the secret arms fund of Haganah after Eliahu Golomb succeeded him as its commander in 1921, but Haganah regarded him as its foe. Hundreds of trade unionists and *chalutzim* had been drawn into Haganah, but many of Jabotinsky's followers were anti-labor. Jabotinsky eventually quit the Zionist Executive and organized the Zionist Revisionists as a separate party whose differences with the Socialists broke into open violence. Subsequently he seceded from the Zionist Organization and formed the New Zionist Organization and a youth auxiliary known as Betar. A paramilitary outfit, Betar was an acronym for B'rith Trumpeldor, named for the one-armed martyr of Tel

Hai. It was also the name of the fortress where Bar Kochba made his last stand against the Romans in 135 C.E. Betar members later became the first cadres of the Irgun Z'vai L'umi, the underground military organization.

THE 1929 ARAB RIOTS

Amid the Zionists' internal battles of the 1920s no one really took the Arab problem very seriously. Putative attempts to find some common ground with the upper class of Arab professionals, landowners, and businessmen got nowhere because the Arabs were adamant in opposing the Balfour Declaration. French and British concessions to nationalist violence in Syria and Iraq provoked greater Arab intransigence in Palestine. When the extremists of the Mufti's party gained the upper hand, Arab tactics shifted from political pressure to religious incitement of the illiterate fellahin. A quarrel in 1928 over Jewish access rights to the Western Wall (the Wailing Wall) of the Haram as Sharif Temple area of the Old City of Jerusalem was blown up into the explosive charge that the Jews wanted to rebuild their temple on the site of the Mosque of Omar. Feelings boiled to a fever pitch for nearly a year amid widely scattered attacks on Jews before the Mufti found the pretext he needed to provoke what became the bloody 1929 riots.

The immediate provocation was a reckless demonstration in front of the Western Wall on August 14, 1929, by members of Betar. It was the eve of Tisha B'Av, the fast day commemorating the destruction of the first two Temples. Beyond the Wall, in the Mosque of Omar, Arab preachers insinuated that the Betar parade was part of an all-out assault on Moslem shrines. Moslem worshipers leaving the Mosque two days later attacked Jews at random. Within a week the outbreak escalated into a nationwide pogrom.

Two events at the 1929 World Zionist Congress were also exploited by the Mufti of Jerusalem to fuel his anti-Jewish propaganda. Jabotinsky's inflammatory speech calling for a preponderant Jewish majority on both sides of the Jordan was distorted into a declaration of war on the Arabs. Ratification of a plan to enlarge the Jewish Agency, by the inclusion of non-Zionists, as authorized by the Mandate, was cited as proof of a Jewish plot to take over all of Palestine.

After six years of frustrating and contentious negotiations, Weizmann had won his fight to transform the Zionist agency into the Jewish Agency for Palestine, a more representative international body in which Zionists and non-Zionists had parity in the administration and building of the Jewish homeland. The chief objective of the extended Agency was to win the support of influential and wealthy Jewish leaders in the United States who were opposed or indifferent to the ultimate political aims of Zionism but sympathetic to the practical work of building a refugee center.

Nine days after the Jewish Agency was constituted on August 14, 1929, the storm brewed by the Mufti's agitation erupted in Jerusalem and Haifa and then spread to Hebron and Safed. In a week-long pogrom inflamed mobs butchered helpless men, women, and children and stabbed to death and mutilated unarmed scholars and teachers. By the time the police restored order, 133 Jews had been killed and 339 injured; Arab casualties, mostly in police action, numbered 116 dead and 232 wounded.

The Shaw Commission that investigated the riots whitewashed the Mufti and blamed Zionist immigration and land-buying for "creating a landless and discontented class of Arabs." Rigorous curbs on Jewish land acquisition and immigration that would have frozen the national home were recommended in 1930 by Sir John Hope Simpson, after an on-the-spot study. These became part of a basic new Palestine policy enunciated by the Colonial Secretary, Lord Passfield, in a White Paper of October 21, 1930.

British obligations under the Mandate were redefined as the establishment of the Jewish national home *and* the protection of the rights of the non-Jewish communities. Both had equal weight, the White Paper said, and were in no sense irreconcilable, but stricter land-transfer regulations and controls on Jewish immigration were imposed. Passfield's introduction of the concept of "equality of obligation" and his rejection "as totally erroneous" of the claim that the Mandate's principal objective was to further the Jewish national home raised a worldwide furor. Hot anger boiled up in Palestine and Weizmann resigned as President of the Jewish Agency. Led by some of the framers of the Balfour Declaration, Conservatives and Liberals in the House of Commons violently attacked Ramsay MacDonald's Labour government.

Under this pressure the British government retreated. Without rescinding the White Paper, it moderated the new policy in a statement embodied in an open letter to Weizmann in February, 1931, in which MacDonald disavowed any intent to limit Jewish land purchases or immigration, but did not repudiate the dual obligation theory.

The government's recantation was forced by Ernest Bevin, who sixteen years later would end the long-drawn-out British inquest on Palestine by junking the Balfour Declaration and repudiating the Mandate. In 1931 Bevin was not a member of Parliament, but as the General Secretary of the powerful Transport and General Workers Union, he controlled fifteen Labour votes in the House of Commons. His warning to MacDonald that these fifteen MPs would vote against the government unless it altered the White Paper policy compelled the reinterpretation. As Foreign Secretary in the postwar Labour government of Clement Attlee, Bevin later changed his tune and became the most hated Briton in the Yishuv.

PRESSURE FOR REFUGEE IMMIGRATION

The uproar over the Passfield proposals had not entirely abated when unprecedented pressures for immigration to Palestine generated by the rise of Hitler suddenly gave dramatic urgency to the national home. There were only 200,000 Jews in Palestine, one-sixth the total population, when the Nazis seized power in 1933. Prospects of a Jewish majority and a Jewish state had dimmed in the face of Arab recalcitrance and Britain's unwillingness or inability to fulfill her commitments. From 1933 to 1936, however, the Jewish population nearly doubled and Jewish capital investment in the country more than tripled with the unanticipated arrival of 140,000 refugees from Hitlerism. These included several thousand who slipped in illegally via Lebanon and Syria. This emigration from Nazi Germany was aided by an understanding between the Jewish Agency and the Reichs Ministry of Economics at a time when Hitler was still encouraging Jews to get out.

Under this arrangement a Jew leaving Germany would contract with a German exporter to transfer certain goods to Palestine. The exporter would pay for them from the blocked account of the emigrant, who was reimbursed in Palestine currency by the Jewish Agency. This transfer plan enabled more than 50,000 Jews to bring most of their assets to Palestine despite bitter protests in some Jewish quarters that it also benefited the German economy.

While this welcome numerical and economic growth stiffened the Yishuv's resistance to edicts limiting the admission of victims of persecution, it became the pretext for a three-year Arab rebellion.

In April, 1936, the Mufti, Haj Amin el Husseini, organized and became the president of a broad-based Arab Higher Committee that was determined to win control of the country, by force if necessary. The far-reaching concessions that Arab nationalists in Egypt and Iraq had wrung from Britain in 1936 had made British installations in Palestine more vital to imperial lines of defense. The Mufti was convinced that an uprising in Palestine would compel the British to sacrifice the Jewish national home rather than jeopardize further their positions in the Middle East and the Mediterranean.

Fearful that the flood of new immigrants might result in a Jewish majority, the Arab Higher Committee called on the Mandatory government to ban immediately all land sales to Jews, to halt all Jewish immigration, and to create an Arab national government. To enforce these demands, the Arabs proclaimed a general strike and an economic boycott of Jews and British, including the withholding of all tax payments.

The boycott quickly turned into a wave of terrorism against Jews, and attacks on public buildings, trains, pipelines, and bridges, and then escalated into full-scale guerrilla warfare. Terrorist gangs recruited by the Mufti shot down Jewish workers in the fields, burned crops, blew up farm buildings, and laid siege to isolated settlements. Neighboring Arab countries sent in arms, money, and volunteers.

Haganah fought off assaults on the settlements but refrained from reprisals. Reluctantly, the British allowed Haganah to train recruits for defensive purposes and grudgingly provided light arms to protect isolated villages. The British needed an entire division to put down the insurrection, which ended when the general strike was called off in October, 1936. Transjordan and Iraq had persuaded the Palestine Arabs "to have faith in the good intentions of our friend, Great Britain."

THE PEEL COMMISSION

The government's reply to the crescendo of violence was the Royal Commission of Inquiry, headed by Earl Peel, whose report was the first official British document to support a Jewish state. The Peel Commission stated unequivocally that the Mandate's principal objective was "unquestionably . . . to promote the establishment of the Jewish national home," but that it should be abandoned because it was unworkable.

To replace the Mandate, the Commission called for dividing Palestine into three separate regions. Jerusalem, Haifa, Bethlehem, Nazareth, and a corridor to the sea from Jerusalem to Jaffa—the "promenade des Anglais"—would remain under British rule; the remainder of the country would be partitioned into Jewish and Arab states. The Jewish state would encompass about 2000 square miles, including Tel Aviv, most of the Galilee, and a narrow coastal strip south of Jaffa, about one-twentieth the area covered by the Balfour Declaration. The rest of the country, including the Negev, was to be part of the Arab state, which would be linked to Transjordan. Within the limits of the proposed Jewish state there lived 258,000 Jews and 225,000 Arabs; one-third of Palestine's Jewish population would thus be left outside the Jewish state.

The tempting offer of a Jewish state, however tiny, was first broached privately to Weizmann by members of the Peel Commission in Jerusalem on January 8, 1937. Years later he recalled that the idea seemed "such a lofty thing that it ought to be treated like the ineffable Name, which is never pronounced in vain . . . and should be approached only with reverence." Early on a Saturday morning in February the father of the idea, Prof. Reginald Coupland, met secretly with Weizmann in a shabby little hut on the grounds of the Girls Agricultural School at Nahalal. The Oxford University historian cautioned Weizmann that the situation in Palestine required "an operation" and that "no honest doctor will recommend aspirins and a hot water bottle." The surgery implied the termination of the Mandate as the price of partition.

Weizmann was so moved as he left the shack and walked through the school's mud-covered grounds that he had to tell someone the news. To a group of farmers working in the nearby fields, he said, "Comrades, today we laid the basis for the Jewish state." Herzl had written the same thing in his diary forty years earlier after the first World Zionist Congress in Basle.

On July 6, 1937, a day before the Peel Commission report was published, Weizmann conferred behind closed doors in Paris with President Emil Edde of the Republic of Lebanon. Their conversation was about plans for an enduring alliance between the Jewish state-to-be and the Lebanese. When they parted, President Edde shook Weizmann's hand and exclaimed, "I salute the first President of the Jewish republic." The meeting was arranged by Eliahu Epstein (Elath), who on May 14, 1948, as official representative of the Jewish Agency, would ask for US recognition of the State of Israel forty-eight hours before Weizmann was elected its first President.

To the Zionists, partition was a lightning flash illuminating the hope of Jewish statehood just when a refuge for the mounting numbers of victims of Nazism was becoming daily more pressing. From Lords Balfour to Peel, official Zionist policy had soft-pedaled the Jewish state question while concentrating on the Jewish national home concept. As relations with the British worsened, and the remote possibility of an Arab-Jewish accord vanished in the smoke of the Mufti's jihad (holy war), the militants of the Left and the Right took center stage in the Zionist movement.

The Revisionists had never desisted from their clamor for Jewish sovereignty and their belaboring of Weizmann for his efforts to seek an accommodation with the British within the framework of the Mandate. At the 1931 World Zionist Congress, Jabotinsky had forced Weizmann out of the presidency of the World Zionist Organization. The Labor Zionists also turned more aggressive in resisting the curbs on the national home once they became the dominant Jewish voice in Palestine in 1930 with the formation of Mapai, the Jewish Labor Party. This merger of Ben-Gurion's moderate Poale Zion and the Left-wing Hashomer Hatzair, and the election of Laborite Ben Zvi as Chairman of the National Jewish Council, gave Labor political muscle. The Revisionists' anti-labor stand and their hostility to a homeland dominated by a socialist proletariat generated a bitter feud with Labor. The power struggle between the two militancies was fought out first in street brawls in Palestine and then in the Zionist Congress, where Labor won a majority for the first time in 1933.

BEN-GURION EMERGES

Three of its leaders—Ben-Gurion, Moshe Shertok, and Chaim Arlosoroff—gained key portfolios in the Jewish Agency Executive, which had already become more or less identical with the Zionist Executive. When Ben-Gurion became Chairman of the Executive in 1935, he was on his way toward becoming the master of the Zionist movement. In effect he was already a shadow prime minister. The Executive had the earmarks of a Cabinet in what was shaping up as a quasi-government. The civil-service cadres for the future government of Israel were being trained in the Jewish Agency departments staffed largely by Labor appointees.

The shift in Zionist leadership from the Diaspora to Palestine marked the real beginning of the three-way struggle for supremacy in Palestine which would end with the emergence of Israel. To prepare for the coming showdown with the Arabs and the British, Ben-Gurion expanded the clandestine Haganah and tightened the Agency's control over it. He also gave the go-ahead to illegal immigration, arms smuggling, military training in caves, and the establishment of home munitions factories.

The Revisionists also engaged in smuggling immigrants and in underground military preparations through the Betar movement. Jabotinsky's refusal to abide by Haganah's policy of no reprisals against Arab violence created a split in Haganah that gave birth to Irgun as the Revisionists' own military force. The Labor-Revisionist conflict became an unbridgeable gulf after the mysterious assassination in 1933 of Arlosoroff on a beach near Tel Aviv, allegedly by a Revisionist gunman.

Interparty relations were further embittered by the controversy over partition that nearly tore the movement apart at the 1937 Zionist Congress. Weizmann saw partition as a historic chance for Jewish independence even in a postage-stamp-sized country. He felt that the Mandate had outlived its usefulness because the British were no longer able or willing to carry it out. He was confident that a Jewish state with definite internationally guaranteed boundaries would be something final that the Arabs would understand and accept. A Jewish state, even in a small part of Palestine, he insisted, could absorb 100,000 immigrants a year and sustain a Jewish population of from 2 to 3 million.

Ben-Gurion also sensed that Britain was eager for a way out of Palestine and an end to her involvement with Zionism. He fought for taking what was offered as a springboard for extending the area of Jewish independence. He felt that the final word on the size of the Jewish state had not yet been spoken. Ben-Gurion regarded the offer of a Jewish state as the beginning of the end of the Mandate, an opportunity the Jews should not turn down completely lest they get nothing.

Weizmann and Ben-Gurion urged the 1937 Zionist Congress to exchange territorial claims and the uncertainties of continued British rule for the benefits of early Jewish sovereignty in an amputated Holy Land. Both men warned that the Zionists faced the alternatives of remaining a minority in the whole of Palestine or of becoming a majority in a compact but truncated piece of it.

Horrified by the thought of a pint-sized state, Ben-Gurion's Left-wing Labor allies fought partition. The Jewish State Party, an offshoot of the secessionist Revisionists, vowed they would never accept "a corner of Palestine." The religious Zionists were outraged at a state not in accord with Biblical frontiers. The Americans, led by Rabbis Stephen S. Wise and Abba Hillel Silver, thundered against partition.

A majority of the Congress delegates were anti-partition, but the conflict was settled by a face-saving resolution. On the one hand it denounced as unacceptable the tentative boundaries outlined in the Peel report; on the other it gave the green light to negotiations with the British government to determine the precise terms for the establishment of a Jewish state. In effect the movement had voted for partition in a viable state that could quickly absorb the expanding Jewish refugee pool in Europe already under the Nazi shadow.

Ben-Gurion accepted the compromise and announced that from then on the purpose of his life was to work for Jewish statehood. Partition, he exclaimed, "was the beginning of the redemption for which we have waited for two thousand years."

The non-Zionists in the Jewish Agency were put on the spot by the Congress's action because they were opposed to a Jewish state. In fact the overwhelming majority of Jews, as late as 1938, were not even Zionists and few of them considered a Jewish state as anything but a quixotic dream.

THE BEGINNINGS OF PARTITION

Initially, Britain accepted partition, but in the face of a renewed Arab revolt and widespread opposition in Parliament, she backed away from it in 1939 on the eve of World War II and ultimately scuttled it entirely. But partition as an idea never died. It remained in suspended animation until it was revived by the United Nations Special Commission on Palestine (UNSCOP) whose 1947 report provided international sanction for the creation of the State of Isreal.

Prime Minister Neville Chamberlain, whose father had offered an area in East Africa to Herzl, never meant to give the Jews a state. He and his Foreign Secretary, Lord Halifax, were more concerned with neutralizing the potentially hostile Arab world in order to protect British positions in the Middle East in the event of war. This required further appeasement of the Arabs, whose guerrilla forces of 1500 mercenaries held out for nearly two years against a regular British army in a civil war aimed at uncooperative Arabs as well as the Jews and the British. Controlled by the Mufti, the Arab terrorists were led by Fawzi el Kaukji, a pro-Nazi Iraqi adventurer who as commander of a so-called Arab army of liberation would be driven out of Palestine in 1948 by the untried forces of Haganah. Before the rebellion spent itself in 1939, it had cost the lives of 450 Jews, 140 Britons, and 2300 Arabs and had destroyed property worth millions of pounds. The British cracked down at the end of 1938, when they arrested members of the Arab Higher Committee, rounded up thousands of rebels, and deposed the Mufti as head of the Moslem Supreme Council. He fled to Syria, where he continued to incite to rebellion as an open ally of the Axis powers.

Until mid-1937 the Nazi government took little interest in Palestine affairs although Axis propaganda against the British in the Middle East consistently exploited Arab grievances. The prospect of a Jewish state, however, created great agitation in Germany as well as among the 2000 German "Aryans" in the Templar colonies in Jerusalem, Jaffa, Haifa, and Sarona. Completely under the influence of the Nazi Party, they sympathized with and supported the Arab rebellion. The German Consul-General in Jerusalem warned Berlin that "with a completely pro-Jewish solution, the German colonists would be compelled to emigrate and German institutions will have to close their gates."

A month before the Peel Commission report was published, the German Minister for Foreign Affairs, Baron von Neurath, advised the German Embassy in London and the legations in Jerusalem and Baghdad that "a Jewish state or a Jewish-led political structure under British mandate is not in Germany's interest." Von Neurath's letter pointed out that Germany was more interested in keeping Jewry dispersed and "therefore has an interest in strengthening the Arab world as a counterweight against such a possible increase in power for world Jewry." The Nazi envoy in Baghdad was instructed to express "the German understanding of Arab national aspirations . . . more clearly than before." A fortnight after the Peel report the Iraqi premier asked the German ambassador in Baghdad for Nazi support in frustrating partition. Simultaneously, the Mufti of Jerusalem informed the German consul-general in Jerusalem of his support for "the new Germany," and Syrian nationalists requested the German consul at Beirut to provide arms and ammunition for the Arab rebels in Palestine. Although Germany was still permitting Jews to emigrate and to transfer their capital to Palestine, Hitler raged against the Peel report as paving the way for "a spiritual center for the international Jewish conspiracy."

Frontiers for the Arab and Jewish states proposed by the Peel Commission were mapped in 1938 by another commission headed by Sir John Woodhead. It offered three alternative plans of partition, none of which was taken seriously. In the interim Britain applied one of the Peel report's suggested palliatives by cutting Jewish immigration to 10,000 annually for five years and curbing Jewish land purchases.

In December, 1938, the British buried partition but called a tripartite Arab-Jewish-British conference in London. Ostensibly it was intended to conciliate Arab opposition to and Jewish doubts about partition. Actually it became the instrument through which Britain imposed her own solution. The conference was doomed to failure from the start when the delegations from Palestine and six Arab states refused to sit at the same table with the Jews or to meet with them under any circumstances.

Two separate but simultaneous conferences were held at St. James's Palace, London, in February, 1939. The Arabs refused to enter by the same door as the Jews and then declined to sit in the same room with them. In one chamber Chamblerlain, Halifax, and Colonial Secretary Malcolm MacDonald talked with the Jews. For the first time Ben-Gurion wore a black morning coat, striped trousers, batwing collar, and gray silk tie as he listened to MacDonald caution the Jews to waive their demands for free immigration and to forget about a Jewish majority and an autonomous Jewish state. In another salon the British leaders pleaded with the Arabs to consent to controlled Jewish immigration and land purchases. Six weeks of talks got nowhere. The Arabs refused to allow another Jew to enter Palestine and demanded an all-Arab state and British withdrawal. Ben-Gurion warned that British bayonets would be needed to enforce a suspension of Jewish immigration.

As the stalemated conference drew to a dreary close on March 14, the day the Nazis occupied Czechoslovakia, an official-looking envelope was delivered by Colonial Office messenger to Dr. Weizmann. Opening it, he discovered that he had received by mistake a confidential letter intended for the Arab delegations. It contained the final British proposals, described as "Command 6019," which were being submitted to the Arabs for their prior approval before publication as the White Paper of May 17.

By the terms of this fateful document only 10,000 Jews would be admitted to Palestine annually for the next five years, absorptive capacity permitting; an additional 25,000 refugees would be allowed in immediately. Thereafter all Jewish immigration would be subject to Arab veto, which meant no Jews at all. Sale of land to Jews was forbidden or closely restricted over all but 5 percent of the country. An independent Palestine government would be set up within ten years in which Arabs and Jews would be represented in accordance with their numbers, dooming the Jews to permanent minority status.

In effect, the White Paper made the Balfour Declaration a dead letter, jettisoned the key obligations of the Palestine Mandate on which British authority rested, and, as some said, turned the land of Israel into the land of Ishmael.

In Parliament the White Paper was denounced by both parties. Labourites labeled it "a Palestine Munich" that a Socialist government would repudiate. Winston Churchill thundered "this is the abandonment of the Balfour Declaration, this is the end of the vision, of the hope, of the dream." The opposition mustered 181 votes in the House of Commons, but it was not enough to block approval.

The moribund League of Nations, through its Permanent Mandates

Commission, unanimously condemned the White Paper as an unlawful breach of the Mandate. This League action would become the basis for the Jewish Agency's contention that Jewish resistance to the White Paper was in defense of the sanctity of an international treaty.

England ignored the League of Nations and the storm of bitter protest that arose throughout the world, having been persuaded by permanent officials in the Foreign, Colonial, and War Offices that Arab power and support were more important than a Jewish state. London reasoned that in a war with Hitler the Jews would have no alternative but to support Britain. The policy of appeasement adopted at Munich in 1938 was extended to Palestine in 1939, when the British miscalculated relative Arab and Jewish strength, as they would again in 1948.

The 1939 Zionist Congress, ending its sessions ten days before World War II began, heard in silence Weizmann's anguished plea for a truce with Britain and his call to stand at her side. Ben-Gurion swore the Jews would "not submit to the conversion of the national home into a ghetto." He announced that Palestine Jewry would fight the war beside Britain as if there were no White Paper and resist the White Paper as if there were no war.

The most imperative form of resistance was illegal immigration, which led to armed clashes with British land and naval forces engaged in enforcing the White Paper. Britain's capitulation to Arab violence was a lesson not lost on the Yishuv as it defied, evaded, and circumvented regulations that frustrated the rescue of fellow Jews. The locked gates of Palestine during the incomparable disaster that befell European Jewry after 1939 converted moderates into activists and turned activists into terrorists. Ultimately, the White Paper policy and its aftermath won over world Jewry and the Great Powers to the need for a Jewish state and precipitated the final struggle for Jewish independence climaxed by British withdrawal in 1948.

chapter

∘ ∘ ∘ ∘ ∘ ∘ ∘ ∘ ∘ ∘ ∘ ∘ ∘ ∘ ∘ | 4 | ∘ ∘ ∘ ∘ ∘ ∘ ∘ ∘ ∘ ∘ ∘ ∘ ∘ ∘

BRITAIN'S ATTEMPT TO STOP
ILLEGAL IMMIGRATION

WHILE PALESTINE JEWRY aligned itself on the side of Britain in the struggle against Nazism, Britain declared war on illegal Jewish immigration as "a serious menace" to her interests in the Middle East. Obsessed by fear of angering the Arabs, the British closed the doors of Palestine to all people from Germany or German-occupied territory, including Poland, unless they held prewar immigration certificates. In May, 1942, the British reaffirmed the policy of "taking all practicable steps to discourage illegal immigration to Palestine" and of doing "nothing whatever . . . to facilitate the arrival of Jewish refugees in Palestine." At the moment this statement was issued the death trains were rolling across Eastern Europe and the mass extermination of Jews by the Nazis was tragically well under way.

A fleet of corvettes, destroyers, and power launches and squadrons of RAF planes patrolled the shores of Palestine to intercept illegal ships. New police posts and radar installations were set up along the coast to guard against night landings. British agents scoured Europe to locate the secret ports from which the ships sailed. Pressure was put on Turkey to close the Bosporus to vessels coming from the Danube via the Black Sea. The tiny, unseaworthy converted cattle and cargo boats stealthily crept from port to port on the Black Sea and the Mediterranean before attempting to run the British blockade. Few were successful, despite the daring efforts of shore-based underground Jewish paramilitary units waiting to smuggle the immigrants to the safety of isolated kibbutzim.

The mass tragedies of the floating coffins hardened Jewish resistance to British rule and gave birth to a campaign of sabotage by Haganah and violence and terrorism by dissident groups. In November, 1940, the leaky tramp steamers *Pacific* and *Milos,* packed with 1800 refugees, were captured and towed into Haifa by British naval vessels. Slated for deportation to the malaria-ridden tropical island of Mauritius for the duration of the war, the desperate passengers were transferred to the British steamer *Patria.* But the survivors of the Hitler terror deliberately blew up the ship just before she was to sail. Over 300 men, women, and children were blown to bits or drowned a hundred yards from the Promised Land. From Panorama Street, atop Mount Carmel, fourteen-year-old Eliyahu ben Hakim witnessed the disaster through field glasses. He never forgot the sight of the floating corpses and dismembered bodies of women and children dragged into boats by fishhooks. In 1944, Hakim, a member of the Stern Gang, helped assassinate Lord Moyne, Britain's resident minister in Cairo, and was hanged for the deed.

Even as bodies from the *Patria* were still being picked up in Haifa Harbor, the British brought in the 800-ton steamer *Atlantic* carrying 1700 survivors of the Danzig Jewish community and refugees from Czechoslovakia and Austria. All were sent to a detention camp at Athlit, after which they were dragged by force, some on stretchers, for deportation to Mauritius. The 75-foot sailing vessel *Salvador,* overloaded with 350 refugees from Bulgaria, reached the Turkish coast in December, 1940, where the British authorities said no Palestine entry permits would be granted to its passengers. Because the Turks refused to allow persons without Palestine visas to land, the *Atlantic* headed out to sea again where it foundered and sank with the loss of 231 people. The survivors were returned to Istanbul but were still denied admission to Palestine. Some finally got there on the SS *Darien* in March, 1941, and were allowed to land only because the ship was in danger of sinking.

The worst tragedy involved the *Struma,* a brokendown cattleboat packed with 769 passengers crowded into cages on a deck measuring 60 by 20 feet. The *Struma* barely limped into Istanbul on December 16, 1941. The Jewish Agency frantically sought Palestine visas at least for the children under sixteen. While the British debated the request, the ship remained in port for two months. Ultimately, the Turks lost their patience and the *Struma* had to leave Istanbul. She sank in the Black Sea, a mile off the Turkish coast. There was only one survivor. The British had finally consented to let the children between eleven and sixteen into Palestine but had failed to advise the Turks.

Soon after the *Struma* went down the walls of Jerusalem, Haifa, and Tel Aviv were placarded with a poster reading: "MURDER—

WANTED FOR MURDER BY DROWNING OF 800 REFUGEES ON BOARD THE STRUMA." Above these words was a photograph of Sir Harold MacMichael, the British High Commissioner.

Once the British victory at El Alamein in the winter of 1942 ended the immediate Axis threat in the Middle East, an undeclared Anglo-Jewish war erupted in Palestine. British police and military forces swooped down on the Jewish settlements in search of illegal arms caches and hidden training camps. In 1943 the British staged a show trial of two British deserters charged with stealing 3000 rifles and 125,000 rounds of ammunition, allegedly for sale to Ben-Gurion. The trial was conducted in a blaze of publicity and the defendants were described by their counsel as victims of "an arms-trafficking gang of the Jewish Agency."

Haganah retaliated by raiding British arms dumps and blowing up British communications facilities, RAF stations, and police launches used to detect incoming immigrant ships. Jewish terrorists blasted British military posts, killed British soldiers, and attempted to assassinate the High Commissioner. Regarding Haganah as little different from the terrorist Irgunists and Sternists, the British staged onerous and often humiliating searches for arms, made wholesale arrests of suspected Haganah leaders, put large areas under curfew, and invoked collective penalties.

The widening chasm between the Yishuv and the Mandatory authorities fed the growing conviction that after the war only an independent Jewish state could cope with the desperate needs of the surviving Jews of Europe. As the frightful tragedy of European Jewry became widely known, American Jewry also turned more militant on the question of Palestine's immediate role as a haven of refuge and on that of its long-range future. United in denouncing the White Paper and in demanding that Washington intervene with Great Britain to open the gates of Palestine, American Zionists and non-Zionists were still divided on the idea of a Jewish state. But the emotional impact of the news of what had happened to European Jewry had converted the rank and file of American Zionists from the cautious, practical posture of the Weizmann and Brandeis wings to uncompromising advocacy of statehood.

After the 1939 White Paper the Palestine and American Zionists took over control of the world Zionist movement. Weizmann and his middle-of-the-road adherents were shunted aside. Convinced that the United States would displace Britain as the decisive force in the postwar world, the Zionists mapped a campaign to win the political and moral support of Washington and of American Jewry. Fearing that Palestine might be cut off during the war, the American Zionist Emergency Council was created to carry on in the United States. Under the vigorous leadership of Rabbis Abba Hillel Silver and Stephen S. Wise, this council became the Jewish Agency's ally for marshaling world opinion for the Jewish cause against Britain.

As hope of moving Britain faded, the Zionists turned to arousing public opinion in the United States in the belief that England could not afford to ignore pressures from America. Weizmann visited the United States three times between 1940 and 1943 in a vain effort to persuade President Franklin D. Roosevelt and Secretary of State Cordell Hull to intercede with Britain. When Washington refused to do or say anything prejudicial to the British war effort in the Middle East, the American Zionist Emergency Council embarked on a carefully planned nationwide propaganda effort to mobilize American support.

Hundreds of local councils were created. Ministers, educators, officeholders, and labor leaders were won over by the thousands. A flood of books, pamphlets, articles, and press releases was produced to inform and influence editors, writers, and news commentators. Speakers carrying the Zionist message fanned out over the entire country. The campaign keynote stressed the need for official intercession by the United States government with Britain. The primary targets were Congress, the State Department, and the White House. A joint Congressional resolution favoring a Jewish commonwealth was on the verge of passage in both houses of Congress in 1944, when objections by the State and War Departments on security grounds forced a delay until December, 1945. The platforms of the Republican and Democratic Parties in the 1944 Presidential election included pro-Zionist planks.

THE BILTMORE PROGRAM

Masterminded by Dr. Emanuel Neumann, this remarkably successful barrage began in May, 1942, with the adoption of a statement of postwar objectives formulated at an extraordinary conference of six hundred delegates from all Zionist parties at the Hotel Biltmore in New York. Proclaiming Jewish statehood for the first time as the official and open goal of Zionist policy, inside and outside Palestine, this statement, which came to be known as the Biltmore Program, superceded the Basle Program of 1897 as the basic Zionist policy. As part of any postwar settlement the Biltmore declaration demanded complete freedom for the Jewish Agency to develop Palestine "as a Jewish commonwealth integrated in the structure of the new democratic world."

This outright request for independent Jewish rule in the whole of Palestine was opposed by Weizmann as a violation of his promise to the British to suspend political pressure for the duration of the war. Some Left-wing Laborites from Palestine fought it because they supported a program for a binational state advocated by Dr. Judah L. Magnes. Ben-Gurion, backed by Dr. Silver and his followers in the Zionist Organization of America, pressed for and won acceptance of the maximalist program, thus paving the way for the final stage of the struggle for statehood.

Meyer W. Weisgal, for many years Weizmann's personal representative in the United States, tells it differently in his autobiography, *Meyer Weisgal . . . So Far,* published in 1972. In Weisgal's view, the first clear and open demand for a Jewish commonwealth in Palestine had been spelled out by Weizmann five months before the convening of the Biltmore conference in an article in the January, 1942, issue of *Foreign Affairs.*

Weisgal's claim that he organized the Biltmore conference is supported by Yehuda Bauer in his scholarly work, *From Diplomacy to Resistance: A History of Jewish Palestine, 1939–1945,* published in 1970. Bauer is silent about Weisgal's assertion that he had acted at Weizmann's behest, but credits the Biltmore Program as adopted with having been "expressed in Weisgal's wording with certain changes."

Weisgal says only that he and Louis Lipsky, longtime leader of the Weizmann forces in American Zionism, worked on the draft of the program for months preceding its adoption, and that their draft, "with stylistic changes, was eventually adopted." The entire program, he insists, was "drawn up in consultation with Weizmann."

But, he adds, "somewhere along the road, Ben-Gurion decided it was important for history that the paternity of the Biltmore resolution be attributed to him, and appear as a victory of his conception over Weizmann's." It is a fact that Weisgal opened the Biltmore conference, and he observes that "if it had been Ben-Gurion's program . . . it would have been inconceivable" for Weisgal to "have been given, or taken, the signal honor." Strangely, Weizmann's own autobiography, *Trial and Error,* published in 1949, does not even mention the Biltmore conference.

Ben-Gurion's triumph over Weizmann climaxed five years of planning that began when the Peel Commission's proposal for partition convinced him that the Mandate and Britain's commitment to help build a Jewish national homeland were doomed. Persuaded since 1937 that the only road to the fulfillment of Zionist hopes was to obtain a Jewish state in as large an area of Palestine as possible, he won over the Labor Party in Palestine at the cost of a split, but he still needed to persuade the world Zionist movement. A Zionist Congress was impossible during the war, but the Biltmore conference, attended by Palestinians and Zionist leaders from seventeen foreign countries, as well as the top figures from the United States and Canada, was well-timed. It could give official sanction to Ben-Gurion's thesis that Zionist policy had to shift from working within the Mandate to striving for an autonomous Jewish regime.

In a long address at the Biltmore conclave, Ben-Gurion mentioned alternate possibilities, such as a British dominion or some form of Jewish entity as an autonomous part of a Near East federation. Aware that attainment of complete sovereignty over all of Palestine was not likely, he used the term "commonwealth" rather than "state." This became the language of the Biltmore Program. The supreme goal, however, was the ingathering of the exiles, to which end statehood was only a means.

In 1943 the entire Biltmore Program was endorsed by the American Jewish Conference, a democratically elected body of delegates representing American Jewry. A passionate address by Dr. Silver in support of the commonwealth idea headed off a segment of Zionists ready to go back on the Biltmore Program in return for non-Zionist support of unlimited Jewish immigration to Palestine.

By 1945 the disclosure of the full extent of the catastrophe that had overtaken European Jewry, and the terrible urgency of providing a refuge for the survivors, had persuaded the overwhelming majority of American Jews that Palestine was the only practical solution. The non-Zionist American Jewish Committee, which had withdrawn from the American Jewish Conference in 1943 because it could not go along with the commonwealth resolution, subsequently joined the united Jewish front for a Zionist-oriented solution to the plight of the refugees. Only the bitter-enders, who organized themselves in the American Council for Judaism, remained aloof.

Worldwide sympathy for the survivors of the Holocaust became "the rock on which the Mandate finally split." There were 100,000 housed in makeshift DP camps in the American, French, and British zones of occupation in Germany and Austria. Several hundred thousand more huddled in the Russian zone but tried to infiltrate the Western zones in the frantic hope of finding their way to Palestine.

MILITANCY IN THE DP CAMPS

Fourteen days after V-E Day the Jewish Agency demanded that Britain relieve the pressure in the DP camps by immediately admitting

100,000 Jews to Palestine. The Agency also called on England to announce that Palestine "undivided and undiminished" would be established
as a Jewish state, with the Agency in control of Jewish immigration.
An international loan was proposed to underwrite the immigration of
"the first million Jews to Palestine."

The DPs' militancy added immediacy to the Agency's action. Hope of
a new life in a Jewish state had buoyed the thinking of the Jews who had
fought Nazism in the European underground as well as those who had
survived the concentration camps. Most of the Jewish partisan cells had
been built around the nuclei of Zionist youth training centers. Flight from
the DP camps spurred illegal immigration, organized and led by Haganah
agents. Relief teams from Palestine attached to UNRRA units, Jewish
military personnel from Palestine demobilized in Italy, and American
Jewish chaplains with the occupation forces encouraged Zionist sentiment
and promoted enlistment in the Haganah.

The British ignored the Jewish Agency's request, insisting that only a
general postwar settlement could deal with the Palestine question. In the
fall of 1945 a letter from President Truman to Prime Minister Attlee created a sensation with its suggestion that 100,000 Jews be allowed into
Palestine without delay. This had been the principal recommendation of
Truman's personal emissary, Earl G. Harrison, who had made an on-the-
spot survey of conditions in the DP camps and reported that immigration
to Palestine was the only hope for the majority of DPs.

When Attlee led the Labour Party to an upset victory over the Churchill government, Palestine Jewry was elated because in 1944 the Labour
Party conference had endorsed the establishment of a Jewish state. Once
in power, the Labour Party made it plain that it had no intention of nul-
lifying the 1939 White Paper, the last remnant of Neville Chamberlain's
appeasement policy. Attlee and his Foreign Secretary, Ernest Bevin, not
only rejected Truman's proposal but ordered tougher measures to halt illegal immigration and to disarm the Jews of Palestine.

Indignation and protests erupted around the world. In Palestine
60,000 marched, in a procession of mourning, led by Bergen-Belsen and
Buchenwald survivors in concentration camp uniforms. In the US many
public officials called upon Washington to deny Britain's request for a
loan. The Jewish Agency in Palestine retaliated by abandoning its long
adherence to self-restraint. On October 21, in the first act of armed revolt
against the British, Haganah raided the Athlit detention camp, overpow-
ered the garrison, and freed 177 illegal immigrants awaiting deportation.
The death of a British constable in the raid was also the first time an Englishman had died at the hands of Haganah. On October 31 Haganah

paralyzed the country's railroad system by dynamiting 100 junction points. Simultaneously, police patrol boats in Haifa and Jaffa ports were blasted out of the water and bombs rocked the British-owned Haifa oil refineries. Britain retaliated by rushing an entire airborne division in from Malta with orders to force its way into the kibbutzim in search of the illegals and of arms dumps.

Before this the Jewish Agency and Haganah had been warning the Palestine government of planned actions by Jewish terrorists. Haganah even resorted to kidnaping and trapping Irgunists and Sternists to prevent terrorism. But while the Haganah hunted down terrorists, its leaders were themselves being hunted by the British. How far the *"Me-Avah"* ("the struggle") against the British should go in direct action created a serious rift in the Jewish Labor Party when some elements objected to the use of force. It was Golda Myerson (Meir), speaking at the funeral of the first Jewish victims of the open warfare against the British at the end of 1945, who coined the slogan *"Ein Breira"* ("There Is No Alternative"). Ben-Gurion and Moshe Shertok, head of the Agency's political department, then warned the High Commissioner that any further efforts by the Agency to aid in preventing terrorism "would be futile." They said they could not ask Jews to keep the peace when the government itself was consistently violating the fundamental law of the land embodied in the Palestine Mandate by barring Jewish refugees.

This defiance, coupled with a national day of mourning and bolder attempts to break through the immigration blockade, was the answer to Bevin's policy statement of November 13, 1945. The Labour government proposed another inquiry by an Anglo-American Committee, to which Truman had consented. At a press conference in London, Bevin mocked the Zionists for "pushing to the head of the queue" and sneered at American eagerness to send Jews to Palestine because they didn't want too many in New York. Bevin's coarse anti-Semitism, as much as his intransigence, earned him the hatred of Jews throughout the world. In Palestine he was gibed at as Israel's George III and an unwilling instrument of her independence. In 1949, when the Hebrew University awarded Ben-Gurion a prize given by an American Jew to the person who had rendered the greatest service to Israel in 1948, the university rector was not jesting when he said that the only other serious contender had been Ernest Bevin.

The new outburst of violence that greeted the Anglo-American Committee in Palestine was a warning that rage and anguish over Britain's callousness had broken the dikes of Jewish restraint. Three RAF stations were wrecked by Irgun. Jews disguised as members of the 6th Airborne Division boldly attacked the huge British camp at Sarafend. In the newly formed joint Haganah-Irgun committee that mapped combined operations and divided responsibilities the British military recognized the beginning of an open Jewish rebellion. They charged the Jewish Agency with being the high command of the revolt and conniving with Irgun in the reign of terror that gripped the country. By the time the Anglo-American Committee report was published on May 1, 1946, Palestine had become "John Bull's other Ireland."

The Committee called for the prompt admission of 100,000 refugees to Palestine, repeal of curbs on Jewish land acquisition, and repudiation of the doctrine of a permanent Jewish minority. Jewish proposals for a sovereign state were set aside in favor of a future independent binational state of Palestine—the plan sponsored by Dr. Magnes and his Ihud (Unity) Society—after a period of British rule under a United Nations trusteeship.

Bevin and Attlee had promised to accept the recommendations of the Committee if it reached a unanimous conclusion, but they refused to carry them out. Truman endorsed the immigration proposal despite warnings from the State Department not to do so unless he was ready to send American troops to Palestine. Britain insisted that either all the recommendations or none be implemented. It was powerless to implement the Committee's findings, London said, unless the United States provided military and financial assistance and until the Jewish militias were disbanded and had surrendered their arms.

TRUMAN URGES 100,000 IMMIGRANTS

When Truman pressed for the immediate objective of opening Palestine to 100,000 DPs, an Anglo-American Cabinet-level committee was set up to explore the problem. On July 26, 1946, this committee produced the Morrison-Grady report that suggested the cantonization of Palestine. Under a modified form of partition, the country would be divided into Jewish, Arab, and central government zones, but major powers would be vested in the central (British) zone, with little autonomy for the Arab and Jewish cantons. An area of about 1500 square miles, 17 percent of Palestine, was assigned to the Jews, who would be barred from the remaining 83 percent. But even in the Jewish canton Jewish immigration would be dependent on the British High Commissioner. Admission of the 100,000

DPs would be permitted within a year of the acceptance of the plan by all parties. To carry out the scheme, the experts foresaw the need for large sums of money. They anticipated that the Jews would provide their own funds, but recommended that the United States furnish $300 million for the Arabs.

While this plan was being concocted, the Palestine government was secretly planning to smash Haganah and the Jewish Agency on the ground that the latter had forfeited its status under the Mandate. Two weeks before the move was scheduled to begin, Kol Hamagen, Haganah's underground radio, announced details of the coming assault. The British had compiled a blacklist of 3000 leading Jewish personalities, terrorists, and Haganah leaders who were slated for arrest. Military operations against the Yishuv called for motorized units to invade forty-nine Jewish towns and settlements.

On June 10, Haganah blasted all of the fourteen bridges linking Palestine with the adjacent Arab lands to demonstrate that Palestine was no longer a safe British base so long as the DPs were barred. Sternists attacked government railway shops in Haifa and Irgun kidnaped five British officers as hostages for two Sternists under sentence of death.

Nineteen days later the British launched their operation to liquidate the Jewish opposition. The Jewish Agency building in Jerusaleum was occupied and all its leaders who had not gone into hiding were arrested. Nearly 2500 officials of Mapai, Histadrut, the cooperatives, and the kibbutzim were taken into custody and interned behind barbed wire in a concentration camp at Latrun. All of the key Haganah commanders as well as the Irgun and Sternist leaders managed to escape the dragnet and lose themselves in the underground. Most of the Jewish arms caches were salvaged by being removed to new hiding places.

British troops surrounded and searched twenty-seven settlements for arms in the first three days of a task-force operation by three divisions. They met with no resistance. Everywhere they found only men and women lying on the ground with legs and arms interlocked and refusing to move. The soldiers had to drag the passive resisters one by one into cages for questioning.

The sixty-nine-year-old Rabbi Yehuda Leib HaCohen Fishman, who had been arrested in Jerusalem on the Sabbath, was refused permission to walk to prison. He was forced to compromise his religious convictions by riding in an armored car after being struck by a British officer. On May 14, two years later, the same rabbi would recite the Sheheheyanu—the traditional thanksgiving prayer—at Israel's ceremony of independence in Tel Aviv.

While the raids were under way, Haganah's secret radio exhorted the Yishuv not to be intimidated even though "Britain has declared war on the Jewish people. Out with the unclean sons of Titus from our Holy Land," the announcer cried. The Irgun underground flooded the country with leaflets proposing the immediate establishment of a Jewish provisional government, a boycott on tax payments to the government, the creation of a Jewish exchequer, and the formation of a united Jewish liberation army sworn to fight until independence was won. On July 22, the Irgun, after a warning that was ignored, blew up a wing of the King David Hotel in Jerusalem, seat of the government secretariat, killing ninety-one Britons, Arabs, and Jews.

Palestine was near the boiling point but Bevin and Attlee continued to stall by planning a new Arab-Jewish round-table conference for September. Jewish Agency leaders, still under arrest in Palestine, refused to come. Those who had been abroad during the June roundup were instructed to ignore the London conference if it was to be based only on the Morrison-Grady scheme. The Palestine Arabs also stayed home, thus making a fiasco out of the London meeting, which was attended only by delegates from the Arab states.

On August 5, 1946, those members of the Jewish Agency Executive who had escaped the British dragnet of June 29 met in emergency session in Paris, with Ben-Gurion presiding. By a vote of 10 to 1, with one abstention, the group agreed to a plan of partition almost identical with what the Peel Commission had suggested in 1937, plus the Negev. The Agency indicated its readiness to appear in London if the agenda included consideration of a Jewish state in an "adequate" area of Palestine, the immediate grant of 100,000 immigration certificates, and Jewish control of immigration in the area of the Jewish state.

Ben-Gurion is said to have voted against going to London under any circumstances. He agreed with Rabbi Silver, who was not present, that the Paris decision undermined the Agency's position by taking the initiative instead of waiting for a specific British offer. Weizmann, then in London, was prepared to accept the admission of 100,000 DPs and the scrapping of the land restrictions as a minimum basis for making a fresh start with Britain.

Nahum Goldmann, later Weizmann's successor as President of the World Zionist Congress, claims in his autobiography that it was he who advanced partition as a way out of the deadlock, and indicated that Ben-Gurion, Shertok, and Weizmann supported him. During the debate, Goldmann received a cable from David K. Niles, Truman's White House aide, advising him that the President was ready to disassociate himself from the whole Palestine question. Truman was so annoyed by Britain's rejection of the Anglo-American Committee's proposals that he was seriously considering withdrawing from any involvement unless the Jewish Agency came up with a specific workable and reasonable plan.

Following the vote in Paris, Goldmann hurried to the US to present the Agency's plan to the State and War Departments and to the White House. Weizmann and other Agency leaders conveyed it privately to the Colonial Office in London. According to Goldmann, Secretary of State James F. Byrnes, who was then in Paris, facilitated his transportation to the US.

There is still controversy over whether Goldmann acted on his own or with the authorization of the Agency Executive. As head of the political office the Agency had opened in Washington in 1943, Goldmann had become embroiled in a bitter dispute with the American Zionist Emergency Council over questions of authority, status, and strategy. The Council also had an office in Washington which directed the propaganda barrage at Congress and the White House.

The Agency Executive opposed the line taken by Dr. Silver as head of the Council, particularly his violent attacks on the Roosevelt and Truman Administrations. Weizmann, who himself had an unofficial band of advisers in Washington that kept him informed, sought to patch up the feud between the Agency and the Council. This group at various times included Niles, Judge Samuel I. Rosenman, Robert Nathan, David Ginsburg, Benjamin V. Cohen, Oscar Gass, and Justice Felix N. Frankfurter.

JUDGE PROSKAUER HELPS

Judge Joseph N. Proskauer, a non-Zionist who was then president of the American Jewish Committee, and Niles and Bartley Crum, a member of the Anglo-American Committee of Inquiry, became Goldmann's chief allies and door-openers. In his autobiography, *A Segment of My Times,* Proskauer wrote that in the summer of 1946 he was invited to Washington by a high official (in a letter to the authors he identified him as Truman) to see if he could reconcile the recommendations of the Anglo-American Committee and the Morrison-Grady experts. After meeting with spokesmen for both, he found the task hopeless.

At this point Goldmann called on Proskauer and revealed to him that the Jewish Agency was for the first time willing to consider partition because of the desperate plight of the DPs. This was a retreat from the Biltmore Program. When Goldmann asked for Proskauer's support, the latter indicated that his position would be determined largely by the stand to be taken by the US government. Proskauer brought Goldmann to the Pentagon to meet Secretary of War Robert P. Patterson, using as the intermediary Gen. Edward Greenebaum, a key figure in the American Jewish Committee and Patterson's aide. Goldmann outlined the Agency's plan to Patterson and then left the room. Patterson assured Proskauer of his agreement that partition was the quickest way of opening the gates of Palestine, but pointed out that the decision was up to the State Department.

With this encouragement, Proskauer arranged for Goldmann to talk to Secretary of the Treasury John W. Snyder and Under Secretary of State Dean Acheson who with Patterson constituted the Cabinet committee on Palestine. Proskauer also enabled Goldmann to see Ernest Bevin and Lord` Inverchapel, the British Ambassador to the US. Proskauer vainly tried to sell partition to Bevin and Inverchapel, but the meeting with Acheson was more productive. Acheson agreed that partition was the only answer and told Proskauer that the backing of the American Jewish Committee would be crucial. From then on the AJC supported partition. On August 8 Acheson reported to Truman that the Cabinet committee favored partition. The next day Niles phoned Goldmann to say that Truman had accepted partition and had instructed Acheson to inform the British government.

In 1971, at funeral services for Judge Proskauer, a message was read from Israel Foreign Minister Abba Eban paying tribute to his "unforgettable contribution to American-Israel relations at the most crucial periods of our nation's rebirth as a sovereign state."

Relations between Goldmann and Silver were strained, Goldmann says, because Rabbi Silver was unhappy at not being invited to join in the talks. Rabbi Silver was then still adamant against partition. On August 11 Goldmann reported to the Jewish Agency Executive in Paris and was authorized to talk to Bevin in London. He met with him once alone and then with Rabbi Wise and Berl Locker. The conversations, which continued until the eve of the 1946 Zionist Congress in December, got nowhere.

In mid-August, 1946, the *New York Times* got wind of what was brewing. The *Times* reported that Goldmann had shown Patterson and Inverchapel the Agency's plan "for the partitioning of Palestine by the creation of separate and independent Jewish and Arab states and the early termination of the British Mandate." The proposal has had "serious consideration by this Government," the *Times* said, adding that the plan "is understood to be included in President Truman's reply to Great Britain on the Morrison-Grady plan."

The *Times* was well informed. Irked by the repeated adjournments of the London round-table conference, Truman, on October 4, 1946, made public another letter to Attlee, reiterating interest in the earliest possible admission to Palestine of 100,000 DPs. The President declared that a solution along the lines of the Agency plan proposing "a viable state in control of its own immigration and economic policies in an adequate area of Palestine instead of in the whole of Palestine" would "command the support of public opinion in the United States." To such a solution, Truman said, "our government could give its support."

Truman's statement was tantamount to a rejection of the Morrison-Grady recommendations, which had already been turned down by Jews and Arabs. More important, however, it introduced publicly for the first time the Jewish Agency's partition formula as a potential major element of American policy on Palestine.

Most American Zionists were at that time hostile to partition. In July, 1944, the *Bulletin* of the American Zionist Emergency Council denounced partition as "an evasion of the issues" and reiterated the demand for "a Jewish national home within the boundaries of historic Palestine."

In October the Mizrachi (Orthodox Zionists) reaffirmed the Biltmore Program and the Zionist Organization of America reiterated claims to "the whole of Mandated Palestine, undivided and unlimited." Dr. Silver denounced the Agency Executive's action as both an "error of judgment" and an arbitrary step since only a World Zionist Congress had authority to make decisions of such magnitude. He charged Goldmann with flouting agreements that neither the Zionist Emergency Council nor Goldmann "would propose a partition plan to the Cabinet committee on Palestine, or to other American officials."

In November, at the convention of Hadassah, the Women's Zionist Organization of America, Goldmann openly advocated abandonment of the Biltmore declaration. He said that further adherence to it was no longer realistic because it represented an unachievable goal in the light of postwar developments. Dr. Neumann, speaking for Dr. Silver and the Zionist Emergency Council, attacked the Agency's partition position, but Hadassah joined the Agency in "reluctant acceptance of the principle of partition of Palestine."

The stand taken by the majority of American Zionists determined the outcome of the first postwar World Zionist Congress in Geneva in December, 1946. Much of Weizmann's former following from Poland, Germany, and Central Europe had been wiped out. Of the 325 delegates, 121 were from the United States; the largest single bloc, 56 delegates, represented the Zionist Organization of America and was controlled by Silver and Neumann.

The Congress was bitterly divided between those who wanted to accept an invitation to the resumed Arab-Jewish conference called by Britain for January, 1947, and those who no longer wanted any dealings with England. Weizmann, Shertok, and Wise favored attending on the grounds that the need to open the doors of Palestine was paramount. Ben-Gurion favored partition but Silver was at least publicly adamant against it.

Silver downgraded Truman's pronouncement, claiming it "did not commit the United States to the Jewish Agency's proposals but indicated only that the United States is prepared to give its support to a compromise between the partition scheme of the Agency and the Morrison-Grady plan." Ben-Gurion, on the other hand, said, "A smaller part of Palestine under sole Jewish control is preferable to a larger part under British or Arab-Jewish control," but he no longer trusted Britain's promises and was fed up with Weizmann.

THE DECLINE OF WEIZMANN

Ben-Gurion and Silver joined forces because they agreed that the time had come to retire Weizmann. They saw eye to eye in regarding him as "an incubus of moderation, characterized by a formal claim to statehood which camouflaged a practical readiness to continue with Britain on a promise of freer immigration." Together with 42 votes from the Revisionists, the Ben-Gurion–Silver alliance squeezed out a narrow 171–154 majority for a resolution that amounted to a repudiation of Weizmann.

Violently anti-British in mood, the Congress decided against taking part in the Arab-Jewish parley. It also went on record as unalterably opposed to "the institution of any trusteeship system over Palestine as a replacement for the present Mandate, which will prevent or postpone the establishment of the Jewish state." Turning down Weizmann's plea that the immediate goal should be a viable Jewish state in an adequate area of Palestine, the Congress committed itself to the establishment of Palestine as a Jewish commonwealth. The United Nations was asked to support "this Jewish people's demand."

Having lost confidence in Britain, the Congress decided that Weizmann, as the leading exponent of cooperation with the British, had to go. Dejected and rejected, Weizmann resigned as President of the World Zionist Organization, but no one was elected in his place because Silver and Ben-Gurion couldn't agree on a successor. Weizmann's position on partition was based on word from Winston Churchill that a Cabinet committee on Palestine had decided to give the Jews full sovereignty in one sector of Palestine after the war. Reporting an off-the-record talk with Churchill in November, 1944, Weizmann said that the Prime Minister had spoken favorably of partition and of a Jewish state that would include the Negev.

Once Weizmann was ousted, Ben-Gurion and Silver divided Zionist authority. Ben-Gurion was given full power in Palestine and Silver was made the chairman of a new six-member American Section of the Jewish Agency. This undercut Goldmann, even though he was a member of the newly elected twenty-man coalition Agency Executive of which Ben-Gurion was the chairman. Ultimately, the American Section became the focus of the dramatic diplomatic efforts at the United Nations. Shertok acted as Ben-Gurion's representative and Goldmann served as a roving emissary. As far as the United States was concerned, power rested with Dr. Silver and his fellow members of the American Section of the Agency: Dr. Emanuel Neumann, Mrs. Rose Halprin, Chaim Greenberg, and Rabbi Wolf Gold.

Despite the official Jewish Agency boycott of the Arab-Jewish conference that convened in January, 1947, members of the Agency Executive met unofficially five times with Bevin, Colonial Secretary Arthur Creech-Jones, and other officials of the Foreign and War Offices. Three of the Jewish negotiators—Ben-Gurion, Shertok, and Yitzhak Gruenbaum—would later be signers of the Israel Declaration of Independence. The Arabs would consider nothing but their own demand of a unitary Palestine under Arab control. The Zionists stood firm on the principle of a Jewish state in an adequate area.

The conversations merely hardened positions on all sides, with Bevin balking at anything that smacked of partition. On February 7 he submitted his own plan to the Arabs and communicated it privately to the Jewish Agency. He offered to admit 4000 Jews per month for two years, with further immigration after that to be determined by an arbitration panel appointed by the United Nations. Bevin proposed that within five years the Jewish minority come under the rule of an Arab majority in a unified and independent Palestine state.

Arabs and Jews refused categorically even to discuss Bevin's scheme.

The Jews turned it down as a new version of the 1939 White Paper, offering even less than the Morrison-Grady scheme and leading ultimately to an Arab state. Bevin had warned both sides that if they did not accept, he would "wash my hands of the whole business" and dump the Palestine problem into the lap of the United Nations.

Bevin wound up the abortive round-table conference on February 14, 1947, by announcing that Britain would "submit the problem to the judgment of the United Nations." Exactly fifteen months later that judgment would lead to the birth of the State of Israel. This is "the only course now open to us," the glum Foreign Secretary confessed to the House of Commons on February 18, in admitting that the last of the postwar schemes had failed to break the Palestine impasse.

What he had in mind, however, was not the surrender of the Mandate, but advice from the United Nations. Colonial Secretary Creech-Jones informed the House of Commons that if the Mandate could not be administered in its existing form, Britain wanted the UN's recommendations on how to amend it. In turning to the UN, Britain offered no solution of her own but sidestepped any promise to abide by whatever the UN suggested unless she approved of the principles involved.

Sentiment for getting out of Palestine had been rising in Great Britain since the closing weeks of the war. The inner circles of the Churchill and Attlee Cabinets had debated the question several times, and Churchill had urged withdrawal on three occasions in 1946. A few weeks before Bevin's announcement Churchill said in the House of Commons that Britain ought to pull out "unless the United States come in with us shoulder to shoulder, to take a half-and-half share of the bloodshed, odium, trouble, expense, and worry." The Attlee government was sharply divided over what course to take. Some ministers insisted on immediate withdrawal, a few were eager to stay on and damn the consequences, but the majority leaned toward some kind of face-saving compromise.

This view was strengthened in the first months of 1947 by renewed violence carried out by the Irgun and the Stern Gang. After twelve British soldiers and police were killed on March 1, when the British officers' Club in one of Jerusalem's security zones was blown up, the British proclaimed martial law in Tel Aviv and parts of Jerusalem. For two weeks 240,000 Jews were cut off from postal, telephone, telegraph, and motor transport services in an attempt at collective punishment. Neither goods nor people was permitted to leave the martial law area. During a four-day screening of the total population of Tel Aviv, British troops separated the sheep from the goats by marking them with different colored dyes on their foreheads. Soldiers heiled Hitler in the Jewish settlements and scrawled swastikas on synagogues.

On March 16 the Jewish Agency's press office was blown up by a time-bomb. This was one of a series of explosions attributed to an anti-Semitic counter-terror squad in the British police force composed of former members of Sir Oswald Mosley's Blackshirts (the British Union of Fascists). The Jewish underground answered back with further attacks on British forces. The British countered by abolishing habeas corpus, legalizing detention without trial, and deporting citizens to the British colonies in Africa. Additional British troops were brought in as intensified searches for Jewish arms caches spread over the country, and the coastal blockade was tightened by an enlarged fleet of frigates and cutters.

Frustration over failure in Palestine added to Britain's cup of bitterness in the winter of 1946–47, when she began to liquidate the Empire. The crisis over Palestine coincided with the surrender of British military and financial commitments in Greece and Turkey and the granting of independence to India and Burma. Simultaneously, the Cold War emerged out of the widening split between the Anglo-American bloc and the Soviet Union over Germany, the Balkans, and the Middle East.

THE UN ENTERS THE PICTURE

Nevertheless, the Arabs and the Zionists were suspicious and apprehensive on April 2, 1947, when Britain asked the UN to convene a special session of the General Assembly to deal with the Palestine question. The Zionists faced heavy odds in the UN, where the Arabs had seven votes and the support of other Moslem nations. There was no assurance that the Commonwealth countries would desert the United Kingdom on the Palestine issue. The attitude of the Russians and their satellites, which had always opposed Zionism, was uncertain. The position of the US State Department was unpredictable.

The right of the Jewish Agency to present the Jewish case to the UN special session was conceded only after a bitter battle: six other Jewish organizations had sought recognition but the Jewish Agency won it. As the sole representative and spokesman for the Jewish cause the Agency was allowed to sit in at meetings of the Political and Security Committee of the General Assembly.

Named as the official Agency representatives were Ben-Gurion, Dr. Silver, Moshe Shertok, Chaim Greenberg, Mrs. Rose Halprin, Nahum

Goldmann, and Dr. Emanuel Neumann. On May 8, 1947, Dr. Silver as the recognized spokesman of the Jewish people, took his place between Cuba and Czechoslovakia on the Political and Security Committee. Observers referred to "the great force and dignity" with which he spoke on this history-making occasion. Shertok appeared before the Committee on May 10 and 12 and Ben-Gurion made the closing Jewish statement on May 12.

In answering a question from India as to whether the Agency recognized a difference between a Jewish state and a Jewish national home, Shertok explained that "the establishment of the Jewish national home is in process" while "the setting up of a Jewish state is its consummation." He reminded the Committee that such consummation "had been intended" by the authors of the Jewish national home policy. The partition plan of the Peel Commission in 1937 "conclusively proved," he added, that the way was definitely left open for the achievement of a Jewish state.

Ben-Gurion attacked the explanation of the British spokesman, Sir Alexander Cadogan, that Britain had for years tried and failed to settle the Palestine problem and had now brought it before the UN in the hope that it would find a just solution. Ben-Gurion declared that the Mandatory power "was not charged with discovering a solution" and "its failure was not in its ability to find the right solution." Britain's failure, he pointed out, was the failure "to carry out the settlement" determined originally by the United Kingdom and later embodied in the Mandate.

Once the United Nations agreed to appoint a special committee of inquiry on Palestine, the debate switched to its composition. The United States favored a body composed exclusively of smaller neutral powers with no direct interests in Palestine, thus excluding the Big Five. Britain supported this view, but the Soviet bloc wanted representation. The Jewish Agency sought to avoid any arrangement by which Britain would be able to play the double role of an object of international investigation and a partner in framing the investigation's conclusions and recommendations. The Agency also objected to the inclusion of an Arab country on the commission. It won on both points when the eleven-nation United Nations Special Committee on Palestine (UNSCOP) was set up comprised of Sweden, the Netherlands, Canada, Australia, Peru, Guatemala, Uruguay, Czechoslovakia, Yugoslavia, Iran, and India.

UNSCOP met first in four organizational sessions at Lake Success in May, 1947. At one of these the Jewish Agency was granted permission to designate two liaison officers with UNSCOP. The appointees were Aubrey (Abba) Eban, who would become Israel's first Permanent Representative to the United Nations, and David Horowitz, later Israel's Director of Treasury and Governor of the Bank of Israel.

The Commission then moved to Palestine, where it conducted thirteen public and eighteen closed hearings at which it heard thirty-four witnesses. The bulk of the testimony came from Jews and officials of the Palestine government because the Palestine Arabs boycotted UNSCOP. The views of representatives of the Arab States were heard in Lebanon when they refused to testify in Jerusalem. All but one of the Jewish spokesmen who appeared before UNSCOP called for partition as a logical solution. Only Dr. Judah L. Magnes opposed partition and urged instead an international trusteeship as a prelude to an independent binational state.

The Jewish Agency rejected a binational state and trusteeship, opposed continuation of the Mandate, demanded revocation of the 1939 White Paper, and asked for the establishment of a Jewish state. Ben-Gurion and Shertok presented the political aspects of the Jewish case. Eliezer Kaplan, David Horowitz, and Peretz Bernstein dealt with economic questions. Jewish historical and religious claims were outlined by Rabbi Fishman and Chief Rabbi Isaac Herzog. Weizmann, who no longer held any official Zionist position, summed up with a vigorous advocacy of partition.

For days before Weizmann was due to testify in the basement of the Jerusalem YMCA, he was briefed by a "brain trust," which included Gershon Agronsky, editor of the *Jerusalem Post;* Eban; Walter Eytan, later Israeli Ambassador to France; Mordecai Kidron, a future Israeli Ambassador to the UN, and Weisgal. As Weizmann tossed out ideas they worked them up and Eban "handled the styling," after which Weizmann made corrections. The final text was set up in one-inch-high type on the press of the *Jerusalem Post* because of Weizmann's failing eyesight. Just before he began to speak the sheets of his speech fell off the table and scattered over the floor. "Weizmann made no gesture to retrieve them," Weisgal recalls, and spoke extemporaneously. While UNSCOP was in Jerusalem, Weizmann invited its members and staff to lunch at his home in Rehovot. Ralph Bunche, UNSCOP's secretary, who sat next to Weisgal, nudged him "as if to say, 'how well I understand this man and how well he understands us Negroes.'"

After completing its hearings in Palestine on July 18 UNSCOP, the nineteenth commission to probe Palestine since 1919, left for Geneva to begin its fateful deliberations. They were held in the magnificent Palace of Nations, the former home of the defunct League of Nations, under the chairmanship of Justice Emil Sandstrom, a Swede. For six weeks Jewish

Agency emissaries engaged in frantic efforts to win over the representatives of the eleven nations to a decision favoring Jewish statehood in as large a segment of Palestine as possible.

Through private contacts with the various delegations and their chiefs, the Agency people kept well informed about the shifting tides of opinion in UNSCOP's debates. Eban and Horowitz had direct access to UNSCOP as official liaisons but the day-to-day unofficial talks and mapping of strategy also involved Shertok, Moshe Tov, Leo Kohn, Gideon Rafael, and Eliahu Sassoon. Weizmann, vacationing in Switzerland, was kept advised by cable and phone daily as the situation in the Palace of Nations shifted for better or worse.

THE UNSCOP REPORT

Several days before UNSCOP completed its work the Agency knew the broad outlines of what would be proposed. It had learned that there would be two reports, a majority position favoring partition and a minority stand advocating a federal state. It even had gotten wind of which countries would sign which report and that Australia would abstain from both.

Eban and Horowitz had been instructed to appear at the entrance to the splendid antechamber of the Palace of Nations at 9 PM on August 31 to receive copies of the reports. Waiting with them was Donald MacGilvray, the liaison officer of the Mandatory government. At 10 P.M. they were still pacing outside the hall where twenty-five years earlier the League of Nations had awarded the Palestine Mandate to Great Britain. An hour later an UNSCOP official darted out of the chamber, threw a swift glance at the three impatient men, and said with a grin, "Oh, here are the expectant fathers." The ceremony of signing the documents was not yet completed.

Exactly at midnight the doors of the chamber opened and members of UNSCOP and their staffs filed out. Enrique Fabregat of Uruguay embraced Horowitz and with tears in his eyes exclaimed, "It's the greatest moment in my life." Judge Ivan Rand of Canada, whose firm propartition stand had been decisive in UNSCOP's majority report, shook hands with Eban and Horowitz. Five minutes later Ralph Bunche came out of the chamber carrying bulky documents. He handed to Horowitz the one that contained UNSCOP's unanimous recommendation for the end of the British Mandate over Palestine, and the majority and minority reports.

The majority report represented a serious diminution of the proposals advanced in August, 1946, by the Jewish Agency, but it went further toward meeting Zionist hopes than any other previous non-Jewish partition plan. It assigned 62 percent of the country, including most of the Negev and the Arab town of Jaffa, to the Jewish state. The country was carved into seven pieces: three were assigned to the Jewish state and three to the Arab state, while the seventh was earmarked as an international enclave embracing the Old and New Cities of Jerusalem. The Jewish and Arab areas were interlocked in a checkerboard design with the various segments of the two states linked only at single "kissing points and junctions." The proposed Jewish state contained a population 45 percent Arab. The Jewish and Arab states would be given independence after they signed a ten-year treaty of economic union, with the economically weaker Arab state to be subsidized by the Jewish state.

This plan was endorsed by Canada, Peru, Guatemala, Uruguay, Sweden, the Netherlands, and Czechoslovakia. The minority report—favoring a federal state with a large Arab area and a small Jewish area, from which Jewish immigration would be barred after the two peoples reached numerical parity—was the suggestion of Iran, Yugoslavia, and India, all three of which had substantial Moslem populations.

The Arabs turned down both plans unconditionally and threatened war if partition was adopted. The Arab League backed them up with a pledge of men, money, and arms. The General Council (Actions Committee) of the World Zionist Organization, meeting in Zurich when UNSCOP's findings were published on September 1, accepted the majority plan, and the Jewish Agency followed suit. The prospect of a sovereign Jewish state prompted a majority of Zionists to take, with resignation, only "a minor part" of what had originally been promised in the Balfour Declaration. Two Left-wing Labor parties, Ha'Avodah and Hashomer Hatzair, refused to go along because they favored a binational state and an interim international regime. The Revisionists held out for a Jewish state on both sides of the Jordan.

The British served notice that they would implement no UN decision unacceptable to both Jews and Arabs, an obvious impossibility. The majority report had been a major diplomatic defeat for Britain, which had not anticipated that partition would be proposed. She had counted on UNSCOP's urging a British-administered binational state and had expected that Arabs and Jews would ask her to stay on.

From September 26 to November 29 the United Nations engaged in a quarrelsome, bitter, and protracted debate over UNSCOP's reports in an ad-hoc committee of the General Assembly representing all member states and in three subcommittees. At the first session of the ad-hoc committee Creech-Jones announced that in the absence of an agreed-upon settlement between Jews and Arabs, the British government "had to plan for an early withdrawal" of its forces and administration from Palestine.

As the UNSCOP reports moved tortuously through the complex UN machinery the minority proposal was shelved and the Arab demand for a unitary Arab state was voted down. The key decision on partition remained in abeyance because the Soviet Union and the United States each hesitated to show its hand until the other had spoken. Both feared pushing the Arab states into the opposite camp because the Palestine issue had become "an Arab-Zionist contest within an Anglo-American controversy about to be drawn into the Soviet-American Cold War."

Russia's position remained enigmatic for months. On May 14, 1947, Andrei Gromyko had created a stir by stating, "It is impossible to justify a denial . . . of the aspiration of the Jews for the creation of a state of their own . . . particularly if one takes into consideration the experience of this people in the Second World War." He suggested that partition and a binational state were possible solutions. While the Russian delegation kept silent in the early weeks of the UN debate, a Jewish Agency team of Shertok, Horowitz, and Eliahu Epstein, all of whom spoke Russian fluently, cultivated the Russian representatives. At one meeting in the Soviet Embassy Semyon Tsarapkin and Boris Stein startled the Agency men by offering a toast to "the future Jewish state."

The stalemate was broken on October 13, when Tsarapkin announced that the USSR would vote for partition. A few hours later Herschel Johnson followed suit for the United States. With the Cold War antagonists on the same side of a major international issue for the first time, a resolution favoring partition became the sole item on the agenda of the General Assembly and its ad-hoc committee.

As it gradually took shape the resolution ordered the termination of the Mandate as soon as possible but no later than August 1, 1948. British armed forces were to be withdrawn progressively, the last to be out of the country by August 1, 1948. By February 1, 1948, the Mandatory power would have to provide a seaport and a hinterland in the territory set aside for the Jewish state as facilities for substantial immigration. The Mandatory power was to turn over its authority in stages to a UN implementation commission of five. Jerusalem would be governed under a UN trusteeship.

Concentrating its entire apparatus on winning the two-thirds vote

needed in the General Assembly, the Jewish Agency grudgingly consented
to almost every whittling-down of the resolution in favor of the Arabs. In
order not to jeopardize votes for partition, it swallowed the severance of
the New City of Jerusalem and its inclusion in an internationalized Holy
City and the exclusion of western Galilee. At the insistence of the US
State Department the Negev, too, was almost detached from the Jewish
state until Weizmann's intervention with Truman caused the President to
send a last-minute change of instructions to the US delegation.

The nerve center of Zionist diplomacy during the crucial days of the
debate was the enlarged Jewish Agency delegation at Lake Success. Eliahu
Epstein, Michael Comay, Arthur Lourie, Mordecai Shiloah, Reuben Zas-
lani, Lionel Gelber, and Walter Eytan had been added to the group that
had worked so effectively in Geneva. Additional members of the staff
were Robert Nathan, Oscar Gass, Gottlieb Hammer, I. L. Kenen, and
Dorothy Adelson. Coordinating this team was Shertok, who also served as
the chief negotiator. The American Section of the Jewish Agency Executive, headed by Dr. Silver, was in almost constant session, deciding on
major policy and mapping day-to-day strategy. A political advisory committee representing all Zionist parties received regular reports on contacts
and negotiations with UN delegations and on proposed lines of action.
Dr. Silver was the forceful and magnetic spokesman who, together with
Weizmann, presented the Agency position at the UN. The legal case and
the pertinent documents were assembled by Dr. Jacob Robinson, an eminent international lawyer who recruited a battery of volunteer attorneys
headed by Abraham Tulin. This documentation would later figure in the
drafting of Israel's Declaration of Independence. In all the world capitals
Jewish Agency envoys launched intensive diplomatic action to bring pressure on the delegates at Lake Success.

Once the Americans and Russians lined up behind partition, the British, who had supported every move aimed at killing it, declared they
would do nothing to help carry it out. Hoping to frighten off some countries, Sir Alexander Cadogan informed the General Assembly sixteen days
before the final vote that since partition could not be put into effect
peaceably, his government would not be a party to its implementation by
force.

Cadogan announced that Britain would get out of Palestine by August
1, 1948, under conditions that made it plain that she intended to prove
that partition was unworkable while allowing the Jews and Arabs to fight
it out. The date for evacuation would be set without prior consultation
with the United Nations. Until the Mandate was surrendered, British rule

would continue wherever their forces remained. Authority would be turned over at one stroke only to the United Nations Committee on Palestine, not in stages to any provisional Arab or Jewish councils the Commission might establish. The British would not permit the United Nations to form interim governments or to recruit Arab and Jewish militias in any part of Palestine still occupied by His Majesty's troops.

The United Kingdom was one of the ten members that abstained when the General Assembly adopted the partition resolution on November 29 by a vote of 30 to 13, after a heartstopping dramatic poll. The very next day, while British police in Palestine stood idly by, the Arabs carried out their threat to resist partition by launching guerrilla attacks on the Jewish population. The scattered outbreaks had already escalated into warfare that was bloodying the country when on December 11 the Colonial Secretary advised the House of Commons that May 15 would be the last day of the Mandate.

chapter

∘ ∘ ∘ ∘ ∘ ∘ ∘ ∘ ∘ ∘ ∘ ∘ ∘ ∘ | 5 | ∘ ∘ ∘ ∘ ∘ ∘ ∘ ∘ ∘ ∘ ∘ ∘ ∘

JERUSALEM CELEBRATES PARTITION

A THUNDEROUS ROAR of *"Mazel Tovs"* spread over Jewish Palestine a few minutes before midnight on Saturday, November 29, 1947. A two-thousand-year-old dream had just come true, and the Yishuv exploded in fervent exaltation and frenzied exultation as if they had just heard the messiah was coming.

Every Jewish ear had been listening hopefully and avidly that evening to the radio account of the minute-by-minute proceedings of the United Nations General Assembly six thousand miles away at Flushing Meadow, New York. When the vote in favor of the UNSCOP plan to create a Jewish state in a partitioned Palestine was announced at 11:30 P.M. (5:30 P.M. EDT in New York), Palestine Jewry became almost incoherent with joy.

In minutes the streets of Jerusalem, Tel Aviv, Haifa, and every Jewish settlement seethed with throngs of men, women, and children, many in nightclothes. The same wave of unalloyed happiness and excitement that engulfed the Jews of Palestine spread swiftly over Jewish communities throughout the world. Jews wept, embraced, kissed, cheered, shouted, and uttered prayers of thanksgiving. Years later many Jews, in Israel and throughout the world, recalled this celebration more vividly than the proclamation of independence less than six months later; some even confuse the two dates in their memories.

British soldiers on patrol in Jerusalem gaily mixed with the celebrating crowds. Grinning Tommies gave joyrides on military vehicles to teen-agers with long sidecurls, girls in shorts, staid matrons, and bearded rabbinical students. From one slow-moving army truck a youngster who had celebrated his Bar Mitzvah that morning kept reciting his Torah portion over and over.

At 3:30 A.M. a huge army tank rumbled into the courtyard of the Jewish Agency building on Jerusalem's King George V Avenue. The Tommie at the wheel waved a bottle of slivovitz, the gift of one of the cheering Jews who clung to the tank's sides as it rolled through the immense crowd gathered to demand speeches from the leaders of Palestine Jewry.

Mrs. Golda Myerson, the American-born teacher from Milwaukee who, as Golda Meir, would later be Israel's fourth Prime Minister, came out on the Agency's first-floor portico. With each word punctuated by shouts and applause, she said, "We have labored for this moment." Her face shining behind tears of joy, the only Palestinian woman member of the Jewish Agency Executive continued, "We always believed that it would come. Now we will have a free Jewish State."

In the throng was Elazar L. Sukenik, professor of archaeology at the Hebrew University, bursting to share another piece of tremendous news. That morning he had returned from Bethlehem with the first three Dead Sea Scrolls acquired in a secret deal from an Armenian. His son Yigael (the surname was later changed to Yadin), Haganah's chief of operations, had warned that the trip to Bethlehem was dangerous, but Sukenik ignored the man who eventually made even more sensational discoveries as Israel's leading archaeologist.

Sukenik was excitedly examining the Scrolls in his study while his youngest son, Mati, twiddled the radio dial in the next room to bring in the news from Flushing Meadow. Hour by hour Mati reported to his father what was happening at the UN while the archaeologist became more enthralled by what he was uncovering. Around midnight he tore himself away from the incredible finds on his desk to join the celebrants. The first news of his discovery he confided to Aviezer Yallin, an eminent Hebrew educator, and Yitzhak Ben Yechezekiel, collector of Jewish folktales, whom he had spotted in the crowd.

The coincidence of the miracle in the UN with the historic cultural event that unfolded in Sukenik's study was regarded by many as highly symbolic, particularly since one of the Scrolls was that of the "War of the Sons of Light [the children of Levi, Judah, and Benjamin] Against the Sons of Darkness [the nations surrounding Israel]."

Before dawn Chief Rabbi Isaac Herzog toured the wildly celebrating city in an open car that threaded its way slowly through curb-to-curb throngs. At Rehavia, a Jewish suburb, he paused to recite the traditional

Sheheheyanu. Speaking in the brogue acquired during his years as Chief Rabbi of Ireland, he was joined by his octogenerian father-in-law, Rabbi Samuel Hillman, and the aged Rabbi Moshe Silver, whose son, Rabbi Abba Hillel Silver of Cleveland, had been a decisive figure in the effort to win UN approval for Jewish statehood.

In Tel Aviv, Haifa, Tiberias, and Safed the news from New York touched off a wild nightlong outburst of singing, dancing, and toasting. Cafés and hotels overflowed as jubilant celebrants greeted friends and strangers alike with endless *"L'Chaims."* Cries of "Long live the Jewish state" and "Long live the United Nations" welled up with uninhibited exuberance. In the synagogues and yeshivas the pious gave thanks that they had been permitted to see the great day.

But only twenty-four hours after the UN vote the joyous celebration was snuffed out by the opening shots of Arab resistance. Ambushes on the roads from Jerusalem to Nathanya and Hadera claimed the first Jewish casualties on November 30. Arab snipers also shot down Jewish civilians that day on the Jaffa-Tel Aviv border and in the Arab quarter of Haifa. A three-day nationwide strike called by the Arab Higher Committee to protest against partition triggered the first assault on the Jewish quarter of the Old City of Jerusalem on December 2. Looting and burning of Jewish property in the New City began. The last phase of the long and bloody fight for independence had started.

A week after the UN had spoken all of Palestine was in turmoil despite Britain's boast that the country was in her undivided control. Roadblocks manned by armed Arab guards had shut off all traffic into the Old City's Jewish quarter. With the Tel Aviv-Jerusalem road under constant attack the New City and its surrounding Jewish suburbs were already in trouble. Scattered raids had begun on the Jewish settlements in the Galilee and the Negev.

The Arab strategy was readily apparent: to keep all the Jewish colonies under day-and-night fire from neighboring Arab villages and to cut communications between the Jewish areas. Because the Jewish population was largely concentrated in Tel Aviv, Jerusalem, Haifa, and in 700 scattered settlements, control of the connecting highways was crucial to the Jews. The Arabs were dispersed in over 760 villages and 25 towns, in addition to large pockets in Haifa, Jaffa, Tiberias, and Safed. With small forces and snipers occupying the heights that commanded the roads, the Arabs were in good position to choke off all Jewish traffic. The cities were isolated from each other and from the settlements in the north and the south.

The Arabs didn't expect a long war. They counted on the ambushes of

Jewish convoys to sever the Jerusalem area from the rest of Jewish Palestine and to starve out the settlements. They were sure that one by one the Jewish colonies in the Galilee and the Negev would have to be abandoned or surrendered and that all of Palestine would fall into Arab hands once the British moved out. Through the road blockades, streetfighting, and bombing in the cities and the weak position of isolated settlements, they banked on proving the impossibility of partition in the hope it would collapse.

Before the UN convened to debate the implementation of the UNSCOP report, the Arabs had declared "a relentless war to repel this attack on our country." On September 19, 1947, three days after the General Assembly debate began, the Arab League held a secret meeting at Sofar, Lebanon, at which it was decided to send troops and arms into Palestine if the UN agreed on partition. The Arab Higher Committee for Palestine swore the Arabs "would never recognize the validity of partition or the authority of the United Nations to implement it."

During the UN debate, the Arab delegates had assailed partition as a violation of the UN Charter and vowed never to recognize it. Then they walked out of the session before it ended. The prime ministers of the seven Arab states comprising the Arab League, meeting in Cairo on December 7, 1947, announced that they would back the Palestine Arabs with arms, money, and troops. They promised that their own armies would march against the Jews as soon as the British Mandate ended. Damascus became the training center for an Arab "army of liberation." Fawzi el Kaukji, the pro-Nazi soldier of fortune who had led the 1936–39 Arab rebellion in Palestine, took command of the "volunteers." They were trained by Syrian Army officers.

Widely publicized assurances to the Palestine Arabs that the Jews had no aggressive intentions against them failed to halt the hit-and-run raids and ambushes. As the fighting spread in December and escalated in January, 1948, into organized Arab onslaughts, Haganah maintained an almost exclusively defensive stance. Open suppression of Arab violence might have been considered provocation that would open the Jews to the charge of breaking the peace. This, it was feared, could precipitate revocation of the UN partition resolution and a proclamation that the country was in a state of civil war. There was a danger that the Jewish state could be lost even before it came into being.

Offensive action on any scale was also not yet possible. Haganah's mobilization had not yet been completed. Arms and munitions were critically short. British arrests of Haganah men and continued searches for and seizures of Jewish arms caches seriously impeded Haganah's preparations.

When Arab snipers hidden in Jaffa mosques and other commanding buildings endangered the Tel Aviv suburbs, Haganah took up defensive positions but were forced out by the British. Haganah offensive activity in the first weeks was limited to punitive raids on Arab villages harboring irregulars and the escort and guarding of convoys.

Opposed to partition and determined to do nothing to see it implemented, British policy was to let the Jews and Arabs fight it out. In practice, however, the British Army carried out instructions from London to hamper the Jews and encourage the Arabs. Some British soldiers took advantage of the Arab rebellion to retaliate for acts of Jewish terrorism against the British forces. There were, however, some instances of British soldiers aiding the Jewish defenders.

While hundreds of Arabs were daily crossing Palestine's land frontiers, Haganah was compelled to maintain its underground character because the British refused to recognize it as a legal force. Long after the Arabs had openly assembled "liberation" units in Palestine from Syria and Iraq, the British were still searching Jewish convoys for arms. In typical "divide and conquer" technique, the British announced on January 20, 1948, that predominantly Jewish or Arab areas would be progressively handed over to whichever side was in a clear majority. In mid-December they had turned over the policing of Tel Aviv and Petach Tikvah to the Jews. This left the British free to concentrate their forces at such strategic points as Jerusalem and Haifa.

British refusal to turn over the administration of evacuated communities to any local authority or to permit the creation of local militia was part of its plan to create an administrative vacuum with consequent chaos in maintaining public security. As the British garrisons departed erupting towns and rural areas of mixed Arab-Jewish population, civil war followed. By not handing over legal or factual control to anyone, the British encouraged Haganah and Arab forces to try to grab possession with paramilitary forces.

The British also refused to protect Jewish road traffic or to allow Jewish self-protection units to accompany the convoys. To do so, they claimed, would be "enforcing implementation of partition." When the first Arab roadblocks began halting Jewish traffic into the Old City of Jerusalem, the British police stood by. As the battle for the roads intensified, the British advised the Jews to evacuate the Old City and the commercial center of the New City. They even suggested the abandonment of the entire Negev.

Lacking either the will or the power to halt the Arab attacks, the British tolerated the infiltration of irregular Arab forces on Palestine soil. The first Arab invasion of Palestine began with a raid on two northeastern settlements on January 9, 1948, by six hundred uniformed "volunteers." Six days later Britain signed a new treaty with Iraq, pledging arms and equipment. With a straight face, Albert Victor Alexander, the British Secretary of Defense, told the House of Commons on February 6 that he "had no reason to suppose" that arms assigned to the Arab states under treaties would "find their way to Palestine." In mid-March, Britain entered into a new twenty-year mutual defense and friendship pact with Transjordan. This alliance assured Transjordan of arms, munitions, and military equipment and the continuation of the £2 million grant for the support of the Arab Legion.

In the House of Commons on the very next day the Colonial Secretary conceded that Fawzi el Kaukji had "slipped through the border guards and gotten into Palestine." The War Office admitted that since November 30 5000 Arabs had crossed into Palestine from Syria and Iraq. By mid-March 15,000 Arab irregulars, including 10,000 Palestinians, were operating in Palestine under the command of Gen. Sawfat Pasha of Iraq who had been appointed by the Arab League.

THE BREAK WITH BRITAIN

In the face of this British policy the Jewish Agency on February 21 advised the UN Implementation Commission that the "Jewish people in Palestine have come to recognize that only their own forces stand between them and annihilation." Confronted with the Britain's so-called neutrality on the issue of Jewish survival or extermination, the Jewish Agency advised the Implementation Commission that "the Jews of Palestine have assumed responsibility which formally rests on the Mandatory Power." This proclamation of self-reliance was in effect the first declaration by the Yishuv of a state of war.

A militarily costly but politically sound decision by the Jewish leadership followed. They determined to defend every settlement, even the most isolated, to disprove the Arab claims, unofficially backed by British spokesmen, that partition was impossible to achieve. This meant no retreat and fighting to the last, however untenable any position was militarily. It necessitated the dispersion of Haganah and Palmach forces in small pockets throughout the country. No concentration in strength anywhere was possible. Supplies and reinforcements had to be sent to all the settlements through Arab-held territory. Tailormade for Arab ambushes of the convoys trying to run the blockade, this tactic gave rise to the desperate battle for the roads.

The first convoy of forty-five trucks and taxis fought its way from Tel Aviv to Jerusalem early in December. Until the Haganah openly assumed escort duty, the only protection the convoys had in running the gauntlet of snipers and guerrillas was the Jewish Settlement Police, almost all of whom were secretly in the Haganah. They suffered heavy casualties because the British refused to let them use the armored cars acquired from the British during the 1936–39 riots.

At first the British insisted that the convoy escorts ride in open half-ton trucks, with no protection even for the drivers. Preceding or trailing the convoys, these trucks were inviting targets. Steel armor plate stolen from British military depots later provided protective fronts and sides for the cabs of trucks running through the blockade.

Similarly, for weeks the Tel Aviv-Jerusalem buses running the Arab gauntlet had neither guards nor armor. Their only protection was a team of boy and girl Palmachniks who rode the buses disguised as students. The girls carried hand grenades and disassembled Sten guns in their clothing.

As the Arabs tightened their hold on the roads and stepped up their attacks on the settlements in the north and south, the success of the convoys in getting through became a matter of life and death for the Jewish community. Some of the bitterest fighting occurred fifteen miles northwest of Jerusalem where the road to Tel Aviv passes through a high and narrow ravine known as Bab el Wad ("Door of the Valley"). In all of February only two convoys successfully fought their way through the roadblocks at Bab el Wad and Kastel, another Arab strongpoint. The number of trucks trying to break through was doubled in March, but on some days not a single vehicle got by. By April 1 the convoy system had almost completely broken down.

Besieged Jerusalem was in desperate straits and in danger of starvation. Communications with the settlements were becoming increasingly hazardous. With the Arabs in almost complete command of the heights controlling the roads, military experts in the US were openly voicing doubts that the Jews could hold on to their scattered outlying areas. If Jerusalem fell and the colonies were overrun or compelled to surrender, the establishment of the Jewish state was in peril.

Nevertheless, the Jews held out, even though the cost was high. After three months of guerrilla warfare the Mandatory government announced the casualties at 1378 dead and 3186 wounded, including 550 Jews killed. By April 3 the UN reported 1256 Jews and 3569 Arabs killed, and 2100 Jews and 3160 Arabs wounded. But not a single Jewish colony had been abandoned and a new one had been established in the Negev. Jerusalem's New City was still in Jewish hands.

Jubilant over their successful convoy ambushes, the Arabs settled down to wait until the British left. They were confident that when food, fuel, and arms were exhausted, the Jews would submit. The first round of Arab victories were "grease on the wheels" of Arab diplomacy. When the United States retreated from partition on March 18, the Arabs felt sure that the Jewish state would die aborning.

"OPERATION NAHSHON"

The Arab strategy and timetable were upset when Haganah embarked on a major change in policy as "anxiety gave birth to daring." April 1 became the turning point of the conflict with the launching of an offensive action "Operation Nahshon," code-named for the man who, according to legend, first jumped into the Red Sea on Moses' order.

The purpose of this first large-scale Jewish offensive was to open the Tel Aviv-Jerusalem road. Supplies for Jerusalem had to be gotten through; thus the safeguarding of the convoys became a prime necessity. This was a grave gamble because it involved open resistance to British authority: its right to search the convoys for arms.

But to seize and hold the steep hills bordering the road involved a major military undertaking. More and better arms were needed than were available. Jewish Agency emissaries in Prague had been feverishly assembling war matériel, but shipments to Palestine were largely being held up until the British evacuated and the state was declared.

Jerusalem's need for food and water was so dire, however, that a decision was made to fly the arms in immediately despite the risk of discovery and confiscation. On March 31, a few hours before "Nahshon" was launched, a Dakota transport landed at Beth Darass, south of Jerusalem, a secret Haganah airstrip only recently abandoned by the British.

The plane landed after dark, refueled, and took off again. Still in its original packing, the load of arms was rushed to Haganah troops poised to strike. All traces of the plane's presence were removed since British officers were due back the following morning to check on rumors of an arms cache. Another cargo arrived by sea on April 3. Together the two shipments brought a few hundred light machine guns (Spandaus) and several thousand rifles, but they made a tremendous difference.

"Nahshon's" key objectives were the roadblocks at Kastel, five miles west of Jerusalem at the eastern end of the highway, and Bab el Wad, a few miles farther away on the western approaches. Kastel, which dominated three miles of the winding highway below from its 2500-foot promontory, was taken on April 4. While the Jews held the village and the segment of road it controlled, one lifesaving convoy was rammed through to Jerusalem on April 6. Counterattacks drove the Jews out of Kastel on April 9. The last Jewish command was "All privates will retreat—all commanders will cover their withdrawal." Shimon Alfasi, who gave the order, died beside his machine gun.

The battle cost the Arabs the life of one of their ablest commanders, Abdul Kader el Husseini, a nephew of the rabidly anti-Jewish Mufti of Jerusalem. Demoralized by Kader's death, the Arabs abandoned Kastel on April 10. At the western end of the road a Jewish task force cleared the hills around the rocky Bab el Wad gorge through which the highway twists up the Judean Hills on its way to Jerusalem. By temporarily neutralizing heavily fortified Arab villages from which the road was under fire, Haganah enabled three more large convoys to slip into Jerusalem.

One got through on April 12. Another, moving bumper to bumper, was badly mauled but got through on April 17. Riding in the lead truck was David Ben-Gurion. Although it arrived on a Saturday, the convoy was blessed by an Orthodox rabbi. "These men hallow heaven and earth," he cried out. Still wearing their prayer shawls, Jews poured out of the synagogues to help with the unloading.

A third convoy, a Passover special of three hundred trucks organized by veterans of British Army Transport drafted for the hazardous assignment, broke through to Jerusalem on April 20, four days before Passover. On the side of each truck was chalked, in Hebrew, "If I Forget Thee, O Jerusalem." An all-day battle at Bab el Wad had delayed the trucks, but they delivered a thousand tons of Passover supplies. This Passover convoy was the last to get through, however, for behind the convoy a new and massive Arab roadblock again made the road impassable. Thereafter, Jerusalem had to make do with what the April convoys had brought.

Meanwhile, a small detachment of Haganah, armed only with a single Browning MG, a handful of mortars, and some small arms, fought off an attack on Mishmar Haemek by Fawzi el Kaukji's irregulars. Ignoring British warnings to get out, the Jews held on from April 4 to 10, when the

Arabs withdrew. Their attempt to sever the Haifa-Tel Aviv road had failed.

In the midst of "Operation Nahshon," on April 10, the Irgun and Sternists raided Dir Yassin, an Arab village southwest of Jerusalem. Conducted without the authority of the Jewish Agency or Haganah, this raid took the lives of 200 Arabs, a great many of whom were civilian men, women, and children. The Irgun and Stern groups suffered forty-one casualties, including four dead.

To this day this raid remains one of the most tragic and controversial aspects of the pre-state fighting. The Irgunists claim that it was necessary from a military point of view to relieve pressure on Kastel, which with Dir Yassin had to be under Jewish control if the Jews were to keep the road to Jerusalem open.

At the time the Jewish Agency voiced its "horror and disgust" at the manner in which this dissident action was carried out. It cabled Emir Abdullah its sorrow at the loss of civilian lives. The Agency statement, calling attention to continued Arab killing of civilians, said it nevertheless "could not excuse the commission of such brutalities by Jews." The Agency made "an earnest appeal to all parties that if armed conflict in Palestine can indeed not be avoided, it should at least be conducted in accordance with the rules of civilized warfare and that in particular the rights of the civilian population should be scrupulously respected."

The Irgunists never admitted that their action was terroristic and not militarily necessary, however, and in March, 1969, the Israel Ministry for Foreign Affairs issued an explanation exonerating the Irgun and Stern groups of the charges made against them. But the Dir Yassin episode has been utilized by the Arabs ever since in their propaganda against the Jews.

Five days later, when the Arabs ambushed a convoy of doctors, nurses, and Hebrew University personnel en route to Mount Scopus with supplies for the Hadassah-Hebrew University Hospital, in which seventy-six men and women were killed and twenty-one wounded, some of the attackers cried out that it was in retaliation for Dir Yassin.

"Nahshon" did not achieve all of its objectives, but six weeks before independence it marked the turning of the tide in the Jews' favor. Starvation in Jerusalem was temporarily averted and morale bolstered as its Jewish defenders knew they had not been forgotten. The British also seemed to have sensed the turn, for early in April they transferred Army headquarters from Jerusalem to Haifa.

Haganah could have opened the Jerusalem road for its entire length, but further offensives in that area were deferred when Jewish forces were deployed northward in preparation for the battle for Haifa.

Haganah and the Arabs were informed on April 18 by the British commander in Haifa that all his forces would leave by April 20 and concentrate in fortified enclaves on Mount Carmel and the port area. Both sides had been preparing for this day during the months in which violence and sabotage spread over the country's only port at which large seagoing vessels could dock. Following four days of continuous forays by Syrian mercenaries, Haganah struck on the night of April 20. Behind a creeping mortar barrage and TNT-filled oil drums rolled down the steep streets from Mount Carmel into the Arab sectors, Haganah quickly overran the Arab strongholds. After one brief counterattack, Arab leadership collapsed. By April 22 the city was in Jewish hands.

THE JEWS TAKE OVER HAIFA

The swift capture of Haifa, which fell to the Jews on April 22 after a thirty-six-hour battle, implemented phase one of Haganah's "Plan D." This was an order to all local commanders "to fill the vacuum left by the British, to capture strategic heights overlooking possible lines of advance by the expected invading armies, and to link Jewish-held territory in one continuous stretch."

Haganah's surrender terms included a bid to the Arabs to remain as free citizens if they refrained from military action. Haganah leaflets in Arabic were scattered throughout Haifa during the closing hours of the battle, urging the Arabs to stay. Arab policemen were asked to return to duty and assurances were given that municipal services would be restored, stores and shops permitted to reopen, and food distributed.

"Stay, stay in Haifa," loudspeakers boomed from Haganah trucks. The same trucks described the rout of the Arab forces and broadcast news of the panicky flight of the Arab leaders. They were identified by name, Haganah having learned their identity by tapping telephone lines. Haganah intelligence had also intercepted nine of eleven convoys bringing Arab reinforcements. A top-level Arab-Jewish parley in the Haifa city hall, and even a plea for British intervention, failed to halt the mass exodus of the Arab population. Propaganda from the Arab Higher Committee urged the Arabs to abandon the battlefield "so that the heroic Arabic armies approaching from abroad" could smash through the country and drive the

Jews into the Mediterranean. Most of the 70,000 Arabs who fled expected to be gone only briefly. They believed they would return in triumph with the conquering Arab armies after May 15. One Palestinian Arab writer recalled that Arab leaders "told us, 'get out so that we can get in.' We got out but they did not get in."

Many Arabs, particularly Christians, had been leaving the city since the previous December, and the panicky flight assumed massive proportions even before the shooting stopped. Those who could afford it took passage in small boats and fishing smacks. Arab captains did a land-office business, demanding fabulous passage money. The well-to-do hustled off in motorboats and chartered tugs, heading for Acre and Lebanon. Others piled into trucks, buses, cars, and carts. A thousand frightened women and children and men who had sought refuge from the fighting in the port area were given shelter by the British. As the long irregular column moved out of Haifa without hindrance, the Arab high command was sure that the withdrawal of Arab workers would paralyze the city. But this too failed to materialize. Tough, burly Yosef Almogi, boss of the Histadrut in Haifa, had recruited a Haganah labor brigade from the Jewish oil workers who had been guarding the Haifa oil refineries to prevent the British from removing crude oils from its tanks.

The Jewish assault on Haifa, the first city to be liberated by force of Jewish arms, was officially blamed on the Arabs. The High Commissioner described it on April 25 as "the direct consequence of continuous attacks by Arabs on the Jews in Haifa over the previous four days." British police headquarters in Haifa also confirmed that "every effort is being made by the Jews to persuade the Arab populace to stay and carry on with their normal lives."

The British military moves around Haifa that preceded the fall of the city were part of the piecemeal withdrawal from the entire country. As the Union Jack began coming down from police and military fortresses in northern Palestine and as British withdrawal commenced, Arab civilians followed. At first a trickle, it became a flood. Haganah had expected a tough battle when it attacked the Arab quarter of Tiberias. There had been fighting around the city for two weeks before the British left on April 18, but the Arabs fled en masse, and on April 18 Tiberias had not a single Arab. A week before there had been 6000 and about the same number of Jews. Within ten days Haganah had cleared the road north of Tiberias and occupied the police post and military camp at Rosh Pina.

The British camps, airfields, and supply dumps, including those left over from World War II, as well as the forty police forts built during the

1936–39 riots were great strategic prizes. As the British began dismantling their installations preparatory to evacuation, they turned over arms,
equipment, and forts to the Arabs. Sympathizers in the Palestine police or
British Army often tipped off the Arabs in advance of the British departure. In some instances British commanders even invited the Arabs to
take over strongpoints before the British had gone. Nevertheless, superior
Haganah intelligence often enabled the Jews to grab many of these places
as fast as the British disappeared.

What matériel the British could not take with them or sell to the
Arabs they ordered destroyed. Eyewitnesses to the military departure compared the abandoned camps and billets all over the country to "a panorama of the sack of Rome." Huge heaps of twisted metal and burnt rubber
littered deserted truck parks where the British had set fire to mobile
equipment too costly to ship home. Tangled electric wires mingled with
broken glass, smashed furniture, and gutted pipes. Some British NCOs
and junior officers sold off condemned equipment and supplies to the
highest bidder, Jew or Arab.

In the weeks before the final withdrawal the black market in British
arms and matériel offered everything from radio equipment to aspirin,
Churchill tanks and jeeps, kitbags and light field artillery pieces. The
Tommies engaged in this clandestine trade preferred the few pounds a
sale brought to seeing the stuff burnt, smashed, or dumped into the Mediterranean. Gen. Sir Richard Gale, who commanded the British garrison
on May 14, was the officer who directed the disposition of all British military stores in the north of Palestine in April and early May. He closed
his eyes to the bargain sales of British quartermaster officers. When he
left Palestine, he was one of the few high-ranking British commanders remembered as a friend of the Jewish community.

THE JEWS CONSOLIDATE THEIR POSITION

As in Tiberias and Haifa, Haganah prepared to strike at Safed immediately after the British moved out of this historic center of Jewish mysti-
cism on April 16. The battle for Safed lasted three weeks, but Haganah
didn't attack in force until May 8. During this period the Arabs had made
good use of the Safed police station and the Tegart Fortress, which had
been turned over to them under orders by the British commander when
they evacuated the city.

The Tegart Fortress, which was part of a number of fortified police sta-

tions recommended by Sir Charles Tegart during the 1936–39 Arab uprising, was especially valuable to the Arabs as it enabled them to keep
every Jewish house in the citadel of Galilee under fire. The tactical value
of this fortress under Arab control was stressed by the British to buttress
their urging to Haganah that it withdraw Jewish forces from this area
early in April. They pointed out that the 2500 Jews couldn't hold out two
hours after the British left, against the 12,000 native Arabs, 600 Iraqi
guerrillas, and 1500 Home Guards.

But when the Jews attacked in force on May 8, Arab resistance
melted. After the capture of two villages on the northern outskirts the
Arab populace began to flee. By May 10 the city was completely in Jewish
hands; after bitter house-to-house fighting the Jews had captured the Tegart Fortress and the police station on the preceding day. In the course of
the struggle the Jews unleashed a Davidka blast, which was immediately
followed by rain. The Arabs had heard that atomic blasts brought on rain,
and the unseasonable downpour following the Davidka shot convinced
them that the Jews had dropped an atom bomb. After this the Arabs fled
the city wildly, and the entire area around Safed came under Haganah
control. (A Davidka was actually a crude homemade mortar whose noise
was more lethal than its missile.)

The Mufti of Jerusalem had planned to make Safed the capital of an
Arab state. But the fall of the city broke the back of the guerrilla forces in
the north and ended the last chance of cutting communications between
the Jewish colonies in the Galilee before the full-scale invasion got under
way. After the capture of Safed by Yigal Allon, in 1972 Israel's Deputy
Prime Minister, the Jews held the entire coast of western Galilee to the
Lebanese frontier and a well-defended belt in eastern Galilee that embraced Tiberias, Samakh, and Safed. Beisan, the last Arab town in Jewish
territory, was taken on May 11.

Twenty-four hours earlier Jaffa had capitulated. The formal surrender
by an emergency committee of four Arab notables who had been administering the city since its officials fled was accepted at 3:20 P.M. by Haganah
commander Amos Ben-Gurion. It was a little more than twenty-four
hours before his father was to proclaim Jewish independence in neighboring Tel Aviv.

An invasion of the Mansieh quarter of Jaffa, a base for Arab raids on
Tel Aviv, had long been considered by Haganah and Irgun. When Haganah decided not to attack, Irgun went it alone. Following a night assault
on April 25, Irgun overran the city's northern sector in three days. In the
heart of Jaffa, Irgun forces ran into trouble and Haganah launched a di-

versionary attack from the south. Once Haganah joined the battle, Arab morale caved in. In a few days the Arab population shrank from 65,000 to 15,000.

The British, who for months had looked the other way while Syrians and Iraqis stormed across the Palestine border to attack Jewish settlements, suddenly intervened. Land, sea, and air reinforcements were rushed in from Cyprus, Malta, and Suez. British troops occupied a buffer zone between Arab and Jewish lines and some Jewish positions were shelled. Fearing that all of Jaffa, like Haifa, would fall to the Jews, the British enforced an uneasy cease-fire for two weeks.

The British show of force was justified on the ground that Irgun's "unwarranted aggression" had so "seriously deteriorated" the situation around Jaffa that the area had "assumed operational priority in the Middle East." Commanding General MacMillan claimed he had halted the fighting because it jeopardized plans for the withdrawal of his forces from Sarafend, ten miles from Tel Aviv, the principal British Army camp in Palestine. Negotiations for its sale to the Jewish authorities at a price of £750,000 were almost complete when London ordered it turned over to the Arabs. When the British began their withdrawal from Jaffa on May 12, Sarafend was handed to the Arabs, free. Haganah drove them out on May 18.

The troop movements renewed suspicion that the British had changed their minds about yielding the Mandate on May 14. But the High Commissioner defended the recall of infantry, guns, tanks, and marine commandos as a step toward keeping the Arab-Jewish war from interfering with the evacuation.

Under the surrender agreement Jaffa became an open city policed by Haganah. Mayor Israel Rokach of Tel Aviv sent Jewish labor battalions into the battered city to restore sanitary facilities and communications. The last British forces left on May 14 in a long convoy of tanks and armored police cars that guarded the line of trucks carrying all but the poorest Arab families to Lebanon.

The loss of Jaffa intensified the flight of the Arab population from Palestine, but the mass exodus, entirely unanticipated, had been gathering momentum for months. Moshe (Shertok) Sharett recalled, in a lecture in 1957, that Israel never dreamed that two-thirds of the Arabs would suddenly uproot themselves and leave. In retrospect, however, it is evident that the Arabs had apparently glimpsed defeat as early as January, 1948, when the British High Commissioner confirmed "a steady exodus of middle-class Arab families who could afford to leave the country."

The Arab newspaper *Ash Shab* on January 30 denounced Arabs who abandoned their homes and businesses as "the first group of our fifth columnists." Inhabitants of Arab villages near Tel Aviv who were "quitting . . . bag and baggage" were accused by the Arab newspaper *As Saruh* on March 30 of having "brought about a terrible disgrace." Less than three months after Jewish statehood, Glubb Pasha, commander of Jordan's Arab Legion, wrote in the London *Daily Mail* on August 12 that "the Arab civilians panicked and fled ignominiously." Villages, he said, were frequently "abandoned before they were threatened by the progress of the war."

Even before the British left Jerusalem on May 14 one high British official noted that "the whole effendi class has gone. It is remarkable how many of the younger ones are suddenly deciding that this might be a good time to resume their studies at Oxford." As the Arab leaders began to leave, doctors, lawyers, teachers, civil-service employees, and labor leaders followed. Dependent largely on the British for public services, the Arab community began to dissolve as the British closed down government offices providing these services. Rumor and panic spread in the Arab quarters. By early May over 200,000 Arabs had gone, and those who remained had been deserted by their leaders. Almost no Jews left the country and not a single Jewish community leader abdicated.

The original boundaries established by the United Nations for the Jewish state in a partitioned Palestine contained a population 45 percent Arab. By May 14 this had shrunk to barely 15 percent. The fleeing Arabs left behind houses, shops, and land valued at millions of Palestine pounds. They abandoned a million acres of land, more than two and a half times what the Jews owned before statehood.

"We stand on the eve of the Jewish state," David Ben-Gurion exclaimed after the fall of Jaffa. Its capture and the earlier liberation of Haifa, Tiberias, and Safed were regarded as a miracle by many pious Jews. Equally astounding was the fact that not a single square mile of territory assigned to the Jewish state by the United Nations partition had been lost in the fighting since November 30. But the Jews were not able to take over some of the thirty-three Jewish settlements located in the area set aside for the Arab state, including the Etzion bloc just south of Jerusalem on the road to Hebron. This was to remain a thorn in Israel's side until a unified Jerusalem area was achieved in the Six-Day War of 1967.

Jewish-held areas had been consolidated and enlarged by the conquest of nearly a hundred Arab villages. In the face of all the grim predictions, the outnumbered and outgunned Jews had routed the forces of the Palestinian Arabs and had badly trounced the Arab Liberation Army from abroad. The roads to the Galilee in the north and to the Negev in the south had been largely cleared. Arab pockets of opposition in the towns and cities had been wiped out, western and eastern Galilee were solidly in Jewish hands, and Acre was on the verge of falling.

Besieged Jerusalem and its Jewish environs, however, were still in peril. The Arabs held the Old City, in whose Jewish quarter 2500 Jews were isolated. Most of the New City was controlled by the Jews but it was still cut off from the rest of Jewish Palestine. Desperate attempts to solidify the scattered Jewish districts around Jerusalem by attacks on Arab sectors of the New City had been only partially successful. The adjacent Jewish colonies north and south of Jerusalem remained isolated and in danger. The seesaw battle to reopen the Tel Aviv-Jerusalem road was still raging when Haganah withdrew its forces to meet the invasion by the armies of the Arab states after midnight May 14.

Part Two

THE MILITARY CONFLICT

c h a p t e r

∘ ∘ ∘ ∘ ∘ ∘ ∘ ∘ ∘ ∘ ∘ ∘ ∘ | 6 | ∘ ∘ ∘ ∘ ∘ ∘ ∘ ∘ ∘ ∘ ∘ ∘ ∘

THE ARABS ATTACK

ON THE DAY ISRAEL came into being five Arab armies massed on its frontiers, determined that it be stillborn. Damascus announced that Syria and Lebanon would invade from the north at dawn on May 15. In the south Egyptian forces in the Sinai Desert concentrated around El Arish under orders to cross into Palestine at one minute after midnight May 14. Egyptian naval vessels had already landed troops forty-five miles south of Tel Aviv at what is now Ashkelon Beach.

"We are not attacking anybody," Egypt's Prime Minister declared. "We are only sending an expedition to keep order in Palestine and to suppress the dissident minority of Zionist terrorists." An Iraqi motorized brigade that had moved westward on the night of May 13 took up positions on the border. Simultaneously, mechanized units of the British-officered Arab Legion reached the Allenby Bridge entrance to Palestine via the main highway from Jordan.

In the Red House, Haganah's headquarters on Tel Aviv's Hayarkon Street, the general staff and David Ben-Gurion, Chairman of the Defense Council, agonized over whether to strike first. Ben-Gurion heatedly demanded a Jewish initiative, while the military strategists urged delay until the British had left and the Arabs' operational deployment became clearer. The experts pleaded that they could not mount an offensive with the resources on hand. They also feared damage to the Jews' UN standing if they were the aggressors. In retrospect Ben-Gurion turned out to be right, but he did not overrule general headquarters.

Few military authorities doubted that the Arabs would swiftly overrun Israel. The Arabs' own timetable, as revealed later in captured documents, called for a blitzkrieg. Haifa was to have fallen on May 20, Tel Aviv and Jerusalem would be taken five days later. Jordan's Emir Abdullah would then enter the Holy City and be crowned king of a wider realm. Egypt's King Farouk had already printed a special Tel Aviv stamp.

On paper the Arabs had a crushing advantage in manpower. The 600,000 Jews, facing a four-front war with their backs to the sea, had to contain and repel invasion by the combined might of millions of Arabs. Ben-Gurion has said that on May 14 the Jews mustered barely 50,000 men and women, only half of whom were armed. By his count Haganah could call on 20,000 trained in Palmach, in the Hish (field units), and in the Allied armies of World War II, plus 22,000 in the Home Guard and youth battalions, 3000 Jewish settlement police, a few thousand Irgun and Stern Gang fighters with no experience in open combat, and a handful of volunteers from abroad.

The Jews believed the Arabs had mobilized 80,000 to 100,000 men on Palestine's borders. Arab commanders were convinced they would face a Jewish force of 100,000, including 20,000 veterans of the Russian Army. Both estimates were far off the mark. Actually, Haganah fielded 25,000 trained and armed troops out of a total of 35,000 effectives, while the Arab armies that entered Palestine numbered only 23,500, according to figures cited by Jon and David Kimche. A similar balance prevailed on most of the fighting fronts, they pointed out in their authoritative work *A Clash of Destinies*. Jon Kimche, who covered the war as a correspondent, and David, who fought in it, asserted that "most of the tales of over-whelming superiority on one side and the heroic inferiority of the other, to which both Arabs and Jews have lent credence, are not substantiated by the actual numbers which were engaged."

In weaponry, however, the Israelis were completely outclassed in the first weeks of the war. The Arabs commanded fighter planes, bombers, heavy artillery, tanks, and armored vehicles, all furnished by the British, "in accordance with treaty obligations," as Ernest Bevin put it. The Jews had no modern planes or artillery or armor and only 22,000 rifles of varying manufacture and degree of obsolescence. A last-minute check on May 13 showed that the Israelis' arsenals contained 11,000 homemade Sten machine guns, 1500 light machine guns, a few heavy machine guns, 800 2- and 3-inch mortars, 75 Piat antitank rifles, and 4 65-mm. guns. There were also 16 Davidkas, caches of grenades, and a supply of Molotov cocktails. There was enough ammunition for only 50 rounds per rifle and 700 per machine gun.

In assessing the grim prospects on the eve of invasion, Haganah com-

manders banked heavily on the safe arrival of arms shipments—
including the "heavy stuff" bought in Czechoslovakia, France, and Italy
—the moment the British blockade ended. Great reliance was also
placed on new manpower expected to pour in from the Cyprus detention
camps and the European DP camps once statehood was a fact.

When the first Jewish army in modern times emerged from the underground on May 14, it had no official name or recognizable uniform and
lacked even a unified command. Its troops wore a hodgepodge of uniforms
of varied style, color, shape, and origin and helmets discarded by half the
armies of the world. On the fateful day Haganah's chief of staff, Gen.
Ya'acov Dori, was immobilized in a Haifa hospital. Yigael Yadin, who
had spent most of his adult life in Haganah, was directing operations,
aided by Dori's deputy, Isaac Sadeh. Battle plans had been blueprinted by
a political strategy group known as the National Command, a nine-man
body representing all political parties. Its chairman was Israel Galili, who
had reshaped Haganah after World War II and mapped its tactics during
the successful battles against the Arab guerrillas and the Arab Liberation
Army. Harassed by doubts that the National Command could cope with a
full-scale war, Ben-Gurion had ousted Galili on May 2 but reinstated him
five days later to quiet the uproar among the kibbutzniks who dominated
Palmach, Haganah's striking force. On May 9 Ben-Gurion abolished the
National Command and became de facto commander-in-chief, with Yadin
as de facto chief of staff.

Negotiations for the merger of Haganah with Irgun and its offshoot,
the Stern Gang, were not complete on May 14, although they had been
under way since February, when tension between the bitterly hostile
forces led to armed street clashes. Pressure of public opinion gradually
forced a measure of cooperation. At the end of March, when the first ship-
ment of arms from Czechoslovakia reached Haganah, it was shared with
Irgun. This was followed by the formation of a joint Haganah-Irgun staff
committee that coordinated operations and divided responsibilities.

In April the Zionist Actions Committee, at the same session at which
plans were made to proclaim independence in May, narrowly ratified an
accord bringing Irgun under national discipline. Ben-Gurion and his allies
fought against the agreement because it did not provide for the total dis-
solution of Irgun and its incorporation into Haganah. Although the peace
pact committed Irgun to act militarily only in accordance with instructions from Haganah's National Command, the Irgunists moved independently on April 25 and attacked Jaffa. They were worried lest some
Jewish Agency leaders, yielding to threats from abroad and listening to

"charmers," might defer setting up the Jewish state. Irgun and the Sternists were prepared to end their underground activities and support the
Jewish state only if there was a firm commitment to immediate independence.

On May 14, Irgun and the Sternists went into action as part of an
over-all plan and turned over their arsenals to Haganah quartermasters.
They retained their separate identities, however, until May 29, when the
provisional government created an official military arm of a sovereign Israel and gave it a name. Order No. 4 united Haganah, Irgun, and the
Sternists into Z'va Haganah L'Israel—Defense Forces of Israel, or Zahal
for short.

Zahal's origins, and the desperate efforts to arm it with modern weapons, were no less incredible than its unanticipated victories which vali-
dated Israel's independence. Zahal was the direct descendant of a
mounted patrol called *Shomrim* ("Watchmen"), formed in the 1880s by
the first modern Jewish colonists in Palestine. In Israeli mythology the
Shomrim are enshrined as Hebrew cowboys who had to hold their own
against Bedouin raiders and knife-wielding Arab marauders to protect the
Jewish settlers. Veterans of Jewish self-defense units in Russia who began
arriving in Palestine after the Czarist pogroms of 1905 expanded the
Shomrim into full-time posses known as Hashomer.

Hashomer provided most of the manpower for the Palestinian battalion of the Jewish Legion that served with the British during World War
I. After the British disbanded the Legion, Hashomer and ex-Legionnaires
formed the nucleus of a new Jewish self-defense corps that came into
being during the 1920–21 Arab riots. Its name was Haganah (Defense)
and it was sponsored by the National Council of Palestine Jews (Va'ad
L'umi) and the World Zionist Organization.

Haganah proved itself in the 1929 riots when it repulsed all Arab
onslaughts on the rural settlements. Thereafter it became a permanent militia organized for local defensive purposes and trained in the use of small
arms. Theoretically, the Jews were permitted to have no arms except ancient shotguns that had to be kept in sealed cases and opened only in the
event of emergency. In the 1930s Haganah, under the guidance of its
commander, Eliahu Golomb, began smuggling arms into the colonies. The
British at first closed their eyes to this traffic, thus giving Haganah a kind
of conspiratorial semi-underground character.

During the 1936–39 Arab rebellion, Haganah expanded into a nationwide force and created its first full-time cadres. More than 2000 of its
members were armed when the British established a special Jewish police

force to protect the isolated villages. Not a single Jewish settlement was taken or evacuated during the revolt because the new colonies had been located and built with defense in mind and were manned by Haganah riflemen.

The core of Haganah's elite units, and its future officers, were the kibbutzniks who learned commando tactics from Brig. Orde Wingate, the T. E. Lawrence of Judea, during the Arab uprising. A non-Jewish British intelligence officer, for whom the children's village of Yemin Orde was later named, Wingate was so outraged at the anti-Jewish attitude of his fellow officers in the British Middle East command, that he secretly allied himself with Haganah in 1937. A tough, unorthodox taskmaster who moved from Army headquarters into a kibbutz to learn Hebrew, Wingate organized the famed Haganah night squads that routed Arab terrorists by surprise raids.

Known to the Jews as "The Friend," Wingate is still a legendary figure in Israel. Haganah and, later, Israeli officers adopted his battle cry of "Follow me!" in leading their men in attack. After Brigadier Wingate was killed in Burma during World War II, his widow sent her young son to live in a kibbutz. She returned to Palestine during the Arab rebellion of 1948. During some of the hottest fighting in the upper Galilee, Mrs. Lorna Wingate wanted to visit Ramat Naftali, a colony founded by kibbutzniks who had been trained by Wingate in the night squads. Warned that it was under Arab siege, she talked her way aboard a Haganah Piper Cub that was flying supplies to Ramat Naftali, and while the plane circled over the kibbutz, she tossed out Wingate's Bible and a penciled note dated May 4: "To the defenders of Ramat Naftali—since Orde Wingate is with you in spirit, though he cannot lead you in the flesh, I send you the Bible he carried in all his campaigns and from which he drew the inspiration of his victories. May it be a covenant between you and him in triumph or defeat, now and always."

In resisting Arab violence from 1936 to 1939, and again in the first months of the Arab war against partition in 1947–48, Haganah adhered strictly to a policy of *havlagah* ("restraint"). Its members were warned that "your duty is to beat off attacks but not to let the smell of blood go to your heads." They were constantly reminded that "our meaning is in our name, Defense, and our only aim is to provide security for creative work." The bitter feud between Laborites and Jabotinsky's Revisionists ended in a complete split over the latter's refusal to accept *havlagah*. As a result they formed a separate paramilitary force called Irgun Z'vai L'umi (National Military Organization) in 1937.

World War II was the crucible in which Haganah was changed from an inexperienced ragtag militia into an organized underground reserve that became the principal weapon in the final struggle for Jewish independence. When the war began, Ben-Gurion pledged that the Yishuv would stand beside Britain as if there were no 1939 White Paper that had slammed the gates of Palestine just when the extermination of the Jews in Europe was getting under way. He also vowed that the hit-and-run resistance to the White Paper policies, spearheaded by Haganah, would continue as if there were no war.

While more than 130,000 Palestinian Jews registered with the Jewish Agency for voluntary war service, the Palestine government shifted from perfunctory searches for Haganah guns to carefully planned mass raids on Jewish armories and hidden Haganah camps. Wingate's night squads were rounded up and interned. The legal Jewish settlement police, armed with British rifles and all secretly in Haganah, were put under close surveillance. Stiff prison terms were meted out as early as 1941 to the staff of the agricultural school at Ben Shemen, which housed 450 refugee children and which had been repeatedly attacked by Arab gangs. A police search had unearthed twenty-seven rifles, five submachine guns, and twenty-three grenades under a tiled floor. A forty-three-man Haganah unit, which had volunteered en masse for the British Army, was thrown into Acre Prison: one was sentenced to life; forty-two, including Moshe Dayan, received ten years. Dayan, Yigal Allon, and Yigael Yadin were among the graduates of the first Haganah officers' school opened at Kfar Vitkin in 1938 and of an advanced course that began at Ein Hashofet in 1939.

Fearful of throwing the Arabs officially into the arms of the Axis, although they were for the most part already there, the Chamberlain government rejected all proposals for a British-commanded Jewish regiment under a Jewish flag. Active recruiting of Jews began only after the fall of France in 1940 and the growing Axis threat to British positions in the Middle East. Before Winston Churchill became Prime Minister he had protested that "it is little less than a scandal that at a time when we are fighting for our lives" Britain should "keep large forces in Palestine instead of arming the Jews." Grudgingly, the British enlisted 30,000 Jews, rightly suspecting they would become part of a postwar Jewish army. Jewish assault units from Palestine led the British advance into Vichy-held Syria, helped quell the Mufti's pro-Axis revolt in Iraq, volunteered for suicide parachute missions behind the enemy lines in the Balkans, and took an honorable part in the fighting in North Africa and Crete.

In 1941 Dayan and his comrades were released from prison, put into

British uniforms, and assigned to join the British-Free French attack on Syria. In a later battle in Lebanon, Dayan lost an eye when a bullet struck the binoculars he was holding. A Haganah company of twenty-three, equipped with its own illegal arms, volunteered to blow up the oil refineries at Tripoli, Libya, in May, 1941. Led by British officers, they left Haifa by motorboat, but were never heard from again. David Raziel, Irgun commander, joined the British Army as a captain after ordering a wartime truce with the British. Before his death in an aerial bombardment in Iraq in 1941, he had won British consent to a foray into Baghdad by Irgunists disguised as Arabs. They planned to destroy installations and kidnap the Mufti, who from his hideout in Iraq had proclaimed a jihad against the Allies.

In 1939 Raziel and his two chief lieutenants, Jacob Viniarsky, alias Meridor, and Abraham Stern, had been captured by the British and interned at the Latrun detention camp. Under the Irgun code, Raziel was free to admit his identity but to say nothing else. Since this impaired his further usefulness, other Irgunists held in Latrun prison tried to depose him in favor of Stern, who had denounced Raziel's armistice as a surrender to the British. According to Boruch Shadmi, an Irgun unit commander, Raziel's supporters appealed to Jabotinsky, Revisionist chieftain, who sent a cable from Paris ordering Raziel's reinstatement. At that point Stern split with Irgun and formed Lohame Herut Israel ("Fighters for the Freedom of Israel"), generally known as the Stern Gang.

Raziel's death in a British uniform, and Stern's at the hands of British police who ambushed him in Tel Aviv in 1942, deactivated Irgun and the Stern Gang until new leadership took over. Irgun was revived in 1943 under the command of Menachem Beigin, head of the Polish branch of Betar, the Revisionist youth movement, who arrived in Palestine in 1942 with General Anders' Polish Army in Exile. His top aides were Viniarsky, Arieh Ben Eliezer, Eliahu Lankin, Shlomo Levi, Samuel Katz, Peter Bergson, and Samuel Merlin. Bergson and Merlin directed propaganda, fundraising, arms purchases, and recruitment operations in the United States and Europe. Stern was succeeded by Nathan Mor (Friendmann-Yellin), whose principal commanders were Yisrael Shein (Eldad), and Yitzhak Jazarnitsky (Shamir).

While the British imprisoned and deported Irgun and Sternist terrorists and adamantly refused to recognize Haganah as an official Jewish security force, they nevertheless sought its help when Erwin Rommel seemed on the verge of overrunning the Middle East. In the event the Wehrmacht captured Palestine, the British planned to abandon the entire country, leaving Haganah to harry the Nazis behind their lines. The underground fighters for this operation were recruited by Haganah from its own veterans and trained and armed at a British commando school in Haifa.

Organized on May 15, 1941, this outfit of partisans became Palmach (a combination of the Hebrew words *"Plugat-Machaz"*—assault companies"), Haganah's striking force, which after the war turned the tactics learned from the British against both Arabs and British. One of Palmach's founders was Isaac Sadeh, a much-decorated veteran of Russia's World War I army who had served with Wingate's raiders. Once Rommel had been turned back, however, and the Middle East was out of danger, the British resumed their hunt for Haganah's camps and for Palmach's officers. A photograph of Sadeh, known as "Big Isaac," hung on the wall of every British police station and in British military headquarters. Most of the Palmachniks vanished into the kibbutzim from which they had come. Each collective settlement had a Palmach platoon or two that divided its time between working in the fields and perfecting what the British had taught them at camouflaged training bases.

All mention of Jewish involvement in the war effort and of Arab support for the Axis was blacked out by the Palestine government. The exploits of Jewish units on various fronts were carefully excluded from the press by the official censor. He also kept a tight lid on the fact that Jewish factories in Palestine turned out all the land mines used against Rommel, as well as parachutes, tents, and precision instruments for the British Eighth Army. Even when spoken by Winston Churchill in 1943 and 1944, terms like "Zionism" and "Jewish national home" were scissored out of dispatches published in Palestine and deleted from radio broadcasts.

In the fall of 1944, three months after the Allies had landed in Normandy, Churchill finally overruled his commanders and authorized the formation of a separate 5000-man Jewish brigade to be attached to the Eighth Army in Europe. Made up largely of Palestine volunteers who had seen action with British units in North Africa and in the invasion of Sicily and Italy, the Jewish Brigade wore British uniforms with a Star of David insignia. Commanded by Brig. Ernest F. Benjamin, a Jewish Canadian-born career officer, the Brigade fought in the final phases of the Italian campaign against Nazi troops and helped police the first liberated areas of Austria and Germany. Many of its members were to play significant personal roles in the postwar underground organization to aid illegal immigration to Palestine.

As the fighting in Europe drew to a close, the Jewish Agency girded for stiffer resistance against Britain, confident that one way or another she would ultimately be forced out of Palestine. In anticipation of this eventuality and because of the likelihood that war with the Arab states would follow, the Agency moved to mobilize and arm Palestine Jewry and to flood Palestine with illegal immigrants.

In March, 1945, at a secret meeting in Paris between Ben-Gurion, Chairman of the Agency Executive, and the high command of Mossad, Haganah's committee for illegal immigration, two Haganah subgroups were created, Bricha and Rehesh. Bricha was made responsible for manning an escape route for smuggling concentration camp survivors to Palestine in defiance of the British blockade. Rehesh was set up as an underground task force to procure arms and military equipment for Haganah however and wherever it could.

chapter

∘ ∘ ∘ ∘ ∘ ∘ ∘ ∘ ∘ ∘ ∘ ∘ ∘ ∘ 7 ∘ ∘ ∘ ∘ ∘ ∘ ∘ ∘ ∘ ∘ ∘ ∘ ∘ ∘

THE SONNEBORN INSTITUTE

THE STORY of the arms procurement—the ships purchased and chartered, the planes, tanks, and guns shipped, and the funds raised to make all this possible—is the unpublicized story of American Jewry's underground or "illegal" participation in the birth of Israel. It was conducted concurrently with, but independently of, the philanthropic effort of the United Jewish Appeal and the political campaign of the American Zionist Emergency Council.

It began early in June, 1945, when Ben-Gurion slipped into New York, grimly determined to get for the Yishuv the resources necessary to win the independence for a Jewish state he was to proclaim. Nettled by what he regarded as a lack of vision and courage among the leaders of the Zionist Organization of America in whom he had confided, he turned for help to Henry Montor and Rudolf G. Sonneborn. Sonneborn, a wealthy industrialist, had been involved in Zionist affairs since 1919, when, shortly after his release from the US Naval Air Force, Justice Brandeis interested him in going to Palestine with Dr. Harry Friedenwald and Robert Szold as the youngest member of the first American Zionist Commission. Montor was then executive vice-president of the United Jewish Appeal and had previously been executive director of the United Israel Appeal. He was not personally close to Ben-Gurion but was widely known in Palestine as "The Fund-Raiser." He knew intimately all the leading Jews in the United States; to most of these, Ben-Gurion was still only a name.

On June 25, sprawled on a divan in a bleak suite of the Hotel 14 on

East 60th Street, in the same building as the Copacabana, Ben-Gurion divulged to Montor what he had in mind. He asked Montor to bring together quickly for a private briefing a small but reliable group of men so committed to Palestine that they would be ready to undertake a major assignment upon whose success the future of Jewish Palestine might depend. Montor agreed and, in consultation with Sonneborn, quickly rounded up a group of prominent Jewish business tycoons, bankers, and industrialists. All of the invitees were contacted by telephone to avoid putting anything in writing. No one was told more than the date, time, and place and the urgent need for his presence at an off-the-record conference with a highly placed personage from Palestine. Not even the wives of those invited knew what it was all about until much later.

It was a blisteringly hot Sunday that July 1 when the group gathered in the living room of Sonneborn's duplex bachelor apartment on East 57th Street. The long meeting—it was to last eleven hours—began at 9:30 A.M Ben-Gurion, in an open shirt, was perspiring heavily as Montor and Sonneborn introduced each man. Ben-Gurion in turn presented the key advisers he had brought along.

With Sonneborn as chairman, Montor recalls, there was no "assembly atmosphere" and no formal agenda. The room was charged with an electric air of excitement even though the real purpose of the gathering was still vague. Ben-Gurion, in a long speech, projected his plans for the State of Israel that was to be born in less than three years.

Years later Sonneborn recalled that Ben-Gurion's speech "seemed at the time remote from reality and tempered by visionary hopes." Yet everything Ben-Gurion predicted in a completely frank analysis of the Jewish position turned out to be unerringly accurate: the Labour Party would win the upcoming Parliamentary elections in England but this would not alter British policy in Palestine; England would yield the Mandate before too long and the Jews would then seize the opportunity to create an independent state; the British would interfere, the Arabs would resist through widespread attacks on the Jewish community, and open warfare would ensue; the Yishuv had at best two years to prepare its defenses and to increase its manpower by massive illegal immigration from the DP camps; the youth of Palestine, if they had tanks, heavy artillery, planes, and guns, would defeat the Arabs.

To arm the Yishuv, Ben-Gurion proposed the immediate expansion of its tiny munitions industry and the stockpiling in Europe for later use in Palestine of the heavy armor and munitions that could not be brought in while England retained control of the country. It was pointed out that

once the Japanese were defeated, immense quantities of surplus arms-
making machinery and military hardware would become available in the
United States at bargain prices.

Kaplan spelled out the potential cost of such purchases and Shiloah
sketched the methods by which arms could be obtained and smuggled
into Palestine.

According to Montor, Ben-Gurion brought with him three key advisers: Eliezer Kaplan, treasurer of the Jewish Agency; Moshe Shiloah, chief
of Haganah intelligence and later Minister to Washington; and Ya'acov
Dori, a trained engineer and Haganah chief of staff. Also present was
Meyer Weisgal, Weizmann's confidant.

Having taken his rapt listeners into his confidence, Ben-Gurion invited them to create an American arm of Haganah. He asked them to be
ready to provide the resources and manpower for this undercover operation, which would have to be conducted with both boldness and discre-
tion. It would be their task, when given the signal, to enlist other like-
minded men and women throughout the country in a fund-raising and
purchasing project that would have to be so secret that not even all the
contributors could be told for what they were specifically giving their
money.

William Sylk recalls that one of those present asked Ben-Gurion how
he could raise funds, ask a man for a $5000 gift without so much as tell-
ing him what it was for. The future Prime Minister responded with a
story about the rabbi who had surreptitiously played a round of golf after
services on Yom Kippur. This caused great consternation when observed
in Heaven and Moses asked God to see to it that the errant rabbi would
have to make a sacrifice for his sin. God told Moses not to worry. But
Moses, watching the rabbi continue his golf, saw him hit a magnificent
drive down the fairway for a long record-breaking hole-in-one.

"Is that your idea of punishment and sacrifice?" Moses asked.

"Yes," God answered. "For an ardent golfer to achieve a lifetime ambition, to make a hole-in-one, and then not be able to tell anyone about
it—that was a sacrifice beyond all normal human punishment."

None of those present at the meeting made a formal pledge or promise, but neither did anyone demur. All sensed that they had become part
of something historic, and they agreed implicitly to make themselves
available without reservation for the cloak-and-dagger mission that Ben-
Gurion had outlined. It was in this spirit that the all-day meeting adjourned, but not before a final word of warning not to divulge the presence of Ben-Gurion and his Palestinian associates at the meeting.

There is considerable difference of recollection as to the names of the

Americans who responded to the invitation and met at this pivotal July 1 meeting. Montor says that anyone who claims "to have total recall of that meeting is pretending to information he does not have, because no notes of any kind were taken." He explains that in the absence of an official record, "quite a few people not present, many of whom became active workers later, have claimed they were there since in retrospect the meeting turned out to have such historic significance."

Ben-Gurion, who may have later jotted down something in his diary, differs from Montor about the identity of those present and even about the date of the meeting. A letter from Ben-Gurion published in the September, 1966, issue of *The American Zionist* mistakenly gives August 1 as the meeting date and says he arrived in New York on that mission on July 18. There is no doubt, however, that the meeting was on July 1.

In his autobiography Weisgal claims that he was the middleman between Ben-Gurion and Montor. As Weisgal tells it, he received a call from Ben-Gurion at the Hotel 14. Weisgal's version is that Ben-Gurion asked him to find thirty Jews who would follow him blindly and unquestioningly do what he asked to mobilize money, arms, and manpower for the state-to-be. When Weisgal said he would give him an answer in twenty-four hours, Ben-Gurion replied, "I suppose you want to discuss it with your boss," meaning Weizmann. To which Weisgal replied, "Exactly." When Weizmann heard the story from Weisgal, he approved. Weisgal says that he then contacted Montor, but he suspected that Ben-Gurion had talked to Montor first and he had suggested that Ben-Gurion talk to Weisgal.

In addition to this group, and Sonneborn and himself, Montor names sixteen other participants: Shepard Broad, Miami; Abe Berkowitz, Montgomery, Alabama; Julius Fligelman, Los Angeles; Max Livingston, New Haven; Dr. Jacob C. Shohan and Joel Gross, Newark; Charles Gutwirth and Jacques Torczyner, New York; Ezra Z. Shapiro, Cleveland; Harold J. Goldenberg, Minneapolis; William S. Cohen, St. Louis; Charles J. Rosenblum, Pittsburgh; William H. Sylk, Philadelphia; James L. Permutt, Birmingham, Alabama; Martin Abelove, Utica, New York; and Albert Schiff, Columbus, Ohio.

Ben-Gurion's letter in *The American Zionist* omits Berkowitz, Shohan, Gross, Gutwirth, Cohen, and Permutt, but mentions Sam Cherr, New York; Philip Lown, Portland, Maine; Eli Cohen, Swampscott, Massachusetts; Adolph Hamburger, Baltimore; and Robert Trevus, Atlanta. "A few others were invited too," Ben-Gurion wrote, but he did not name them.

There is still other evidence in a reconstructed portrait prepared in

1953. Ben-Gurion, with his sense of history, wanted some memento of the July 1 meeting, which he has several times described as the most important day in the history of Israel. (In March, 1967, when Ben-Gurion visited the United States, he made this statement in his Los Angeles hotel room in an interview with Mrs. Justin G. Turner of that city.) He requested that Sonneborn give him a picture of the living room in which the meeting was held. Sonneborn delegated to his associate, Rusty Jarcho, the task of creating this memento for Ben-Gurion.

The room had been dismantled, so Jarcho commissioned an artist, Leo London, to recreate it in color from Sonneborn's memory of it, as well as from replicas of similar antique pieces in museums. From this painting a negative was made and around it was placed a layout of photographs of the twenty-two persons who were present at the meeting. Fifty mounted copies of this reconstructed photograph were produced, with one sent to each participant (accompanied by a memo from Sonneborn describing each of the valuable antiques in the room).

Jarcho recalls that the list of those present was compiled by asking each participant who sat next to him at the meeting. This photograph includes twenty-two people as the participants in the meeting. It does not include Ya'acov Dori, whom both Montor and Ben-Gurion recall being present as one of the Israeli experts. It differs from the Montor recollection in that it eliminates Torczyner, Abelove, and Permutt. It adds Samuel Cherr, New York; Barney Rappaport, Connecticut; and Samuel J. Zacks, Toronto.

When Ben-Gurion received his copy of the picture in Israel, he took it to a meeting of the Cabinet and asked each of them to give their opinion as to the most important day in the history of Israel. After each Cabinet member had spoken his piece, Ben-Gurion passed around the picture of the room in which the conference was held and said that the day of this meeting was in his opinion the most important day, for without the $11 million that was raised for arms by what came to be called the Sonneborn Institute, Israel might not have been able to repel the Arab invaders successfully when they stormed across Israel's borders after midnight of May 14–15, immediately following the proclamation of independence.

Out of the July 1 meeting was born the nameless, nationwide secret movement that became the American section of Haganah. Its operations began in the early fall of 1945 after Britain's Foreign Secretary Ernest Bevin confirmed Ben-Gurion's prediction that the new Labour government would not budge from the 1939 White Paper. One morning in September, Sonneborn received a mysterious telephone call from an Englishman who said, "I'm trying to locate the Sonneborn Institute. Perhaps you can help me." Unwittingly a cover name had been coined. Sonneborn gave no sign of recognition but agreed to meet the caller for lunch. The man was Sir Simon Marks, who in 1917 had been one of Weizmann's young associates and who later became one of England's foremost merchants. He handed Sonneborn a four-word message from Ben-Gurion: "The time has come."

The next day the Sonneborn Institute opened headquarters in a small suite of rooms in an unmarked office on West 57th Street. Later the group was to take over the entire seventeenth floor in what came to be known as Kibbutz Pentagon. Similar unidentified branches were established in major cities. Each of the original trustworthy group recruited collaborators of his own. Within a fortnight the entire country was covered by a network of volunteer committees whose secret parlor meetings gave their activities a truly conspiratorial character. The movement had no officers, directors, or letterhead. Its unofficial leader was Sonneborn, who presided at luncheon meetings of the high command every Thursday at 12:30 in a private dining room of the Hotel McAlpin. There visitors from Palestine brought confidential instructions and Institute leaders from around the country reported on progress.

The Institute's first assignment was a private fund-raising effort that gained more than $1 million for the purchase and shipment of machinery, tools, dies, and blueprints for the Yishuv's munitions industry. Armed with specifications, a cadre of Haganah experts, headed by General Dori and Chaim Slavin, director of the hidden defense factories, fanned out over the country. For months they scoured scrap-metal yards, used-machinery lots, Army and Navy stores, surplus-munitions dumps, and government offices disposing of World War II matériel, snatching up whatever was available. The Sonneborn Institute paid the bills and set up the intricate channels through which the goods reached their destination. Every crate got by the British customs inspectors and some of the contents were still in use during the Six-Day War in 1967.

A second undertaking involved the Sonneborn Institute in helping Haganah locate, buy, and transport guns, used planes, ammunition, and explosives. This was not yet illegal but it was carried out in secret because British security agents were doing all they could to thwart it. The actual arms smuggling was done by a tightly knit group of Haganah agents who arrived in New York in 1947. They included Zev Shind, father of the Israeli Merchant Marine; Hy Issachar, builder of El Al, the Israeli airline; Shlomo Shamir, organizer of the Israel Navy; Yehuda Arazi and his twin brother, Tuvia; and Teddy Kollek, later Mayor of Jerusalem. Kollek, the coordinator of fund-raising, was also in charge of the main purchasing center in the Hotel Empire at Broadway and 63rd Street. He found the Irish stevedores on New York's waterfront helpful allies in getting arms out of the country because of their traditional dislike of the British.

Haganah's New York base was at the Hotel 14, where Ben-Gurion had first divulged his plans to Montor for what became the Sonneborn Institute. This inconspicuous and rather undistinguished hotel was owned by Ruby Barnett, whose wife, Fanny, was an ardent Zionist who had many times served as confidential secretary to Dr. Weizmann and other Zionist leaders while they were in New York. It was jocularly referred to by the visiting Palestinians as "Kibbutz 14" because several suites and rooms at the hotel were reserved for Haganah emissaries, including Ben-Gurion, who lived there under a variety of aliases. Its location, three doors east of the swank Jewish city club, The Harmonie, was also extremely handy because of its proximity to the Jewish Agency headquarters on East 66th Street.

In the Hotel 14, Yehuda Arazi, chief organizer of the arms-procurement program, recruited his most important American agent, Adolph (Al) Schwimmer. A World War II Ferry Command pilot, Schwimmer became known to Haganah while serving as a TWA flight engineer. With Ray Salk and William Sosnov, he bought and reconditioned scrapped transport planes from surplus US war stocks and set up a cover organization, Schwimmer Aviation Co., to enlist mechanics, pilots, and gunners. Planes were flown to an operations base at Burbank, California, where Bill Gerson and Al Auerbach, US Air Force veterans, and an unnamed retired US Marine Air Force major supervised their overhauling. Eleanor Rudnick, owner of a fleet of crop-dusting planes, made her private airport south of Los Angeles available for testing and crew training by Leo Gardner, son of a rabbi and a World War II US pilot, and Sam Lewis, a flying buff.

In Honolulu, Schwimmer contacted a dealer with a large supply of spare engine parts and surplus arms. Machine guns flown in from Hawaii in crates labeled "Engines" narrowly escaped a search by FBI agents at Burbank. Schwimmer and Arazi enlisted Hank Greenspun, a New York-born Nevada newspaper publisher and World War II combat officer, for a brief but fantastic career as a gun-runner. Before Greenspun was through he had plundered a Naval arms depot in Hawaii, acquired an airport and two airlines in Panama, and posed successfully as a confidential agent of Chiang Kai-shek in Mexico. When he was arrested, he pleaded guilty to violation of the Neutrality Act in order to spare Haganah embarrassment. His exploits cost him his citizenship and a fine of $10,000 but he was later pardoned. Others too risked reputations in the desperate effort to arm Haganah. Some Jewish manufacturers slipped nonexplosive war matériel into cartons of export goods that eventually turned up in Haganah warehouses abroad.

Social workers and rabbis were among the active participants in producing the collection of "pots and pans"—the guns, trucks, small arms, and drill presses that reached Haganah piecemeal from collection points in New York, Florida, and California. Haganah war matériel—labeled "Czechoslovak Crockery"—was often stored temporarily in the basements of public buildings, synagogues, Jewish community centers, and Hillel Foundation offices. Teamsters Union locals cooperated in trucking heavy items to ports.

One fund-raising pitch that added forty used US Army trucks to Haganah's arsenal was made before a crowd of crap-shooters in the cellar of a Midwestern city hall. Escorted to the game by one of the city's leading criminal lawyers, a Sonneborn Institute member, the social worker who made the appeal was told that he could have everything in the next ten pots. From time to time high-school and college students were arrested on charges of illegal possession of pistols and rifles that they were caching for Haganah in loft buildings, factories, and private homes. One of these, Joseph Untermeyer, son of the poet Louis Untermeyer, was acquitted after a passionate defense by Paul O'Dwyer. The former Presidential yacht USS *Mayflower,* which had been acquired for Haganah, was loading guns in Panama when the Panamanian government withdrew its registry at the request of the US Embassy.

Directly or indirectly, virtually every Jewish organization was linked in some way to the Sonneborn Institute and its many auxiliaries, but few talked about it. On Friday night, May 14, worshipers in Congregation Sons of Israel, Woodmere, Long Island, heard their rabbi, Irving Miller, describe for the first time what the Jews of Woodmere, Lawrence, Hewlett, and Cedarhurst had been doing for many months to procure arms and war matériel for Haganah. Without mentioning names, he revealed the existence of a short-wave radio transmitter aboard a Jewish-owned yacht anchored in Hewlett Harbor. It had been part of the communications network through which Haganah arms-buyers in the US received their instructions from Paris and Tel Aviv. Aboard that same yacht Moshe Shertok, the Jewish Agency's chief negotiator at the United Nations, had often met with friendly delegations.

More than one Jewish radio amateur was admonished by the FCC for sending and receiving messages on behalf of Haganah in technical violation of the international treaty governing radio communication. British intelligence and Arab spokesmen repeatedly complained about such infractions. One American ham operator who had been cooperating with Haganah was the first to give Tel Aviv the news that Truman had recognized Israel. At 10:28 P.M. on May 14 this amateur contacted Station ZC6LA in Tel Aviv and talked to Joseph Baer, the engineer who had patched together an underground Haganah transmitter from bits and pieces left after the British dismantled the official government station. The American reached Baer several times between 10:35 and 11:25 P.M. EDT (4:35 A.M. and 5:25 A.M., Tel Aviv time, May 15). He also managed to raise the ZC6XY operator in the US Consulate in Jerusalem.

A second major clandestine project of the Sonneborn Institute provided ships and crews for the Bricha agents smuggling refugees out of Europe via tiny ports in southern France, Italy, and the Balkans. It began with the purchase of a pair of corvettes from the Canadian government. Manned almost entirely by former American Merchant Marine seamen and ex-GIs, and outfitted with surplus US Navy equipment, the two 925-ton vessels delivered 5200 Jews to Palestine before being captured by the British. One unloaded its first "cargo" on the high seas onto small craft and made a second round trip before being caught. Samuel Zemurray, the banana king, who was president of the United Fruit Co., had a key role in locating available vessels in Caribbean ports.

All told the Sonneborn organization bought eighteen ships that carried over 75,000 Jews to Palestine illegally. One of its purchases was the *Exodus from Europe 1947,* for whose dedication in Baltimore Harbor in 1947 some of the Institute leaders made a rare public appearance. Other groups made noisy claims about what they were doing, but the Institute could not deny them without risking exposure. Doggedly and anonymously, it continued this phase of its work without recognition or the desire for it.

When private fund-raising for Haganah was discontinued at the beginning of 1948 because it was producing only a small part of what was needed, the Sonneborn Institute switched to public activity. At the end of 1947 Eliezer Kaplan had returned to Tel Aviv from the United States with a depressing report on the prospects of substantial funds for arms. Ben-Gurion wanted to leave for the United States at once with Kaplan, but was overruled, and Mrs. Golda Myerson took on the assignment.

In an emotion-drenched speech before the General Assembly of the

Council of Jewish Federations and Welfare Funds in Chicago, late in January, 1948, she described the dangers the Yishuv faced unless it were adequately armed. She asked for an immediate $25–30 million—five times what Kaplan had said was possible—to enable Rehesh to buy what its purchasing missions had already taken options on. Her listeners —the key leaders in organized Jewish fund-raising—gasped but quickly provided the cash through bank loans secured by future contributions in the local communities. In this way over $28 million became available in the next four months.

When the chief of the Rehesh mission in Paris cabled that he could buy tanks if he had $10 million, he was instructed to close the deal. Similar good news went to Prague, where negotiations were under way for planes and heavy guns. On Mrs. Myerson's return to Palestine, Ben-Gurion said, "Some day, when history will be written, it will be said that there was a Jewish woman who got the money which made the state possible."

On February 16, 1948, Sonneborn wrote to his collaborators that "certain confidential activities" carried out for two and a half years were ended with the "successful accomplishment" of the mission. That same day he assumed the open leadership of the newly incorporated "Materials for Palestine," which collected immense quantities of noncontraband goods through a campaign for cash or gifts-in-kind. Thousands of volunteers engaged in fund-raising projects for the new organization, which provided the Yishuv with ambulances, medical supplies, hospital equipment, blood plasma, clothing, and shoes, and made available to Haganah heavy trucks, jeeps, barbed wire, steel sheeting, rubber tires, tents, field glasses and telephones, messkits, cable wire, burlap bags for sandbags, and compasses.

After May 14 "Materials for Palestine" became "Materials for Israel." It continued its operations, publicly and undercover, until March 7, 1955, when Sonneborn wrote a letter to his key people, announcing the disbanding of the group and a final public dinner, "Sigum Hasifer" ("Mission Accomplished"), at the Hotel Pierre on March 22. Its work was taken over by the Israel government as the Israel Purchasing Mission in the US.

When, shortly after statehood, Ben-Gurion was able to incorporate Haganah into a unified Israel Army (Zahal), unauthorized fund-raising for Haganah still persisted in the United States. The Jewish Agency even met with resistance when in July, 1948, it ordered the disbanding of Americans for Haganah, an organization founded chiefly to counteract the flamboyant money-raising activities of the American backers of Irgun and the Stern Gang. While sensational newspaper advertisements and wild claims won headlines and a following for the Hebrew Committee for National Liberation, Americans for a Jewish Palestine, the Committee for a Jewish Army, and the American League for a Free Palestine, Haganah quietly undertook to sign up American volunteers for Mahal (from the initials of the Hebrew words *"Mitnavdee Hutz-L'Eretz"*—"Overseas Volunteers"). Irgun's announcement that Barney Ross had enlisted in a so-called George Washington Legion triggered a State Department clampdown on passports for American citizens seeking to join the fighting forces in Palestine. Unlike Mahal, this outfit never got off the ground, but its founder, Samuel Weiser, fought in the defense of Jerusalem.

MAHAL

HAGANAH'S RECRUITING for Mahal in the United States was done surreptitiously through cover agencies such as Land and Labor for Palestine, the Palestine Vocational Service, and Service Airways, Inc. The first sought volunteers for crews on immigrant ships and for combat service, the latter flying personnel. Under the guise of offering information to prospective settlers in Palestine, Land and Labor for Palestine and the Palestine Vocational Service spread the news through seamen's journals, blind advertisements, and word of mouth on college campuses that jobs were available for deck officers, engineers, navigators, stewards, radio operators, and able-bodied seamen, with or without experience.

The Intercollegiate Zionist Federation, the B'nai B'rith Hillel Foundations, and rabbis steered volunteers to the New York headquarters of the two organizations. The National Jewish Welfare Board's Bureau of War Records files, which listed the names of thousands of decorated World War II GIs, were carefully combed for pilots, bombardiers, and navigators. One over-eager recruiter brought the FBI down on him by advertising in the *New York Times* for crews for a nonexistent airline.

A Haganah detail, commanded by Wellesley Aron, an ex-British Army major attached to the Jewish Agency staff of Moshe Shertok, processed the American volunteers. Interviews were held in New York in a suite at the Hotel Empire and at several rundown hotels in the Herald Square area. Some preliminary screening took place in other cities. Californians were interviewed in a Hollywood projection room. After Aron signed up the recruits and gave them travel instructions, they were temporarily housed in transit camps on private estates in Westchester County and New Jersey. The FBI knew what was going on and occasionally passed on warnings. Once in a while they even picked up an obstreperous and drunken recruit who was making a nuisance of himself in a bar. Aron's biggest headache was caused not by the FBI but by tearful mothers who came to plead with him not to send their sons to die in Palestine.

Most Mahalniks from the United States and Canada reached Palestine either as students or tourists bound for France and Italy, or as crew members of ships headed for the immigrant smuggling fleet. One Mahal detachment from the US was interned in Lebanon when the SS *Marine Carp* made the mistake of docking in Beirut.

The clearinghouse for all volunteers was Paris from where they moved into a Haganah pipeline run by Nachum Shadmi. Housing, documents, medical examinations, transportation, and assignment to training camps in the south of France and Italy were handled from a small office on the Avenue Wagram managed by Ruth Berman. Pilots, gunners, and airplane mechanics, carrying forged papers identifying them as businessmen or tourists, and students without training, were sent on to Palestine by commercial flights or on immigrant ships. Less essential Mahalniks wound up in the eleven camps for escaped DPs from Germany and Austria maintained by Haganah around Marseilles, Milan, and Bari.

Ostensibly refugee centers, the camps were actually advance training bases of Gahal (*Guitz Hutz-L'Eretz*), Haganah recruits from the DP camps. Palmach missions in all the DP camps and at the Cyprus detention centers directed premilitary and paramilitary courses in first aid, signaling, grenade-throwing with stones, and arms drill with wooden guns made in camp workshops. When French and Italian police dropped in to ask why refugees spent so much time running through rocky fields, fighting with sticks, climbing trees and walls, and tossing stones, they were assured it was all a rehabilitation program carried out on doctors' orders.

The Mahalniks who had fought in World War II were at first amused and then irked by the elementary guerrilla tactics they were being taught. Haganah did not initially regard Mahal as a significant military asset, except for the specialists, and so it devoted its meager resources to Gahal, thousands of whom were awaiting transport to Palestine. The Gahalniks were always hungry because their food supplies were chiefly rations from the International Refugee Organization. Training on half-empty stomachs, the DPs often pilfered food from French and Italian farmers. Frequently half the trainees in a camp remained idle so their boots could be worn by others on training assignments.

During the weeks of training, the Mahalniks often had their passports lifted by Palmach, not only to keep them in camp but because Haganah needed the documents for other illegal activities. Haganah secrecy was part of its tradition, but it also provided the advantage of avoiding embarrassment to the French and Italian governments, whose intelligence services knew all about the Haganah training camps. The camps' clandestine nature, however, enabled Paris and Rome to plead ignorance when the British brought pressure on them to close the camps.

When the Gahalniks were loaded into the immigrant ships, the Mahalniks went along. If the ships managed to run the British blockade, the passengers went directly from the secret landing places on the Palestine coast to Haganah bases. If the ships were intercepted and sent to Cyprus, they were accompanied by Palmach officers who continued the training in the detention camps. From 1946 until May, 1948, Haganah maintained constant communication with Cyprus through emissaries who, after making their way to Cyprus on fishing boats, slipped into the camps with forged documents or burrowed under barbed-wire fences. Hundreds of Gahalniks reached Israel from Cyprus in time to join the first battles against the Arab invaders. For two weeks after May 15 the British permitted unrestricted immigration from Cyprus. Only after the United Nations Security Council adopted its first truce resolution on May 29 did the British halt the movement of people of military age.

Mahal was a genuine international brigade made up of Christians and Jews, white and black, from thirty-five countries. All of the Jews and most of the non-Jews served without pay, although some non-Jewish pilots earned as much as $1200 a month. In Mahal's ranks were veterans of the Spanish Civil War, the Russo-Finnish War, the Jewish Brigade, De Gaulle's Free French, partisans from Poland and the Balkans, and men who had seen action at Guadalcanal and Iwo Jima, in the Italian and Normandy invasions and the Battle of the Bulge. Finnish volunteers included some who had fought with the Germans against the Allies, one of whom sported a Nazi decoration. Mahalniks from England who signed up prior to May 14, 1948, did so knowing that they risked arrest for treason. In South Africa the Jewish Ex-Servicemen's Association opened training camps where 5000 potential Mahalniks took refresher courses under officers who had led South African troops in Europe and North Africa.

A postwar census by Israel's Ministry of Defense identified 2400 foreign pilots, gunners, ordnance experts, radar specialists, tank drivers, airplane mechanics, and other technicians as having served in Israel's armed forces. Actually, there were probably twice that number in Mahal because many did not bother to register as volunteers. Mahalniks are believed to have accounted for almost 10 percent of Zahal's forces in the first weeks of the war. According to Netanel Lorch, historian of the War of Independence, the unique contribution of the foreign volunteers was their technical know-how, combat experience, devotion, and willingness to sacrifice.

Mahal's official rolls listed 500 each from France and Great Britain and 300 each from the United States and South Africa. One authority, however, counted 450 from Canada alone, more in proportion to its size than from any other country. There were 661 Mahalniks in the Israel Air Force, in which English was the language spoken because almost all of them hailed from the United States, South Africa, Great Britain, and Canada. Veterans of the Allied air forces, they not only flew most of Israel's foreign-made bombers and transports, but also trained Israel's first pilots. The South Africans contributed 36 trained pilots who became instructors of Israeli flying cadets at a Haganah base outside Rome. Three Dakotas contributed by the South African Mahalniks were in constant use on the Marseilles-Haifa run to transport men and equipment. After the war these planes became the nucleus of El Al.

Mahal pilots and ground crews arrived in Palestine early in 1948, before there were any fighting planes. Rounded up in Prague, in November, 1947, by Ehud Avriel, Haganah's most resourceful arms-buyer, they became the first unit of Mahal. Israel's infant Navy and Medical Corps also utilized many foreigners.

Hardly any of the English-speaking Mahalniks knew Hebrew. Mahal was a word few of them knew before they landed in Palestine. The Israelis hadn't heard it either and they spelled it out phonetically for the foreigners. Many volunteers had joined up because they had seen the Nazi extermination camps while serving with the Allied armies; others came because they had relatives in Palestine. A surprisingly large number paid their own way and some even brought their own weapons. Most of those from English-speaking countries had not belonged to any Zionist organization.

The most celebrated Mahalnik was Col. David ("Mickey") Marcus, a much-decorated American World War II officer, who helped map Haganah's military tactics and played a major role in building Israel's famed "Burma Road," before he was accidentally killed by an Israeli sentry. Mahal also attracted some deadbeats: one bemedaled Latin American turned out to be a phony general with no military experience, but he came with a small arsenal; an American posing as a psychiatrist used his fake medical credentials to free some disillusioned Mahalniks from dangerous duty; another American, who never ranked higher than sergeant, represented himself as a former combat officer; the Canadian contingent included a full-blooded Indian who left a trail of bad debts. On the other hand, there were such men as the deeply pious Catholic French captain known only as "Eitan" and the Swedish merchant seaman who deserted his ship in Haifa to join Palyam, Haganah's sea arm.

The commander of the English-speaking Mahalniks in the ground forces was Ben Dunkelman, who grew up in a Toronto home known as "Kibbutz Dunkelman" because it was visited by so many prominent Zionists. His mother had been president of Canadian Hadassah and his father had held the same office in the Canadian Zionist Organization. A 240-pound six-foot-two giant, Dunkelman had been a border watchman in Palestine as a boy of seventeen. He landed in Normandy on D-Day with the 3rd Canadian Infantry and came out of the war a major. In 1946 Mrs. Lorna Wingate and Samuel Zacks, president of the Canadian Zionist Organization who was part of the Sonneborn apparatus, persuaded Dunkelman to head Haganah's arms procurement in Canada. Later he and Lionel Drucker, an RCAF pilot, became Mahal's chief Canadian recruiters. One of those they enlisted was Buzz Buerling, Canada's top World War II ace, who had shot down thirty-one Nazi fighters; he died in a flaming Haganah plane that crashed on an airstrip outside Rome in April, 1948, while en route to Palestine.

chapter

o o o o o o o o o o o o o $\boxed{9}$ o o o o o o o o o o o o o

MILITARY STRENGTH IN PALESTINE

DESPITE MORE than two years of feverish efforts, the Yishuv was desperately short of arms and had only a makeshift army when the Arab rebellion broke out on December 1, 1947. Crippled by the military embargo and British searches and seizures, Haganah had to hold out with what it had, plus the meager output of the underground Ta'as workshops and occasional consignments smuggled in from abroad, until May 14, when the British blockade was lifted.

Haganah's tiny arsenal had been acquired by the Palestine Flower Growers Association, one of the many disguises for Rehesh, after World War II. Agents of Munya Mardor, Rehesh chief, later director-general of Israel's weapons research authority, snatched what they could from abandoned Axis and Allied stocks in the western desert of Egypt. Some of it was hauled to Palestine in trucks still emblazoned with the Afrika Korps insignia.

Rehesh also bought black market rifles and machine guns from friendly British quartermasters and from Arabs who robbed British armories. The demobilized Jewish Brigade came home with sidearms and anything else they could carry. Some small-arms cargoes got through from Europe early in 1948 hidden in steamrollers, cement barrels, and heavy machinery. Guns accumulated in Rhodes, packed in crates of books and cereals, were slipped past Arab stevedores and British inspectors at the Haifa docks. Rehesh even managed to bring in fifty-two rusting American halftracks snatched up in France and Germany.

The need for secrecy limited the production of the camouflaged ordnance factories that turned out homemade Sten guns, small mortars, grenades, and explosives. Little of the smuggled-in arms-making machinery, bought with funds raised by the Sonneborn Institute, could be made operative until the Mandate ended for fear it would be confiscated. Sheet steel from the United States helped convert trucks into boxlike armor-plated vehicles with enough protection to repel small-arms fire. One of the strangest products of Ta'as was the Davidka, the homemade mortar invented by David Leibowitz, director of Haganah's heavy ordnance section. Lacking artillery, Haganah fighters had to carry loads of dynamite with lit fuses to Arab positions and then race back under fire to their own lines.

Leibowitz's device was a huge slingshot that tossed an 80-pound shell of explosives and steel casings, not too accurately, a distance of 600 yards. The barrel, made of a section of steel sewage pipe, served as a launching pad. The 300-pound contraption needed four men to haul it across open fields and terraced hills, but Palmach loved it because its devastating blast created havoc. Fired for the first time on March 13, its noise woke everyone in Jaffa and Tel Aviv. Only sixteen Davidkas were made, but some of its shots helped capture Safed and Jaffa. There is still an argument whether it was named for its inventor, later proprietor of the Machon Garage in Tel Aviv, for King David, or for David Ben-Gurion. Leibowitz also produced the "USA" rifle grenade (*"Unser Shtickel Arbeit"*— Yiddish for "Our Piece of Work").

Too conspicuous to be effectively hidden in a country as small as Palestine, none of the planes, artillery, tanks, and antiaircraft and antitank guns stockpiled at secret airfields and dockside warehouses in Italy, Yugoslavia, Czechoslovakia, and France could be brought in until the British left. Nevertheless, arms concealment became an organized but risky business since possession of illegal weapons was a capital offense. The entire Yishuv was linked to Haganah's intelligence system to protect buried arms depots. Whatever arms the Jews possessed had to be the kind that could be hidden under a woman's skirt or cached in the ground deep enough to foil mine-detectors. Waitresses, policemen, cabbies, newspapermen, and fruit dealers were all part of the network that protected the arsenals. Every Jewish-owned truck and taxi was fitted out with a secret gun compartment. The British reluctance to search women was exploited by having women passengers in buses and taxis secret arms on their persons to get Haganah weapons through checkpoints. One intelligence officer moaned that in order to locate all Haganah arm depositories, the British would have had to dig up the entire country from Dan to Beersheba. Despite Haganah's resourcefulness, it is doubtful whether the groundwork for a Jewish army could have been laid in advance had the Palestine Mandate been held by Russia, Germany, or Japan, all of which had fewer scruples about executing anyone caught with illegal arms.

The only fully trained force at Haganah's command at the end of 1947 were 3000 Palmach fighters, one-third of them girls. In addition there were 5000 raw Hish field troops, who were in training two days a month with sticks and ancient shotguns; the Home Guard, composed of older men who had seen action with Haganah in the 1920s and 1930s; and women and fourteen-to-seventeen-year-olds trained in signaling and communications. Outside of Haganah's defense operations in the first months of the revolt were the Irgun and Sternist separatist units whose campaign of terror was aimed at forcing the British Mandatory regime to leave as a prerequisite to Jewish independence. Neither group adhered to Haganah's policy of confining attacks on the British to blasting railway and supply lines and military installations and guarding the landings of illegal immigrants.

Having repudiated its truce with the British in 1944, Irgun waged war on the British by blowing up government offices and police stations, raiding arsenals, killing British soldiers in retaliation for the deaths of Jews, and whipping British officers in reprisals for the flogging of Jewish youngsters caught with weapons. Irgun's most daring coup was the liberation in 1947 of arrested terrorists in Acre prison. Two British policemen, taken hostage for the four Irgunists sentenced to death for their part in the Acre breakout, were released only after Haganah's forcible intervention, lest the Jewish case then before the United Nations Special Committee on Palestine be endangered. Haganah also foiled an Irgun plot to blow up the British Army's headquarters in Tel Aviv.

Anticipating the execution of the convicted Irgunists, the Sternists kidnaped two British sergeants and hanged them forty-eight hours after the four condemned Irgunists went to the gallows. Before that the Sternists had murdered Lord Moyne, the British Minister in Cairo, and narrowly missed assassinating Sir Harold MacMichael, the British High Commissioner to Palestine. The majority of the Yishuv abhorred terrorism but refused to inform against their own people or to deny shelter to Jews hunted by the British, even when Haganah moved against Irgun and the Stern Gang.

From a part-time militia that, like the Minutemen of the American Revolution, sprang into action on short notice and then melted into the general population, Haganah expanded into an underground force of partisans after October, 1947, when mobilization began. Ben-Gurion had to overcome strong opposition to the military buildup and to the vesting in the Jewish Agency of full control of Haganah. Only then were the National Command and full-time general staff created.

Palmach's three brigades were commanded by Yigal Allon, later Minister of Labor and Deputy Prime Minister, Ya'acov Dori, and Yigael Yadin. Top commanders were known only by code names and officers wore no identifying badges of rank. When not on duty, officers and men lived normal lives: every unit was organized on a conspiratorial basis. The Haganah uniform was a khaki shirt and shorts, indistinguishable from the garb of truck drivers and lawyers, doctors and cabbies, farmers and writers, all of whom were in Haganah. To its troops Haganah was known as "The Aunt" or "The Organization." Pistols were referred to as "sprinklers" and rifles were called "pipes"; "plums" or "cherries" were bullets.

After the first call-up many Haganah conscripts spent the time between fighting in house-to-house solicitations for funds to buy food and equipment and to help support their families. A national military budget did not yet exist.

Military preparations were greatly impeded by constant British raids on the widely dispersed training bases. They were tucked away in isolated villages, in caves near the Dead Sea, on the grounds of the Hebrew University, in a field behind the Bet Hekerem teachers' seminary, in secondary schools, and in synagogue basements. On the outskirts of Tel Aviv and Jerusalem there were well-camouflaged rifle ranges. Mortar-firing was practiced in the kibbutzim. Squad and platoon commanders attended night courses in remote villages. An elaborate alarm system gave warning of the approach of British troops or police. Often they roared up to a school or first-aid station on the basis of an informer's tip, only to find an evening class listening to a lecture or a nurse attending patients. To avoid traps or ambushes, training bases were regularly switched from place to place.

By early 1948 Haganah had an artillery unit with no artillery and an air force of obsolete British reconnaissance planes that had been salted away at Kibbutz Afikim after being reconditioned. The twenty-one Austers and three Piper Cubs had been bought at auction in November, 1947, when the British had declared them available for sale as scrap. Civilians called them "primuses" because their droning noise was like the primus gasoline stoves widely used in Palestine. At the end of March the air arm had grown to thirty planes, but none capable of fighting. Bomber and ground crews were being trained by the first Mahalnik pilots and by Jewish RAF veterans. One of these, Aharon Remez, who had seen repeated action over Germany as a fighter pilot, became the first commander-in-chief of the Israel Air Force. Son of David Remez, who was to be a signer of the Israeli Declaration of Independence, in 1968 Aharon became Israel's Ambassador to Great Britain.

The primuses of the infant air force protected convoys, transported food and medicine to settlements under attack, and shuttled VIPs. Ground communication was maintained by messages dropped in bottles. Occasionally a crude bomb held in the pilot's lap was tossed out of the window.

The first fighting units of the Israel Navy were four immigrant ships the British had captured in 1946 and 1947 and left to rust in Haifa Harbor. Under the noses of the British, Haganah's Palyam quietly overhauled the two former Canadian corvettes and the two one-time US Coast Guard cutters and readied them for action on May 15.

Exaggerated reports of these intensive preparations, coupled with the decisive victories in April and early May over the Arab guerrillas, cloaked the Yishuv's basic military weakness. Fantastic tales of Haganah's immense store of arms created an image of a massively armed Jewish community. Some correspondents wrote about a Haganah army of 80,000 men equipped with artillery, tanks, and planes. A week before May 14, *Newsweek* said that "reliable reports indicate the Jews have at least 30 up-to-date fighter-bombers in reserve in Palestine." American and European newspapermen flying to and from assignments in Palestine told of encountering Haganah emissaries on a variety of arms-buying missions. "Big men with ruddy faces" who had been ordering "agricultural machinery" was how Quentin Reynolds described them.

Only two arms shipments of any consequence arrived before May 14. The first was a planeload of rifles and ammunition flown in from Czechoslovakia at the end of March in response to an urgent message from Tel Aviv. Code-named "Balak 1" (from Balak, King of Moab), the guns turned the tide of Operation Nahshon. The Skoda weapons were assembled with the help of Col. Melvin Krulewitch, a retired US Marine Corps veteran of both World Wars who is credited with having devised Haganah's table of military organization. He had arrived a few weeks before with retired Col. Harry D. Henshel, Gen. Omar Bradley's World War II supply chief, to help untangle the transport of military supplies. A second load of arms early in April included 20-mm. guns.

Both deliveries were the first results of the large-scale buying missions established by Rehesh in Prague and Paris in December, 1947. The Czechs had become cooperative in January, 1948, following a breakthrough conference in New York between Andrei Gromyko and Moshe

Shertok. At first Ehud Avriel, the Rehesh chief, posed as "Mr. Ueberall," the representative of an unnamed South American republic. The Czechs were not fooled, and with the encouragement of the Russians they were ready to do business. Mikhail Bodrov, who became Russia's first Ambassador to Israel, headed the Soviet intelligence section that collaborated with Rehesh in procuring arms in Prague and Vienna.

In February, 1948, Avriel made his first purchase from Skoda of 10,000 rifles and 450 heavy machine guns, the "Balak 1" consignment. On April 23 he closed another deal with Skoda for artillery and concluded arrangements to train pilots and for Czech aid in dismantling planes for crating. The Czechs were simultaneously selling to the Arabs, and one shipload of Arab guns from Skoda was highjacked by Haganah intelligence in a Balkan port.

In Italy, Yehuda Arazi contracted with a small aviation company at Castiglione del' Lagota to use its landing field as a base to which planes reconditioned by Al Schwimmer in the United States were flown. On May 10 the Italian Air Ministry grounded ten Haganah-owned planes that had been outfitted with machine guns and were due to be flown to Palestine by Irish pilots. Other planes were sitting on airstrips outside Geneva, awaiting the signal from Tel Aviv.

During the first week in May, Avriel bought ten Messerschmitts from Skoda at $500,000 apiece. Because Palestine was beyond their flying range, they had to be disassembled in Prague and trucked in pieces to Italy. From there they were flown to Palestine in the bellies of Schwimmer's C-46s. The first of them did not arrive until May 20.

Much of the heavy equipment Rehesh had bought and stockpiled in Europe got to Palestine in the surplus C-46s, Constellations, and B-17s acquired and rebuilt in the United States by Schwimmer's undercover operations. The air and ground crews he had hired flew the planes from camouflaged airstrips in the United States to Italy. Some took off from Florida, limped across the Atlantic to the Azores for refueling, and landed in Yugoslavia. Five found their way to Panama, where Hank Greenspun's previously acquired airline sent them to Italy by way of Dutch Guiana, Dakar, and West Africa. From Britain, Mahal pilots brought surplus aircraft to Rhodes. Two Bonanzas, flown from South Africa by former RAF pilots Boris Senior and Cyril Katz, made it to Tel Aviv on May 10 via the Sudan and Egypt. Senior, the key man in recruiting South African air personnel, had obtained forty Kitty Hawks sold as scrap by the South African government, but he could not get them out of the country; he paid

Jewish dealers £6 apiece for them, although they were offered as a gift. Several surplus American Norsemen, purchased through a dummy company in Spain, also became part of the Haganah air fleet.

In anticipation of the arrival of the first tanks, Moshe Dayan made a hasty trip incognito to the United States early in May for a secret course in handling armored equipment. Using training manuals provided by the Sonneborn Institute, Dayan and several other Haganah officers practiced maneuvers on surplus tanks in the privacy of David Greenberg's estate at Hopewell Junction, in New York's Dutchess County. On the same tanks Jewish scientists tested Israel's first antitank guns.

By these unorthodox and roundabout ways Haganah amassed 204 planes, 39 naval craft, 40 tanks, 416 heavy guns, 24 heavy mortars, 6500 medium and heavy machine guns, an assortment of armored vehicles, 53,000 rifles, and several million rounds of ammunition for delivery in Palestine after May 14. Their availability proved to be the critical factor in the final decision to declare sovereignty.

chapter

∘ ∘ ∘ ∘ ∘ ∘ ∘ ∘ ∘ ∘ ∘ ∘ ∘ |10| ∘ ∘ ∘ ∘ ∘ ∘ ∘ ∘ ∘ ∘ ∘ ∘ ∘

THE PRE-PROCLAMATION
MILITARY APPRAISAL

THE LAST WORD had not yet been spoken on May 12 when Chief of Staff Yadin was called by Ben-Gurion to an emergency session of the National Administration (Minhalet Ha'am) and asked to detail the chances of survival if the state was established. Ben-Gurion was determined on independence, however great the risks, but it became Yadin's responsibility to weigh the military pros and cons of a proclamation of independence. Like the other military leaders, he was not a member of the provisional government, and it is interesting that none of the military men were invited to sign the Declaration.

The likelihood of invasion was virtually a certainty, Yadin informed the nine men and one woman seated around a plain square table in the Jewish National Fund Building on Herman Shapira Street in Tel Aviv. Two other members of the Administration were trapped in Jerusalem and a third was in the United States. The Etzion bloc of settlements south of Jerusalem was being overrun by the Arab Legion, he solemnly announced, amid stony silence broken only by Golda Myerson's sobs. The chance of throwing back an invasion was far from certain, Yadin said matter-of-factly. He had no fighting planes and his so-called air force was no military factor, and weapons and ammunition were dangerously short. Without minimizing the handicaps resulting from Arab superiority in armor and planes, Yadin quietly pointed out that the one factor operating in Israel's favor was the imminent British departure. This would permit full-scale mobilization for the first time and would assure the arrival of arms shipments, including considerable artillery and fighting planes.

As Yadin spoke he knew that thirty freighters loaded with knocked-down planes, heavy guns, and ammunition had already dropped anchor outside Palestinian waters, waiting for midnight, May 14, when they could safely make for the docks of Haifa and Tel Aviv without British interference. The ships had sailed from France, Italy, Greece, and Yugoslavia during the first week in May on orders of Rehesh agents who had received instructions from the Haganah communications center in Tel Aviv.

After Yadin left the room the discussion was brief. One or two members were sufficiently frightened by the picture he had drawn to vote No, but the majority said Yes when Ben-Gurion asked if they were ready to vote for proclaiming independence on May 14.

Before the thirteen-hour session adjourned, the Cabinet also rejected a last-minute offer by Emir Abdullah of Jordan to call off the invasion if the Jews would defer the proclamation of independence and let him annex all of Palestine to his kingdom. Two of the ten in the room were ready to talk about a deal, but the majority stood firm for independence after hearing Golda Myerson's report of her secret talk with Abdullah on May 10.

In October, 1947, before the United Nations had voted to partition Palestine but after the British had announced their impending withdrawal, the Jewish Agency had tried to reach an understanding with Abdullah. In the closing weeks of the Mandate his attitude became crucial. If he did not move against the Jews, neither would the other Arab states. If he ordered his Arab Legion to march, the other Arab armies would follow, not only because of treaty commitments, but because Egypt, Iraq, Syria, and Lebanon did not trust Abdullah. The Arab League states were united in opposition to Zionism, but they were at loggerheads on how to prevent the emergence of the Jewish state. The chief reason for the disunity was Abdullah's ambition to grab the areas of Palestine set aside for an Arab state, as well as Jerusalem. Abdullah was well aware that the Mufti of Jerusalem and the politicians in Syria were scheming to set up a rival Arab state in Palestine, with the Mufti as its head. To thwart this planned encirclement by his enemies, Abdullah was willing to come to terms with the Jews.

In mid-November, 1947, Abdullah agreed to a private meeting with Mrs. Myerson, who was then chairman of the political department of the Jewish Agency, at Naharayim on the Jordan. The Bedouin monarch arrived incognito at the meeting, which took place in the living room of Pinhas Rutenberg's house near a power station. In the presence of Eliahu

Sassoon and Ezra Dannin, the Jewish Agency's experts on Arab affairs, Abdullah assured Mrs. Myerson that he would not join in any attack on the Jews. If the United Nations decided on partition, he would incorporate the areas earmarked for the Arab state into his kingdom. He pledged friendship to a Jewish state, spoke of the Mufti as a common enemy, and agreed to another meeting after the United Nations vote. Before they parted, Abdullah asked Mrs. Myerson how the Jews would feel about including the Jewish state in an enlarged Jordan. Told that it was out of the question, he dropped the matter but hinted that he would need some territorial concessions from the Jews to impress his fellow Arab leaders.

No second meeting was held after November 29, 1947, but discreet contact was maintained between the Jewish Agency and Abdullah's agents. As the reports of combined Arab war plans grew more ominous and Abdullah himself became more bellicose in his public statements, Mrs. Myerson sent him a message inquiring if his earlier promise was still valid. Abdullah replied that a Bedouin was a man of honor and that a promise to a woman was never broken. At the same time he renewed his previous suggestion that the Jews should consider ceding to him part of the territory assigned to them by the United Nations in order to raise his prestige in the Arab world.

Although the answer was an unequivocal No, Abdullah nevertheless made another appointment with Mrs. Myerson. This time, however, he refused to come to Naharayim because news of his talks with the Jews had leaked out. He insisted that Mrs. Myerson come to Amman and undertook to arrange the security precautions. In Tel Aviv, Mrs. Myerson was made up as an Arab woman and driven to Haifa. She was accompanied only by Ezra Dannin because Sassoon was pinned down in Jerusalem by the Arab siege. From Haifa they traveled in an inconspicuous car to Naharayim, where a limousine sent by Abdullah was waiting. The Jordanian chauffeur was a member of Abdullah's household and knew all about the rendezvous since it was to be held in his house on the outskirts of Amman. En route to the Jordanian capital, the limousine was halted ten times at checkpoints through the lines of the assembling Arab Legion and the forward units of the Iraqi Army.

Mrs. Myerson's mission was to try to keep Jordan out of the war, thus preventing an attack on Jerusalem and preventing the Iraqis from invading via Jordan. The one-hour audience was cordial but changed nothing. Abdullah said war could still be averted if the Jews were ready to postpone independence and to halt immigration. He informed Mrs. Myerson that once the British left, he would take over all of Palestine and after a year merge it with Jordan. Within his enlarged kingdom Abdullah was prepared to grant autonomy to the Jews in the areas they inhabited and to give them equal representation in the Jordanian Parliament. Mrs. Myerson turned down his proposals as totally unacceptable, but she was empowered to consent to Jordan's annexation of the territory of the proposed Arab state.

Abdullah did not deny his earlier agreement but explained that the situation had changed. "Then I was alone, but now I am one of five," he said, implying that the power of decision was no longer his alone. He was courteous and even gallant, but adamant. When the Iraqi-born Dannin, who spoke Arabic fluently, warned Abdullah that he was in mortal danger from his own allies, the Emir thanked him profusely (among the assassins of Abdullah on July 20, 1951, were collaborators of the Mufti). The meeting broke up after Mrs. Meyerson advised Abdullah that if he turned his back on his promise of 1947, war was inevitable because the Jews would resist invasion.

On the way back from Amman, the Arab chauffeur drove past heavy Iraqi equipment and artillery moving toward the Palestine frontier. Alarmed lest an armed sentry recognize his passengers, the driver let them out two miles from the border at 3 A.M. on May 11. Unarmed, they walked to Naharayim, where a Haganah scout picked them up.

While Mrs. Myerson was conferring with Abdullah, rumors of what she was prepared to offer gained currency. On May 11, two days before the Arabs surrendered Jaffa, there were hints that the Jews would not retain the city but planned to use it as a bargaining point with Abdullah: if he came to terms, he would be given the Jaffa port as an outlet to the Mediterranean. On May 12, after Mrs. Myerson had reported to the shadow cabinet, the Associated Press quoted a Jewish Agency spokesman as saying, "We still hope for an agreement with Abdullah." The rumors were baseless.

chapter

o o o o o o o o o o o o o 〔11〕 o o o o o o o o o o o o o

THE BATTLE FOR JERUSALEM

To GAIN CONTROL of the vital Hebron-Bethlehem-Jerusalem Road, Abdullah's Arab Legion had been pounding at the Etzion bloc of Jewish settlements in the Hebron mountains, fourteen miles south of Jerusalem, since May 4. The four Jewish villages—Kfar Etzion, Massuot, Ein Tzurim, and Revadim—had been under constant attack by Arab irregulars beginning in December, 1947, but had beaten them off at the cost of heavy casualties. From mid-March, 1948, the only contact between Etzion and the rest of Jewish Palestine was by occasional convoy and Piper Cubs that landed on the strip carved out on the side of a mountain bordered by a deep chasm.

The four isolated kibbutzim were among the thirty-three Jewish settlements excluded from the territory of the Jewish state, but Ben-Gurion had overruled Haganah's advice to evacuate every colony that was untenable. He insisted on defending and holding every inch of Jewish soil. The heroic stand of the Etzion bloc, which sat athwart the invasion route from the south, was crucial to the defense of Jerusalem. So long as the Etzion villages held out, Arab traffic between Hebron and Jerusalem was under Jewish fire while the defenders of Jerusalem won time to consolidate their positions and prepare for the main attack on the city.

On May 11 the Arab Legion launched an artillery bombardment and a massive assault by armored vehicles on the Etzion colonies. In the two-day battle that followed the outnumbered defenders were almost entirely wiped out and many civilians were shot down by neighboring Arab villagers after Mordecai Dieschler, Haganah commander, surrendered on radioed orders from Jerusalem. The survivors were taken prisoner and sent in Arab Legion trucks to Hebron along a road lined with jubilant Arabs who spat upon the Jews and screamed, "Slaughter the Jews." The wounded were evacuated by the International Red Cross to Jerusalem. Hannah Hurnard, a Protestant missionary who saw some of them on the night of May 13 in the Mission Hospital, wrote in her diary: "Down there in the cellars it was like a scene from the experiences of Florence Nightingale in the Crimea. Bodies with every conceivable kind of wound. What a price in sacrifices and maimed young lives the Jewish state will have to pay."

In the squat pinkish Haganah headquarters building overlooking the Mediterranean—the Red House in Tel Aviv—Yadin and his staff read the last message from Etzion which had been received at 9:30 A.M. on May 14: "Men and women are sent toward Hebron. The wounded are transferred to Bethlehem. Greetings from the men of Massuot. This is the end of the Etzion bloc. Tonight we shall not be here any more."

That night Dieschler lay exhausted on the tiled floor of the Hebron police station with the other Etzion prisoners. An Arab policeman, who had lived and worked in Haifa, leaned over the twenty-nine-year-old Haganah officer to apologize for the lack of food and to explain that the captives would soon be moved to Jordan. Lowering his head even more, the Arab whispered, "Had Mordecai heard? The Jews had proclaimed their state this afternoon."

The day before, in Jerusalem, a British officer had informed the Jewish Agency that the Arab Legion was no longer under British command. At the United Nations a British spokesman assured the Security Council on May 14 that the last two units of the Legion had left Palestine. Just before High Commissioner Cunningham left Jerusalem for Haifa on the morning of May 14 a correspondent asked him, "Is it true, sir, that your Transjordan Arab Legion has taken the Etzion bloc?" Cunningham brushed the question aside, saying, "As of 23:59 hours last night [one minute before midnight, May 13] the Arab Legion ceased to be under my command, so I cannot answer your question."

When the Arab Legion began its assault on Etzion on May 4, it was still commanded by British officers and thus part of the forces at Cunningham's disposal. The blow at the Etzion bloc was part of Abdullah's plan to clear the road to Jerusalem so that his troops could get there before the Egyptians or the Jews seized the city. The last-ditch stand at Etzion upset Abdullah's timetable and gave the defenders of Jerusalem a few more hours to prepare.

The bodies of the Etzion martyred dead were received in Jerusalem on the morning of May 14 as the battle for control of the Holy City and its approaches erupted just before the last of the departing British Army had left. While the Arab Legion moved into strategic positions north and south of Jerusalem, Haganah, Irgun, and Sternist units launched "Operation Pitchfork," the objective of which was to occupy the heart of the New City evacuated by the British and to link up isolated Jewish sections. For two days armed Jews had been concentrated along the stretch of the British security zones in anticipation of the race to seize key buildings and strongpoints before the Arab irregulars could entrench themselves. Haganah sappers had already cut down back fences to prepare for street-to-street fighting.

Shortly after 10 A.M. the Jews fanned out in four columns on a signal from the Haganah command post in Schneller's, a former Lutheran orphanage in the old German quarter. One company took over the Italian Hospital on the Street of the Prophets and hoisted the Israeli flag. The main post office fell swiftly to a second unit, aided by Jewish civilians who had been hidden there for several days. The same detachment captured the headquarters of the British Criminal Investigations Department, hated symbol of the enforcement of the 1939 White Paper regulations. It also took over the law courts building, the Bank Leumi, the Russian Compound, the Generali Building, the French Notre Dame Hospital complex, and the King David Hotel.

A third unit swooped down on the railroad station, overran the Arab residential quarters of Abu-Tor, Baka'a, and Talbieh, and laid siege to the Allenby Barracks, which the British had handed over to three companies of Iraqis. Irgun fighters stormed the Old City and got within 150 yards of the beleaguered Jewish quarter when they were virtually wiped out. North of the Old City the Irgunists drove the Arabs out of the Sheikh Jarrah quarter of the New City and temporarily linked it up with Mount Scopus, seat of the Hebrew University and the Hadassah Hospital. This Arab suburb had fallen to Haganah at the end of April, but the British, by a show of force, compelled the Jews to give it up because it straddled the British evacuation route. Although the British commander had promised to turn it over to the Jews after May 14, it became a base for Arab snipers attacking the Jewish quarter of the Old City. Sheikh Jarrah was later recaptured by the Arab Legion, thus cutting off the university and the hospital on Mount Scopus from the rest of Jewish Jerusalem until the Six-Day War of 1967.

The Christian Arab quarter of Katamon, a strategic height to the south, was also occupied by Haganah in a swift dash on May 14. It had first been taken on May 2, just before the beginning of negotiations for a truce to cover all of Jerusalem. But again the British forced the Jews to withdraw, this time by dropping a few bombs into the Jewish Montefiore quarter. The Hadassah Hospital in the New City was snatched from the Arabs by a ruse. Just as the last British guards pulled away, Mrs. Molly Bar-David, a journalist and housewife, engaged the Arab sentry at the gate in small talk while another woman began to shout at him in Hebrew. While Mrs. Bar-David was offering to act as an interpreter, a Haganah detail marched up to the gate. "Excuse me, we're taking over," the young Haganah officer said, and walked into the building with his men.

By the time the weary troops heard the news of the Declaration of Independence in Tel Aviv, and broke out in singing and toasting the new state with many a *"L'Chaim,"* most of the New City had been secured by the Jews. On I-Day the defenders of Jerusalem included about half of the eighty American students at the Hebrew University who were studying under the GI Bill. They had elected to stay and fight in defiance of a warning from the US Consulate that any Americans taking part in the war would forfeit their passports. The other half had left before the British departed. One student from North Carolina who spoke Hebrew with a Southern accent fired the Jews' only mortar, while a poet and a Reform rabbi manned a machine-gun post.

Notwithstanding the initial gains in Jerusalem on May 14 and 15, the city remained in deadly peril. From the dominating heights encircling Jerusalem, Arab artillery began shelling the northern Jewish suburbs in a day-and-night bombardment. To the south the advancing Egyptians and the Arab Legion threatened Ramat Rahel and Talpiot. A company of teen-agers was rushed to the outskirts of Ramat Rahel to dig trenches and erect barricades. Other youngsters risked flying shrapnel as they collected bottles from abandoned Arab homes, to be converted into Molotov cocktails.

In the Meah Shearim labyrinth of alleys, where the New City's most pious Jews were already observing the Sabbath at sundown May 14, Haganah officers initially met with resistance and curses as Sabbath desecrators when they tried to set up roadblocks. The ultra-Orthodox residents, who regarded the Jewish state as a heresy, refused to take orders in Hebrew, which they considered a holy tongue not to be defiled by common use. Borya Cymberg, the Haganah unit commander, had to speak in Yiddish before he could organize forty-eight caftaned and sidecurled residents of Meah Shearim into a labor detail by pointing out that the defense of Jerusalem was literally a matter of life and death. They had never before worked on the Sabbath.

Arab control of the Latrun salient blocked the Tel Aviv-Jerusalem road and held Jewish Jerusalem in a tight vise until Israel's "Burma Road" was carved out through rough mountain trails weeks later. The heaviest fighting in and around Jerusalem came after D-Day (D for deluge), May 15, when the Arab armies poured over the borders in a coordinated attack. When the Arabs invaded, some wisecracking younger Israelis began replying to the traditional Israeli greeting of *"Shalom"* with *"Chatzi-Shalom"*—Half Peace. By May 15, Jerusalem was running out of food, ammunition and guns were scarce, water was strictly rationed, and heavy casualties had greatly reduced available manpower. Except for the fighting men and the daring volunteers who distributed water rations, the streets were virtually deserted. Hungry and isolated, Jewish Jerusalem was in desperate straits on the first Sabbath of independence.

The Haganah commander was Col. David Shaltiel, who had come to Palestine from Germany in 1923 and later served in the French Foreign Legion. When he took over the Jerusalem district command in February, no one really expected the city would become a battleground. The area for which he was responsible extended from Jerusalem to Bab el Wad in the west, Atarot in the north, Kfar Etzion in the south, and Beit Haarava and Sodom on the Dead Sea in the east. With limited funds available from the Jewish Agency, his instructions were to steal or buy arms. He had to get his officers on the spot. Together with David Horowitz, the civilian Jewish chief, Shaltiel had to recruit, train, and organize for defense while the city was in danger of starvation as a result of the Arab blockade. On the eve of independence, Shaltiel's effective fighting forces consisted of 1000 Haganah men, not all armed, three armed platoons of Irgun, and 200 armed Sternists. The few available machine guns were carried from place to place to create the illusion of Jewish strength.

Shaltiel's most agonizing concern was the fate of the 2500 Jews trapped in the Old City's Jewish quarter since the beginning of the siege in December, 1947. Tel Aviv had refused to heed his plea to evacuate the Old City Jews because of the immense difficulty in providing them with food and arms. At no point did the Jewish sector of the walled city abut on any Jewish-held district of the New City. All traffic between the two points had to cross a corridor occupied by 20,000 Arabs.

On May 13, when the British pulled out of the Old City, Moshe Russnak, the Haganah commander, had orders to seize every British position as fast as it was evacuated, but not to shoot first. A cease-fire had been theoretically in effect for the Old City since May 1, but the Arabs kept the Jews under continuous sniper fire. At noon British Army trucks, loaded with teakettles, cooking stoves, crates, trunks, and unwrapped portraits of the Royal Family, moved out to the north. At 2 P.M. British officers handed two rifles to every Jewish and Arab policeman in the Old City. Before leaving, the British commander went to the door of A. Mordecai Weingarten, leader of the Jewish quarter, and handed him the keys to the Zion Gate. "From the year A.D. 70 until today, the keys of Jerusalem have never been in the hands of the Jews," the officer declared. "This is the first time in eighteen centuries that you are so privileged."

Haganah had no use for Weingarten, not only because of his friendly relations with the British, but even more so because he was suspected of having tipped them off to the identity of the secret Haganah commander, Abraham Halpern. Smuggled into the Jewish quarter in the guise of a medical orderly, Halpern had been expelled in March, when Russnak replaced him. The British never ceased trying to drive Haganah out of the Jewish quarter by rigorous arms searches. The occasional trucks of food, fuel, and medicines the British convoyed through the gates from the New City were methodically checked for weapons. Sometimes the trucks hid Haganah men posing as religious functionaries or disguised as old men. British sentries were occasionally bribed to look the other way while taxis carrying armed Jews entered the Old City. In this way the Haganah force of eighteen teen-age boys and girls who had guarded the Jewish quarter since December expanded to 120 by May 13. There were also 65 young volunteers and a handful of Irgunists.

The last food convoy arrived on April 28. Riding in a British armored car with the convoy was Dr. Abraham Laufer, who brought badly needed medical supplies for the Old City's two-story Hadassah Hospital. Most of its patients, old people suffering from incurable diseases, were housed on the second floor. On the street floor nurses examined Jews of military age, cared for victims of sniper fire, and taught older men and women first aid. In the cellar the Haganah garrison waited.

To make up for the shortage of arms, youngsters learned to filch ammunition and even rifles from British soldiers. Children collected empty cigarette tins tossed away by the British: filled with explosives bought from compliant Tommies, the tins became homemade grenades. An arms census on the night of May 13 showed that the defenders of the Jewish quarter had only two machine guns, a 2-inch mortar, seventeen rifles, forty-seven submachine guns, forty-five pistols, five hundred grenades, two hundred kilograms of explosives, and a thousand fuses.

At 6:15 P.M. teen-age runners carried instructions to Haganah details posted near the British positions to be prepared to move. Twenty minutes later all the British positions overlooking the Jewish quarter were captured by Haganah. Many Arabs fled in panic from the Old City, fearing that Haganah might overrun the entire walled area. It could have happened had Haganah had the men and the guns and had it wanted to fire on Christian holy places, including the Holy Sepulcher, near where the Arabs were dug in. This was the last chance to save the Jewish quarter. Five days later the Arab Legion moved in and began bombing the ancient Jewish area to smithereens. A Palmach unit that captured adjacent Mount Zion outside the walls on May 18 made a temporary breakthrough to the Jewish quarter via the Zion Gate, but was compelled to withdraw.

With the British gone the Arab irregulars confidently expected the Jewish quarter to fall in a matter of hours. The British had predicted a massacre and quick capture by the Arab Legion. On May 14 Russnak radioed Haganah headquarters at Schneller's: "Help us immediately. Otherwise we will not be able to hold out." Shaltiel ordered him to "Hold out at any cost." Fighting remained sporadic until 7:30 P.M. of May 15, when the Arabs began a heavy artillery attack on the Jewish quarter and Haganah was ordered to shoot back.

For thirteen harrowing days and nights the Jewish quarter withstood the battering before capitulating on May 28. Most of the Haganah men were already dead and the surviving defenders had been squeezed into a tiny perimeter of 100 square yards in three courtyards. Ammunition was exhausted. Over 400 had died in the battle and more than 1000 were wounded. The civilian population consisted largely of elderly pietists and younger members of the Neturei Karta sect, who opposed Jewish independence as blasphemy. Before the siege, few Jews in the Old City had ever held a gun. When the Jewish quarter fell, 345 men and a few women were taken prisoner and sent to Amman; 1300 women and children were evacuated to the New City under the supervision of the International Red Cross.

Two of the siege's survivors claim to have been the last Jew out of the Old City in 1948: one was Elitzur Ben Gur, who served nine months in a Jordanian prison; the other is Rabbi Shaaryeshu Cohen, who was carried out on a stretcher with the other wounded and taken to Amman, and who in 1967 was praying at the Western Wall as the Deputy Mayor of the reunited city.

During the nineteen years the Jordanians controlled the Old City, they desecrated or destroyed thirty-six synagogues and houses of study and defiled the ancient Jewish cemetery on the Mount of Olives. When the Six-Day War reunited Jerusalem, the Israelis found the bodies of sixty-two men and women who had died in the 1948 battle for the Jewish quarter. Forty-eight had been buried by the Arabs in a mass grave and fourteen were the remains of unburied bodies. These heroic dead were interred with military honors as one of the first acts after the recapture of the Old City.

IN THE TEL AVIV AREA

In Tel Aviv, already happily celebrating the first hours of independence, the initial good news from the Jerusalem front and Jewish victories in the north on May 14 evoked great jubilation.

At 10 A.M. Beisan, an Arab strongpoint in the plain of Esdraelon, seventy-four miles from Tel Aviv, was taken through trickery. The commander of a single Haganah company attacking the town deceived the defenders into believing that the reinforcements they counted on had been wiped out and that he would use artillery unless the garrison surrendered. Haganah's only artillery were two 3-inch mortars and eight shells while the Arab relief column was actually on the way. To impress the Arabs, Haganah set irrigation pipes in "firing" position and fired one round from the real mortars. In minutes the Arab commander sent word he would capitulate at noon, but yielded to a demand for a 10 A.M. deadline.

An amphibious assault captured Napoleon Hill (where Napoleon had been defeated in 1799), paving the way for the fall three days later of Acre, just north of Haifa, which had been earmarked for the Arab state. Hours before the Arab armies moved down from the north most of western Galilee was in Jewish control. Besieged Naharia, the principal Jewish stronghold in western Galilee, had been relieved that morning by an infantry battalion ferried from Haifa in motor launches and fishing boats.

At the moment the Declaration of Independence was adopted the Jews held virtually every square foot assigned to them by the United Nations vote, but anxiety rather than exhilaration pervaded Haganah's Tel Aviv headquarters. Despite the first successes of Jewish arms, no member of the general staff left his post on May 14 to attend the signing ceremonies a few blocks away. The men in the Red House on Yarkon Street knew that hard fighting and heavy casualties would follow once the Arabs crossed the frontiers.

At 3:40 P.M. four of the twenty Hispano-Suiza antiaircraft guns in Jewish Palestine were wheeled into position around the Red House, on the seafront between today's Dan Hotel and the French Embassy. At the Sde Dov Airport on the outskirts of Tel Aviv two of Haganah's nine licensed pilots, on duty in the seven-foot-high wooden box that passed for a control tower, made a bet as to when the invasion would start.

Sde Dov's commander, Boris Senior (later Col. Ron Eldor of the Israel Air Force), had just arrived in the Haganah operations room to report on an observation flight during which he had seen the Arab Legion trucks carrying the Jewish prisoners from Etzion to Hebron. After a catnap in one of the tents pitched on the field, Senior took off again at 5 P.M. in his Bonanza and headed northeast to reconnoiter along the Syrian border. At 6:30 P.M. "Balak 3," code name for an American DC-4 chartered by Haganah, rolled to a stop at Sde Dov. The first plane to land in Israel since independence, "Balak 3" had been flown nonstop from Czechoslovakia with a load of sixty machine guns, two hundred rifles, and ammunition. Haganah soldiers tore the guns from their crates and kissed them, Vaseline and all, before sending them off to the front. With Lydda Airport in Arab control (the Israelis didn't capture it until July 13) and the Haifa airfield barred to the Jews until June 30, Sde Dov played an important role in the early days of the war as the main air entry to Israel.

When Senior returned at 7 P.M., Tel Aviv was blacked out in compliance with the Haganah first order of the day by Israel Galili. He had also ordered air-raid shelters made ready and had banned large open-air public gatherings. Ben-Gurion, who had rushed from the independence exercises to the Red House for a briefing on the dangerous security situation, was still there when Senior reported that the roads into Jewish Palestine were choked with hundreds of Arab military vehicles, the advance guard of the invasion.

Yadin and his associates were sweating out a high-stakes gamble. Among the freighters anchored outside Tel Aviv on May 13 was the 1200-ton *Santa Chiara,* codenamed "Borea." Only the National Administration and the highest Haganah commanders knew what she carried. The vessel had sailed from Marseilles on May 5 with five 65-mm. howitzers, 60,000 artillery shells, 200 heavy machine guns, some tanks, several thousand rifles, and 4 million rounds of rifle ammunition in her hold. The howitzers were Yadin's ace in the hole, but if the British confiscated them, he was even worse off than when he had reported to the Cabinet on May 12.

On the night of May 13 the *Santa Chiara* received orders to head for the dock at Tel Aviv. Just outside the port the arms ship was apprehended by two British destroyers. One, HMS *Pelican,* took the freighter in tow to Haifa, where she was to be searched from top to bottom. Against this contingency the cargo had been buried under 450 tons of rotting onions covered by crates of canned tomato juice. The smell was so overpowering that the British seamen did not dig too deep. At 12:05 A.M., May 15, the *Santa Chiara* was released and she returned to Tel Aviv, arriving just after dawn during the first Arab air raid on the city.

The first Egyptian bombs fell on Tel Aviv at 5:25 A.M. while Ben-Gurion was broadcasting to the United States from the Haganah radio shack at Mahaneh Yonah (Camp Jonah). Ben-Gurion interrupted his speech to say, "At this very moment enemy planes are bombing Tel Aviv." That was the first word of the attack to reach the outside world.

The raid was by two British-built Spitfire Mark 9 fighter-bombers, with the markings of the Royal Egyptian Air Force. The planes swept in low from the west and roared over the city's rooftops. One climbed and circled watchfully 3000 feet over Tel Aviv, while the other dropped a stick of 250-pound bombs and then dived for a strafing attack. Boris Senior, who was spending the night in a hotel near Sde Dov, heard the bombers and then the crash of bombs. Certain that the airfield was the target, he grabbed a parked jeep and reached the field in three minutes. There, ahead of him, was Ben-Gurion, still in pajamas covered by a coat, the attire in which he had made his broadcast. A hangar and an ammunition shack were blazing from a direct hit. On the second run the Spitfires damaged the Reading Power Station, but one of the planes was hit in its coolant tank by a blast from a heavy machine gun on the seashore. As the Spitfire limped off over the Mediterranean, Senior hopped into his Bonanza and gave chase. Near Herzliah the Egyptian aircraft crash-landed and the pilot was captured by a member of the Home Guard. Israel's first prisoner of war was brought to the makeshift hospital at Sarona, Israel's first capital, where his head was bandaged by Leah Zwanger. Then he was taken to the Red House for interrogation. The Spitfire was salvaged with parts cannibalized from junked British planes, and on May 30 it joined the Israel Air Force. The Egyptian airman was repatriated in February, 1949, after the Israeli-Egyptian armistice.

While Sde Dov Airport was being bombed and strafed, one of the Dakotas that Senior had acquired in South Africa arrived over the field from Italy—and the jittery Israelis almost shot it down. After contacting the control tower by radio, the South African pilot was allowed to land, still unaware that the state had been proclaimed or that war had broken out. Instead of flying gear, he wore a hunter's felt hat with a pheasant feather, and duck-hunting garb. Seeing armed men all around him as he taxied to a stop, he asked in English, "Excuse me, is this the Jewish city of Tel Aviv?" Just then another wave of Egyptian planes came over and the Israeli soldiers grabbed the startled flyer and pushed him toward an air-raid shelter, shouting, "Rutz!" ("Run" in Hebrew). "I want Tel Aviv, not Rutz," the unidentified non-Jewish pilot protested, until the falling bombs taught him Hebrew fast.

An Irgun-chartered plane with British markings also narrowly missed being shot down later that afternoon because Sde Dov's radio had been knocked out. On board the DC-3, which had left Paris around noon of May 14, were Peter Bergson, Samuel Katz, Yaacov Meridor, and a half dozen other Irgun leaders. They had come to explain to Irgun chief Begin why an arms ship had not arrived as promised on May 14. The SS *Altalena* (Vladimir Jabotinsky's nom-de-plume), bought by Irgun at the end of 1947, was held at a French port while Irgun committees around the world sought the money to buy weapons and equip the 1000 Irgun recruits who would be aboard the vessel. When the Irgunists landed, the Haganah commander at Sde Dov told them he had his single antiaircraft gun trained on the plane because the Egyptians had used similar DC-3s in their bombing runs.

The four air attacks that pounded Tel Aviv on the first Sabbath after independence caused little damage and resulted in only four civilian casualties. No sirens sounded during the raids and civilian defense wardens had a tough time keeping the populace from wandering through the streets to see what was happening. While the radio blared warnings to obey regulations, civilians dodged the wardens to see for themselves how the city was reacting to independence under fire.

The greatest danger was that a bomb might hit one of the arms and supply ships moving into the harbor and start a chain of explosive devastation. Some of the vessels were hastily moved out to sea, but those that had already docked were unloaded during the bombardment. The rabbis granted a special dispensation to permit the stevedores to work on the Sabbath.

In *Assignment Weapons* Pinhas Vasa described how "we were unloading explosives from barges into trucks from the 'Shelev' cooperative when the planes came over, bombing and strafing the crowded harbor. A direct hit would have caused a chain reaction among the hundreds of tons of TNT, devastating not only the port, then Israel's only functioning harbor, but large areas of the city as well.

"The drivers abandoned their trucks and rushed to find shelter." Vasa and his assistant, Isaac Weinman, "jumped into the two leading trucks, started them again and drove out of the harbor area. Grizzled 'Shelev' veterans then hopped into the next line of trucks, as younger drivers, ashamed of their momentary cowardice, helped us move the explosives under enemy fire and disperse them in orange groves north and west of Tel Aviv. The port manager, Zipstein, donned a steel helmet, and shouted to the tugboat skippers to move the explosive-laden barges out of the harbor into the open sea. Four of the stevedores were killed in the raids but the port and the city were saved."

The *Santa Chiara* was hit during the first raid but suffered no serious damage, and by dusk all of her precious cargo had been safely unloaded, including the five howitzers. They turned out to be Krupp mountain howitzers, so old that in Hebrew slang they became known as "Napoleonchiki." Leon Kaufman, a former French artillery officer who reported to Haganah headquarters an hour before the *Santa Chiara* arrived, turned out to be the only man in Israel who knew anything about such weapons. At the waterfront warehouse where the guns were stored after being taken off the ship, Kaufman showed a Haganah crew how to reassemble them. Then he went off to the front as commander of the artillery unit to which the "Napoleonchiki" had been assigned.

Yadin became so excited at the safe delivery of the *Santa Chiara's* cargo that he dropped everything in the operations room of the Red House and hurried to Ben-Gurion's house on Keren Kayemet Street with the good news. Ben-Gurion shouted to his wife, Paula, to bring the cognac and the three of them drank a thankful *"L'Chaim"* to a big gamble that had paid off.

chapter

∘ ∘ ∘ ∘ ∘ ∘ ∘ ∘ ∘ ∘ ∘ ∘ |12| ∘ ∘ ∘ ∘ ∘ ∘ ∘ ∘ ∘ ∘ ∘ ∘ ∘

THE INNER STRUGGLE: UNIFYING
THE ARMY

THE LEAST TOLD, very highly significant, and most sadly tragic aspect of the story of independence is the long-smoldering internal fight between the old-line Haganah command and David Ben-Gurion for a unified army and command under the direct leadership of the Defense Ministry. It was complicated by the political party structure of the leadership of the armed forces—with the Haganah and the Palmach largely under the control of the Mapam, the party to the left of Ben-Gurion's Labor Mapai, and the forces of the Irgun (Etzel) and the Sternists (Lehi) under the control of the Right-wing Revisionists.

In essence Ben-Gurion wanted a unified army directly under the sole control of the National Administration (the shadow cabinet that was to become the provisional government) administered through the Defense Minister, himself. The opposition wanted the continuance of a so-called National Command, a nine-party body representing all political parties, but dominated by its chairman, Israel Galili. Appointed by the Jewish Agency in the prestate days as its representative in dealing with the chiefs of staff and the operational chiefs of the Haganah and its military brigades, Galili was respected and admired as the unquestioned chief of the Haganah.

The clash came to a head with a letter, dated May 2, from Ben-Gurion to the "General Staff and National Command" which said that after noon, May 8, with "the new arrangements in the administration of the Yishuv and security affairs, there is no further place for a representative of the

Jewish Agency Executive on the National Command as Chief of Command and this is to notify the abolition of that post and the termination of Israel Galili's appointment to the post. The Security Forces staff will hereafter receive its instructions only from the Head of Security, or his delegate."

On April 18, at a meeting of the National Administration, after paying tribute to "the effective legacy" of Haganah, Ben-Gurion had said that what was still lacking was "that full discipline which is imperative in an army." On May 3, at another meeting of the National Administration, the day after he had sent the letter to Galili, he reported that the Jewish Agency Executive had transferred security matters to the National Administration and voted to abolish the post of Chief of National Command.

In an article published twenty years later in the anniversary issue of the newspaper *Maariv*, Ben-Gurion recalled that neither his fellow Cabinet members nor the Haganah leadership realized the implications of the change from an effective underground effort to national militia. Before the British withdrawal he had asked the Haganah command to prepare a budget. They brought him estimates double the previous year's. When he showed surprise, they believed he had been overwhelmed by their temerity.

"We're in a war situation," they said apologetically.

"Actually," Ben-Gurion wrote, "I had been amazed by their naïveté. I asked them, 'Will that budget suffice for tanks, cannons, and planes?'"

He recalls that one of the participants later told him that Galili remarked, "The old man is nuts. He wants tanks, cannons, and planes."

Ben-Gurion's action and words—the crystallization of sentiments previously expressed privately to Galili—met with strong dissent from two members of the National Administration, Zisling and Bentov, representatives of the United Workers Party (Mapam). The party's daily, *Al Hamishmar*, broke a vow of silence to which the Hebrew papers adhered in security matters and launched an open attack against Ben-Gurion. It argued that the fighting capacity of the Jewish forces would be greatly diminished by adapting the Haganah "to the apparatus of an accepted Regular Army by disbanding the Palmach, eliminating the experienced and loyal commanders of the Haganah . . . disbanding the Palmach would mean breaking the backbone of the Haganah." The paper also criticized centralizing all security affairs "in the hands of one man, in Ben-Gurion's hands."

Negotiations meanwhile had been consummated whereby the Haganah and the Revisionist groups, the Etzel and the Lehi, would be coordinated with the national army, to which Haganah willingly agreed. On Independence Day, just before the proclamation, Menachem Beigin, the Revisionist leader, announced that he was placing Etzel at the disposal of the provisional government, and by June he went even further when he ordered his armed forces to join the national army, although temporarily; until fully integrated, they were to function under their own commanders.

But although there was some coordination, on various local fronts it was not achieved either before or immediately after statehood, and the final liquidation of Etzel as an entity did not occur until more than a month after Independence, on June 22, when Ben-Gurion persuaded his Cabinet to allow him to take action against the SS *Altalena* in Tel Aviv Harbor, where her crew was unloading arms under the direct order of Beigin. He had refused to turn over the arms on board the ship to the national army still controlled by Haganah leadership, persisting in a demand that he be allowed to turn the arms over to Etzel units.

The problem was further complicated by the fact that the heavily laden *Altalena* had been ordered to sail for Israel on June 11, the very day a four-week truce had been signed through UN mediation which specifically forbade the importation of arms during the truce. At first, after conferring with Galili and Levi Eshkol, later to be Israel's third Prime Minister but who was then high in the Haganah command, Beigin agreed to unload the *Altalena* secretly at some lonely beach as was being done regularly. But on June 17 he reneged, saying that his associates believed that the arms must go not to the High Command, but to various Etzel units serving with the army.

At a meeting on June 20 with his Cabinet, Ben-Gurion had said, "This affair is of the highest importance. There are not going to be two states and there are not going to be two armies. Beigin will not be allowed to do as he likes." Unwillingly, the ministers accepted Ben-Gurion's decision to use force if Etzel leaders refused to give in despite all warnings. Thus the *Altalena* was sunk, at great cost of life, and Etzel units throughout the country were arrested and its units broken up. Later, its men were enrolled as individuals in the national army. Though two Cabinet members resigned in protest and Ben-Gurion is still the subject of much criticism and everlasting hate on the part of some for this action, he did break up Etzel as a partially independent military group.

It is generally agreed that Ben-Gurion chose to have the Etzel showdown, with its final elimination of individual terrorist military groups, despite the abhorrence of the idea of Israelis killing Israelis. But he still hadn't won his battle for control of the army. While it seemed as though he had won his even more significant battle with the Haganah leadership on June 27, when its commanders had taken oaths of allegiance to the army and the government, there was still a strong opposition that manifested itself two days later, after Ben-Gurion announced a thorough reorganization of the army.

This brought about letters of resignation from the top former Haganah command, Galili, Yadin, Eliahu Cohen (Ben-Hur), and Ayalon. In his report to the provisional government he called the development an "attempt at revolt by the army." Accused of seeking to "impose his dictatorship on the army," he played his trump card on July 6: if his recommendations were turned down and the post of Chief of Command was revived for Galili, he would resign.

Although the Mapam ministers compared him to a dictator and the Cabinet members were generally unhappy about the controversy, led by Shertok and Kaplan they supported his position. Ben-Gurion had taken over completely; Galili retired to his kibbutz, embittered and thoroughly defeated.

But when the state was proclaimed on May 14, Ben-Gurion had not yet triumphed in his desire to create a unified army. It was still so Haganah-oriented that it would not give recognition to and fully utilize the non-Haganah-trained manpower in Israel that had previously served in British and other foreign militias.

Part Three

THE DECLARATION OF INDEPENDENCE

chapter

o o o o o o o o o o o o o o 13 o o o o o o o o o o o o o o

THE CEREMONY OF THE SIGNING

THE END of 1878 years of Jewish statelessness was proclaimed at 4:32 P.M. on Friday, May 14, 1948 (5th Iyar 5708, in the Hebrew calendar), at the Tel Aviv Museum on Rothschild Boulevard when David Ben-Gurion concluded the thirty-two-minute ceremony of Israel's Declaration of Independence with the matter-of-fact statement: "The State of Israel is established! The meeting is ended."

It was appropriate that the new state was born in its newest, most dynamic, and largest city, one of the few Israel communities that didn't exist in the Biblical era. For Tel Aviv—whose coat of arms consists of a beacon light to the Jews of the world and a gate of entry to the Jews of the Diaspora—is almost completely a product of the immigrants who comprise the overwhelming majority of the people of Israel.

There was no count taken of the number of persons present at the ceremonies and published estimates have ranged from one hundred to four hundred; nor does anyone know how many invitations were issued. Invitations were sent to all members of the Va'ad L'umi, the Jewish Agency, the Zionist General Council, mayors and municipal department heads, party leaders, representatives of the Zionist and national funds, and newspaper editors and correspondents. Generally, people were invited on an organizational rather than a personal basis.

The Museum was chosen as the site for the ceremony, instead of the larger Habimah auditorium, because it was believed that its limited seating capacity would make for greater secrecy and security. It is likely that about 250 people were present, possibly fewer, and the largest single group present were newspaper editors and correspondents.

The invitations, which were sent by messenger on the morning of

May 14, were from the Minhalet Ha'am (National Administration) and had no personal signature. Ben-Gurion, who was to head the new government, normally would have signed them, but Zeev Sharef, the Administrative Secretary, has said that he didn't want to bother him, and besides the time was too short. The invitation read:

> Dear Sir:
>> We have the honor to invite you to attend the
>>> Session
>>> of the
>>> Declaration of Independence
>> which will be held on Friday, 5th Iyar 5708 (14th May, 1948) at
>> 4 P.M. in the Hall of the Museum (16 Rothschild Boulevard).
>>> We urge you to keep secret the contents of this
>> invitation and time of the Council meeting.
>>> Those invited are requested to arrive at the Hall at
>> 3:30 P.M.
>>>>>>> Yours Faithfully,
>>>>>>> The Secretariat
>>> This Invitation is Personal;
>>> Dress: Dark Festive Attire.

The secrecy invoked and the style of dress requested were honored partially in the breach. The morning newspapers, in what might have developed into a serious breach of security, announced that the new state radio service would begin broadcasting at 4 P.M. with the transmission of the ceremonies. And although Tel Aviv's two chief rabbis, Issar Y. Unterman, Ashkenazic, and Yaakov Moshe Toledano, Sephardic, wore frock coats and silk tophats, two Left-wing members of the United Workers Parties who were to be Cabinet members in the provisional government, Mordecai Bentov, Minister of Labor, and Aharon Zisling, Minister of Agriculture, were in white shirts open at the neck and without jackets or neckties. The generally shirtsleeved Ben-Gurion wore a dark suit and a tie for the historic occasion.

However, for the most part the site of the ceremony was known only to the invitees until about 3 P.M., when military police began blocking off the area around Rothschild Boulevard. Inevitably, this resulted in the neighborhood's becoming jammed with people.

Sharef, who in 1972 was Minister of Housing, after previously having been Minister of Finance and Commerce, was the unquestioned generalissimo who organized and managed the Declaration ceremonies; he was also more than that—the Secretary of the National Administration and

National Council, the capable chief civil servant of the emerging provisional government; a well-ordered man, trusted by everybody, he had the capacity for large plans and small details. Working closely with him was Shelomo Kaddar, later an official of the Municipality of Jerusalem, who as his deputy had labored since the previous October in making plans for the functioning of the administration of the new state. He supervised a large part of the details and coordinated the work of others who were pressed into service.

In charge of the preparation and issuance of invitations for the ceremony was Abraham Rifkind, a member of the staff of the Keren Hayesod. Having handled this sort of responsibility in 1946 at the twenty-second World Zionist Congress in Basle, Rifkind compiled lists of those to be invited and he handled, prepared, and distributed the invitations and planned for the physical arrangements. It was an assignment he took only twenty-eight hours before the meeting. Assisting in the envelope-addressing and -stuffing was a fellow employee, a young lady who later became Mrs. Rifkind.

The initial intention was to deliver the invitations, or at least as many as possible, on the evening of May 13, but then it was decided that nighttime delivery might arouse suspicion and endanger security, so delivery was made by messenger on the morning of May 14.

To forestall criticism on the choice of those invited, invitations were issued not to individuals as such, but to representatives of institutions and organizations. Only one protest was registered, according to an account Rifkind wrote years later for *Maariv,* and that self-effacing. Yaacov Fichman, the poet, complained that "there are greater writers than I, such as Uri Zvi Greenberg or Shimoni. Why were they not invited?" To which Rifkind answered, "We did not invite Fichman, the poet, but Fichman, the President of the Writers Association."

Rifkind claims that an effort was made to have the text of the Declaration enscribed on a scroll, and that a Torah scribe was summoned from the Orthodox community of B'nai Brak, but he found that he could not complete the task on time because of the delay that would result from his having to stop and wash his hands ritually each time he encountered letters that formed part of the name of God.

Otto Walisch, later president of Israel's Advertising Union, handled the physical details of the meeting at the Museum. Rifkind provided Walisch with £50 (about $200) to cover the expenses of readying the Tel Aviv Museum for its historic meeting and instructed him to pay cash for everything he purchased, not to buy everything in one store, and not to reveal to anyone the purpose of his purchases or preparations in order to avoid suspicion of what was being planned. The secrecy striven for was so strict that the Museum officials, though they had been told to cooperate with Walisch, didn't know what was being planned for their building.

Walisch first arrived at the Museum at 2 P.M. on Thursday, May 13, and spent all afternoon and most of the following morning getting it prepared. He was aided by Israel Dimant, a carpenter (who later owned a Tel Aviv furniture store), Shlomo Shayowitz, a painter-decorator, and an anonymous cleaning woman who scrubbed the floors, polished the chairs, and otherwise cleaned the building.

To provide a suitable background for the blue and white Israeli flags and to hide some nudes hanging on the walls of the Museum's main hall, Walisch covered them with two shades of a thick gray material that blended with the national colors; a nude sculptured torso in the entrance lobby was draped with a gray shroud. The windows were covered with blackout curtains because of fear of an air raid during the ceremonies.

A large photograph of Theodor Herzl, founder of modern Zionism, was of course a necessity, but to get a portrait of adequate size was not easy. This problem was solved by requisitioning a comparatively small portrait that hung in the Keren Hayesod Building and mounting it in a large frame, thus giving an impression of size.

Of primary importance was getting a parchment scroll on which to enscribe the Declaration, the final version of which was still not complete. But there was no parchment in all of Tel Aviv, except possibly in suburban Abukebir, but fighting was raging there and it was too risky to go through the lines, and so it was decided to use a substitute. At Bar-Levy's on Allenby Street, Walisch found a synthetic that looked like and easily passed for genuine parchment. This explains why all accounts of the signing ceremonies refer to the parchment.

But Walisch, aware of the historic implications, wanted to be certain that the "parchment" would hold up through the years. He brought the synthetic to the Institute of Standards on Dizengoff Street for quick tests, but the laboratory technician thought his request was insane and refused to cooperate. Unable to explain the reason, Walisch was driven to a homemade test: he tore off two slivers, placing one in water and setting the other on fire. As it neither burned well nor disintegrated in the water, he was convinced that his substitute parchment would endure. Even Dorit Rozenne, Sharef's secretary, who typed the final draft of the Scroll of the Establishment of the State of Israel (its official name), has always referred to the parchment on which the thirty-seven founding fathers signed their names.

Most accounts and recollections aver that the signers put their names on a blank sheet of parchment, but Walisch denies this. When he was given the text of the Declaration in a Museum anteroom, with the hall already full of invited guests, he affixed it with glue to the upper section of his imitation-parchment scroll, which he had attached to a wooden handle. Rolled halfway down for the signatures, the upper half, to which the typewritten text was appended, was covered.

Following the completion of the ceremonies, Kaddar took the scroll for safekeeping to the vaults of the Anglo-Palestine Bank on Herzl Street as previously arranged. There it remained until after the first truce when, some six to eight weeks later, Walisch reclaimed it and on the synthetic parchment inscribed the full text by hand on what is now the official scroll of Israel's Declaration of Independence. He told the authors that it was for years his best-kept secret.

The broadcasting of the proclamation ceremonies was set up under the direction of Zvi Lurie. Among the many technical problems that beset him, caused in large part by lack of proper equipment, which all had to be smuggled into Palestine, was the hiding of the large antennas so they wouldn't be visible to pilots of the Egyptian bombers when, as expected, they flew over Tel Aviv. In the evening he inaugurated the Kol Israel broadcasts in which Ben-Gurion made his first public address as Prime Minister.

In a last-minute flurry of activity Walisch hung paintings depicting a panorama of Jewish history to replace the nudes he had previously covered up. Among them were Minkowsky's "Pogroms," Chagall's "Jews Holding a Scroll of Law," Hirshenberg's "Exile," and similar works.

A few minutes before 4 P.M. a fleet of rented American limousines rolled up to the Museum with the designated signers, members of the National Council in Tel Aviv, for the ceremony; they were to become the provisional government, the Cabinet, and the legislative body who were to govern the country for a year until the first duly elected Knesset of 108 men and 12 women, including 3 Arabs, took office on February 17, 1949.

The final text of the scroll was brought to the Museum by Sharef. On his drive to the Museum from the Keren Kayemet Building, where the National Council formally approved the text, Sharef was accompanied by Nahum Nir (Nir-Rafalkes). Their driver, who had been instructed to hurry, was stopped by a policeman who held the car up as he prepared to give them a ticket.

Only after explaining that the Mandatory government no longer existed and that he therefore had no authority to give a ticket, but more important that they were carrying the Declaration of Independence and that the proclamation of the state would be held up if they were delayed, were they allowed to proceed without the issuance of a ticket for a traffic violation.

The last member of the Cabinet to enter the Museum, to the accompaniment of riotous cheers and the waving of flags by the crowd on the street, was David Ben-Gurion. As he and Paula started to climb the outside steps leading to the front door of the Museum, she was blinded by the strong sunlight and the flashbulbs and tripped on the first step. Falling heavily, she injured her right eye and was obviously in great pain as she proceeded, with Ben-Gurion holding her arm. Seated next to Quentin Reynolds, in a special section for VIPs, she nevertheless translated the proceedings for him from the Hebrew while applying a cold compress to her eye with a handkerchief dipped periodically in a glass of ice water brought to her by an attendant. Reynolds later joshingly offered to bear witness as to how she got the black eye. None of the three Ben-Gurion children was present; one of them, his son Amos, was in the Army.

Ben-Gurion and ten other members of the thirteen-man provisional Cabinet who were present, and Sharef, as secretary, were seated at a table at the south wall of the Museum under the Herzl portrait. At a table placed at a right angle to the main dais, thus forming a T, sat the fourteen other members of the National Council in two facing rows of seven each. Opposite them, in a semicircle, were tiers assigned to other dignitaries.

The reading and the signing of the Israel Declaration of Independence began precisely at 4 P.M. in the low white concrete building that was the former home of Meir Dizengoff, the founder and first Mayor of Tel Aviv. The members of the Palestine Philharmonic Orchestra, who had been secretly assembled in one of the Museum's second-floor galleries not visible to the auditorium, had been scheduled to start the playing of "Hatikvah" on a cue from a boy stationed downstairs that would flash a red light on the conductor's podium. But the music of the orchestra, to be piped into the auditorium by a two-way loudspeaker hookup, didn't come through. The boy, who was to flash the signal as Ben-Gurion opened the meeting with three raps of his gavel, was pushed back by the crowd from his vantage point and there was no signal. The formal ceremony marking the birth of the State of Israel thus opened with a slight change of plans—there was no musical accompaniment when the crowd spontaneously broke into the strains of the national anthem as Ben-Gurion opened the meeting.

Not at all perturbed by the change, he announced, "I shall now read to you the Scroll of the Establishment of the State which has passed its first reading by the National Council." In a room fifty-four feet long and twenty-six feet wide, with high mullioned windows on two sides, he proceeded to read the ten paragraphs of the Preamble, which set forth the historic background for the Declaration. Suddenly, the sixty-two-year-old Israeli leader raised his voice as he read the pivotal eleventh paragraph of the proclamation:

"Accordingly, we, the members of the National Council, representing the Jewish People in Palestine and the World Zionist Movement, are met together in solemn assembly today, the day of termination of the British Mandate for Palestine: and by virtue of the natural and historic right of the Jewish People and the Resolution of the General Assembly of the United Nations, we hereby proclaim the establishment of the Jewish State in Palestine, to be called Medinat Yisrael [the State of Israel]."

At these words, in the solidly packed hall, which was uncomfortably hot because of the movie cameramen's lights, the whole gathering rose as one, cheering and applauding, many of them in tears.

Ben-Gurion rapped his gavel for order and continued with his reading of the seven additional articles that concluded the 979 Hebrew words that comprise the document. It took him seventeen minutes in all before he asked everyone to stand "to adopt the Scroll of the Establishment of the Jewish State." *

With the audience seated after the historic affirmation by acclamation rather than by individual vote, Ben-Gurion announced that any members of the National Council who wished to express reservations to parts of the Declaration could do so at its next meeting, scheduled for Sunday. This was in accord with the decision agreed upon earlier that day when the Council affirmed the Declaration at a first reading after several members had objected to specific aspects of the document.

Ben-Gurion then called upon the venerable Rabbi Yehuda Leib Ha-Cohen Fishman, whom he had personally arranged to have flown from Jerusalem to attend the ceremony, to pronounce the traditional Hebrew thanksgiving prayer—the Sheheheyanu. In a trembling voice the seventy-four-year-old rabbi, who was to be Israel's first Minister for Religious Affairs, intoned the words known to Jews wherever they live: "Blessed be Thou, O Lord our God, King of the Universe, Who has kept us alive and made us to endure and brought us to this day. Amen."

The last business of the meeting, before the actual signing of the Proc-

* The full text appears in Appendix II (see pp. 405–407).

lamation, was Ben-Gurion's announcement of the first decrees of the new state: the hated British White Paper of 1939, with its curbs on Jewish immigration and land sales, was declared null and void, and all other Mandatory laws, to avoid a legal vacuum, were declared valid and in effect until Israel could adopt new laws.

Sharef then called the roll of the Council members to sign the Declaration. Starting with Ben-Gurion and ending with Shertok, he read the names of the thirty-five other members of the Council. Actually, only twenty-five were present to sign their names—eleven of the others were under siege in Jerusalem and one member was in the United States. They affixed their names in alphabetical order to the bottom half of the Declaration. As the members of the National Council in besieged Jerusalem had agreed to the issuance of the Proclamation, space was reserved in the proper order for their signatures on the document.

As his name was called, each signer walked to the middle of the main dais, where Shertok sat next to Ben-Gurion. As they signed, Shertok helped smooth the scroll.

As an aftermath of the bitter discussions about including references to Almighty God and religion in the proclamation text, Rabbi Fishman added the words "With the help of God" after he affixed his signature.

The American-born Golda Myerson, one of the two women signers, was crying uncontrollably as she signed. David Zvi Pinkus went to her side in an effort to be comforting.

Herzl Vardi (Rosenblum), as he was called up to sign, was told in a commanding voice by Ben-Gurion to "Sign Vardi, not Rosenblum." In the emotional excitement, he has recalled, he did as he was told and signed "Vardi," which was the pseudonym he had used for signing newspaper articles. When he asked Ben-Gurion later what prompted this request, Ben-Gurion replied that he wanted more Hebrew names to appear on the document. Though he legally changed his name to Vardi in 1949, Rosenblum never really used the changed name and he always lamented the fact that the name Vardi will forever remain on the Declaration, a name most people don't associate with him.

The feeling of the signers, in their moment of exultation, is perhaps best described by Chaim Shapira, who later said that as he signed the Declaration, he felt he was reliving the words of the psalmists: "When the Lord caused us to return to Zion, we were as dreamers." He adds, "It was a dream, a dream which we had never believed would come true in our lifetime. A miracle had happened!"

When Shertok, who was to be Israel's first Foreign Minister, signed

the document, the last to do so, he received a tremendous ovation in recognition of the extraordinary role he had played in New York as the
chief representative of the Yishuv in the political struggle at the United
Nations following the partition vote of the previous November.

Certainly the most politically sophisticated of all the signers and
whose fears for the future were based on the greatest knowledge of the international situation, Shertok has recalled that he signed the Declaration
with "a sense of excitement together with a clear premonition of danger
such as a man might feel while standing on a cliff, ready to leap into a
yawning chasm. We felt as though we stood on a very high crest, where
roaring winds were brewing about us, and that we had to stand fast."

With Shertok signing his name, the seventy-man Palestine Philharmonic Orchestra, conducted by Joseph Kaminski, struck up "Hatikvah."
As its last plaintive notes faded, Ben-Gurion spoke up: "The State of Israel is established! The meeting is ended."

Later, alone in his office at Haganah headquarters, Ben-Gurion wrote
in his diary: "At 4 P.M. the Declaration of Independence. The people are
profoundly happy. And I am filled with foreboding."

Still later at home, in talking about the military reports he was receiving, he said to his wife, Paula, "I feel like the bereaved among the rejoic-
ers."

TO POSTPONE OR NOT POSTPONE
THE PROCLAMATION

THERE IS STILL a reluctance on the part of the signers and others closely involved, particularly the Israelis, to reveal the inner doubts of those who opposed the proclamation, almost as though it were treasonable or at least cowardice to have held such a view. When in 1961, Eliezer Whartman, an Israeli journalist, taped interviews with the surviving signers, he didn't get very far when he tried to pin people down on this score. There is no doubt that the driving force for immediate statehood was Ben-Gurion and that he made the ultimate decision. He persuaded the Jewish Agency and the Va'ad L'umi to go along with the proclamation of statehood, even though some of its key leaders opposed at least the timing.

In a 1971 interview in the *London Observer* Mrs. Meir said of him, "If ever there was a man who altered the trend of history it was Ben-Gurion. If there had not been a man who would take the risk of decision in 1948, the State of Israel would not then have come into existence. And if not then, when; or even whether."

There is much controversy as to the views of Shertok; certainly he had questions as to the wisdom of the timing of the proclamation after his discussions with Secretary of State George C. Marshall, US Chief of Staff during World War II, who sought to prevent war in the Middle East and had serious doubts as to the Yishuv's ability to defend itself against the Arabs after proclaiming the state. But Ben-Gurion has always said that Shertok did not oppose the proclamation. Whether he did when he left

America and changed his mind in Tel Aviv after sensing the public attitude and seeing Ben-Gurion privately is the unanswerable question.

In *Ben Gurion: The Armed Prophet* Michael Bar-Zohar, who had
considerable access to Ben-Gurion's diaries and his confidence in the writing of his book, tells a story attributed to Eliezer Livne. A few days before
Shertok returned to Palestine, Livne recalls asking Ben-Gurion, "Why
don't you announce that the State will be proclaimed on that date?"

To which the answer is said to have been, "I don't want to do that
until Shertok is back here."

"But he'll be against it," Livne said.

To which Ben-Gurion is reputed to have smilingly replied, "Don't
worry. I shall see to it that as soon as he steps off the plane he'll be kidnaped by my military secretary, Nehemia [Argov], and brought to my office. And I'll promise you he'll have a different opinion when he leaves!"

Bar-Zohar comments, "Whether or not this actually happened is not
known. Several persons claim to have knowledge of it, but Ben-Gurion
has never admitted it. However, the fact remains that when Shertok addressed the General Committee of Mapai (which certainly had doubts
about the immediate proclamation as late as early in May), he made a
magnificent speech in favor of proclaiming the State. His doubts and fears
had completely vanished to the great surprise of the Mapai leaders."

Shertok himself, in his book *At the Gate of the Nations,* firmly denied
that he was against the proclamation of statehood on May 14. He says he
went back to Israel to deliver a report on his conversations with General
Marshall, as he felt it was his duty to do, but even at the moment when
he received Marshall's warning not to trust the optimistic military fore-
casts of his generals, Shertok told the American Secretary of State that the
Jews of Palestine had reached a point from which there was no turning
back, that they couldn't pass up the historic opportunity offered by the
UN partition decision and the British withdrawal as the Mandate ended.

That Shertok was warned that he would be misunderstood in reporting Marshall's views to Ben-Gurion, the National Council, and Mapai was
the tenor of the recollection given to the authors on July 5, 1967, by
David HaCohen, Shertok's lifelong friend who for many years has served
as secretary of the Knesset's Foreign Affairs and Defense Committee. Ha-
Cohen met Shertok at La Guardia Airport, immediately after his interview with Marshall, while he was en route from Washington to Palestine.
After Shertok had confided the substance of his discussions with Marshall
to HaCohen, in the privacy of a phone booth, HaCohen advised Shertok
not to report Marshall's views to Ben-Gurion.

"But I knew this was advice he wouldn't take," HaCohen said. "It would have been contrary to his character to have accepted my advice. Whether he agreed or not, Shertok, a precise and lucid person, had to report to the proper authorities what he had been told, to state the facts fully and frankly. If Shertok had opposed immediate statehood, he would have said so bluntly without hiding his opinions behind the views of Marshall. He was a man of unswerving moral integrity, a fierce fighter, but not stubborn or mulish."

On the other hand, on May 3, at a midnight session of the American Section of the Jewish Agency, Shertok voted with Dr. Nahum Goldmann on the acceptance of an American truce proposal that would have involved postponement of the proclamation of independence. The vote was 4 to 2, with Dr. Silver, Dr. Neumann, Mrs. Halprin, and Rabbi Gold voting to reject the proposal originating with Dean Rusk that a representative group proceed to Palestine by Presidential plane to conduct peace negotiations.

The American peace proposal had been reported earlier that evening by Shertok at a three-hour joint session of the American Section Executive and the larger Political Advisory Committee. The American plan called for a ten-day adjournment of the UN General Assembly during which time representatives of the Jewish Agency, the Arab Higher Committee, and certain states would journey to the Middle East on a special Presidential plane for on-the-spot truce negotiations, an offer that, it was felt, the Arabs would accept.

A considerable minority led by Dr. Goldmann were willing to accept a proposal for a truce for as much as three months if, as Dr. Goldmann argued, two absolute conditions were met: the disassociation of the truce from trusteeship and an American guarantee of help in the event of an invasion by the Arab states in view of the fact that the Arabs were not barred from acquiring arms during the truce.

Those opposing delay argued that there was a possibility of early American recognition of a Jewish state, once it was declared, and that such a truce would involve recognition of the concept that an international authority could impose its will on the Yishuv. Everyone understood that the ultimate decision would have to be made by the Palestine members of the Agency Executive on the basis of military considerations and that the psychological and political pressures for statehood among the Jews of Palestine was so great as to make postponement almost impossible without a serious split of the Yishuv.

Even after the official midnight vote of the American Section Executive the matter came up for further discussion the following morning at a resumed joint meeting of the American Section Executive and the Political Advisory Committee. At that meeting those opposing deferment of a proclamation of independence, in addition to Dr. Silver, Dr. Neumann, Mrs. Halprin, and Rabbi Gold, were Leon Gellman, Rabbi Israel Goldstein, and Dr. Joseph B. Schechtman.

Those indicating willingness to accept deferment, under variously stated conditions, in additon to Shertok and Dr. Goldmann, were Jacob Greenberg, Rabbi Yitzhak Meir Levin, who was to be one of the signers of the Declaration, Dr. Siegfried Moses, Jacob Rivtin, Louis Segal, Dr. Otto Wolfsberg, Baruch Zuckerman, and Zvi Herman. These expressions of viewpoint were cabled to Palestine.

Dr. Goldmann explained his thinking many years later after the publication in *Unzer Wort,* a newspaper published in France, of a statement he made at a small private meeting of the French Section of the World Jewish Congress that he was among those who argued in 1948 that it was premature to proclaim the Jewish state before arriving at an agreement with the neighboring Arab states. After publication of this view generated wide and infuriated criticism, Dr. Goldmann, in a press communiqué issued in Israel on January 15, 1967, explained that "in the light of the experience of the past eighteen years, I was not certain whether it would not have been worthwhile to do in 1948 what I had advised then. Incidentally, I was not the only one who gave this counsel. I believed at the time that there were prospects to prevent a war if we postponed the proclamation of the State for a short while and took advantage of those days for an attempt to come to terms with the Arabs. I repeat that I did not advocate—nor had it ever occurred to me—delaying the proclamation of the State until we reached an agreement with the Arabs. Such an idea is utterly absurd. On the contrary, I was in favor of proclaiming the State without any delay because I believed that time was working against us. Therefore, I did not, and could not, say that we should have waited for agreement with the Arabs before proclaiming the State. All I said was that it would have been desirable to wait for a short time to try and prevent a war."

In a later interview with the authors in New York, Dr. Goldmann amplified the thinking behind his position—which, he said, Shertok had supported—that a delay of a few weeks in the proclamation of independence might have averted the costly War of Liberation and might even have changed the whole course of later Arab-Israeli relationships.

His thinking was based on the fact that the Arabs had their backs against the wall as they realized that both the United States and the Soviet Union would recognize the Jewish state. With this fact of politics in mind and given a little time, Dr. Goldmann stated, the Arabs might well have accepted a peaceful face-saving compromise. Dr. Goldmann claimed that he had been told by sources in the Egyptian Embassy that this was possible, although he can't be sure that Cairo had been informed that its embassy in Washington had engaged in such talks.

Goldmann said that a two- or three-week delay in the independence proclamation would not have hurt the cause of eventual statehood and that without the resulting War of Liberation, the continued hostility and fighting with the Arab states that has since plagued Israel and the Middle East might have been averted.

He also points out that the State Department had documentation on the great pressure campaign being conducted by American Jewry in behalf of statehood, and that Under Secretary of State Robert Lovett had called him to the State Department early in May to show him a "black book" of evidence that might be published. This threatened publication and the possible halting of all American financial aid to Palestine, including an embargo on the transmission of United Jewish Appeal funds, made precipitate action on statehood very dangerous.

The veteran Zionist leader admitted, however, that he understood how Jewish diplomats and supporters in the United States could see the need and value of postponement whereas Palestinians couldn't be so cool as the problem there was different. "If I were in Israel, I might have felt different," he admitted.

No one really opposed the idea of statehood and the ending of the British Mandate; it was just that they feared that a premature proclamation might end with the destruction of all the progress already achieved in the Yishuv. In Palestine this caution dictated the views of such influential leaders as Eliezer Kaplan, David Horowitz, and Joseph Sprinzak—all close associates of Ben-Gurion. There was also some opposition from Mapam leaders who still held out for a binational state rather than the all-Jewish state that was being proclaimed.

But Ben-Gurion correctly sensed the situation. With the British Empire beginning to disintegrate, he felt that independence might never come to pass if the Jewish state were not proclaimed promptly. In this he was fully supported by the Revisionists and the dissident Irgunists and Sternists, who announced that if the state were not proclaimed by the governing Jewish powers, they would proclaim it themselves.

Aside from the support in the United States of the majority of the Silver-led American Section Executive, a strong voice favoring the immediate proclamation of independence came from Dr. Weizmann, despite his historic differences with Ben-Gurion and his lifelong reputation for compromise. A few days before the proclamation Ben-Gurion asked Meyer Weisgal, Dr. Weizmann's closest confidant, to get Dr. Weizmann's views for him. As telephone and telegraphic communication between Palestine and the US was closed, he arranged for air passage to Nice for Weisgal from where he phoned Dr. Weizmann. After informing Dr. Weizmann that Ben-Gurion sought his views on the immediate proclamation of statehood, Dr. Weizmann, speaking in Yiddish, asked, "What are they waiting for?" Weisgal then sent a cable to Ben-Gurion: "The answer is yes."

Weizmann also conveyed his feelings to Ben-Gurion through Shertok, just before his return to Palestine. "Moshe," he said, "don't let them weaken, don't let them swerve, don't let them spoil the victory—the Jewish state, nothing less." Then, to emphasize his view, Dr. Weizmann telephoned Shertok at the airport before he left for Palestine to urge him to repeat his message: "Proclaim the Jewish state—now or never."

Ben-Gurion has issued many and conflicting statements on the proclamation through the years, though he has steadfastly refused to admit that he had any questions as to the ultimate decision, although he may have had fears and doubts.

He once told the writer, D. R. Elston, "The state has been here all the time—from 1918 onward at the very least. It was just a question of filling up its corners with more people and formulating it in the conventional design. We did not fight in 1948 to establish the state. We fought to defend it. The UN gave it international sanction and then ran away. We brought it about ourselves."

Discussing the odds pro and con for a successful confrontation with the Arabs after the issuance of the proclamation, Ben-Gurion told Moshe Pearlman many years later that he was influenced by the recollection of his experiences in London during the Nazi bombardment. "I have seen what a nation is capable of doing in an hour of supreme trial," he said. "I have seen what man can do. This is what the Jewish people can do."

In 1952 he philosophized, "The rebirth of Israel is unlike that of many states in recent days. It was not something restricted to the bounds of the people which brought it about, or of the land in which it took place. It was not by chance that the question of it was debated in the highest forum of modern mankind—the [General] Assembly of the United Nations. And if it be the case that it was determined and decided, in effect, by virtue of our own exploits and military strength, and our own victory in battle, yet in principle it was settled and accepted by the nations of the world and, among them, by the two outstanding powers of our times, the United States of America and the Soviet Union."

Sometimes Ben-Gurion denigrated the celebration of Independence Day, as in Los Angeles, on February 7, 1967, when he told Mrs. Justin Turner, in answer to the question as to what was the most important day in Israel's history, that it was not May 14, 1948, but rather July 1, 1945, when he met in New York with the group of influential American men who organized the Sonneborn Institute and agreed to work under cover to provide the Jews of Palestine with the arms that would be necessary to win independence. "This," he said, "was the most important day in the history of Israel."

THE FIGHT OVER THE TEXT

A DEBATE OVER whether there should be a reference to "Almighty God" in Israel's Declaration of Independence delayed the final approval of the text to scarcely more than two hours before the actual signing ceremony at the Tel Aviv Museum. This debate took place at the third meeting of the National Council ("The Thirty-seven") which convened at 1:50 P.M. in the hall of the Jewish National Fund Building on Herman Shapira Street. But with Jerusalem under siege and closed to all but very limited air traffic, only the twenty-five members who were to sign the Declaration later that day were present.

The previous day the shadow cabinet (also known as "The Thirteen" and the National Administration) had debated the religious issue. Aharon Zisling and Mordecai Bentov led a fight of the Left wing against the inclusion of any reference to "Almighty God." Moshe Shapira, who argued that he couldn't conceive of any omission of the divine name in a document to be signed not only in the name of the Jewish community of Israel but also for world Jewry, urged inclusion of "The God of Israel" or at least "The Almighty and Redeemer of Israel."

No agreement was reached at this meeting and it was suggested that the matter be turned over to a subcommittee composed of Ben-Gurion, Rabbi Fishman, Shertok, and Zisling with authority to agree on a final text to be placed before the National Council on May 14. Ben-Gurion assented on condition that everyone agreed to the inclusion of "Almighty God" and the omission of any reference to "Redeemer."

The final compromise used the Hebrew phrase *"Tsur Israel,"* which could be translated into English as "Rock of Israel," a phrase open to various interpretations that would satisfy all points of view.

Ben-Gurion had worked on the Declaration the night before the meeting of the subcommittee at his home on the morning of May 14. He had removed all of the "whereases," inserted a new first paragraph, shortened other paragraphs, and made other slight changes. But except for cutting the draft by about 25 percent from that considered at the earlier meeting of "The Thirteen" and eliminating the "whereases," the final document was largely the work of Shertok. It was this that the subcommittee offered the National Council for approval.

In opening the meeting of the National Council, Ben-Gurion said, "This day is one of prospects and perils. We have not had such possibilities and such dangers for ages: (a) the Mandate has expired, foreign rule is gone, and we must establish a Jewish regime; (b) war has been declared on us and that war will be intensified with the invasion of regular Arab armies." He presented two documents for approval: the Declaration and a Manifesto that he called the first constitutional paper needed to create the instruments for a Jewish regime.

The first speaker was Meir Wilner, a Communist, who, after protesting the Council's lack of democratic procedures, urged a number of amendments guaranteeing additional civil liberties and support for the "forces of progress, people's democracy, and peace . . . as opposed to the antidemocratic and militaristic forces."

Abraham Granovsky (Granott) of Mapai urged the inclusion of some mention of the DP camps and the additional guarantee of the freedom of language as being more specific than freedom of culture, this in deference to the equality of the Arab language with Hebrew.

The Revisionist Herzl Vardi criticized the phraseology for its implied acceptance of the UN partition of Palestine, with its limitations of the boundaries of the new state being those defined by the UN.

Aharon Zisling of Mapam, while admitting the right and guarantee of religious observance to those who desired it, reopened the discussion on this subject by urging the elimination of the phrase "With trust in the Rock of Israel," which he said, "forces upon us a formula which is not in accordance with our real feelings."

Shertok answered all four speakers on their suggestions for changes. He rejected the Communist charge that democratic procedures were not followed on the grounds that there wasn't time for any other course of action. And he defended the draft phraseology the critics sought to change.

David Zvi Pinkus of Mizrachi suggested the addition of the words

"The land of Israel is the land destined for the Jewish People according to the law and the Prophets in that land."

At this point Ben-Gurion said, "The debate is closed," and commented:

· "Mr. Wilner's grievance about antidemocratic procedures is justified, but there just isn't time for meetings in the emergency crisis.

· This is a proclamation, not a constitution. At a meeting on Sunday, May 16, the formulation of a constiution will be discussed.

· Boundaries are not spelled out in the proclamation; they have been left 'open to the course of events.'

· Each of us, in his own way, believes in the Rock of Israel as he conceives it. I should like to make one request: don't let me put this phrase to a vote."

Ben-Gurion then asked that the text of the Declaration be adopted unanimously. When there was continued opposition and expressions of desire to vote on aspects of the text, Ben-Gurion said that the signers could voice their opinions at a later meeting, after the state came into being. He said that he would, however, refuse to allow anyone to sign the document while noting reservations to particular paragraphs.

"Now I ask all those in favor of the present text as a whole to raise their hands."

All members raised their hands.

Felix Rosenblueth (Pinhas Rosen) presented the Manifesto, which, he said, was deemed necessary to fill a legal void "in the area of jurisdiction." It covered three major points:

1. It established the National Council ("The Thirty-seven") as the legislative authority and the provisional government for the State of Israel, and empowered it to adopt emergency legislation.
2. It retroactively abrogated the White Paper of 1939 and subsequent regulations of 1939, 1940, 1941, and 1945 with their limitations on immigration, land transfer, and Haganah.
3. With these exceptions it authorized the continuance of laws and regulations of the Mandate until changed by the new authority.

There was some opposition by the Leftists on the principle that democratic procedures were being violated, but Ben-Gurion prevailed, arguing that it was necessary to grant power for use in an emergency war situation. The Manifesto was adopted by a rising vote as the National Council adjourned until the 4 P.M. meeting for the signing of the Declaration of Independence.

The name of the new state was also a controversial question that was not definitely decided until late in the evening of May 12 at a meeting of "The Thirteen." Many had expected—in fact, a number of newspapers published it as a definite decision—that the name of the new state would be Judea. Staunchly urged by Yitzhak Gruenbaum and others, this was largely voted down because it referred only to the area immediately surrounding Jerusalem. Zion was similarly rejected because it was the name of a hill overlooking the Old City, although one argument advanced in its favor was that with "z" being the last letter of the alphabet, "Zion" would have an advantage in roll-call votes at the UN. One member suggested "Ever," from the root word *"Ivri"* ("Hebrew"). Berl Repetur preferred "Jewish State," which Gruenbaum preferred to "Israel."

There was strong support for "Eretz Israel," long the traditional name among Jews, but this meant all of ancient Palestine, and some felt that this would have been contrary to the UN resolution of authorization for the Jewish state. Meir David Levinstein, of the Orthodox Agudat Israel, was among those who urged the choice of "Eretz Israel" over "Israel," which he regarded as a shortening of the historic name. But Ben-Gurion and others were against a two-word name.

The great majority of the thirty-seven signers preferred "Israel" or "Eretz Israel," so when Ben-Gurion finally proposed "Israel," the choice was popular. It was adopted by a vote of 6 to 3. Four members of the National Administration were absent. It was selected only after voice tests to see how "Israel government," "the Navy of Israel," "Israel Consul," and "Israel citizen" sounded.

Most people agree that it was Ben-Gurion who actually chose the name, and many published versions give him credit for first suggesting it. He has said that he couldn't say who first suggested "Israel" as the new state's name, but that he strongly supported its choice. Shertok and others credit David Remez with first suggesting it. But Itzhak Ben Zvi, Israel's second President, said that a writer, Aharon Reuveni, suggested the name "Israel" as far back as three days after the UN partition resolution, and he showed a newspaper clipping from the *Palestine Post* of December 5, 1947, in which Reuveni made the suggestion in an English-language article.

Ben-Gurion, writing about the argument over the new state's name, said in the newspaper *Davar* of January 29, 1965, "Seven members [*sic*] voted for the name of Israel. Aharon Zisling opposed it and any other name which would be objectionable to Arabs living in the state because of its emotional or religious association with Jewishness. Pinhas Rosen suggested the state have two names: Israel to be used in Hebrew, and one to be used in Arabic, something like Western Palestine or a combination of Israel and Western Palestine. Shertok said, 'I too prefer a name that will not compel the Arab citizens to identify with the Jewish people.'"

Ben-Gurion then quotes himself as saying, "If Arabic pronunciation or meaning is what bothers you, then I suggest coopting Shertok to the committee which will make the final decision regarding the state's name."

The name finally chosen, Israel, is a Hebrew word for the "Children of God." The literal meaning, "He who strives with God," was given as a surname to Jacob, grandson of the patriarch Abraham, after Jacob wrestled with the angel ("Thy name shall be called no more Jacob, but Israel; for as a prince hast thou power with God and with men, and hast prevailed"—Genesis 32:29). Thereafter the twelve tribes of Israel, headed by Jacob's twelve sons, were referred to collectively by Hebrew prophets as "Children of Israel" or "Israelites." The name later gained wider connotation as a synonym for all of Jacob's descendants, the Jews, and in this usage is often to be found in the ritual of Jewish religious services.

Although ratification of the official text of the Declaration and the decision on the inclusion of *"Tsur Israel"* in it did not happen until just before the signing ceremony, Moshe Shertok decided on the previous evening that there should be an official English translation. Conscious of Ben-Gurion's determined stand on the inclusion of a reference to God in the text, he assumed that the religious reference would be included— and he knew that the rendition of this phrase would be the main problem of the English translation.

Working late at night in the home of Eli Kerschner, Shertok and his aides struggled with this delicate problem. Fay Doron, the assistant editor of an English-language monthly who had been designated to direct the English-language unit of Kol Israel, argued for "With trust in Almighty God." She pointed out that non-Jews, for whom the translation was intended, would not understand "Rock of Israel" and would expect the proclamation of the Jewish state to refer to "God" rather than "Providence." As a final sentimental argument, Miss Doron suggested that in honor of the Orthodox settlers at Etzion, which had just fallen after a heroic and deadly battle, *"Tsur Israel"* be translated as "Almighty God."

"You've convinced me," Shertok said. Thus the meeting, which had begun at 10 P.M., was concluded at 4 A.M. after a night during which the participants had subsisted on black coffee while referring time and again to the Bible, the American Declaration of Independence, and Churchill's speeches as models for the English text of the Declaration.

Ironically, the English text as first published abroad did not contain the words "With trust in Almighty God." An overzealous censor deleted it from the press cables because it was part of the last paragraph, which gave the time and place of the signing of the Declaration and which he had been instructed to keep secret. Thus the reference to God, which had been so bitterly debated and which was held to be so important in terms of American and other overseas public relations, did not appear in the first and most important news stories that appeared throughout the world on May 15.

Miss Doron was right. Americans voiced surprise and chagrin that the Declaration contained no reference to God. The omission in the American press was the result not only of the censor, but also of some early versions of the document which had been sent to America before a final text was approved in Tel Aviv.

But the phrase "Almighty God" was included in the first English-language broadcast of the Proclamation over Kol Israel, following the completion of the signing ceremonies at the Museum. Appropriately, the honor of making that broadcast was given to Miss Doron.

chapter

o o o o o o o o o o o o o 16 o o o o o o o o o o o o o

THE AUTHORS
OF THE PROCLAMATION

THERE IS NO DOUBT that the final editing and changes in Israel's
Scroll of Independence was the work of David Ben-Gurion. Nor is there
any doubt that Moshe Shertok was largely responsible for the so-called
final version that Ben-Gurion cut and revised. But there were many other
hands involved in the writing of some dozen or more earlier drafts or
legal documents prepared prior to the one completed in Tel Aviv on
Wednesday evening, May 12, by Shertok with some help from the four
other members of the committee named by the National Administration
—Remez, Rosenblueth, Shapira, and Zisling. The subcommittee had
given this Hebrew draft only one reading because of the lack of time, and
in Sharef's judgment, was in effect the work of Shertok.

A careful and sometimes florid stylist, and with a good legal mind,
Shertok had started most of the paragraphs with "Whereas," and he had
written a lengthy twenty-two paragraph document influenced by Thomas
Jefferson and the American Declaration of Independence and having
some of the qualities of a legal brief espousing the rights and bases for Israel's independence.

Ben-Gurion objected to the use of "whereas" on the ground that it
was not Hebraic in style,* and he took exception to such phrases as "a
flourishing community," and "courageously and valiantly," and to specific
references to the "Plan of Partition." Following objections voiced by

* The full text of this version appears in Appendix IV (pp. 411–413).

others—among them Bentov, Fishman, Shitrit, Zisling, and Shapira—
a committee of Ben-Gurion, Fishman, Shertok, and Zisling was appointed to make revisions for consideration at the Friday-morning meeting of the National Administration that was to precede a meeting of the
larger National Council, which was formally charged with the approval of
the Declaration before its public presentation at the Museum ceremonies.

Shertok always contended that the changes made by Ben-Gurion in
the structure of the document weakened its logical sequence. He said that
he never objected to word changes, deletions, or the addition of some
phraseology, but he believed that "whereas" as a link between the paragraphs gave the text a continuity leading to a climactic impact—the actual proclamation—that began with "Therefore."

Thinking and planning for the proclamation went back as far as April
12, 1947, when the Zionist General Council (Actions Committee), the
highest-ranking Zionist policy body between meetings of the Zionist Congresses, voted to establish a state after the end of the Mandate and created
the thirty-seven-man Moetzet Ha'am (National Council) and the thirteen-man Minhalat Ha'am (National Administration), which was eventually to become the Cabinet of the provisional state. This was thirteen
months before the actual proclamation and seven months before the UN
partition resolution.

Core of the National Council of thirty-seven were nine Palestine-
based members of the Jewish Agency and fourteen members of the Executive of the Va'ad L'umi. A group of thirteen—Ben-Gurion, Perez
Bernstein, Itzhak Gruenbaum, Eliezer Kaplan, Moshe Shapira, and Golda
Myerson from the Agency and David Remez, Meir Grabovsky, Zvi Lurie,
G. Landauer, David Pinkus, and Mordecai Shottner from the Va'ad L'umi
and Abraham Granovsky of the Jewish National Fund—were set up as
a Joint Emergency Committee to prepare for statehood. When this committee disbanded in March, 1948, its legal committee had framed a legal
code and drafted a proposed constitution that outlined a government
structure and its ministries and had established a school for training diplomats and administrative personnel, compiled a roster of experienced
Jewish and British civil servants willing to serve a future Jewish state, in-
stituted vigorous recruiting for Haganah, and otherwise planned for the
future.

Serving on this legal committee, among others, were Dr. Bernard Joseph, Dr. Haim Cohn (later Attorney General and Supreme Court Justice), Shabtai Rozenne (later Israeli Ambassador to the UN), Professor
Edward Vita, Yehuda Galoni, and Uri Heintzheimer (A. Yadin; later As-

sistant Director of the Ministry of Justice). A committee in Tel Aviv, headed by Dr. Felix Rosenblueth, paralleled this work. Among its most active members were Zvi Berinson, then legal advisor to the Histadrut and a former member of Rosenblueth's law office, now a Supreme Court Justice; Mordechai Beham, an attorney; and Henry E. (Zvi) Baker, an Englishman who had served as an Assistant Attorney General in the Mandatory government and later became President of the Jerusalem District Court.

In the United States, following the partition resolution, the Jewish Agency named a committee of legal experts headed by Dr. Leo Kohn to begin drafting a constitution for the Jewish state that would serve the needs of Shertok and his associates in their appearances before the United Nations and also provide a legal basis for the Palestinians similarly at work.

Dr. Jacob Robinson, legal adviser to the Jewish Agency in New York, an eminent international law authority, who as a member of the Lithuanian Parliament had served on many of his country's delegations to international conferences, and Sir Hersch Lauterpacht in London also prepared comprehensive memoranda, outlining the legal position of the Jews of Palestine based upon such precedents as the Balfour Declaration, the League of Nations Mandate, the United Nations decisions, and other international agreements.

An early precursor, what could probably be called the first draft of a Declaration of Independence, as apart from legal memoranda, was prepared by Zalman Rubashow (later Zalman Shazar, third President of Israel) for the April 12, 1948, meeting in Tel Aviv of the Political Committee of the Zionist General Council (Actions Committee), of which the American Zionist leader, Dr. Israel Goldstein, was chairman. This document was approved by two fellow members of a drafting committee, Dr. Otto Wolfsberg of Israel and Dr. Samuel Margoshes, then a Yiddish journalist in New York.

As read by Rubashow, then as later one of the most beloved literary figures in the country, the key paragraph said:

"Whereas, after twenty-seven years of an oppressive foreign regime that had received Palestine as a trust on behalf of the world to establish a National Homeland for the Jews, that trust has not been fulfilled; now therefore, the Jewish nation will establish its own state and independence in its homeland. The Jewish State to be established will be ruled by justice, freedom, and equality for all inhabitants, regardless of race or creed. We call upon the Arabs of Palestine and the neighboring states for an alliance of peace and cooperation. Together we shall build a state as citizens with equal rights and in mutual respect, for our freedom is your freedom. Our lives are dedicated to defense, and the Lord of Israel will be our mainstay."

Overlong and literary in tone, the draft summarized Jewish history from the earliest days. In its original form it was published in the newspaper *Davar,* of which Rubashow was then editor. It was not so much a declaration of independence as a declaration of intent. A shorter Hebrew version was prepared by Chief Rabbi Isaac Herzog, according to the journalist Jon Kimche, who says he shortened it even further, to about two hundred words in an English translation. That this version was widely distributed in Zionist circles is probably why it was erroneously published in a number of English-Jewish newspapers in the United States and Canada, in the period immediately before May 14, as the official Israel Declaration of Independence.

At about the same time as the Jerusalem draft reached Tel Aviv, Rosenblueth sent members of the National Administration a lengthy memo in which he proposed two proclamations: one to summarize the events leading up to independence and authorize the provisional council of government to assume powers and administer the state; the second to spell out the structure of the new government and outline the functions of the Cabinet ministers. It also would authorize the continuance of the majority of Mandatory laws and regulations until changed by the new government.

The proposals from both the Jerusalem and Tel Aviv legal committees were essentially similar and complementary. They sought to meet the problems of transition from the British Mandatory government to a Jewish-controlled administration, and they endeavored to cope with the inevitable inner problems of party and personal rivalries and conflicts by setting up general guidelines.

With these memos as a basis, Rosenblueth asked Zvi Berinson to formulate a first draft of a proclamation of independence. Justice Berinson has told the authors that he prepared this document himself, that it was shorter than the first proclamation, and that he doesn't know if a copy is extant. According to Moshe Gurary, then executive director of the Jewish Agency office in Tel Aviv, and who served as secretary to a Shertok subcommittee on the text of the Declaration, Baker, Beham, and Heintzheimer worked on this draft. Heintzheimer, who had arrived only a few days earlier from Jerusalem, was the only man who participated in the preparation of the drafts in both cities. Rubashow and Remez, both fine Hebrew stylists, were privately shown this version and had a hand in its final formulation. Today Israel's President declines to comment further on the role he played in the drafting of the proclamation that was completed on May 10, except that he told the authors that he had a hand in its editing. This draft still referred to May 15 as the last day of British rule. Some sections of its text that did not give the name of the new state are preserved on the scroll as finally adopted. Beginning its last paragraph with "And placing our trust in the Almighty," this draft as given to Shertok and his committee consisted of twelve paragraphs and was only half as long as the later twenty-two-paragraph Shertok draft, which concluded with the same reference to God.*

The Shertok revision—with its logical presentation of the history of the Jewish claims to Palestine from the days of their forcible exile and dispersion through the first World Zionist Congress, the Balfour Declaration, the League of Nations Mandate, the Jewish settlement in Palestine, the Nazi period, and the United Nations decisions for the establishment of the state and for partition—was the document presented to the May 12 meeting of the National Administration. It was the sort of orderly legalistic brief that one would expect from Shertok's precise mind.

The meeting was also presented with the Robinson and Lauterpacht memos designed to set at rest, in legal terms, any doubts that a proclamation of independence was not in accord with the UN partition resolution. Robinson's thesis was that the Jewish nation had actually come into being as a nation from the moment the UN General Assembly resolution was adopted on November 29, 1947. He asserted that the UN resolution had not created the legal right that existed, and he pointed out that the conditions for establishing a state and maintaining its sovereignty had been fulfilled: the Mandatory government, together with its arms and militia, had withdrawn; the UN Implementation Commission did not exist and hence exercised no control, and thus there existed no deterrent to a Jewish provisional government's assuming the prerogatives of government set forth in the UN resolution and itself holding elections for a constituent assembly and proclaiming sovereignty. Though differing in small details, similar conclusions were reached by Lauterpacht.

It was at this meeting that the decision was made, largely at Ben-Gurion's insistence, not to delineate the boundaries of the state in the proclamation, Ben-Gurion arguing that the American Declaration of Independence set no boundaries. Following the other objections, criticisms, and textual revisions suggested, this meeting adjourned at 11 P.M.,

* The full text appears in Appendix III (pp. 408–410).

just forty-nine hours before the end of the Mandate. Shertok was charged
with making further revisions in the draft preliminary to another meeting
of the National Administration on Thursday, May 13, at 6 P.M.

One meeting was held by Shertok and his subcommittee in Gurary's
office on the morning of May 13. A number of suggestions were made
and recorded in interlinear notations made on Shertok's handwritten
draft, the original of which is now in Gurary's possession.

With Gurary's help Shertok ironed out a final text for the meeting
that evening, after which it was retyped in five copies by Esther Gordon,
Gurary's secretary. In order to obviate any possibility of leaks of the text,
Gurary asked her to take her lunch in the office.

Gurary recalls that they had particular problems with the phraseology
of Paragraph 3, dealing with the first Zionist Congress, and Paragraph
15, outlining the new state's dedication to the principles of liberty, open
immigration, equality of social and political rights without distinction of
race or religion, and the safeguarding of the holy places of all religions.
After the phraseology was worked out, Shertok asked Ben-Gurion to go
over the wording with him.

After this revised draft was typed Gurary asked Shertok what he
should do with this handwritten version. Shertok, apparently unaware of
its historic import, shrugged his shoulders, and so Gurary kept the original (during the war, it was stored in a vault for safekeeping).

It is this draft that was presented to the meeting of the National Administration on the evening of May 13 and that Ben-Gurion took home
with him that evening, to edit and cut down. It was the basis of the final
text that Ben-Gurion presented the following morning at his home to the
fellow members of his subcommittee, Rabbi Fishman, Zisling, and Shertok. Aside from the complete elimination of "whereas" and a general
shortening, the major change made by Ben-Gurion was the relegation of
Shertok's opening on the long exile of the Jews to Paragraph 2 and the
introduction of a new first paragraph characteristically reflecting his love
of the land of Israel:

"The Land of Israel was the birthplace of the Jewish people. Here
their spiritual, religious, and national identity was formed. Here they
achieved independence and created a culture of national and universal significance. Here they wrote and gave the Bible to the world."

A comparison of various sources, including official Israel Yearbooks,
yields variations in the text of the English translation of the Declaration
of Independence. A first translation was prepared by Shertok and Fay

THE FIRST CAPITAL

THE CHOICE of a capital city for the new Jewish state was a concern of the Yishuv leadership at least six months before the state came into being. Jerusalem was the sentimental choice, but because of the problems its selection would have generated at the UN and the fact that the city would inevitably be a battle scene, it was eliminated from any serious consideration.

Already displaying his fondness for the Negev which was to lead him eventually to make his home at Sde Boker, Ben-Gurion was in favor of Kurnub, a settlement in the Negev near Dimona now known as Mamasheet. But he knew it was impractical because of its inaccessibility and the fact that the Jews didn't control the area, and he never pressed for it.

Golda Myerson suggested Mount Carmel, but this site overlooking Haifa Bay was almost automatically ruled out after the British made it known that they planned to use Haifa Harbor as their final evacuation enclave.

Two small communities, Zichron Yaa'qov and Herzliah, delegated emissaries to plead their cases, with Herzliah pressing the sentimental argument that it was appropriate that the first capital of the Jewish state bear the name of the founder of political Zionism.

But the final choice lay between Sarona and Nathanya, with Sarona winning out because it was adjacent to part of Tel Aviv, and had more facilities readily available that could be adapted to the needs of governmental offices.

With Israel having arisen phoenixlike in large part from the ashes of Nazi Germany, it is ironical that Sarona was originally settled some seventy-five years earlier as a German colony by a religious sect, the Templars, and had been largely deserted by their youthful third- and fourth-generation descendants, who under the nationalistic impetus of Nazism returned to fight for Germany in World War II. Those who remained in Palestine were interned by the British during the war and later transferred to Australia, where they eventually settled. An observer, noting the hundreds of gabled stone farmhouses converted into government offices, and the dirt roads of the town built by German farmers, described the first capital as "Bavaria in the desert."

During the war period, the British converted Sarona into a police camp. As anti-British violence developed in 1946 the camp was enclosed with barbed wire and the Jews took to calling it the "Bevingrad" of Tel Aviv. When the British left the Tel Aviv area, they gave the keys to Sarona to the Municipality of Tel Aviv.

Following the British evacuation of Sarona, Haganah took it over as a training center, renaming it Mahaneh Yehoshua (Camp Joshua) in memory of a Haganah leader, Yehoshua Globerman of Kibbutz Yagur, who died in combat in one of the early battles for the control of the Jerusalem-Tel Aviv road. It became the headquarters for the Tel Aviv District Haganah command, the assembly area for the first imports of Czech arms, and the taking-off point for punitive expeditions against the suburbs of Arab-controlled Jaffa.

But before May 16, when the provisional government was to meet for the first time in Sarona—renamed Hakiryu ("The City") by the Israelis—difficulty was encountered in getting Haganah to give up its comfortable headquarters and in making financial arrangements with the Tel Aviv Municipality. Arrangements were finally concluded and the Tel Aviv authorities sent forty-nine-year contracts to the Jewish Agency for the government offices leased. Sharef recalls that he found this packet in government files, still unsigned, ten years later.

One of the problems that plagued Sharef most in setting up the government offices was the shortage of office furniture. His problem was partially solved when a boy ran up to him with a message from a port officer in Jaffa: "A ship stuck in port here is loaded with stuff you can use. Come and get it." The "stuff" was a cargo of office furniture from Czechoslovakia—ornate hand-carved desks and chairs and telephones in a variety of colors that ranged from vermillion to gamboge—all consigned to none other than the Emir Abdullah of Transjordan.

chapter

○ ○ ○ ○ ○ ○ ○ ○ ○ ○ ○ ○ 18 ○ ○ ○ ○ ○ ○ ○ ○ ○ ○ ○ ○ ○

THE SIEGE OF JERUSALEM

THE BIRTH of the Jewish state was only hours away when His Britannic Majesty's last High Commissioner made his exit from Jerusalem, but the city that had witnessed so many miracles would share in this one only through a simple and symbolic act of faith. Its participants were ten of the eleven members of the National Council in Jerusalem. The thirty-seven-man body was due to convene in Tel Aviv at 1 P.M. on May 14 to consider the Israel Declaration of Independence, prior to its formal adoption later that afternoon.

Established on April 12, the National Council had not yet met. Meetings called for May 4 and 5 had been postponed because the Arab siege and the desperate shortage of air transport made it impossible for the Jerusalem delegates to attend. In the last weeks before independence Jewish Agency headquarters in Jerusalem had been cut off much of the time from the main Jewish institutions and events in Tel Aviv. Tenuous communication was maintained via short-wave radio and two tiny training planes owned by the Agency. The flimsy Piper Cubs could carry only a pilot and one passenger on the risky hop from an improvised dirt runway in Jerusalem to Tel Aviv. The only other link with Tel Aviv was a Haganah-operated wireless telephone hidden on the upper floor of an apartment house that was almost constantly under fire.

The Jerusalem members of the National Council had complained often and bitterly to Tel Aviv over the lack of dependable transportation. Their continued inability to reach Tel Aviv during the decisive days before May 14 gave rise to rumors that Ben-Gurion was not eager to have them come. Some of those stuck in Jerusalem were said to have been lukewarm to immediate independence, and their votes might have resulted in a postponement.

Only two of the Jerusalem members reached Tel Aviv for the independence ceremonies. Mrs. Golda Myerson, who had been in and out of Jerusalem many times by plane and convoy since the outbreak of the Arab revolt, was headed for the city on May 13 for a final meeting with the High Commissioner. On the return trip her seat on the plane had been reserved for Yitzhak Gruenbaum, Minister of Agriculture-designate in the provisional Cabinet, and a former deputy in the Polish parliament. Halfway to Jerusalem the plane developed engine trouble and had to turn back. Gruenbaum had been booked to fly the air shuttle several times before May 13, but each time he was bumped by a Haganah officer with a higher priority.

On the night of May 12, Rabbi Yehuda Leib HaCohen Fishman, oldest member of the Jewish Agency Executive, had been flown out of Jerusalem to enable him to attend a meeting of the thirteen-man National Administration. Because of his age a special effort had been made to bring him to its final sitting, May 13, the meeting at which the text of the Declaration was agreed upon, subject only to editorial revision by a subcommittee on which Fishman served. Gruenbaum was also a member of the National Administration, but he did not reach Tel Aviv until weeks later.

At 9:15 A.M. on May 14, Gruenbaum and nine of the ten other Jerusalem members of the National Council trapped in Jerusalem—exactly a *minyan*—gathered in the second-floor conference room of the Jewish Agency building. They had arrived separately and by roundabout routes, ducking snipers' bullets and picking their way through shellpocked streets. Through the sandbagged and black-taped windows of the big white structure standing back from deserted King George Avenue they could hear the rattle of gunfire and the thud of mortar shells.

These ten, and an eleventh who never arrived, had confidently expected to be witnesses to and participants in the unfolding miracle for which Jews had prayed for two millennia. History was being made only forty miles away, but isolated as they were, it might just as well have been on the moon. They were aware that independence had been set for May 14, but only those with handwritten personal invitations knew the exact time and place. None of the prospective founding fathers in Jerusalem had received one. Although they were familiar with the general tenor of the Declaration of Independence as it was taking shape, they had not been directly involved in its formulation and had not seen any of the preliminary drafts. Nevertheless, they were prepared to align themselves in spirit and de jure with whatever was to be done in Tel Aviv.

The chairman of the meeting of ten, Yitzhak Ben Zvi, called them to order. In a brief session the ten unwilling absentees from Tel Aviv recorded themselves as in favor of independence, and Ben Zvi communicated the unanimous decision to Tel Aviv by radio. Thus the delegates who were not in Tel Aviv became the first to commit themselves to the independence of Israel, hours before the actual signing of the Declaration. News of their action, when conveyed to the assemblage in Tel Aviv by Ben-Gurion, evoked thunderous applause.

Besides Ben Zvi and Gruenbaum the men who voted in absentia, without knowing that a place was being left for their signatures to be inserted later, were Daniel Auster, a future mayor of Jerusalem; Eliahu Berligne, Dr. Abraham Katznelson, and Zorah Warhaftig, members of the Executive of the expiring Jewish National Council; Rabbi Wolf Gold, Eliahu Dobkin, and Moshe Kolodny (Kol), members of the Jewish Agency Executive; and Dr. Abraham Granovsky, Chairman of the Jewish National Fund. Saadia Kovashi, head of the Yemenite Jews Federation, the eleventh belated signer from Jerusalem, was unable to cast even an absentee ballot because the fighting on May 14 kept him from reaching the Agency building.

The Jews of Jerusalem had risen early on May 14, quietly jubilant but grimly aware that the fate of the Jewish state struggling to be born depended on the outcome of the battle for the city in which Jewish history was enshrined. It had suffered twenty sieges and been destroyed countless times and won and lost by many nations in its millennial existence, but no people had adhered to it for so long and with such stubborn and singleminded devotion as the Jews. To Christians, Jerusalem was hallowed because of its many associations with the life and death of Jesus. To Moslems it was equally holy as the site of shrines second in importance only to Mecca and Medina. To Jews it was the heart and soul of the Promised Land.

The Jewish people's tie with Jerusalem has been traced to around 3000 B.C.E., when Abraham entered Palestine and was greeted near Jerusalem by Melchizedek, king and high priest of Salem. On a rock atop Jerusalem's Mount Moriah, Abraham prepared to sacrifice his son Isaac to God, thus initiating the covenant between the Lord and Israel. King David made Jerusalem an important religious center when he brought to it the gold-lined ark that Moses had ordered made to contain the Ten

Commandments and then established his capital there in 1003 B.C.E. David's son, Solomon, built the first Temple on Mount Moriah about 995 B.C.E. After the Babylonians obliterated Solomon's Temple in 586 B.C.E. and the Jews went into captivity, the exiles "by the waters of Babylon" took an oath of eternal fealty to Zion and Jerusalem (Psalm 137): "If I forget thee, O Jerusalem, let my right hand forget her cunning. . . ." Renewed through centuries of persecution, dispersion, and messianic hope for the "ingathering of the exiles," this pledge made Jerusalem the singular spiritual, cultural, and national focus of Jewish life.

Separation of Jerusalem from the Jewish state had been agreed to with heavy hearts as a condition of the United Nations' partition plan. When the Arabs attempted to thwart by force the partition that created the Jewish state and made Jerusalem the focus of their rebellion, Ben-Gurion and his colleagues determined not to yield the city, regardless of cost. Zionism without the city of Zion had again become unthinkable.

When the Arab revolt began on November 30, 1947, Jerusalem had 100,000 Jews, 30,000 Moslem Arabs, and 25,000 Christians, some of whom were converted Arabs. A majority of the non-Jews dwelt in the walled Old City, together with 2000 Jews, "among the relics of antiquity and the shrines of many religions." The bulk of the Jewish population lived in the modern New City and in the surrounding suburbs.

The Jewish quarter in the southeast corner of the Old City was surrounded by Arab and Christian quarters. It consisted of a cluster of thirty-six synagogues, numerous religious schools and institutions, a hospital, and stone houses whose ultra-pious residents—the spiritual descendants of Jews who had clung tenaciously to Jerusalem despite natural and man-made disasters—occupied themselves chiefly with prayer, religious studies, and Cabbalistic and messianic speculations.

The Jewish quarter had grown up around a series of courtyards adjacent to a sand-colored wall, 160 feet long and about 60 feet high. Its 24 rows of hewn stone aboveground and an estimated 19 tiers belowground constitute what is known as the Western Wall (*Kotel Ha'Maaravi* in Hebrew). According to ancient Jewish tradition, the Wall is a remnant of King Solomon's Temple. Christians derisively called it the Wailing Wall because it was the place to which Jews went to mourn the destruction of Jerusalem and the Temple.

Modern scholars have identified the Wall as an outcropping of a stone retaining wall raised by King Herod in 18 B.C.E., when he rebuilt the second Temple that had been erected in 516 B.C.E., after the return from Babylon, on the site of Solomon's edifice. It was Herod's Temple that was razed by the Roman legions under Titus in 70 C.E. Some archaeologists believe that digging now under way at the Wall may establish that part of the belowground layers of stone go back to Solomon's era. The gray walls of the Old City were put up by the Turks in the sixteenth century, reputedly on foundations of Solomon's Temple. Some historians of the Masonic Order claim that masons brought by King Solomon from Tyre, in Lebanon, to build his sanctuary were the founders of Masonry.

The Western Wall, whatever its origin, is also one boundary of Haram es Sherif, a large enclosed plaza containing two of Islam's most venerated shrines—the silver-domed Aksa Mosque and the gold-domed Mosque of Omar, or Dome of the Rock. The latter was built by Caliph Abdal-Malik—not Omar as is generally believed—in the seventh century over the site of Herod's Temple after the Arabs captured Jerusalem from the Byzantines in 638 C.E. "Rock" in the mosque's name refers to the stone from which the Prophet Mohammed is supposed to have ascended to heaven; it is also the very spot that Jewish tradition identifies with Abraham and Isaac. One order of Christian knights, in the mistaken idea that the Mosque of Omar was the ancient Jewish Temple, took the name "Templars" after the Crusaders had captured the mosque.

The Western Wall has no formal place in Jewish ritual, but as a religious and national symbol it has always exerted an immense emotional impact on Jews. Praying at the Wall became a deeply significant act of religious devotion for the pious and a dramatic demonstration of commitment to the land of Israel for other Jews.

From the days of the first dispersion the Jews built their synagogues with the ark facing toward the site of Solomon's Temple as a sign of attachment to the city of David. The magic words "Next year in Jerusalem" have been recited for generations as part of the Day of Atonement and Passover services. "Renew our days of old" is the ancient plea for the restoration of the Temple and the rebuilding of Jerusalem heard in synagogues daily for 2000 years.

The breaking of a glass underfoot by the groom during the Jewish wedding ceremony symbolizes the destruction of the Temple and serves as a reminder that no happiness is really complete while the Jewish people are separated from the Holy City. The destruction of the Temples in Jerusalem in 586 B.C.E. and 70 C.E. is still memorialized by Tisha B'Av, an annual day of mourning, lamentation, and chanting of dirges.

After each catastrophe some Jews always returned to Jerusalem. To pray in Jerusalem was equivalent to standing before the throne of God, whose earthly abode had been the vanished Temple. The defilement of the

Temple by the Greeks had triggered the Maccabean revolt of 168–165 B.C.E., paving the way for Jewish independence and the rededication of the Holy of Holies. When the Bar Kochba revolt of 132–135 C.E. failed and the Romans again laid Jerusalem waste, they forbade the Jews to enter Aelia Capitolonia, the new pagan city erected on its ruins. But the Jews never stopped coming, individually and in small groups.

They were there during the Byzantine era and during the sanguinary power struggles of successive Moslem dynasties. Even during the time of the Latin Kingdom, established by the Crusaders, the Jews were not entirely wiped out. Lonely pilgrims, refugees from Europe who had fled before the marauding armies of Crusaders, and immigrants from Babylonia, the Arabian Peninsula, and Egypt slowly created a community around the Western Wall after Saladin regained Jerusalem from the Christians in 1187. Exiles from Spain and Portugal in the fifteenth and sixteenth centuries gave the settlement new strength. The dream of physical reconquest of Jerusalem died in the disasters of false messiahs, but the spiritual link with Jerusalem remained unbroken. By the middle of the nineteenth century, when Sir Moses Montefiore built the first houses outside the walled city, the Jews numbered more than half of Jerusalem's 18,000 people.

Until the division of Jerusalem that followed the establishment of the State of Israel, the Jews' right to pray at the Western Wall had been sanctioned by centuries of custom and internationally recognized in the Mandate for Palestine. The area around and the approaches to the Wall had not been in Jewish hands since the Romans leveled the city. And it remained so until June 6, 1967, when the Israelis occupied the Old City during the Six-Day War and reunited the severed city under Jewish sovereignty.

On May 14, 1948, the psalmist's prediction—"Our feet shall stand within thy gates, O Jerusalem . . . builded as a city that is compact together"—was no more than a fond hope. It was not even that in December, 1947, when Golda Myerson and Dov Joseph, a Canadian-born lawyer and veteran of the 1917–18 Jewish Legion, were sent to Jerusalem to head a clandestine emergency committee to prepare for the coming siege.

Step by step, Joseph built up a shadow administration that took over municipal functions from the fading British civilian authorities and began stockpiling food, water, fuel, and medical supplies. Despite British interference, the Emergency Committee also worked closely with the city's Haganah command in preparing for the takeover of strongpoints occupied by the British the moment they left.

Crucial nonmilitary duties were assigned to a hastily recruited Home

Guard (Mishmar Ha'am), whose members were identified by a "uniform" of raincoat, beret, baton, and armband. The Home Guard registered the entire population, issued identity tags to children, organized blood donors, built and maintained bomb shelters, and enforced blackout regulations. It also guarded water cisterns, manned roadblocks, served as fire wardens, collected fuel oil, supervised food distribution, gave first-aid instruction, and helped maintain public order.

Inoculations against cholera and typhoid were administered by the staff of an emergency health council that merged the resources of Hadassah, the health department of the Va'ad L'umi and Histadrut's Kupat Holim. Regulations were drafted for testing drinking water and the sewage system and for the distribution of serums and blood plasma. Hadassah doctors and nurses were mobilized for medical services and the Mogen David Adom (Jewish Red Cross) operated ambulances and cared for the wounded.

Because everything the city needed to survive had to come via the Tel Aviv-Jerusalem coastal highway, which passed through Arab-held territory, the Emergency Committee was also involved in the desperate seesaw struggle for control of the roads. Even Jerusalem's water was piped from wells at Ras el Ein, twelve miles east of Tel Aviv, and some of the pumping stations were in Arab hands. Any break in the convoy supply line would quickly create hunger because New Jerusalem was cut off from the countryside, its traditional source of food. The Jewish quarter of the Old City was dependent on what the British allowed to pass through the gates—and that was just enough to maintain the population from day to day.

Fearing rationing and price controls, Jerusalem's storekeepers at first ignored the Emergency Committee's order to build up a three-week stock of food. Food hoarders sold at outrageous prices. The ultra-Orthodox Neturei Karta staged demonstrations to protest "Haganah's eating of our food."

Only strict rationing and ingenuity kept starvation at bay. By the beginning of March, Jerusalem had no meat, eggs, milk, butter, or vegetables for anyone but children, pregnant women, and hospital patients. Risking land mines and snipers, women and children combed the open fields after dark for edible weeds. To save fuel, the number of bakeries permitted to operate was cut from twenty-six to five at the end of April, thus slashing daily production to less than a third of a loaf per person. Bakers who ignored price-fixing were dealt with by rump courts set up to punish ration violators and speculators.

In the Old City the Jews constantly faced hunger. There were some weeks when not an ounce of food reached them, because even when the British let a convoy through, it was blocked by armed Arab guards. The British tried to force the evacuation of the Jewish quarter by deliberately holding up convoys that they suspected also carried men, arms, and ammunition.

Women stood in line for hours in the hope of getting some of the matzoth brought into the New City by the last convoy to get through from Tel Aviv before all-out war began. By then the individual food ration was down to 800 calories daily; it had dropped to 500 for a while, less than that allotted in some Nazi concentration camps, before the Passover convoy arrived. One family gorged itself on ten hardboiled eggs sent in by the mail plane from Tel Aviv. The average meal during the siege consisted of two pieces of bread, a cup of tea, and a vitamin bonbon.

Hundreds of starving dogs and cats were chloroformed. Molly Bar-David, an American journalist who wrote for the *Palestine Post* and *Hadassah Magazine,* regularly scrounged scraps for her dog, Peter, from the guards at a British military hospital near her home in Talbieh, the last suburb in Jewish hands. Occasionally, British Tommies from the hospital brought fresh food they had swiped from their mess, and Mrs. Bar-David shared it with neighboring families.

Anticipating that the Arabs would cut the pipelines, Jewish engineers in the British-administered municipal water department conducted a secret house-to-house survey of wells and cisterns in the Jewish areas. Old and unused ones were cleaned and repaired, new ones were built and instructions were given for filling them with rainwater. This added 22 million gallons and, together with other water resources, provided enough to hold out for 164 days on a ration of 5 quarts a day per person. The Home Guard showed the people how to build indoor watertanks against the possibility of snipers' bullets puncturing outdoor tanks. Trucks of the Palestine Potash Co. were outfitted with watertanks for distributing rationed water; many truck drivers died at the hands of snipers. Few flower gardens survived despite pathetic efforts to save them by sprinkling with waste water.

There were no oil reserves because Jerusalem lacked storage facilities. In April the gasoline supply scraped bottom when the British halted fuel convoys. The trickle that got through was stored in jerrycans and tins. Some oil was snatched from abandoned Arab homes. Fuel for heating, refrigeration, and private cooking was severely restricted. Private cars almost vanished and buses and taxis were scarce. Garbage was carted off by donkeys.

Despite hardships, the Jewish population remained calm, retained its

sense of humor, and even planned for after May 14. Two pious Jews returning from the synagogue were overheard discussing the siege. Said one,
"We can be saved either by a miracle or by a natural event." "And what
natural event?" asked the other. "The coming of messiah, of course," was
the reply.

This was more than a witticism, for the ultra-Orthodox Neturei Karta
sect regarded the coming Jewish state as a calamity. Since it was being established not by messiah but, as they saw it, by impious Jews who flouted
Jewish law, the Neturei Karta reacted to the state's imminent birth as an
occasion not for joy but for mourning. To this day the Neturei Karta observe Yom HaAtzmaut, the anniversary of independence, with lamenta-
tions. At the height of the siege community-minded Jerusalemites met in
the basement of Hadassah's health center on Strauss Street to blueprint
the city's first YMHA. Sitting with them was an expert from the United
States, Louis Kraft of the National Jewish Welfare Board, who had
braved a convoy trip from Tel Aviv.

As the Arab noose tightened around the city, the United Nations, the
International Red Cross, and other neutrals made futile efforts to restore
peace through a truce or by declaring Jerusalem an open city. The British
imposed a forty-eight-hour cease-fire in the Old City on May 2, bringing
its people their first respite in months. Six days later High Commissioner
Cunningham enforced another precarious halt in hostilities in the Old
City and around its approaches by ordering tank and artillery fire on both
Arab and Jewish positions whenever fighting broke out. He made a final
try on May 12, this time to protect the evacuation route of the British
forces from Arab-Jewish crossfire.

In his farewell radio address on the night of May 13, General Cunningham sadly conceded British errors but appealed to Jews and Arabs to
settle their differences lest war destroy Jerusalem. "Sometimes 'here we
did right' and no doubt at other times 'there we did wrong,'" he confessed, but "if it shall be by our going we bring eventual good to the people of Palestine, none of us will cavil at our departure." His parting
words, before a brusque "Goodbye," were, "Let peace for the Holy Land,
which must certainly come, have its source in the Holy City, to flow there
from over the whole country."

During the last five months of Cunningham's administration, some
3000 Jews, Arabs, and Britons were killed and about 5000 injured in an
undeclared war. Nevertheless, Jews and Arabs alike agreed that he had
done his best but was frustrated and trapped by policy made in London.
Harry Levin's *"Shalom"* to Cunningham, in the last "Kol Hamagan"
broadcast before it surfaced as the radio voice of the Jewish state, was sin-

cerely meant. The many good deeds of the British in Palestine since 1917 were recalled and the hope was voiced that the Jews and English might yet come to recognize each other as friends.

After listening to Cunningham's epitaph to British rule, Hannah Hurnard, the British Protestant missionary who had come to Palestine to help convert the Jews, wrote in her diary, "It was sensible and good, with no sentimental nonsense about it. He ended abruptly with 'Goodbye.' It broke over me for the first time that Britain, our nation, was leaving the Holy Land." But, Miss Hurnard added, she and her fellow missionaries in the Mission Hospital Compound in Jerusalem were not leaving: "Our home is cleaned from top to bottom. We face whatever is coming with a clean house and clean bodies. We all managed to bathe yesterday and I washed my hair. So we turn to the future and new chapter that begins for Palestine."

Two hours after the British pullout and six hours before the new chapter began, a United Nations Truce Commission was still engaged in a frustrating and fruitless last-minute attempt to end the fighting that had engulfed the city. Appointed on April 23 by the Security Council, the truce unit, consisting of the American, Belgian, and French Consuls, was in session in the highly exposed French Consulate overlooking the Jaffa Gate and Mount Zion. The Jewish authorities in Tel Aviv were represented by Walter Eytan, who was unable to return from Jerusalem to Tel Aviv until mid-June, although he was slated to be the first Director-General of Israel's Ministry of Foreign Affairs.

Eytan found the meeting's atmosphere nervous and tense because "bullets were whizzing past or hitting the building all the time." There was neither bread nor water in the Consulate and the wine cellar was empty. The French Consul's immediate worry was how he would feed his six children. Like the rest of the city, the French Consulate was out of touch with events elsewhere: its radio was dead and telephone service was erratic. A Jewish employee who dashed out in search of refreshments returned breathlessly with only bad news: the Belgian Consul's chauffeur had been wounded; the Polish Consul was trapped in a ditch under Arab fire; the former British Consul, now calling himself the British "political representative," was sending snide messages to the Jewish Agency from his temporary quarters near the Damascus Gate.

As the tramping feet and grinding wheels of the British Army moving out of Jerusalem resounded on the morning of May 14, life in the embattled city had become a series of makeshifts. Emergency food, water, and fuel rationing was the order of the day. Home bread deliveries were stopped to conserve fuel, of which there was only an eight-day supply on hand; house-to-house collections—some called them seizures—of fuel oil from central heating tanks were stepped up. Restaurants and housewives cooked on wood-burning stoves—if they had something to cook. All but two taxis, reserved for emergencies, were ordered off the streets. Several small diesel engines and a generator flown in from Tel Aviv were hooked up as an auxiliary power station in the event that Arab saboteurs in the Jerusalem Electrical Corp. cut off power. Householders ran to and from cisterns under sniper fire. Children made a game of searching for mallow, a spinach-type of plant that became a food fad of necessity.

Business was at a standstill: the mails, courts, banks, and railroad had suspended operations; factories and offices, isolated by sniper fire and shelling, were closed for lack of raw materials and because of absent workers. Only the birds, who never left the city, seemed unaffected as they perched on tree branches stripped of foliage by gunfire.

If some of the birds had been carrier pigeons, the city would have exulted, for the most oppressive fact of life on May 14 was the almost total absence of communications with the outside world. Isolation was so complete that even the Truce Commission lost contact with United Nations headquarters at Lake Success. Not until May 15, at its last meeting, did the Truce Commission get the news, belated and by then meaningless, that on May 14 the General Assembly had designated the Quaker leader Harold Evans, as Mayor of Jerusalem. He never did get there.

When the electric power went off before noon as a fuel-conservation measure, all radios not powered by batteries became useless. Much of the telephone service broke down soon after, enveloping the city in a virtual news blackout. No newspapers arrived from Tel Aviv or Haifa. The one-page edition of the English-language *Palestine Post* and the single-sheet mimeographed *Yediot Yerushalayim* ("News of Jerusalem"), published by the combined Jerusalem staffs of the Tel Aviv Hebrew dailies, were so scarce that they became collector's items. The lucky ones with short-wave receivers picked up some news from the BBC and the Arab stations. But the majority of the population lived on rumors: what someone had heard from someone else; hearsay in the synagogues; gossip of housewives as they queued up for food and water rations.

Unable to get through the ring forged by the Arab Legion, the foreign press corps found itself trapped without adequate communications. They had been relying on short-wave transmitters in the British and American Consulates and the uncertain plane service to Tel Aviv to get their stories out. When the British "Blue Train" cable system moved to Amman on

May 12, most of the correspondents stayed in Jerusalem on the assurance of the Jewish Agency that it would fly copy to Tel Aviv until it could install new communications facilities.

Kenneth Bilby of the New York *Herald Tribune* claimed that the Agency reneged on its promise. He recalled the two weeks from May 14 as "a newspaperman's nightmare." Every day, he said, the correspondents "would wiggle from their front line hostelry, the Pantiles Hotel, to the Jewish Agency's press office in Ben Yehuda Street. They composed glowing eyewitness accounts of the battle for the Old City and turned them over to Walter Eytan, Gershon Hirsch, and other Agency officials. The dispatches got no further. There was no wireless set in operation and the vague promises of a liaison plane to airlift copy to Tel Aviv never materialized." Not until the US Navy flew in a high-powered transmitter and installed it in the American Consulate were the correspondents able to send one pooled message a day, according to Bilby.

Carter Davidson, the Associated Press correspondent, remembered driving back to the Pantiles Hotel, a two-story building one block from the King David Hotel, with the other newsmen after watching Cunningham's take-off to Haifa from Kalandia airport. On the way they had to remove, stone by stone, a barricade erected across the road of the Arab quarter through which they had to pass. The Arab owners of the Pantiles, where some twenty-four American, British, and Australian correspondents were living, had already fled, but two Arab boys stayed on and prepared what food the newsmen could scare up. Davidson recalled shaving that morning with beer from the cache that had been laid in because of the water shortage.

The Pantiles was in the direct line of fire between Arab snipers on the walls of the Old City and Haganah troops in the New City. Davidson still has the American flag that as a symbol of neutrality the newsmen tied to the handle of a garden rake and lashed to a dented radio antenna on the roof. They entertained themselves by singing updated verses of a parody to the tune of "Lili Marlene" written in 1947 by Clifton Daniel of the *New York Times* for a farewell party for Homer Bigart of the *Herald Tribune*. One of the eight original verses went like this:

> Far from Jewish Jaffa and Arab Tel Aviv,
> Rabbi Homer Bigart prepares to take his leave,
> Leaving behind him the Jewish state
> He helped create by working late.
> Farewell to thee, Rehavia,
> Farewell, Jerusalem.

Bigart had acquired the nickname "Rabbi" because of a letter from an angry anti-Zionist reader to the Paris edition of the *Herald Tribune*. Because of Bigart's alleged pro-Zionism, the letter-writer referred to him as "Rabbi Homer Bigart."

On the night of May 14 the reporters in the Pantiles pulled the mattresses off the beds and slept in the hallways, protected from flying shrapnel by the hotel's stone walls. At daybreak on May 15 they found themselves on military real estate controlled by Israel: a Haganah unit had taken up a position between the Pantiles and the Arab-held walls. Escorted to the command post of Col. Moshe Dayan, they were duly accredited as war correspondents. When Davidson moved from the Pantiles to the Salvia Hotel, in Arab territory, the Israeli authorities suspected him of consorting with the enemy. Somehow he managed to get a cable through to the Associated Press in New York, which wired London, which telegraphed Amman, which got word to Davidson's Associated Press colleague Dan DeLuce in the Arab sector of Jerusalem. The message gave him Davidson's new address—they were only a mile apart.

Farnsworth Fowle, then a CBS correspondent, was one of the last to leave British press headquarters in the David Building—which the press corps called the "Snake Pit"—because he waited to see whether Jews or Arabs would move in first. When Haganah occupied the building, he found himself within the Jewish lines. It was Fowle who first passed along to the Jewish authorities in Jerusalem the dramatic news that President Truman had recognized Israel. Shortly after midnight he was on the way to the main post office when he picked up the bulletin from the BBC. Near the Catholic Terra Sancta College, not far from the American Consulate, he talked with Haganah guards and Jewish policemen, wearing for the first time the blue-peaked caps "liberated" from the former British police. Only a few hours earlier 400 Jewish police, who had been released from their oath of loyalty to the British, had been hired on probation by the Jewish Emergency Committee.

For a few moments they were much too busy guiding military vehicles to listen. Stray bullets were flying high overhead from Arab roadblocks. So their reaction to the news was immediate and practical: "Fine—that means we can get arms." When the flash finally reached Walter Eytan in the Jewish Agency building, he was skeptical. "How one wished it were true, but surely the man was a babbler," Eytan wrote in his diary.

Eytan's reaction was not surprising. It was not until the early hours of May 15 that most residents of Jerusalem heard what all had expected but few dared to take for granted: Israel had been reborn. Few in the Holy

City actually heard the reading of the Declaration of Independence as
broadcast from Tel Aviv. Jerusalem received no copies of *The Day of the
State,* the newspaper published collectively on May 14 by all the Tel Aviv
papers, which contained the text of the Declaration and the new government's first pronouncements. Jerusalem didn't know whether it had happened or if it had been postponed. Contributors to and participants in a
miracle, Jerusalemites found it hard to believe until it stared them in the
face—the next day. The few who did hear Ben-Gurion's words over the
radio saw a good omen in a simultaneous flight of storks and many of
them made a wish on seeing them. While Tel Avivians danced in the
streets on Friday evening and Jews paraded in Haifa, any public celebration would have been too dangerous for Jerusalemites, even if they had
known that the state had been proclaimed. NBC correspondent John
Donovan, however, remembered attending several all-night parties at
which armed Haganah troopers dropped in from time to time for a quick
"L'Chaim." He marveled that no one was accidentally shot as the exuber-
ant celebrants fired off their sidearms in all directions.

In the Hadassah Hospital in the Old City, patients badgered nurses
for news and nurses asked the doctors, "Will we proclaim a state?" No
one knew for sure, but one doctor reported hearing Haganah radio calling
all Jews to tune in to Tel Aviv at 4 P.M. The first man brought to the hospital on the morning of May 14, where Dr. Abraham Laufer was ready
for Jewish casualties, was a British deserter. He wanted to fight for the
Jews but Haganah assigned him to Dr. Laufer as an orderly.

In the Old and New Cities the wounded were being cared for not
only in Hadassah hospitals and casualty clearing stations but in Christian
mission hospitals. Mrs. Bertha Spafford Vester, senior member of the
American colony in Jerusalem, worked side by side with nurses in the
American Mission Hospital on the Street of Prophets, in the center of the
fighting on May 14 and 15. In 1917 a sheet from one of the hospital's
beds had been used as the white flag under which Jerusalem was surrendered to General Allenby.

Hannah Hurnard had risen before sunup to catch enough water for
her morning tea in the St. George Mission just outside the Old City, and
then she went to hunt for fresh vegetables and fruit. When she returned
after 9 A.M., she heard the singing of the pious Meah Shearim residents as
they labored to build roadblocks before the coming of the Sabbath. In her
diary she wrote, "It is all happening as I imagined. Everything that goes
on seems interesting and life is overflowingly full. Our home is a little

heavenly oasis in the midst of The Valley of the Shadow of Death." At that moment a bullet ripped through the branches of the acacia tree outside her window.

While doctors and nurses at a Haganah rest camp at Arnona excitedly discussed the broadcast from Tel Aviv, some patients slipped away to join the attack on Arabs who had holed up in the Russian Compound in Jerusalem. At Kiryat Meier a small plane flew over the Haganah camp and dropped copies of the Declaration of Independence. It was not the final version as adopted in Tel Aviv, but no one knew or cared. Amnon Lor, a sixth-generation Palestinian, welder by trade, and Palestine's champion ballroom dancer by night, stood at attention with his comrades as the leaflets fluttered from the sky. Exhausted and grimy from hours of digging trenches, Lor and his comrades listened joyfully as the camp commander made a brief speech. Then they toasted Israel's birth in lukewarm tea, ate an early supper of hardboiled eggs and bread, and resumed digging.

At Degania, the pioneer kibbutz on the southern shore of Lake Galilee and the Jordan where they still remembered the days of Captain Trumpeldor, American newspaperman Thomas Sugrue watched the colonists feverishly preparing for the promised Arab invasion. When they heard the news from Tel Aviv, "we had a heavy feeling at Degania," wrote Sugrue, "because we knew we would be attacked and we decided to work on Saturday, even though it was the Sabbath."

Yigal Allon, captor of Safed, was walking in the hills of Naftali at sundown on May 14, preparing for an assault on Malkiya, when a girl radio operator came running with a message from Israel Galili, deputy Haganah commander, telling of the statehood proclamation. Allon knew it was coming, but like most other Haganah officers, he was so preoccupied with the hour-to-hour business of making sure that what had been done in Tel Aviv would not be undone that he almost forgot the reality of the great moment. In Haganah, Irgun, and Sternist camps everywhere, officers and men heard all or parts of the Tel Aviv broadcast with weapons in hand.

In Jerusalem, Irgun leaders breathed a sigh of relief when they learned that independence had been voted. Their chief, Menachem Beigin, had made arrangements to proclaim independence on their own in Jerusalem on May 14 if for any reason Ben-Gurion had deferred action. The Cinema Edison, at Chancellor and David Yellin Streets, Israel's largest movie house, had been chosen as the site for the Irgun proclamation. Ben-Gurion was aware of this plan since Revisionist headquarters in Paris had warned him by cable that failure to proclaim the Jewish state "would be a rebellion against the people's will."

At Haganah headquarters in Jerusalem, Harry Levin, Kol Hamagen's best-known announcer, heard the broadcast and then wrote in his diary, "The tension of weeks burst today. A tremendous weight has been lifted. The war is only starting but we are our own masters in our own land. Can't fully grasp it yet." Then he went home. On the kitchen table he found a note from his wife, who was out working on military maps: "Please don't get killed today."

Unlike the memories of the events of November 29, 1947, that remain indelibly vivid for tens of thousands of Jews, few people retain similarly distinct images about May 14. It is remarkable how many people can recall the most minute details of what they were doing on the day the United Nations adopted the partition resolution and how few can remember anything about May 14. What is even more significant is the number of people who have blurred both days into one. When asked about May 14, scores of them described events that actually took place on November 29.

The late Moses Eskolsky, an American who was then on the *Palestine Post* editorial staff, recalled that the events in Tel Aviv were cause for joy but that those in Jerusalem were more personal, pressing, and perilous. The siege conditions, bombarding, and starvation rations stand out more clearly in Jewish memories than what was taking place in comparatively secure Tel Aviv, Eskolsky said.

A battery-operated short-wave radio in the *Post*'s plant kept its staff tuned in on the agony of the Etzion settlements whose defenders repeatedly asked for a *"zippor"*—a "bird," Haganah talk for aircraft. They were calling for one of Haganah's handful of Piper Cubs from which bombs or grenades were occasionally tossed. The nearby Etzion bloc was being overrun by the Arab Legion almost at the same time as Israel's founding fathers were getting ready for its birth in Tel Aviv. This heightened Jerusalem's mood of depression, according to Eskolsky, at a time when the Old City's Jews were making their last stand and Arab mortar fire was pouring down on the New City from the surrounding hills.

Because Independence Day was on the eve of the Jewish Sabbath, and no daily papers appear on the Sabbath, the *Post* had the frustrating experience of sitting on the momentous story for twenty-four hours. The big headline spelled out in wooden type in the *Post*'s Sunday edition told no one anything he didn't already know. All through the siege the *Post*, under the editorship of Gershon Agronsky, missed only four printed issues, and these four were published as a matter of pride in mimeographed editions. As Palestine's only English-language daily, the *Post* was a particular irritant to the British. Whatever else it had to omit as paper ran short, the *Post* never failed to carry "Column One," written by David Courtney, a former British intelligence officer who went underground as Roy Elston when ordered out of the country. During World War II, he had directed a radio propaganda unit whose non-British staff included many Jewish refugees from the Balkans and Central Europe. From headquarters in Jerusalem's Convent of St. Pierre, Courtney beamed anti-Nazi broadcasts in Czech, Polish, German, and other languages to Nazi-occupied Europe. After his outfit was demobilized he became a Reuters correspondent in Jerusalem and gradually found himself bitterly critical of British policies vis-à-vis the Jews. His *Post* column was a tremendous morale-booster to the Jewish community, but Courtney's British countrymen ostracized him, gibing that he was writing "the fifth column," not the first.

A full moon that lit up the Jewish state's first Sabbath eve was the city's only illumination. The populace sweltered and thirsted on the hot night of May 14 but paid no heed to the shrill warnings from the Arab radio that by morning the Jews would be dead or driven into the sea. Rachel Ben Zvi, whose husband had presided earlier that day at the symbolic independence ceremony in the Jewish Agency building, spent her first night in free Israel caring for seventy children from Rumania and Iraq at the Pioneer Women's youth farm and school at Talpiot on the isolated southern edge of Jerusalem. There was no phone link to Jerusalem, but an overworked walkie-talkie maintained contact with Haganah headquarters at Moriah. While the children dug trenches, Mrs. Ben Zvi went to the Haganah post at Talpiot and over the walkie-talkie heard the voice of her son Amram assuring her "We'll get to you by tonight." Two months earlier another son, Eli, had been killed in the defense of Kibbutz Beit Keshet in Galilee. Amram's men, forty of them, arrived after midnight. They had made a six-hour roundabout trek to bypass Arab positions, bringing with them arms for the defenders of Ramat Rahel near Talpiot.

Israel's first day of independence dawned radiant, but Jerusalem remained isolated. Hurrying pedestrians in the New City that Saturday morning heard someone playing a Chopin étude on a piano and passed the aging Mrs. Judah L. Magnes (she died in 1968) taking her daily ten-minute walk, which she hadn't missed since the siege began. Her husband was in New York, having fought to the end for a binational Arab-Jewish state; when independence was proclaimed, he had gone to congratulate his old friend Dr. Chaim Weizmann. Norman Bentwich, another supporter of binationalism who had served as Attorney-General under the British, was in Geneva. Of the Ihud leaders, only Martin Buber was in Jerusalem on May 14. At about 8 P.M., in the apartment that the Harry Levins shared with David and Idie Goldberg, an American couple who had settled in Palestine, Dr. Buber heard a rebroadcast of the proclamation ceremony over one of the few battery radios in Jerusalem.

It was a solemn, worried community of people that heard the news of the proclamation in beleaguered Jerusalem. Virtually none of the city's leaders, civilian or military, was able to attend the ceremonies in Tel Aviv. Even if they had had any way of getting there, they were too busy defending Jerusalem, and they would have felt guilty of desertion if they had found a way to get to Tel Aviv.

The next morning more than one worshiper attending Sabbath services in the synagogues of Jerusalem felt that he was hearing the whisper of messiah saying "Amen" to ancient prayers being fulfilled.

chapter

∘ ∘ ∘ ∘ ∘ ∘ ∘ ∘ ∘ ∘ ∘ ∘ ∘ 19 ∘ ∘ ∘ ∘ ∘ ∘ ∘ ∘ ∘ ∘ ∘ ∘

TEL AVIV IS BOMBED

IT WAS APPROPRIATE that the day, May 14–15, on which Israel was born should end for David Ben-Gurion with a radio broadcast to the United States. The message was delivered shortly after 5 A.M., May 15 (Israel time), from the Haganah Radio Center at Mahaneh Yonah (Camp Jonah) on Hayarkon Street, near the present site of the Sheraton Hotel, because—as Ben Gurion phrases it—"our people in the United States demand that I broadcast to them."

The request to the new Prime Minister for the broadcast was received by Yaakov Yanai, officer in charge of the Haganah Communications Center, who picked up a message from a ham operator in New Jersey: "American Jewry requests Ben-Gurion to broadcast tonight. Awaiting reply."

Yanai relayed the message to Mordecai Shiloah, one of Ben-Gurion's closest advisers, but was turned down: "Not tonight. It's out of the question. The Old Man's asleep."

When Yanai received additional messages and the word that from thirty to forty American stations were ready to pick up the broadcast, he went directly to the Ben-Gurion home on Keren Kayemet Street. Paula Ben-Gurion opened the door and said, "Don't bother him. It's still the middle of the night." But when Yanai insisted, she allowed him to go up to Ben-Gurion's bedroom. Sitting on his bed, the Israeli leader agreed to the broadcast.

Still wearing his pajamas, with a coat over them, and in shoes and socks hastily brought by Paula, Ben-Gurion drove with Yanai to the transmitter, about five minutes away. In the car and at the station, while Yanai was handling technical details for the relay, the Prime Minister jotted down notes for his talk on a scrap of paper.

There wasn't time to send recording machines to Mahaneh Yonah to record the speech, but fortunately for posterity Yeshayahu Lemberger of

the Haganah Signal Corps (now Yeshayahu Lavie, Director-General of
the Ministry of Posts) thought to instruct Ralph Ellinger, who had recorded the Museum ceremonies, to tune in on the short-wave broadcast
and to make a recording right off the air.

In his broadcast in English, Ben-Gurion stressed several points: the le-
gality of the independence proclamation under the UN resolution; the
Arab violation of the UN Charter in declaring war on Israel; the dangers
facing Israel, its need for help, and its determination to fight alone if necessary.

Ben-Gurion started broadcasting shortly after 5 A.M., and when bombs
began to fall at 5:25, he interrupted his remarks to say, "At this very moment, enemy planes are bombing Tel Aviv."

"I was still broadcasting," Ben Gurion later recalled, "when the first
Egyptian bombs fell on Tel Aviv. I included this information in my
broadcast but I could not continue as the crash of bombs exploding quite
near Camp Jonah drowned out my own words."

After the broadcast Ben-Gurion left by car to go to Sde Dov Airfield
and the nearby Reading Power Station, which were taking the brunt of
the enemy attack. He has recalled, "Returning home, I saw the faces of
all Tel Aviv peering through its windows; it was just sunrise. There was
no hint of fear or panic, and I knew in my heart: they will stand up to it."

A few hours later, between 7 and 8 A.M., the first radio messages after
independence to contacts in Europe were sent by Haganah Radio. The
first, addressed to "Or" (code name for secret Haganah headquarters in Geneva), reported. "To Or and Friends [code name for Shaul Avigur and
Pinhas Sapir, Haganah representatives in Europe in charge of arms pro-
curement] from Hillel [code name for Israel Galili]. Tel Aviv bombed this
morning by three Spitfires attacking airfield and power station. Scored direct hits, but no great damage. Etzion bloc fell because aircraft lacking and
no reinforcements available. Aerial reconnaissance reports heavy concentration enemy forces on border. 'Balak 3' [code name for chartered American Skymaster with arms from Czechoslovakia] arrived and encouraged."

A second message read: "To Or and Friends from Hillel. Our Lady
[code name for Haganah arms ship, SS *Borea*] freed by British authorities
after midnight. She arrived safely Haifa port and unloading now. Rush
TNT by air immediately as explosives urgently needed. Answer at once.
Our antiaircraft brought down Spitfire which can be repaired and used.
Pilot captured."

The arms were coming through, the careful planning was starting to
pay off, and the battle for Israel's liberation was beginning to be hopeful
right from the first day of independence.

chapter

o o o o o o o o o o o o o o o o ☐20☐ o o o o o o o o o o o o o o o o

NORMALITY IN TEL AVIV

EVEN WITH A historic proclamation of independence in the offing, life
in a big city goes on with a normality that is both comforting and incredible. Tel Aviv, with its population of 174,000, was no different on this
pleasant day in May that began with a sunrise at 4:45 A.M. and ended
with a sunset that heralded the coming of the Sabbath at 6:34 P.M. The
weather was mild, with the temperature ranging from a low of 54 to a high
of 73. The climate was in this general range throughout Israel; no rain
marred the festivities on either Friday or Saturday, although it did cloud up
a bit on Saturday.

Galila Triffon and Jacob Hasson announced their engagement on Friday afternoon, almost as Israel's independence was being proclaimed. Earlier that morning Naomi Less of Ramat Gan gave birth to twins. A
Matchless motorcycle belonging to a Mr. Marcus of Ben-Yehuda Street
was stolen, as was a black Morris car belonging to A. Birk of 8 Brenner
Street.

There were no movies on Friday evening, but that was a normal closing for the Sabbath. On Saturday evening, however, despite the intermit-
tent bombings, the movies were open in this nation of avid moviegoers.
Three new films were featured: *In the Stream of Life* at the Esther Cinema; *Demon in the Flesh* at the Allenby; and *Queen Without a Crown* at
the Mograbi. Four soccer games were played on Saturday morning, as
scheduled. Immediately after the first two Egyptian bombings, Hapoel Tel
Aviv played Hashahar Nissim; Hapoel Hakovesh met Ramat Gan Maccabi; Hapoel Petach Tikvah fought it out with Kadima Hapoel; and the
Maccabi Menachem met the Kadima Hakoach. The Chamber Theatre announced the premiere of a new play, *He Walked in the Fields,* by a new
writer, Moshe Shamir.

As able-bodied young men enlisted and were drafted for the army, a few speculators and black marketeers plied their trade and were brought before the bar of justice. Pinhas Vinograd was fined for selling at the price of fresh butter "renewed Australian butter" containing a high percentage of "foreign fats." Itzhak Goldman was fined for marketing A-class eggs at the price of extra-class eggs. The court invoked heavy fines of £100 ($280) on each of the offenders, and others were fined for price-gouging and food-hoarding.

To keep living costs down and to prevent inflation, the Price Control Committee announced new prices for foods on Friday. A liter of milk was priced at 100 mils (28¢), extra-class eggs were set at 39 mils (about 9¢), a kilogram of cheese was valued at 320 mils (almost $1), and a kilogram of fish at 640 mils (about $2).

Yehezkiel Saharov, the newly appointed Inspector General of Police and Prison Services, issued a call for police recruits as he divided the Yishuv into four police districts and announced that "all former forms of organization and police administration in this country are canceled herewith. The new police force," he said, "will adopt the West European system of organization." He also announced uniforms for the new police force: "For the time being, policemen on duty shall wear khaki uniform, with gray visored caps. There will be no insignia until the state emblems are decided upon."

The Treasury announced higher taxes on cigarettes. The Dan Company's Bus Lines announced a sharp curtailment of services because so many of its drivers had been mobilized. All local insurance firms joined together to create the Palestine Mutual Insurance Fund Against Emergency Risks Ltd., and insurance of property against emergency damage was made compulsory.

Advertisements for a £5 million emergency war loan appeared in the newspapers along with obituaries published by the families and friends of those who had fallen in battle in the defense of Etzion and Safed. The war loan theme was "10–30," which meant that if you bought a £10 bond, you might be eligible later to buy $30 worth of American merchandise. The bonds were on sale in a tent erected on a vacant lot in the middle of the city.

By sheer force of willpower Mrs. Celia Nechama Amidror gave birth to what was probably the first baby born after the State of Israel came into formal being after midnight of May 14–15. An ardent freedom fighter, who was an officer in the underground Irgun Z'vai L'umi, Mrs. Amidror had been arrested six times by the British police, the last time in 1945. Released in the summer of 1947 from the notorious Bethlehem Prison, she became pregnant shortly thereafter. This is her story:

"I felt the first labor pains on Friday and asked my husband to take me to Balfour Hospital. He said I must be 'off my rocker'; according to our calculations, I still had two weeks to go. But I persisted, and he took me. The doctors said he was right—that I was two weeks ahead of schedule, and they couldn't keep me in the hospital that long. They sent me back home.

"On our way home, as we passed the Rothschild Boulevard, I saw the street filling up with people. I asked, 'What's going on?' Someone said that the state was going to be proclaimed that afternoon. I became obsessed with the idea of giving birth the moment the state came into being. A neighbor told me that although the state would be proclaimed that afternoon, it would come into being only at midnight, when the British Mandate terminated.

"My husband said it was impossible to give birth according to an historical timetable. But I told him to wait and see. I listened to the Voice of Haganah broadcast of the actual proclamation ceremonies from the Tel Aviv Museum. The moment they began singing the 'Hatikvah' I had some more contractions. My husband muttered, but rushed me back to the Balfour Hospital's maternity ward.

"They examined me again," she continued, "said it was against the laws of nature, but agreed to let me stay overnight just in case I turned out to be right. I kept looking at my watch. Tension and pains mounted as the hour approached midnight. There was no one else in the maternity ward, and although quite a few women gave birth to children throughout Israel on May 15, I was the only one who timed my labors parallel with the termination of British rule.

"At midnight I yelled 'It's the end of the Mandate, we are free!' A great sense of relief came over me. I drifted over to physical and spiritual release. At five minutes past midnight, the doctor congratulated me: 'It's a boy, Mrs. Teplitzky'—that was my name then—'a healthy, robust boy.'

"It was the first baby born in the Jewish state. He is a soldier now. His name? Israel, of course."

Among other babies born that day—according to the records of the Kupat Holim's Bellinson Hospital in Petach Tikvah on the outskirts of Tel Aviv—were (on May 14) Rivka, daughter of Mr. and Mrs. Aharon Podlinski; Bat-Ami, daughter of Mr. and Mrs. Jacob Miller; Dorit, daughter of Mr. and Mrs. Mark Levita; and Amikam, son of Mr. and Mrs. Aharon Shapiro; and (on May 15) Rachel, daughter of Mr. and Mrs. Akiva Ashkenazi; and Moshe, son of Mr. and Mrs. Meir Rovkovski.

chapter

∘ ∘ ∘ ∘ ∘ ∘ ∘ ∘ ∘ ∘ ∘ ∘ ∘ ∘ ∘ 21 ∘ ∘ ∘ ∘ ∘ ∘ ∘ ∘ ∘ ∘ ∘ ∘

PERSONAL RECOLLECTIONS

INDEPENDENCE DAY IN ISRAEL was a day of action and preparation for the conflict that lay ahead, which is probably why there is so little in first-hand recollection—letters, diaries, and the like—written immediately after the event. But one exception is a letter written to Dr. Weizmann in New York by Dr. Ernest David Bergmann, the scientific director of the Weizmann Institute who was later to be the first head of Israel's Atomic Energy Commission. In a letter written in his own hand at dawn on May 15, after the Arab invasion had begun and Tel Aviv had been bombed, Dr. Bergmann described the reactions of the entire thirty-five-man staff of the Institute as they gathered—five minutes before the independence ceremonies were to begin at the Tel Aviv Museum—in the Physics Laboratory, where its short-wave radio equipment was located.

Using Institute stationery, from which he had crossed out Palestine in the Hebrew and English address and substituted "State of Israel," Dr. Bergmann said that the group, all members of Haganah, wore their uniforms, and in almost deathly silence, except for the sounds of the pumps and hum of the machines, stood at attention as "Hatikvah" was heard over the radio.

The letter began apologetically, Dr. Bergmann saying he felt that he was almost "committing a sin in interrupting the laboratory work," but that "I feel very deeply the desire to speak to you." After telling of the fifteen-hour meeting he had attended in Tel Aviv on May 13 with the Institute's scientific staff, at which they had discussed the regrouping and mobilizing of the Institute's resources to fulfill the immense responsibilities

Bergmann had accepted for them in connection with the War of Libera-tion, he expressed the realistic optimism they all felt as he concluded his letter to the Chief, saying, "We will have a bit of trouble in the war, but even that will not help the Arabs. They first will have to create their own Weizmann Institute if they want to succeed."

But other recollections—as recorded years later—help recreate the picture of what people were doing and how they felt as the state was being born. Of course, as time passes and actions become memories, per-sonal identification with an historic event is both magnified and dimin-ished. The time lapse creates a new perspective as reality becomes legend. This resort to memory—oral history—in trying to recreate an event is fascinating if not always completely factual.

These recollections are often mere vignettes and, unrelated as they are, do not lend themselves to an orderly or logical sequence. But individually and collectively these sidelights offer a panoramic portrait not otherwise available. Though not important individually, these recollections are sig-nificant in the aggregate as a part of the total picture.

This is true even of what may be apocryphal stories, such as the story of the Tel Aviv teen-ager who, bravely preparing to march off to combat, kissed his grandfather and said, "I shall not live to see the Jewish state, Grandpa, but you will." Or that of the young waitress, serving breakfast and showing the blue concentration camp number tattooed on her arm, who said on the morning of May 15, "This is the first time in my life that I've been happy."

It is to fill in this picture of a people as it faced a war of life or death that we present the Independence Day recollections of a number of men and women, gathered some twenty years later.

· BENNY MAHRSHAK, writer, poet, former political education officer of Palmach: "On May 14, 1948, I stood on the steps of the communal rest house at Kibbutz Ma'leh Ha'hamishah facing the Jerusalem highway. The building was completely shattered by shells and bullets which pounded it into rubble. It was Friday and I was wondering where to stage our weekly entertainment program for troops off duty. Suddenly, one of the younger sol-diers came running. 'Benny, come to the radio!' he yelled. 'Forget about the show, they are proclaiming a state. . . .' "

· JAFFA YARKONI, the songstress, known as The Torch Singer of Inde-pendence: "On May 14, 1948, I was passing through the Carmel Market in Tel Aviv when someone opened his window and I heard Ben-Gurion's voice on the radio proclaiming the state. I stood transfixed in the busy market, and then forgot my errand and rushed back home to rejoin my unit."

· NATHAN FRIEDMAN YELLIN (MOR), former commander of FFI (Fighters for Freedom of Israel—also known as the Stern Gang): "On May 14, 1948, I was in our underground headquarters at 18 Ben Yehuda Street in Tel Aviv. I heard the whole proceedings on the radio, and the moment the state was proclaimed and they began playing 'Hatikvah' I grabbed my hat and jacket and left the headquarters. My friends asked me where I was rushing and I told them—'Home! There is no longer any need to remain underground. Foreign rule is over, we're now in a state of our own! It was my first night home in many, many months. . . .' "

· LEON KAUFMAN, businessman, former artillery officer: "I was in Tunisia when the War of Independence broke out. I sailed to France and volunteered for Haganah. On May 15 I disembarked from an immigrant ship in Tel Aviv. The moment I stepped ashore someone asked me if I had served in the French Army. I said yes, artillery. They grabbed me off the quay and rushed me to another part of the port where Israel's first antiquated guns, the 65-mm. so-called Napoleonchiks, were being prepared for action. I accompanied the first four pieces into the battle of Degania under Moshe Dayan's overall command. We saved Degania and the Jordan Valley."

· DAVID EYTAN, official, former commander of Yeshiva volunteers in Jerusalem: "I was commanding a platoon set up by the Hebron Yeshiva. The Arab Legion attacked us [Saturday]. We were a strange sight in our long *kapotehs* [coats], *tallis* [prayer shawls], and *streimels* [fur hats]. The commanding officer took one look at us and said, 'Listen to me, men. The Arab Legion brought up a brass band for the triumphant victory parade it expects to stage in Jerusalem. If the Arabs learned to play music, you guys will learn to be soldiers.' In the end, our platoon was assigned to the 'religious commando.' We hid Sten guns and grenades under our *kapotehs* and specialized in close combat at night, after the Maariv prayers."

· THE LATE PRIME MINISTER LEVI ESHKOL: "On May 15, 1948, I was attending an emergency session of the supreme command and general staff, to decide upon measures and countermeasures in face of enemy invasion."

· GEN. YIGAEL YADIN: "On May 14 and 15 I was in a small room at the Red House. I could not leave the operations center and this was the reason I did not attend independence proclamation ceremonies."

· GEN. ITZHAK RABIN, later Chief of General Staff and Israel Ambassador to the United States: "On May 15, 1948, I was engaged in the battle of Beit-Mohsir, on the road to Jerusalem. Our brigade, Harel-Palmach, suffered numerous casualties. I heard about the independence proclamation by chance, after it happened. On that day one thought was uppermost on my mind: the enemy must not break through to Jerusalem."

· LT. COL. ARYEH SA'AR: "On May 15 I was in command of the so-called 'Orphan Convoy.' This was in the last twenty-four hours of the British Mandate in Palestine. Our unit, the Givati Infantry Brigade, received orders to seize the Latrun crossroads, together with the police fortress, monastery, and three surrounding villages the moment the British tanks which protected the Arab irregulars entrenched there moved out on their way to join the evacuation ships in Haifa port.

"The plan, known as Operation Maccabi, was for our brigade to link up with the Harel Brigade of the Palmach which defended the Jerusalem sector, hand over to Harel thirty-five trucks with ammunition and supplies, and mop up enemy resistance in the hills on both sides of Bab el Wad, the narrow gorge and most vulnerable bottleneck on the road to Jerusalem.

"Harel and other units defending Jerusalem were desperately short of 3-inch mortar shells. The few 3-inch mortars they had were the only 'artillery' in besieged Jerusalem. Having shells for them was a matter of life and death to the city. I was appointed in command of the breakthrough force, which was supposed to spearhead the convoy. We waited in Hulda, the last Jewish outpost on the road to Jerusalem, which at that time served as Givati head-quarters. On Friday afternoon, May 14, 1948, we heard on brigade radio that independence was proclaimed in Tel Aviv. To be quite frank about it, it left us quite cool. As far as we were concerned, the Jewish state came into being the moment we went into battle against the Arabs. What was said or written in Tel Aviv mattered less at the moment than what was done at the battle-front. And our possibilities were limited.

"We waited all night, and at dawn of Saturday, May 15, only one truck out of the promised thirty-five materialized in Hulda. We were told that all other supplies and available forces were diverted south to meet the Egyptian Army's invasion, which posed an unexpected threat to Tel Aviv. Our Second Battalion of Givati Brigade was also ordered to pull out of the Latrun sector and face the Egyptians. But my orders were not amended or canceled and I decided to go on. Luckily, the only truck that arrived at Hulda was loaded with boxes of 3-inch mortar ammunition and I figured even one truck of mortar shells can make a hell of a difference in Jerusalem.

"We moved out at dusk on Saturday the fifteenth of May. We had three armored cars in front, then the armored truck with the cargo, then a soft-skinned truck with food rations, and two more armored cars bringing up the rearguard.

"Between Latrun and Bab el Wad we ran into an Arab roadblock. When we halted to remove it, heavy fire was opened on us from all directions. We fought our way through and moved on to the next barrier. The leading vehicle blew up on a mine. We pushed it into a ditch, transferred the crew to the other cars, and continued on our way in utter darkness without lights. Another minefield claimed the second armored car several minutes later. At midnight we had negotiated only a few miles of the road, and the leading scouts reported it was impossible to go on. The Arabs had dug deep ditches across the highway, heaping high banks of stones and rubble on both sides.

"We needed bulldozers, engineers, and daylight to move on, and by then it would be too late to do us any good. We manhandled the armored truck up the steep slope of a hill. The soft-skinned truck and an armored car turned over into a ditch and were abandoned.

"On the crest of the hill was a narrow path leading to the Arab village of Deir Ayoub, our rendezvous with Harel troops. The village was still in Arab hands, but we were confident that Harel would take it. The rearmost armored car got stuck in the rutted path. We left it and moved on. Soon the last armored car broke its rear axle. The armored truck with the precious cargo kept moving, perhaps because we pushed and heaved it by hand over rocks, boulders, and ditches. All the time snipers and machine guns kept firing at us in the darkness but did not hit anything.

"Dawn broke over the Judean Hills in the east as we approached the outskirts of Deir Ayoub. One of my men found a sheet of paper tacked to a tree. 'The minefield begins here' was written in Arabic. We halted, unwilling to risk the last truck after getting it that far.

"We heard shooting, shouts, and the roar of engines. Our scouts returned with the commander of the Harel unit which took the Arab village. 'Where is the convoy of thirty-five trucks?' he wanted to know.

"I pointed to the single armored truck. 'This is the convoy.' He shrugged. 'Poor little orphan convoy, so much trouble for one single truck.'

"The name stuck. Since then, it was known as the 'Orphan Convoy.' We returned on foot to our base in Hulda, bypassing Arab positions. From time to time we were fired on, but reached the village safely. Later on, we learned that the mortar ammunition really did save Jerusalem. The Arab Legion attacked them that day, and the shells our 'Orphan Convoy' brought up at such great cost beat back the enemy onslaught. And there was another aspect to our operation on May 15. When the High Command looked for an alternative route to besieged Jerusalem, they remembered the crazy mountain track we had negotiated and built Israel's famous 'Burma Road' along it. First people moved on foot, carrying mortar shells or sacks of flour on their backs. Then jeeps moved along our track. Then armored trucks and in the end full-fledged convoys. So the 'Orphan Convoy' of May 15 made sure, in its own way, that Jerusalem remained Jewish, the capital of the State of Israel."

· POLICE COMMISSIONER MAX KAHAN: "I was the operations officer of 23rd Battalion facing the Syrian invasion in eastern Galilee. When I hear the date May 15, 1948, my mind automatically supplies the figures forty-four-six-two. These are not measurements or a secret code. On May 15, 1948, we had two 3-inch mortars with fifty shells. We fired six rounds that day and were ordered to save the remaining forty-four shells for the next day's battle.

Today, Lake Huleh has been drained, new roads crisscross the reclaimed swamps, and no isolated settlements are left in the area. But in 1948 we had to defend a dozen villages with two mortars and forty-four shells against the Syrian Army, its bombers, and massed artillery fire. Somehow we did it. We came through. We survived and emerged victorious. Today, when I drive near the settlement of Hulata, see its manicured lawns and well-tended gardens, neat little houses surrounded by orchards, children playing in nursery schools, and elegant cars in front of the rest house, my heart misses a beat as I remind myself that in 1948, on May 15, this village was nearly overrun by the Syrians."

· SHLOMO GOREN, LATER CHIEF RABBI OF THE ISRAELI ARMED FORCES AND CHIEF RABBI OF TEL AVIV. On May 14, 1948, he was in command of an outpost on the edge of Jewish Jerusalem. "I did not hear the Declaration of Independence because we were under attack from the Sheikh Jarrah positions near the Old City. I was told by people who listened to the radio that the state had been proclaimed. It all looked so distant and unreal to me that I remained unmoved. We were under artillery bombardment then and the historical event in Tel Aviv looked strange and divorced from reality. We expected an armored attack by the Arab Legion on Saturday and I ordered my men to round up civilians and start digging antitank ditches in the streets populated by Neturei Karta zealots. I went to talk to the Neturei Karta rabbis, to convince them that circumstances demanded desecration of the Sabbath for defense purposes. Our discussion was long and tiring. The Neturei Karta people favored surrender to the Arabs. But in the end I obtained their permission to dig antitank ditches. We worked all night between Friday and Saturday. Neturei Karta people joined us too. Some of them cried from emotion, despite their misgivings and lack of confidence in the power of arms. We trusted in God's help, but the antitank ditches helped us too."

° ° ° ° ° ° ° ° ° ° ° ° ° ° |22| ° ° ° ° ° ° ° ° ° ° ° ° °

PRESS COVERAGE

HOW THE NEWSPAPERMEN and radio commentators covered a major historic event generally provides a story within a story. This was true in Tel Aviv at the birth of Israel when a small, but for the most part distinguished, group both competed and cooperated with one another as they observed, and in some cases almost participated in, the events of the day. Mainly sympathetic to the Zionist cause, although often griping at restrictions and fancied discriminations, they were also among the most vociferous and active celebrants of the occasion.

Although the time of the ceremony was supposed to be kept a secret, no self-respecting reporter didn't know it was to be at 4 P.M., and most of them probably knew the site, although when they had assembled at the Jewish Agency press headquarters on Ben Yehuda Street at 3:30 P.M., to be taken to the Museum, it had still not been announced officially.

Joseph Heftman, editor of *Haboker* and chairman of the Hebrew Journalists Association, and the editors of the Hebrew dailies, however, had been informed by Sharef in confidence of the time and place, and as preparations were made for coverage by members of their staffs, many of whom were stringers or tipsters for the foreign correspondents, the news inevitably leaked. But secret censorship at the cable office effectively kept this information within Tel Aviv. Later the Jewish Agency public relations officials admitted that an error had been made in not informing the correspondents of the censorship.

A post office employee at the cable desk who had been acting as censor noticed that many of the correspondents were including the time and place of the ceremony in their dispatches—something not included in the Tel Aviv papers—and he carefully eliminated these facts from the stories, thus giving rise to one of the biggest bloopers in the press coverage.

Even after the ceremony was concluded, when there was no reason for hiding the time or place, he continued to do so by eliminating from the cables the last paragraph of the text of the English translation of the actual proclamation:

"With trust in Almighty God, we set our hand to this Declaration, at this session of the Provisional State Council, on the soil of the Homeland, in the City of Tel Aviv, on this Sabbath Eve, the Fifth of Iyar, 5708, the fourteenth day of May, 1948."

Thus the reference to God in the Proclamation, which had been so bitterly debated, and which was held to be so important in terms of American and other overseas public relations, did not appear in the first and most important news stories that appeared throughout the world on May 15.

One foreign correspondent, after opening the invitation he received at noon, felt that it said, "Your company is requested to meet the messiah after an absence of 1878 years." Simon Eliav, the United Press correspondent, put this widely experienced feeling in his dispatch when he described a wrinkle-faced Yemenite cleaning woman, who still went barefoot, as saying, "This is the coming of the messiah for which I set out from Yemen twenty-five years ago."

Eliav beat his fellow correspondents on two aspects of the story from Tel Aviv. Despite the fact that all correspondents had been told that there was no need for cabling the text because it was being released simultaneously in New York and London, he decided, after weighing the pros and cons, to cable the full text.

All the foreign correspondents had received an advance copy of the Declaration earlier in the morning with the provision that it could be filed immediately, but had to be slugged "For Release Not Before 14 GMT [Greenwich Mean Time], May 14." The UP man forgot this slug —by mistake, he said; deliberately, according to his fellow correspondents. As a result other correspondents, who followed instructions, began to receive agitated cables from their own offices, demanding to know why they were restricted to withhold the release while the UP teletypes were already clicking out the text. When the error was called to the attention of the cable office, the restriction was lifted and all the correspondents sent wires to their offices, announcing that the text could be released immediately.

Eliav also got his color story of the actual proceedings at the Museum off to his office in advance of the competition because he wrote his eye-witness running story from the cable office on the basis of the description of the event as it came over the air while his competition actually witnessed it. By sending an assistant, Miss H. Boas, to the Museum and foregoing actually seeing the ceremony himself, he was able to get his story to New York ahead of the others.

Later Eliav was stopped by censorship from filing his story of the de-tails of the actual bombing of Tel Aviv that night by the Egyptians. He made a strong protest to the censors, but to no avail.

The first wire-service account of the impending proclamation of state-hood to reach New York, however, was the Associated Press story. Arieh Dissentchik, onetime Editor of the Hebrew daily *Maariv,* the AP stringer in Tel Aviv, scored this coup over his colleagues by tipping off the decla-ration through a message couched in Hebrew prayer that he sent from both Tel Aviv and Haifa.

Early on Friday he had cabled AP headquarters in New York this message: "Tonight in Palestine the Sabbath prayer over the candles, 'May we worship You in the rebuilt Temple as we worshiped You in ancient times,' will have, in part, come true."

The censor in Haifa had not understood the message hidden in the ca-bled prayer and he had not been informed of the Tel Aviv ban on press cables. So the enterprising reporter had already received an okay on his story from the New York cable desk before the ceremonies began. The story was released on the AP circuit with a Haifa dateline. Dissentchik, like his fellow stringer Eliav, also wasn't present at the Museum for the actual ceremony; he followed it at home on the radio with his family, but for a different reason: with each paper and news service limited to only one Museum ticket, Dissentchik wasn't present because of the seniority of both the chief of the Tel Aviv AP Bureau and the editor of *Maariv,* the late Dr. Ezriel Carlebach.

The AP had taken to filing stories in duplicate from Tel Aviv and Haifa, not to evade censorship, but to insure greater speed in getting sto-ries out of the country after Old Jerusalem was cut off from the rest of the country when the siege of the Holy City began after partition was voted by the UN.

Until then it had been fastest and surest to file news stories from Jerusalem, via the "Blue Train" cable link to London. But when the fight-ing closed this down, the quickest way to get a cable out of Palestine was through Haifa, where Cable and Wireless Ltd. had its chief operational base and sent stories to London via Cyprus and Malta. Cable and Wireless Ltd. operated out of Haifa because the city was adjacent to such major British installations as the naval base and Iraq petroleum refineries. It was possible for AP to do this double filing because it had an American staff correspondent in Haifa.

A phone call to and a cable sent from Haifa gained time because of the limited cable facilities at the Tel Aviv post office and the heavy file there, where the majority of correspondents were located, as a result of which it sometimes took longer for a story to get from Tel Aviv to Haifa than from Haifa to London.

Dissentchik states that he didn't use Haifa to beat censorship, for as a Jew he wouldn't deceive Haganah. As a matter of fact, he says, the Tel Aviv censor was conscious of the use of the prayer to tell the story, liked it, and passed it. It was only then that the stringer phoned the story to Curtis, his colleague in Haifa.

Most of the correspondents were at the Museum, actually watching the ceremonies from seats in the entrance hall lobby to the main auditorium. Among them were Gene Currivan of the *New York Times;* I. F. Stone of *PM* and the *Boston Globe;* Asher Schwartz of the Jewish Telegraphic Agency; Quentin Reynolds of *Collier's* magazine, who later was to describe the ceremony in a book, *Leave It to the People;* Robert St. John, who put his recollections in a full-length biography, *Ben-Gurion;* Arthur D. Holtzman, Israel correspondent for the Mutual Broadcasting System and *Pathfinder* magazine; Jon Kimche of the London *Evening Standard;* and Edwards of the London *Daily Telegraph.* M. Z. Frank, an American freelance, arrived late and had to observe the ceremonial as a part of the crowd outside.

Schwartz and Currivan made their way on foot to the cable office and were able to file their eyewitness reports ahead of the other reporters, who, going by car from the Museum, were delayed by the happy and excited crowds thronging the streets. With the breakdown of incoming cable communications Schwartz did not receive the normal flow of JTA stories detailing the news and reactions from other world capitals. To service the local press in Tel Aviv, Schwartz had to rely on the news he received over a Hallicrafters radio receiver hastily installed in his home. Nevertheless, he recalls, he was one of the prime sources of incoming news for Ben-Gurion, relayed to him by his secretary and adjutant, Nehemia Argov, and Mrs. Ben-Gurion.

Among the half-dozen photographers at the ceremonies, the most noted was Robert Capa of *Life* who had arrived a few days earlier. By

dint of his personality and reputation, Capa took over. It was his "Hey,
B.G., please, a little smile," that brought a smile to the face of the harried
but happy white-bushy-maned leader of Israel. People who watched Capa
almost felt that Ben-Gurion wouldn't start the proceedings until Capa
nodded that he had enough photographs. Also very much present was Ben
Oyserman, of British Paramount News, who had come to Tel Aviv for the
ceremonies after having flown earlier that morning from Jerusalem to
Haifa with departing British High Commissioner, General Sir Alan Cunningham.

If not for Arthur Holtzman of station WMCA, New York, and his
radio engineer, Ralph Ellinger, a German-Jewish refugee who was a radio
technician for Haganah, there would have been no actual recording of the
ceremonies at the Museum. Assigned by Holtzman to record a few choice
excerpts of the ceremonies for the Mutual Broadcasting System, Ellinger's
father, with whom he conducted the Palestine Recording Service, told
his son to record the entire ceremony.

"I was sure the people in charge of planning had thought of recording
everything for posterity, but I was surprised to learn no one had paid attention to this detail," he recalls. "So it was fortunate that my late father,
who founded the Palestine Recording Service, known as Radio Doctor,
which I still conduct, advised me to record everything from beginning to
end. We dragged the two heavy recording machines into the Museum,
placed the microphone in position, and waited for the ceremony to begin.
We missed the first two or three minutes of the ceremony, either because
we had forgotten to plug in the wires from sheer excitement or because
someone had stepped on the cord and jerked it out of the socket. But we
got the rest of it on records."

As the possessor of a valuable unique collection of heavy metal-cov-
ered records (no tape-recording equipment was available in Palestine at
the time) Ellinger owns this recording. "It took several court rulings," he
says, "to decide that the records are my private property." Along with Ellinger's recording of Ben-Gurion's radio message to the United States and
the commentary with its on-the-spot descriptions of the Egyptian bombing of Tel Aviv later that night, against a background of the bombs themselves, this material is part of the album *Israel is Born* that Holtzman
compiled years later. At the time his news reportage was flown to the
United States by Teddy Kollek, when he left Israel on May 16, for broadcast over the Mutual network.

Most of the correspondents wrote their stories of the Museum ceremonies at the Scopus Club, headquarters of the Israel press information

office, and later they assembled at the Armon Hotel on Hayarkon Street, not far from the Scopus. The Armon was the press hotel, just as the Café Kassith, a sidewalk café on Dizengoff Street, was the meeting place for the Hebrew and Yiddish literati, actors, and musicians, the Kaete Dan was the base for the diplomatic corps and officials, the Gat Rimon was for VIPs from abroad, and the Park Hotel for the flyers from America and South Africa.

Sometime after the ceremony Quentin Reynolds was at the Kaete Dan with Sam Federman, its co-owner, who went behind the bar, picked out a bottle of Veuve Cliquot 1937, pulled the cork, and wordlessly filled two glasses.

Reynolds, who knew a little Hebrew, felt that the traditional Hebrew toast, "L'Chaim" ("To Life"), didn't seem quite important enough for the occasion. Remembering another Hebrew phrase, he toasted, "Am Israel Chai" ("Israel Lives"), which Federman repeated as they drank, but not before adding a second toast, "To the Baby." "To the baby nation?" Reynolds asked. Federman shook his head. His wife had gone to the hospital that morning. For two weeks the whole press corps had been speculating about when the Federman baby would be born and offering names for it. "If it arrives," Reynolds said, predicting a boy, "you've got to name him Israel." It was a boy, born a few moments after the bombing of Tel Aviv in the early hours of the morning of May 15, and he was named Israel.

Later Reynolds acted as host for a party of newspapermen at the Armon at which champagne flowed like water and great quantities of alcohol were consumed.

A little before midnight many of the reporters at the Armon gathered for the news broadcasts. American stations couldn't be tuned in, but the BBC was describing the events with icy precision. Shortly after midnight the Haganah station carried the startling news that Truman had recognized the state.

Reynolds has written that when he awoke Saturday morning at 5:30, he saw four Spitfires circling the port at about 5000 feet. Ignoring the ack-ack from machine guns and Brens, they descended to about 500 feet and dropped their bombs, which hit barely 100 yards from the docks. Everyone awake watched in awe and with a feeling of impotence as the Spitfires dropped their loads and then turned south. Four hours later they returned. Little damage was done and the unloading of the ships went on uninterrupted.

The next night at 7, Reynolds, at the invitation of Moshe Brilliant, participated in the first public broadcast of the Israel Broadcasting Station.

Plans for the twice-daily broadcasts in English, which he was to help inaugurate, had been carefully prepared. On the broadcast, which was called "I Was There," Reynolds said:

"There is no fear of what the night may bring in this land, the land where the kings and prophets of the past now live. The fight which they began two thousand years ago, the fight for which so many of them gave their lives, has finally ended in victory. The years since they lived and fought for Israel may seem long to us, but to the spirits of the great ones, they have passed as quickly as sand pouring out of an hourglass, and today they see their prophecies and visions come true. Perhaps if our mortal ears could be attuned to the celestial celebration, we might hear the sounds of music and we would know then that once again David has picked up his lyre to celebrate in song the fact that his dream of a strong united Israel has finally come true. And in chorus of joy we could, I am sure, hear the voice of Zedekiah, King of Judah, rising in triumph: once the King of Babylon slew his two sons and put out his eyes, but tyrants can destroy only the bodies of men—never the dreams of men.

"Moses will be there too, not alone, as he once stood on Mount Neboh, but one of a huge happy company. And if our eyes could pierce the veil that separates us from Valhalla, we could see the smile on the face of Moses and see his lips form the words he once heard: 'This is the land which I have sworn to Abraham, Isaac, and Jacob, saying, To thy seed will I give it.' And Moses must be content tonight for at long last it has come to pass. . . .

"If our eyes could pierce the veil, we would see the spirits of all who fought for freedom joining in this chorus. We would see two others reading the Declaration of Independence which made this a free nation today. They would be nodding with satisfaction and when they had finished reading it, Thomas Jefferson would turn to Citizen Tom Paine and say, 'There's something familiar about this, Tom. It's a lot like that little thing you and I wrote back in 1776. And it bears the same name: Declaration of Independence.' And Thomas Jefferson would laugh and say: 'After all, Paine, this young Moshe Shertok, who had so much to do with the writing of this new Declaration of Independence, has read and studied everything that either of us ever wrote. Maybe we helped him a little and we may feel a bit proud.'

"Then the two old gentlemen would chuckle a little, and walk over, the better to hear the music, and they would feel very much at home with the prophets and kings who once fought to make Eretz Israel a united

free nation—just as my colleagues of the American press and I feel at
home here tonight."

Reynolds, who was followed on the air by Ben-Gurion, waited with
Paula in the reception room outside the glass-enclosed studio while the
Prime Minister spoke, because Ben-Gurion had suggested that he would
drive Reynolds home after the broadcast. Paula's eye was still black and
blue as a result of her fall on the steps of the Museum.

Of his ride back from the broadcast, Reynolds recalled asking Ben-
Gurion, "How long will Tel Aviv have to take this bombing?"

"God knows," Ben-Gurion said wearily. "We have some fighter aircraft on the way but it is impossible to hurry them. They are on slow
ships. Meanwhile our people will have to suffer. There is something horri-
ble about watching planes bomb a defenseless city, knowing there is abso-
lutely nothing one can do about it."

Reynolds then said, "There is a report that in retaliation you are
going to order the bombing of Cairo. Is that true?"

"Bomb Cairo?" A rueful smile flitted over the tired face of Israel's
new leader as he answered, "With what? A week from now we could
make such a threat because I hope by then we will have planes here, but
tonight we can make no threats because we could not carry them out."

With his eyes closed and his head resting against the back seat, Ben-
Gurion then said, almost as if thinking aloud, "They can bomb us and
murder our civilians. They can kill us, but they will never kill this nation
of ours." With that his voice trailed off and he was fast asleep. Ever vigi-
lant as the protector of her husband, Paula leaned over and put a warning
finger to her lips.

After five minutes of silence the car lurched and Ben-Gurion was
thrown against Reynolds. Opening his eyes and smiling apologetically, he
continued, "I think I dozed off. We were talking about—about—I
think you asked me how we could win with no defense against their air
attack. Is that it?"

It wasn't, but Reynolds recalls nodding, to which the Prime Minister
answered, "You see, we have a very large army. Our enemies will have to
kill every member of that army in order to beat us."

Puzzled, Reynolds repeated, "A very large army?"

"Yes," Ben-Gurion said. "We have an army of 750,000."

"But that's the entire population," Reynolds interjected. (Actually the
figure was 650,000.)

"That's right," he answered calmly.

The press in the new state of Israel—fiercely competitive and with strong party and personal loyalties before and after statehood—all cooperated on the joint newspaper published on the day of independence, *Yom Ha'Medinah (The Day of the State)*. The one-sheet broadside printed on two sides appeared at 5 P.M., one hour after the declaration ceremonies began. Printed in Hebrew, at the plant of Hapoel Hatzair, with a Hebrew and English dateline, it carried the headline "LAST DAY OF FOREIGN RULE" under the front-page logotype.

One of the anomalies of this front page is the list of signatures appended to the proclamation of the National Administration, the new provisional State Council, announcing the abolition of the 1939 White Paper and all of its restrictions. Dated May 14, it carried the signature of Chaim Weizmann as President, although he wasn't elected until May 16 and he was never to sign the Declaration itself.

Earlier, with Sharef himself reading the final proofs at the Hapoel Hatzair printing plant, the first number of the provisional government's official *Gazette* had been printed with the official Hebrew text of the Declaration and Proclamation. Sharef took the first two copies to Ben-Gurion at his home. Later Haganah planes flew over the city, dropping copies of the *Gazette* and leaflets urging subscriptions to the Independence Loan.

chapter

○ ○ ○ ○ ○ ○ ○ ○ ○ ○ ○ ○ ○ |23| ○ ○ ○ ○ ○ ○ ○ ○ ○ ○ ○ ○ ○

TELLING THE WORLD

THOUGH IT WAS the Sabbath, Israel's Foreign Office, under the direction of Moshe Shertok, began work on the morning of May 15. In the Red House on Hayarkon Street, the headquarters of the Histadrut, Shertok and his secretary, Mrs. Eiga Shapiro, went to work on their first job: the sending of cables to all countries, officially informing them that the State of Israel had been born.

Mrs. Shapiro had been summoned to work by an early-morning call from Shertok, and she found him waiting for her when she arrived at the Red House. Aside from Shertok's driver, she was the only member of the staff of the Jewish Agency's Political Department to be in Tel Aviv, which with statehood became the Foreign Ministry; the others were stuck in besieged Jerusalem. She was there by accident, having arrived a few weeks earlier with Sharef and his family in an armored car in which there was an empty seat; she had come to spend a day or so with her family, whom she hadn't seen since November, and she had stayed on, although with a sense of guilt for having abandoned Jerusalem, because Sharef decided there should be someone from the Political Department in Tel Aviv as preparations were being made for the proclamation.

With Mrs. Dorit Rozenne, Sharef's secretary, helping her with the cables in French, the notification cables were completed by 2 A.M. When it came to drafting the cable to Iceland, neither lady knew how to spell "Reykjavík." With no atlas or encyclopedia available, a minor crisis was averted only by the appearance of Francis Offner, correspondent of the *London Observer* and the *Christian Science Monitor,* who knew the correct spelling.

Mrs. Shapiro didn't leave the building until the cables were completed, and she doesn't recall eating all day. All that she and the others knew of what was going on was the aerial bombardment that began in the morning and continued intermittently all day. Until the ladies convinced him that it was too dangerous, Shertok stood at the window of his office facing the Mediterranean and watched the Egyptian planes flying over Tel Aviv.

With the cables completed Shertok and Mrs. Shapiro drove to the Western Union office on the top floor of a building on Allenby Road near the main post office. Shertok, still unaccustomed to being a Cabinet officer, started to take the cables to the Western Union office himself, until his secretary reminded him that this would be improper work for the Foreign Minister. He then allowed her to deliver the cables.

Then a major crisis almost developed, laughable now but typical of the impromptu arrangements under which the new government was operating. After counting the words, the officials in the cable office courteously but firmly demanded payment for the cables. Mrs. Shapiro said the Jewish Agency had a charge account, but one of the officials wryly observed, "The Jewish Agency has a charge account, the Foreign Ministry so far has none." Admitting his recognition of the importance of getting the cables off at once, the official said he had to abide by regulations and he insisted on cash payment. Ultimately, when Shertok joined Mrs. Shapiro in the office, the official accepted the Foreign Minister's personal guarantee.

Shertok and his minuscule Foreign Office moved to Sarona on May 16. Aside from his secretary, there was only one member of his staff to assist him: Levi Allon, later Ambassador to Panama. The plan for the Foreign Ministry had been formulated by Walter Eytan, principal of the Jewish Agency's Public Service College. Immediately following the UN partition decision, he and his students, working mainly from books on how foreign ministries of other nations operated, drew up a plan—"Outline Plan for the Foreign Office and Foreign Service of the Jewish State"—the first draft of which was completed and submitted on January 9, 1948. Eytan has since held many top positions in the Foreign Service.

THE ILLEGALS

THE VERY FIRST ACT of Israel's founding fathers after they had proclaimed independence on the afternoon of May 14 was to repeal the hated British laws curbing Jewish immigration. The epic struggle for the unrestricted right of the Jews to return to the land from which they had been exiled for nearly 1900 years had been won largely by defying these regulations with a tidal wave of Jewish immigration that made the British position in Palestine untenable and undoubtedly hastened the British departure.

Many in the tightly packed hall of the Museum wept openly as Ben-Gurion slowly read the Preamble's seventh paragraph, which paid tribute to those who had "continued to migrate to Eretz Israel, undaunted by difficulties, restrictions, and dangers." Then a storm of shouts and cheers almost drowned him out as he announced that Israel was flinging open its gates to any Jew who wanted to come.

Of the 120,000 Jews who entered Palestine between 1939 and the 1947 United Nations vote partitioning the country, nearly 40,000 arrived as illegals. (Ben-Gurion himself had come in 1906 on a passport borrowed from S. H. Michelson, his *cheder*—Hebrew school—classmate, whose father was the rabbi of Plonsk. Because Ben-Gurion was of military age, the Russians would not let him leave, and so he traveled under the name of young Michelson, who was sixteen months younger.)

All of the illegals reached the Promised Land via an underground railroad in Europe and a fleet of weatherbeaten vessels that brazenly eluded the British warships, planes, and soldiers barring the way. This illegal immigration was stepped up in the early months of 1948 as thousands of illegals outwitted the five divisions, plus RAF and Royal Navy units, that were mobilized for what Winston Churchill called "a squalid war" to guard the gates of Palestine against the tiny remnant of European Jewry.

A few months after he left the country the commander of these forces—General Cunningham, the last British High Commissioner—wrote in *International Affairs* that "every Jew brought to Palestine during the last 12 years, up to the termination of the Mandate, was brought in under the protection of British bayonets."

Illegal immigration on a small scale had been under way for more than a decade before the 1939 White Paper. In 1927 the French authorities in Syria winked at the smuggling of Jews over the border after they had been trained at an agricultural colony in Syria. On a summer night in 1934 the 2000-ton Greek tramp steamer *Velos,* relic of the white-slave traffic, landed the first illegal immigrants from Europe on the coast of Palestine. The 300 Polish *chalutzim* (pioneers) went by train from Warsaw to Athens and sailed from the port of Piraeus. A second run by the *Velos* that same year failed when RAF planes and police boats turned it back.

The 1936 Arab riots impelled the Jewish Agency temporarily to halt illegal immigration for fear it might handicap diplomatic efforts to get the British to increase the legal quota. Imposition of new immigration cuts recommended by the Peel Commission in 1937 gave birth to Mossad Aliyah Beth, the Jewish Agency's Committee for Illegal Immigration. From headquarters in Paris, Mossad emissaries moved in and out of Berlin, Vienna, Bucharest, Sofia, Prague, Athens, and Istanbul, making deals with the Devil himself to save Jewish lives.

In 1938 the Nazis were still encouraging Jewish emigration by all possible means while Hitler's Foreign Office was taking diplomatic steps to block the formation of a Jewish state. Otto von Hentig, the Foreign Office's Middle East expert, however, felt that a Jewish state would relieve the Third Reich of a large number of needy Jews and would "make it possible, when we are attacked by world Jewry, to deal with official representatives, and not, as heretofore, with anonymous and therefore irresponsible elements."

Pino Ginsberg, a Mossad agent, received a Gestapo permit in the summer of 1938 that enabled him to open training camps in Germany to prepare Jews for illegal runs to Palestine. Moshe Auerbach, who dealt with Adolf Eichmann, had a similar go-ahead in Vienna. The first transport of 400 young pioneers organized by Ginsberg left Berlin in March, 1939, on a train provided by the Nazis. Nazi officials accompanied it as far as Vienna, where it was joined by another group assembled by Ginsberg and Moshe Bar-Gilead. Armed with Mexican visas and ostensibly bound for Mexico, the *chalutzim* sailed on the Greek passenger ship SS *Colorado* from the Dalmatian port of Susak. At sea, however, the *Colorado* transferred its passengers to the SS *Otranto* for the final leg of the journey to Palestine.

Once word of Auerbach's activities got around Vienna, he was besieged by shady characters eager to sell or lease leaky tubs. Even Gestapo men tried to cut themselves in on sub-rosa transportation deals. By the end of 1938 Mossad's Scarlet Pimpernels were sending more than 1000 illegals a month into Palestine on salvaged cattle and cargo boats that left from Black Sea and Mediterranean ports. With the quiet help of countries of exit, large groups, ranging from 300 to even 1400, were slipped into Palestine at one time, including 5000 rescued from the Hitler terror.

In the two months between May 24 and July 20, 1939, British patrol forces on land and sea "captured" 3507 illegal immigrants, the Colonial Secretary informed the House of Commons. During that period, he said, 4000 more were known to be on the high seas and between 500 and 1000 were believed to have entered undetected.

The *Tiger Hill,* with 1400 passengers aboard from Poland and Rumania, was beached off Tel Aviv on September 2, 1939, the night Hitler invaded Poland. Although fired on by a British patrol, most of the refugees were taken off safely by Palmach units. In the late summer of 1939 Ginsberg arranged with the Gestapo for the evacuation of 10,000 German Jews on four ships that were to leave Emden and Hamburg the week the war broke out. The ships never sailed and Ginsberg had to flee to Holland.

The risks Mossad was taking were so appalling to some Zionists that illegal immigration became a hotly debated issue at the twenty-first World Zionist Congress, which met in Geneva on the eve of World War II. Hostilities forced Mossad to shift its headquarters from Paris to Geneva, and some of its people stayed on in Vienna and the Balkans until Italy's entry into the war in 1940 and the Wehrmacht's sweep through the Balkans in 1941 and 1942. Before the death trains began rumbling across the continent, Mossad was able to rescue many Jews by cramming them into unseaworthy hulks that limped across the Black Sea and into the Mediterranean. Some of the floating wrecks went down with no survivors. Only a pitiful few got through the British blockade. In a temporary shift of operations to the Middle East and North Africa, Mossad slipped 400 Jews from Syria, Iraq, and Lebanon and 1000 from Morocco into Palestine in 1941.

Two years later Mossad set itself up in Istanbul after it got wind of a secret message from the Colonial Office to the British Ambassador in neutral Turkey. Warned against encouraging Jews in occupied Europe to escape, he was nevertheless authorized to give them entry visas to Palestine if they managed to reach Turkish shores. On the strength of this news, Ehud Avriel, Levi Schwartz, Bar-Gilead, and Teddy Kollek resumed organizing transports for Palestine via Turkey. When the Russian armies rolled through Rumania toward Hungary in the fall of 1944, Mossad agents followed and began sending small boatloads of refugees from Constanza on the Black Sea to Eretz Israel.

These risky exploits expanded after the war into a massive and clandestine exodus organized by Bricha ("Running"), Mossad's newly established escape section. When the British obdurately refused to let the survivors of the Holocaust into the Promised Land, Haganah retaliated with a calculated policy of trying to drown the White Paper in a flood of illegal immigration. The strategy was to increase the Jewish population in Palestine while winning world sympathy for the Zionist cause by dramatizing the results of Britain's broken promises.

In March, 1945, Mossad's high command, at a meeting in Paris, confided to Ben-Gurion that Bricha agents were already in touch with Jews freed by the advancing Allied armies in Eastern and Central Europe. After meeting with the concentration camp survivors, Ben-Gurion went to New York to raise the money needed to underwrite the underground railroad Bricha was organizing and to buy, equip, and man the ships that would carry the illegals to Palestine.

After the German surrender most of the millions of displaced persons of all nationalities whom the Allies found in their areas were repatriated within sixty days after V-E Day. The vast majority of the 100,000 Jews among them, however, were fiercely determined to quit Europe forever. Even after they were moved to separate camps to spare them further indignities at the hands of liberated Polish, Ukrainian, and Slovak slave laborers, the Jewish DPs found life intolerable. Shattered by their experiences in the concentration camps and embittered by British stubbornness and the inaction of other countries that kept the doors of Palestine shut, the DPs eagerly welcomed the strangers who spread the word of a secret route to the Jewish Homeland.

The schools, theaters, newspapers, and political parties in the camps gave rise to a miniature Jewish state in exile. The camps themselves became way-stations to Eretz Israel, and their inhabitants saw themselves as front-line fighters for a Jewish Palestine. DP came to mean "Destination Palestine." In the summer of 1945 Ben-Gurion toured all the camps and generated tremendous excitement by telling the DPs, "You are not only needy persons, you are also a political force." Bricha agents in the camps gave assurance that the Yishuv was waiting to welcome the *Sheerith Hapletah* ("the Surviving Remnant") with open and loving arms.

This emboldened the Central Committee of Liberated Jews, a federation of camp committees in the American zone of Germany, to demand the opening of Palestine to the DPs. After winning grudging official recognition from the American occupation authorities, the Central Committee made common cause with similar groups in the French and British sectors in plotting to break the British blockade to Palestine. The DPs themselves fired the opening shot in what became "an astonishing war of illegal immigration which quickly caused a great power to retreat."

Bricha's "Operation Escape" was carried out in three stages. In phase one Bricha located scattered Jews in Poland, Hungary, and Rumania and shepherded them over secret routes to the DP camps in one of the Allied zones of Germany, or to temporary emergency centers in Austria and Italy. The hazardous second stage involved moving the refugees from the camps to obscure ports and lonely beachheads on the Mediterranean, Adriatic, and Black Seas where the illegal ships waited. The third stage was running the illegals through the gauntlet of the British Mediterranean fleet, RAF patrols, a coast guard, and 100,000 troops.

The two main lines of migration led from eastern Poland into Czechoslovakia and Austria into Italy and from Germany into France. A smaller stream flowed from Rumania, where Mossad bluffed its way into control of the Red Cross, through Hungary to Vienna and then on to Italy. By early 1946 there were 1000 Bricha men and women operating the escape route that extended through seven countries, with twenty-four staging points along their borders.

The trek of Polish Jews to Bricha's western "collection" stations, which began at the end of 1945, became a mass exodus in mid-1946. Nearly 100,000 fugitives from Poland, who had encountered anti-Semitic violence on their return from Russia, were led by Bricha to the DP camps in the Western-occupied zones of Germany and Austria. This influx so enraged Lt. Gen. Sir Frederick Morgan, the British chief of UNRRA operations in Germany, that he publicly denounced "the secret organization" stimulating it. His sneering gibe at "well-dressed and well-fed rosy-cheeked" Jews arriving from Poland, who "certainly do not look like persecuted people," created an international uproar. After June 30, 1946, when the British banned new DPs in their sector, the infiltratees were directed by Bricha into the American zone. This aspect of the migration was masterminded from Mossad's headquarters in the thirteenth-century Old-New Synagogue in the Prague Ghetto. Once the refugees reached Prague, they were sent on to Vienna and then funneled into the American zone.

At the end of 1946 the camps housed 250,000 men, women, and children, 186,000 of them in the American zone. On April 21, 1947, the US military authorities, who had previously turned a blind eye to Bricha's operations, barred infiltratees from Eastern Europe from receiving shelter in the DP camps. A month earlier a confidential US Army memo issued in Bremen alleged that "every Zionist-indoctrinated Jew who arrives in the American zone is an unconscious asset to Moscow." The document charged that "this intensely vocal group is, unconsciously or not, helping to increase strained relations between London and Washington over the Palestine crisis . . . to Russia's obvious benefit." The DP camps answered back with posters urging an immediate march on Palestine.

The US Army memo was an echo of British attempts to halt the flow of illegal immigration by diplomatic measures and by efforts to apprehend the leaders of the underground movement. The Rumanians refused to interfere with "legal" immigrants holding valid entrance visas for Central or Latin America. The Russians ignored British protests. The Italians, Dutch, and Belgians promised stricter border controls, but public sympathy for the DPs was too strong for more than token enforcement. The governments of France, Italy, and Yugoslavia also did nothing to impede Bricha—in fact, they often allowed local officials to be helpful in connection with sailings of immigrant ships.

Unofficially, JDC, the American Jewish relief agency, supported Bricha with funds, food, medicine, and transportation. It frequently prevailed upon friendly American commanders to turn their backs at the right time and tacitly permitted Bricha to use trucks bearing the JDC shield. When Bricha delivered the illegals to the DP camps, JDC was the chief provider. On several occasions JDC officials were called on the carpet by the US State and War Departments, which protested against the constant new arrivals in the camps. Moe Leavitt, JDC's chief executive, warned that the only way to seal the borders against illegals was to kill the Jews as they crossed. Jewish chaplains in the Allied armies, particularly the American, were also deeply involved in Bricha's work—at least one was threatened with court-martial or expulsion from the area—and they were especially helpful in collecting rations contributed by Jewish soldiers and in encouraging them to conduct campaigns for money and clothing.

Bricha was manned chiefly by Haganah men who had served in the

British Army's Jewish Brigade in Europe. First contact with concentration camp survivors had been made by Brigade units on the Italo-Austro-Yugoslav border as they marched westward into Germany, frustrated troops who arrived too late to participate in the actual fighting against the Nazis. While still in British uniform, members of the Jewish Brigade requisitioned food and clothing for the refugees and trucks for transporting them. Many Brigade members changed clothes, dogtags, and places with DP camp residents to enable the latter to reach Palestine sooner. Some Canadian, American, and British non-Jewish troops did the same. A relative of Field Marshal Bernard Montgomery was so shocked by what she saw in the DP camps and by her country's attitude toward the DPs that she joined Bricha.

Bluff and bravado, bribed officials, forged visas, and the compassionate aid of the ordinary people in France, Italy, and Czechoslovakia enabled Bricha to crack sealed frontiers and to escort thousands over mountains, across flooded rivers, and through dense forests. The DPs were smuggled in buses and trucks and on foot, moving by night and hiding by day to avoid British informers. It was a terrible ordeal for the refugees but they endured it stoically because they were going home, and for that no danger was too great.

Bricha's chief was Yehuda Arazi, son of a Polish rabbi, who was only seventeen when he joined Haganah in 1924. Two years later he enlisted in the Palestine police force to keep an eye on them. He was an officer in charge of the police political department when Haganah ordered him to resign in 1936 and assigned him to organize the acquisition of illegal arms. In the guise of salesman for a citrus fruit company he returned to Poland, where he bought a small factory that built steamrollers. In the hollowed-out insides of the rollers he sent 2250 rifles and 250 machine guns to Haganah.

Arazi got out of Poland a few days before the Nazi invasion, and became simultaneously one of the chiefs of Haganah intelligence and a British agent. In the latter role he was sent to sabotage the Rumanian oilfields. On the side he bought and stole arms in the German-occupied Balkans and cached them away for postwar use. Known as "the Man with the Seven Faces," Arazi persuaded British intelligence to buy a Greek ship and turn it over to Mossad for illegal immigration. He convinced them that the Rumanians and Germans would ignore the vessel after she made a few round-trips between Constanza and Haifa, since this would brand her as being anti-British. Thereafter, he argued, she could be fitted with torpedo tubes and used for offensive purposes in the Black Sea.

When the SS *Doron* made her first "cover" voyage, she landed 800 Jews openly in Palestine. The red-faced Palestine authorities and British Naval Intelligence beached the *Doron* and ordered Arazi's arrest, but they could never find him.

In 1945 he turned up in Cairo in the uniform of a British sergeant-major from the Jewish Brigade. His false papers called for him to be flown to Milan, where he took command of Bricha. The Italian black market and the postwar snafu in the British occupation forces were made to order for Arazi's amazing operations. When the Jewish Brigade in Italy was ordered to North Africa for demobilization at the end of 1945, Arazi created a phony military outfit by forging the necessary documents, and then manned it with Jewish Brigade veterans who made their way back from Palestine.

With faked orders and counterfeit gasoline coupons, Arazi's nonexistent unit "borrowed" vehicles, requisitioned farms and remote country homes to house the "troops"—the DPs arriving from the north—and organized military convoys that delivered them to the beachheads. Each Palestinian soldier donated two bottles a week from his army liquor ration to Arazi's "liquor bank" on which drafts were made to pay for needed supplies, including lifebelts. Once he traded a case of whiskey for the complete map of the minefields around southern Italy. Filched from the files of the Italian Admiralty at Taranto, the map was needed to minimize the hazards facing the illegal ships that sailed from Italian ports. Arazi became a master at bribery, but he could not have done what he did without the volunteer help of thousands of rank-and-file Italians.

On the Italian and French beaches, where the ships awaited the DPs, Palmach commandos stood guard. Sometimes the vessels came so close to shore that the DPs were able to embark by walking out on long planks. At other times a wire stretched from ship to shore was used to guide and pull rubber dinghies loaded with refugees. The first of Arazi's ships from Italy, carrying only thirty-five Jews, left in August, 1945, from La Spezia. In seven round-trips it delivered 1200 people. Arazi's impunity in buying off or sweet-talking Italian harbor authorities, police, and mayors became legendary. Once, however, a ship was searched by the Italian police because they suspected Arazi of smuggling Fascist refugees from Spain.

The temper of the illegals and Arazi's resourcefulness were evident in the case of the wooden cargo vessel *Fede*. She was about to sail from La Spezia for Sardinia, her manifest showing her to be carrying a cargo of salt, when the British held her up at gunpoint in April, 1946. Only after international protests, backed up by Arazi's threat that the passengers would commit suicide one by one, was the *Fede* allowed to sail. Lacking passports, they devised their own: "Mr. —— has been found qualified by the representatives of the Yishuv for repatriation to Palestine. By authority, Ezekiel 37:25: 'And they shall dwell in the land that I have given unto Jacob, my servant, wherein your fathers have dwelt; and they shall dwell in it, even they, and their children, and their children's children forever. . . .' "

Competing with Haganah's Mossad in illegal immigration was the Irgunist American League for a Free Palestine, one of whose leaders was the American writer Ben Hecht. The League's sensational newspaper advertisements in the United States helped stir American public opinion, but only one of its ships made it to Palestine. The SS *Ben Hecht,* with 599 illegals aboard, arrived March 8, 1947, and its passengers were quickly transferred to Cyprus.

In three years the audacious Arazi and his intrepid band along the underground railroad smuggled 84,000 escapees, from newborn infants to the bedridden aged, out of seven countries and delivered them to Mossad for the clandestine sea journey to Palestine. Mossad had snatched up almost anything that would float, from junked ferryboats, converted icebreakers and corvettes and antiquated steamboats, to fishing schooners, ancient freighters, and salvaged houseboats. This was the ragtag fleet the British hunted with cruisers, destroyers, reconaissance planes, radar spotters, and shorebased informers all along the eastern Mediterranean. Floating wrecks jampacked with human wrecks were rammed and fired on at sea, their pleas for food and water ignored, and when captured, they were attacked by boarding parties with guns, clubs, and waterhoses.

Only six of the sixty-three Mossad blockade-runners that reached Palestinian waters beween June, 1945, and January, 1948, were able to land their human cargoes in Palestine by breaking through the tight British air and naval network. Guided to secret bridgeheads at night by Palyam naval detachments, the ships unloaded the *maapalim* (immigrants without visas) under the protection of Palmach infantry units. Provided with false identity cards, the exhausted DPs and their pitiable belongings were trucked to hiding places in remote settlements to escape British searching parties. After being treated by waiting doctors and nurses, the aged and sick were carried ashore on the shoulders of young *chalutzim.*

Until the summer of 1946 apprehended illegals were confined in detention camps, the largest of which was at Athlit, eight miles south of Haifa. After Palmach commandos smashed their way into Athlit, freed 200 detainees, and scattered them around the country, the British began sending the illegals to Cyprus. The new policy was first applied on August 31, 1946, when 1208 concentration camp survivors, including 400 women, fifty of them pregnant, were taken off the *Yagur* and the *Henrietta Szold,* which had been at sea for twenty-nine and fifteen days, respectively. While the captured vessels were surrounded by two cruisers, several destroyers, and a flotilla of police launches, the DPs were herded onto the prison ships *Empire Rival, Ocean Vigour,* and *Runnymede Park.* An infantry division, reinforced by tanks, cut off the Haifa port area from the rest of the city while the transfer was under way. Nevertheless, thousands of enraged Jews streamed toward the docks and three were killed when the troops opened fire.

The horror stories of the DP ships, and the pathetic scenes in the port of Haifa, made international headlines and created sympathy and support for a Jewish state. Britain defended the deportations on the ground that it was fighting "a sinister traffic organized by unscrupulous persons" who sought "to exploit the sufferings of these unfortunate people." Admission of the refugees outside the established quota was likely "to have an adverse effect on the hope of a general settlement" in Palestine, the British insisted.

Mossad's strategy was twofold: to bring Jews into Palestine and to arouse world opinion against the British. Whether the ships got through or not, Mossad won. By rushing in so many illegals that Britain would run out of room to hide them, Mossad counted on forcing Britain to ameliorate her policy and ultimately to get out of Palestine.

Mossad's greatest propaganda victory, and the most fatal incident for Britain in her war against illegal immigration, was the odyssey of the SS *Exodus.* It began late in 1946 in Baltimore when an anonymous buyer, acting for the Sonneborn Institute, paid $40,000 for the SS *President Warfield,* an old Chesapeake Bay excursion boat that had been sold for $8000 to a scrap dealer. A three-decker with an elongated funnel and a wooden hull covered with a narrow iron shield, the 4000-ton *President Warfield* had ferried thousands of American troops across the English Channel during World War II.

Located by Capt. William Ash, Secretary of the Masters, Pilots and Mates Union, and a professional seaman, the *President Warfield* underwent three months of secret reconditioning in Baltimore Harbor to enable her to accommodate 4000 passengers. Sonneborn Institute agents provisioned her with immense quantities of dehydrated food, blankets, medical supplies, and maritime paraphernalia. Moses Schloss, owner of a Baltimore maritime equipment firm, personally drove a truck to the harbor for many days so that the ship's cargo would not become known.

On March 7, 1947, the *President Warfield,* loaded with ballast, left Baltimore's Pratt Street Dock flying the Honduran flag. Her announced destination was Shanghai, where she was supposed to be sold to a Chinese river ferry company. All but five of her crew of sixty-nine were volunteers, Jews and non-Jews, recruited by Haganah from among US Merchant Marine veterans and members of Zionist youth societies. One of the crew was the Rev. John Grauel, a Unitarian minister from Worcester, Massachusetts, who carried credentials as a correspondent of *The Churchman.* The listed captain was Bernard Marks of Cincinnati, but the man in charge was Ike Aronowicz, a young American who had served in the US Merchant Marine before settling in Palestine.

In the summer of 1946 Aronowicz received his second mate's papers from London's Prince Edward VII Maritime College. Mossad then sent him to Norfolk, Virginia, where he met Zeev Schind, one of Haganah's ace arms-buyers, and Captain Ash. Twenty hours after the *President Warfield* steamed out of Baltimore, she limped into Norfolk, having sprung leaks in heavy weather. On March 22 she sailed again, reaching Marseilles on April 10; Aronowicz now took command. To avoid British intelligence agents, who had picked up the trail at the Azores when the *President Warfield* stopped for refueling, Mossad moved the vessel to Porto Venire, an inlet seven miles from La Spezia, Italy. There bunks were installed for 4500 people; a pipe perforated with tiny holes was welded along the ship's entire circumference and then linked to the central steam system to provide hot steam for repelling British boarders at sea.

When the *President Warfield* was shifted westward to Port-de-Bouc, near Marseilles, two British destroyers took up positions nearby. On July 6, the squat riverboat, her single stack belching greasy smoke, inched her way from Port-de-Bouc to the tiny port of Sète on the Golfe du Lion. Waiting at quayside was a convoy of trucks Bricha had hijacked from British Army depots in Italy to transport thousands of DPs to southern France. They had been temporarily housed in five large villas outside Sète, "borrowed" by Bricha from ex-collaborators. All the 1600 men, 1282 women, and 1672 children had visas for Colombia, manufactured by Mossad in Paris. Leaving Sète without a pilot or chief engineer—they had been bribed by the British to walk off—the *President Warfield* flirted with disaster before she reached the high seas. On the way out of the harbor she hit a pier, damaging the forward hold, fouled up her propellors on the shallow bottom, and finally ran aground on a reef. Just outside French territorial waters Aronowicz unfurled a handmade Zionist flag, a Mogen David cut from the blue ribbons of women's dresses and sewn onto a white sheet. He also broke out a banner identifying the ship as *Yeziat Europa 1947* ("Exodus from Europe 1947").

For seven days and nights the floating sardine can made her way across the Mediterranean, shadowed by British warships and a flight of Lancasters. In the suffocating bunks sickness took a heavy toll among the aged. Water and food shortages and the collapse of the sanitation system worried the crew. But the passengers played chess, studied philosophy, talked politics, got married (rabbis performed 116 weddings), died in childbirth, and prayed.

When the *Exodus,* the thirty-fourth ship in Mossad's "armada," reached Palestinian waters on the night of July 16, all of Palestine knew of her progress. Posters informed the public she was nearing the homeland, and announced that her crew would send the Yishuv a message at 10 P.M. on July 17 over the underground Haganah radio, 45-meter wavelength. After Aronowicz radioed his position to Tel Aviv, he was instructed to get as close to the shore as possible and to beach the *Exodus* just north of Gaza.

At 2 A.M., July 17, seventeen miles off Haifa, the British cruiser *Ajax* signaled the *Exodus* to stop its engines and not to resist a boarding party. From the bridge of the destroyer that headed for the *Exodus* the fluttering Zionist emblem, bleached by the sun, might have looked like a white flag of surrender. When Aronowicz suddenly changed course, the *Exodus* was rammed from three directions and might have been sunk but for the iron sheathing around her hull. Her steering gear smashed and her engine room flooded, the *Exodus* floated helplessly as a party of British Marines scrambled aboard. The desperate refugees and the crew resisted with fists, live steam, boiling oil, teeth, and even can openers, but they were no match for small arms, tear gas, and concussion grenades. In a six-hour battle three Jews were killed and 120 wounded. Among the dead were sixteen-year old Hirsch Yakubovich, whose parents had died in Hitler's gas ovens, and First Mate William Bernstein of Philadelphia.

On July 18, the day on which UNSCOP completed its hearings in Palestine, the *Exodus* was towed into Haifa. The sick passengers were taken to hospitals, but the rest were forcibly transferred to three British transports fitted out with wire cages on their decks. While the Yishuv declared a fast and staged a day-long protest strike and members of UNSCOP watched unbelievingly, the transports departed on July 21, presumably for Cyprus. Instead, they headed back to Port-de-Bouc, where they remained from July 29 to August 23. Colombia refused to admit the deportees because their visas were invalid. The French offered asylum to all who wished to come ashore, but only eighty-three, the sick, accepted. The others refused to go anywhere but to Palestine despite the torrid heat in the floating ovens.

The British government then issued an ultimatum: either the refugees disembarked in twenty-four hours or they would be moved to the British zone in Germany. When the seagoing prisons sailed again, everyone believed they were bound for Cyprus. Instead they steamed via Gibraltar, the English Channel, and the North Sea to Hamburg. Habeas corpus proceedings in Gibraltar and London and intervention from Washington and Paris failed to budge the Colonial Office. Arriving at Hamburg on September 9, eight days after UNSCOP had recommended Jewish statehood through partition, the DPs were driven ashore by clubs, tear gas, and waterhoses. Some resisted and thirty-three were injured as the refugees were carried, pushed, and shoved, screaming and struggling, back onto hated German soil and deposited in detention camps near Lübeck. It was almost exactly two months since the *Exodus* had left Sète. Many escaped from Lübeck in a few months with the aid of Bricha. By the spring of 1948 more than half of the *Exodus*'s passengers were back in Palestine or Cyprus; 300 of them fought in the first battles of Israel's war of liberation.

(In 1968, 429 people in Haifa were asked if they knew what the *Exodus* was. On a Kol Israel radio program some said it was a nightclub; they were right. Others said it was a discothèque; they were right too. In fact, there are ten restaurants and four entertainment spots with that name in Israel. Only one of the 429 had the right answer. He knew because he was Ike Aronowicz, who now lives in a kibbutz. On July 16, 1967, five of the *Exodus*'s crew met at the Smithsonian Institution's Museum of History and Technology in Washington to mark the twentieth anniversary of the "ship that launched the Jewish state" by dedicating a plaque and a model of the historic vessel.)

The *Exodus* tragedy wiped out the last shred of good will for Britain in Palestine but it did not halt illegal immigration. Between November 30, 1947, and May 12, 1948, fourteen ships with 22,000 unauthorized passengers arrived. The seaworthy 4500-tonners, SS *Independence* and SS *Ingathering of the Exiles* (formerly *Pan York* and *Pan Crescent*), left Burgos, Bulgaria, on December 25, 1947, with 15,169 illegals. They sailed in defiance of orders from Ben-Gurion who had been warned by the United States, under British pressure, not to let the vessels leave if he valued

American support at the United Nations. This time, however, the British merely redirected the ships to Cyprus, where their passengers were debarked on January 1 and January 5, 1948, respectively.

Although the British blockade remained in force almost until the last hour of the Mandate, by the end of 1947 Britain had lost the war against illegal immigration. As one observer commented, the Jews' "willingness to die at each stage of the homeward journey" had "blackmailed a great power which would not kill its obstreperous wards and which could not otherwise prevent this mass migration."

Nearly 28,000 Jewish refugees celebrated news of Israel's proclamation of independence behind the barbed wire of British internment camps in Cyprus where some of them had spent as much as a year and a half. From August, 1946, to mid-May, 1948, more than 65,000 had passed through the camps.

Five were so-called summer camps on the seashore near Famagusta, a cluster of tents with a capacity of 12,000; twenty miles away in the hills were two winter camps of Nissen huts with accommodations for 14,000. Under pressure from the JDC two special camps were opened for married couples with newborn infants and a third for 2000 orphaned children. At their peak the camps housed 31,400 escapees; 2000 babies were born and 150 DPs died there.

Each month the British permitted 750 Jews to leave Cyprus for Palestine as part of the White Paper immigration quota. An estimated 1500 made it to Palestine illegally, and the remains of their escape tunnels can still be seen. Those not of military age were released after May 14, reaching Palestine on the Mossad ships that had been interned in Cyprus. Men and women of military age remained in confinement until February 11, 1949, after Britain had recognized Israel. Only then did the remaining 10,210 internees complete the last lap of the long road to the Promised Land.

The last illegal ship diverted to Cyprus was named the *State of Israel,* but there are still arguments over which ship's passengers first set foot on Israeli soil after independence was voted. No refugees came ashore on May 14; the only ship carrying immigrants that entered an Israeli harbor that day did not dock until May 16.

At exactly 4 P.M., just as the independence ceremonies were beginning in Tel Aviv, the 5000-ton SS *Argentina,* a modern Italian liner, threaded her way into Haifa Harbor. The port was so clogged with British transports loading troops and equipment that the *Argentina* could not tie up at the passenger quay and had to move more than a mile off shore.

On her regular run from Genoa and Naples to Haifa, the *Argentina* was due to call at Alexandria, Egypt, on May 13, remain there one day, and then go on to Haifa. Her 520 passengers included 375 DPs with forged Mossad immigration permits, fifty returning Israelis traveling on private or official business, sixty-five Christian tourists and pilgrims, and thirty Egyptians. On May 11, two days out of Genoa, the *Argentina*'s captain received an urgent message to change course and head for Haifa. Haganah had persuaded the owners that if the ship docked first at Alexandria, the Egyptians might intern the Israelis and immigrants as enemy aliens and impound the liner.

All night the *Argentina* remained off shore. At dawn on Saturday May 15, when the immigrants went on deck and saw the Israeli flag flapping in the breeze from the Port Administration building, great shouts of jubilation arose. A delegation waited on the captain and asked him to lower the British flag, which was flying alongside the Italian emblem, and to replace it with an Israeli standard. When the captain answered that he didn't have an Israeli flag, a Hashomer Hatzair group from Hungary produced a blue and white pennant given them by a Zionist society in a small Carpathian town. A youngster shinnied up the mast, removed the Union Jack, folded it neatly, and tossed it to the deck. Then he tied the Zionist emblem to the mast with a piece of wire. (Tova Steinfeld, the first woman to land from the *Argentina* on May 16, was the first Israeli woman to settle in the Syrian village of Banias after the Israeli forces occupied it in June, 1967. She later managed the Banias Café, in the former Syrian Army Officers Club.)

The first ship to reach Tel Aviv after independence was the SS *Teti*, an old 1000-ton Greek coaster. She dropped anchor off the main breakwater at 5:45 A.M. on May 15 while the city was undergoing its baptism of fire from the air. Chartered by the Jewish Agency's immigration department for legal sailings, the *Teti* was not a part of Mossad's operations. Manned by a Greek crew, the *Teti* left Marseilles on May 8 flying a Panamanian flag of convenience. Its 189 passengers included 42 foreign newspapermen, press photographers, and newsreel teams. They had arranged this form of transportation through the Jewish Agency's press office in order to cover the birth of Israel. Although they missed the events in Tel Aviv on May 14, they had front-row seats for the first Egyptian bombing raid.

Also on board were some 30 Israeli and Jewish Agency "apparatchiks" and 116 immigrants carrying legal British certificates of entry. They were the last to require such permits as well as the first to come ashore with Israeli visas stamped on their certificates. At journey's end the weary new-comers entered the country through a temporary hall adjoining the dock over whose entrance hung a simple sign in Hebrew that said "Welcome Home." The first to come through and be received by Meier Lemberg, who had just returned from a night-long tour of air-raid duty, was Samuel Brand, age seventy, a survivor of Buchenwald. Told that Ben-Gurion was waiting to greet him before going to the first session of the Israeli Cabi-net, Brand tearfully waved a slip of paper that said, "The right to settle in the land of Israel is hereby given." Signed by the Immigration Depart-ment of Israel, it was the new state's visa Number One.

Another group of 320 immigrants, who had arrived in Haifa port from Cyprus on May 15 on the SS *Kedma,* beat the *Teti* passengers ashore but they were not officially registered by the Israeli authorities. The 5000-ton *Kedma,* owned by Jewish maritime interests in Palestine but flying the British flag, had sailed from Haifa on May 12 to pick up 320 immigrants from the blockade-runner *Ben Hecht,* which had been in-terned in Cyprus. The *Kedma* left Famagusta on May 14 and got word of Israel's independence while at sea. The British flag was immediately low-ered and the Israeli flag hoisted, and the *Kedma* was thus the first Israeli flagship to enter an Israeli port.

Because of the Sabbath the passengers were not to disembark until Sunday, May 16. But the immigrants refused to stay on board: "We waited fourteen months in the Cyprus camps and we are not going to wait another fourteen hours," one Jew shouted in Yiddish. Fearing a riot, the skipper ordered the *Kedma* tied up at the passenger quay without permission from the port authorities, and the refugees swarmed ashore. A minor Jewish Agency official ran from office to office, vainly seeking someone willing to assume responsibility for registering the newcomers on the Sabbath. In the end he accepted the captain's passenger list, signed his name at the bottom of each page, and wrote at the top of each page, "Immigration formalities waived because of government closure." (One of the *Kedma* immigrants was Abraham Tayar, from Tunisia, who was mar-ried in one of the Cyprus camps and later became a member of the Knes-set from Haifa.)

The 10,000-ton Rumanian steamer SS *Transylvania* also arrived on May 15. Then the biggest and most modern ship linking Haifa with Eu-rope, the *Transylvania* had left Constanza on May 10 with 637 passen-gers, 227 of whom had British certificates. The rest were tourists, busi-nessmen, and pilgrims bound for Istanbul and Beirut. The Jewish immigrants stepped ashore in Haifa on May 16.

The Jewish Agency subsequently registered 1189 immigrants as having arrived in Israel on May 15–16, but the actual number was 1347. Not all of the immigrants bothered to register or wait for official processing. Many of these May 15–16 immigrants rushed off to join the Israeli Army, and some were killed in action on May 30 during the battle for Latrun and to date have not been identified. Because they had joined up without documents, when the bodies were collected for burial during a cease-fire, there was no way of knowing who they were.

Two schooners, the *Narkiss* and the *Narkissa,* also played a role in the drama of May 14–15. At 9 A.M. on May 14 the twin converted fishing boats were only three miles out of Tel Aviv when they received orders from Haganah not to attempt to put into port until after the state was proclaimed. Both vessels were part of Mossad's fleet and their passengers were illegals transported by Bricha from Poland and Rumania to Italy.

The ships had left Porto Venire on May 1. The 120-ton *Narkiss* normally carried a crew of twelve and one hundred tons of fish. This time she carried 160 men, women, and children crammed into narrow wooden shelves affixed to the bulkheads. Her captain was Benny Krawetz of Haganah's Palyam. The slightly smaller *Narkissa* took aboard 149 DPs. The two-week journey across the Mediterranean was uneventful for everyone except Mr. and Mrs. Wolf. She was in her ninth month of pregnancy when the *Narkiss* sailed, and a Haganah doctor had refused to let her make the trip, but he relented when she pleaded for the right to give birth in the Promised Land. During most of the journey, her husband squatted on the floor of the stinking, airless hold, gripping her hand. When the *Narkiss* reached Israeli waters, the immigrants began to cheer wildly and burst forth with "Hatikvah."

Amid the noise and excitement Mrs. Wolf went into labor and was carried to a small shack on the deck, which served as the *Narkiss*'s infirmary. There was a doctor on the *Narkissa,* but before Captain Krawetz could move the *Narkiss* close enough to bring the physician aboard, Mrs. Wolf, with the aid of an old woman, gave birth to a son, one of the several children for whom the claim is made of being the first Jewish baby born in the State of Israel.

As the doctor washed the baby with water from a fire-righting bucket and placed him on a white towel spread out on the wheelhouse roof, Krawetz received word from Tel Aviv to change the *Narkiss*'s name to *Nitzahon* (Victory), to prevent confusion with *Narkissa.* At the same time *Nitzahon* and *Narkissa* were ordered to move to within half a mile of the port. Krawetz radioed back: "We must dock at once, we have a newborn baby aboard." The reply was immediate: "You must wait until docking facilities are available. We also have a new baby on our hands—its name is Israel."

That was about 5 P.M. All through the night the Wolf baby cried. There was no milk, no diapers, not even hot water. Saturday morning Egyptian fighter planes zoomed over the *Nitzahon,* which had unfurled a handmade Israeli flag and painted its new name in Hebrew on its side. Then she hoisted anchor and raced out of the fire zone. Each time *Nitzahon* approached the harbor Tel Aviv flashed a message to wait. Not until Sunday morning, May 16, was Krawetz allowed to bring the schooner into port, followed by *Narkissa.*

At the dock an ambulance was waiting for Mrs. Wolf and her infant. Nineteen years later Lt. Itzhak Wolf of the Israeli Army Parachute Corps was one of the heroes of the Six-Day War, which preserved the independence proclaimed a few hours after he was born.

Part Four

THE DIPLOMATIC STRUGGLE

chapter

o o o o o o o o o o o o o o 25 o o o o o o o o o o o o o

AS THE CLOCK TICKED AT THE UN

TWO MINUTES BEFORE the proclamation meeting in Tel Aviv ended at 4:32 P.M., the Political Committee of the United Nations General Assembly opened its session at Lake Success at 10:30 A.M. EDT. The Committee had been charged with making its recommendations to the General Assembly so that it could act before the termination seven and a half hours later of the British Mandate at midnight Palestine time (6 P.M. in New York).

The Russians, adamant in favor of partition, sought to prevent the adoption of any resolution before the Mandate ended that could possibly impair the validity of the 1947 partition resolution and that might continue British influence in Palestine or UN supervision of Palestine. The Arabs stalled because they wanted to prevent the UN from taking any new action to place Jerusalem under its protection, because they hoped the Transjordan troops would capture Jerusalem once the Mandate lapsed. The United States delegation wanted UN action on a mediation or temporary truce proposal before the end of the Mandate that would, at least from a technical point of view, legally forestall the state, establish UN control over Palestine, and halt the immediate war that the Arabs threatened once Israel was proclaimed. The result was a filibuster as the UN raced against the clock.

The Political Committee had two matters to dispose of: the report of Subcommittee 9 on a plan for all Palestine, and that of Subcommittee 10, which was charged with developing a trusteeship plan for Jerusalem.

It was after 1 P.M. when the Political Committee by a vote of 31 to 7

adopted Subcommittee 9's resolution authorizing the appointment of a
UN Mediator in Palestine to be chosen by a General Assembly committee composed of representatives of China, France, USSR, Great Britain,
and the United States. The Soviet bloc voted "No" and the Arabs were
among the sixteen abstaining. With Dr. Julius Katz-Suchy of Poland insisting on the time-consuming procedure, over twenty votes were taken in
the committee as each paragraph in the subcommittee's report was voted
on separately. Relieving the largely inoperative Palestine Commission
from "further exercise of responsibilities under the General Assembly resolution of November 29, 1947," the new UN Mediator would be empowered to arrange for common services in Palestine, assure protection of the
Holy Places, promote peaceful adjustment of the future of Palestine, and
cooperate with the Truce Commission appointed by the Security Council
on April 23, 1948. This was later accepted by the necessary two-thirds
vote of the General Assembly.

In the mad fight against time US Delegate Francis B. Sayre suggested
that sandwiches be served while the Political Committee debated the
problem of a temporary regime for Jerusalem. But with the Arabs and the
Russians filibustering, and no agreement reached at Lake Success by 3:45
P.M., the matter was placed, without a vote being taken directly, before
the thrice-postponed plenary session of the General Assembly which was
scheduled to meet at Flushing Meadow at 4:30 P.M.

The members of the Political Committee hurriedly piled into cars for
the twenty-minute ride to Flushing Meadow, but it wasn't until 4:40
P.M.—just a little more than an hour before the official end of the
Mandate—that President Jose Arce of Argentina, who was serving as
President of the General Assembly, opened the 135th meeting of the
General Assembly with two statements: he would keep the session going
until its work was done and he would limit each speaker to five minutes.

The Russians challenged the five-minute limitation and Dr. Arce, putting his ruling to a vote, was upheld 36 to 11, with 3 abstentions. Arab
and Soviet-bloc spokesmen followed one another with their five-minute
addresses until 6:01 P.M., when the Franco-American plan for Jerusalem,
which needed a two-thirds vote, was defeated when it only got 20 votes,
with 15 against and 19 abstentions, including Great Britain.

For different reasons the Jews, the Arabs, and the Russians were all
delighted since no action was taken before the Mandate officially ended.
The Russians were elated with the elimination of Britain as a Mideast
power. The Jews were delighted because no legal technicality was enacted
that might make the proclamation of independence a direct violation of

UN action. The Arabs envisioned no barrier to an early triumph of their armed forces in Jerusalem.

Awni Khaldi of Iraq voiced the Arab position at 6:01 P.M., when he proposed that since it was impossible to complete action before the Mandate ended, all efforts to formulate a program of UN action be halted. "The whole game is up," he told the General Assembly, in what seemed to be the day's climax at the UN—that is until the news of American recognition.

But even these two climaxes were not enough to halt the talk at the UN. For some inexplicable reason the debate continued for another two hours, until Dr. Arce adjourned the session at 8:32 P.M. But with the partition resolution of November 29, 1947, still legally valid, Israel became the first-born of the UN.

It was the realization of the prophecy of Amos (9:11–15), which coincidentally, by centuries of Jewish tradition, was chanted that Sabbath by thirteen-year-olds celebrating their Bar Mitzvah:

> In that day will I raise up the tabernacle of David that is fallen, and close up the breaches of it; and I will raise up his ruins, and I will build it as in the days of old,
>
> That they may possess the remnant of Edom, and of all the nations, which are called by my name, saith the Lord who doeth this.
>
> Behold, the days come, saith the Lord, that the plowman shall overtake the reaper, and the treader of grapes him that soweth seed; and the mountains shall drop sweet wine, and all the hills shall melt.
>
> And I will bring again the captivity of my people of Israel, and they shall build the waste cities, and inhabit them; and they shall plant vineyards, and drink their wine; they shall also make gardens, and eat the fruit of them.
>
> And I will plant them upon their land, and they shall no more be pulled up out of their land which I have given them, saith the Lord, thy God.

chapter

∘ ∘ ∘ ∘ ∘ ∘ ∘ ∘ ∘ ∘ ∘ ∘ ∘ ∘ |26| ∘ ∘ ∘ ∘ ∘ ∘ ∘ ∘ ∘ ∘ ∘ ∘ ∘ ∘

JOY AT THE UN

"THIS IS MARVELOUS. This is what we've been waiting for," was the surprised but delighted reaction of Dr. Abba Hillel Silver after I. L. Kenen, press officer of the Jewish Agency delegation in New York, told him that President Truman had recognized the State of Israel. It was about 6:20 P.M. as Kenen handed a slip of yellow paper, an International News Service teletyped news bulletin, to Jewry's chief spokesman at the United Nations, the Chairman of the Jewish Agency–American Section.

Heralded by the traditional four bells that precede an important news flash, the bulletin received at the UN's press office at Flushing Meadow said: "The White House tonight recognized the provisional government of Israel de facto." After tearing the sheet off the teletype, UN Bureau Chief Pierre Huss ran out of his office toward the Assembly Hall, where he met Kenen and handed him the news. Kenen hurried down the steps and burst into the Assembly Hall, where he headed for the Jewish Agency delegation seated in boxes located to the immediate right of the podium. Rabbi Silver read the bulletin to his fellow delegates, among them Mrs. Rose Halprin, Dr. Emanuel Neumann, and Dr. Nahum Goldmann. To the bewilderment of the delegates, they rose and broke into cheers, halting the proceedings.

Seated next to Dr. Silver, when Kenen brought him the news of the Truman recognition, was Lionel Gelber, youthful Canadian historian and international expert who was a member of the team of technicians working with the Agency delegation. Assigned to maintain liaison with Dr. Philip K. Jessup and Dean Rusk, Gelber immediately went over to the US delegation to advise Jessup of the Truman action.

Whether the Jewish Agency delegation was completely surprised by the news of the Truman recognition is moot. Abba Eban, who as top figure among the Agency's experts maintained close relations with Dr. Weizmann and Epstein, as well as with Shertok and Silver, in a statement to the authors said that he knew from Weizmann and Epstein that the Truman recognition was expected. Dr. Neumann has stated that Bartley Crum had told him a few weeks earlier that a Truman recognition could be anticipated once the state was declared. But no one really knew for sure whether Truman would follow Clark Clifford's advice and overrule the State Department, and it is doubtful that if as many people knew or thought they knew what Truman would do, the secret would not have been as well kept as it was.

The news spread like wildfire. A few minutes later Arab delegates were talking excitedly to Dr. Jessup of the US delegation, demanding an explanation of the unexpected American action. But Dr. Jessup and the other American delegates could neither confirm nor deny the news: they were taken as much by surprise as anyone. When John Rogers, New York *Herald Tribune* UN correspondent, was told about the Truman recognition, the incredulous newspaperman pointed to the American delegation, still busy on the floor making a last stand for a trusteeship or mediation plan, and said, "Don't you think they'd know about it if the news were really true?"

Everyone sought confirmation. In a public question on the floor Dr. Alberto Gonzales Ferandes, Colombian Delegate, said, "I simply wish to have information from the delegation of the United States concerning the truth of the information." With US Ambassador Warren Austin not present, Francis B. Sayre, who was in charge, walked slowly to the stand and said, "There is no official information that we have." Baffled and embarrassed, the American delegates maintained silence until a half-hour later, when after checking with the State Department, Dr. Jessup confirmed the news and read the text of Truman's recognition statement.

After checking with Washington, the very embarrassed US Ambassador to the UN, Warren Austin, issued an explanatory statement that evening which said that "the recognition by the President of the provisional government as the de facto authority of the new Jewish state is the practical step to be taken in the present development of the difficult question of Palestine." To repeated rumors that he would resign his post, Austin expressed his annoyance the next day at the "very peculiar way" the rumors of his resignation kept cropping up. He said, "If you ask me if I have resigned, I have not. If you ask me whether I'm going to resign, I am not."

The Arab reaction against the United States was violent. Mahmoud Bey Fawzi, Egypt's chief delegate, excitedly shouted that in the changed circumstances, "it is an unworthy mockery" for the UN to continue talking about a UN peace agent for Palestine as proposed by the United States. He denounced the whole work of the Assembly and its Political Committee in the previous four weeks as "a mere fake." In some of the harshest words ever directed against the US delegates, the Egyptian charged that "something behind the scenes was being done," that "the hope of humanity is being shamelessly betrayed."

Faris el-Khouri of Syria assailed Dr. Sayre's statement that recognition of the Jewish state did not affect a truce for Palestine by recalling that Ambassador Austin had told the Security Council that its Truce Commission should operate on the basis of a political standstill.

Even the often conciliatory Dr. Charles Malik of Lebanon accused the United States of betraying the Arabs. "For four weeks we were dupes," he said, "and the whole thing was a show and a game."

Dr. Guillermo Belt, Cuban Ambassador to the United States, a consistent foe of partition, brought laughter from the delegates when he said, "It develops that the representatives of the Soviet Union and Poland are better informed on Washington's plans than the US delegation." When asked about the US position, one delegate told another that he didn't know: "I haven't seen an announcement for twenty minutes."

In an address charging that American policy on Palestine was "completely devoid of principle" and that American efforts to undermine partition were largely responsible for the Arab-Jewish warfare, Soviet Deputy Foreign Minister Andrei A. Gromyko indicated that his government would recognize Israel when, he said, "The Jewish state is in existence."

But it was Guatemala that was to be the second country to recognize Israel. As Arab spokesmen denounced the United States, Jorge Garcia Granados had put in a call to Guatemala City for authorization to announce recognition. When he couldn't get his call through and he saw Assembly President Arce arranging his notes for a closing speech, Granados decided not to wait any longer and he took responsibility on his own as he announced Guatemala's recognition. A few minutes later his call came through and the Foreign Minister endorsed the action of his UN representative who had played so important a role in pushing through the partition resolution the previous November.

When Dr. Silver heard the news of the Truman recognition, he reached the apex of his career as a Zionist leader. With Israel recognized by the United States, he, as an American, could no longer be its official spokesman at the United Nations. But in the years of his leadership of American Zionism he had carved a unique place for himself in the history of the Jewish people. His was the joy of leadership at an historic moment that brought to fruition the contributions of such Americans as the Friedenwalds, Gottheil, Brandeis, Mack, Frankfurter, Wise, Goldmann, Lipsky, Neumann, Goldstein, Weisgal, Halprin, Magnes, Henrietta Szold, and countless others.

THE ROLE OF AMERICAN ZIONISTS

THE HALF-CENTURY campaign of political Zionism began its triumphant push with Herzl at Basle, achieved international recognition with the issuance of the Balfour Declaration and the Versailles Peace Treaty that created the British Mandate, and came to its successful climax with the UN partition resolution of 1947 and the proclamation of independence in 1948.

Thousands of men and women played their roles in this historic undertaking. But in the final push three men dominated: Ben-Gurion, Weizmann, and Silver. Ben-Gurion gave his unswerving faith and courageous leadership to the people of the Yishuv; Weizmann contributed the soft suave hand of diplomacy that enabled him to maintain friendly relations with a Truman who had developed a horror of Zionist pressure and official American Zionist leadership; and Silver lit the fire under American public opinion that made it a nonpartisan political issue that finally triumphed in the UN and led to American recognition of Israel.

The mobilization of American public opinion by the American Zionist Emergency Council under Rabbi Silver's leadership was one of the most broadly conceived and brilliantly executed public-relations efforts in American history.

In *Jews in the Mind of America,* by Herbert Charles Stember and others, there is a striking indication of how American public opinion was changed on the question of Palestine. Based upon polls taken by the Gallup, Roper, and other organizations, many of which were privately sponsored by the American Jewish Committee, this change is noted.

"In December, 1944," the Stember book says, "only about a third of the population was aware that Palestine was ruled by Great Britain. In

May 1946, persons who knew this were still a minority; at the same time, almost three-quarters of the people said they had 'little or no interest' in the news about our [US] policy toward Palestine."

Stember goes on to say that between late 1945 and 1947 there was a considerable increase of interest in Palestine and its problems. He said that by then "about a half the public claimed to have followed the developments there, and three-quarters or more said they had heard or read something about the situation."

Though the polls reveal that many Americans had reservations about specific aspects of aid for the Jews in Palestine, such as loans, and about possible American intervention, a poll taken in March, 1948, two months before the proclamation, indicated that "half the population believed such a state should be encouraged. Only ten per cent felt it should be opposed, and about a fifth thought the U.S. should take neither position."

Stember summarizes: "Whatever the day-to-day vascillations of American policy and opinion, more Americans by and large sympathize with the Jewish than the Arab cause."

Today some Israelis seem inclined to minimize the role played by American Zionism in paving the way for the Jewish state; they are inclined to believe that only the sacrifice of people of the Yishuv could have created a Jewish state. No one denies this basic truth and no one seeks to minimize the roles played by Ben-Gurion and Shertok and their many aides. There are also those who would brush aside the role played by Dr. Weizmann in keeping diplomatic channels open, preferring to believe that it was the Silver-directed campaign alone that paved the way for recognition. But that is no more correct than the contention of those devoted to building the Weizmann legend who believe that his personal relationship with President Truman was the decisive and major factor.

The ultimate achievement that was the birth of Israel was the result of a three-pronged effort—coordinated for the most part, but not always —in which the three major strong-willed personalities agreed, in the final instance, that the end of the British Mandate, at a time when the world was developing an awareness of guilt for the Nazi Holocaust, was a propitious time that might never come again for the proclamation of the State of Israel.

The organized Zionist effort in the United States goes as far back as Herzl and the first World Zionist Congress shortly before the turn of the century; it even had such early-nineteenth-century precursors as Mordecai Noah and the poet Emma Lazarus. In 1824, before attempting to set up a temporary "city of refuge" for Jews on Grand Island, near Buffalo, Noah said, "We will return to Zion as we went forth, bringing back the faith we carried away with us." In a series of sixteen articles, "Epistle to the Jews," published in *American Hebrew Magazine* in 1882–83, Miss Lazarus wrote of the need for "a free Jewish state . . . a home for the homeless . . . a nation for the denationalized."

Dr. Richard Gottheil, after attending the first World Zionist Congress in Basle, organized the Federation of American Zionists in 1898 on his return to New York. He became its first President, and Rabbi Stephen S. Wise was its first Secretary. Other early leaders of this organization, which was to become the Zionist Organization of America, were Dr. Aaron Friedenwald, Benjamin Szold, Lewis N. Dembitz, Rabbi Max Heller, and Rabbi Judah L. Magnes. A little later among the leadership were Louis Lipsky, Jacob de Haas, Bernard G. Richards, Henrietta Szold, Louis D. Brandeis, Julian W. Mack, Felix Frankfurter, Harry Friedenwald, Robert Szold, Emanuel Neumann, Rabbi Solomon Goldman, Morris Rothenberg, Rabbi Abba Hillel Silver, Rabbi Israel Goldstein, Edmund I. Kaufmann, and Louis E. Levinthal, among many others.

But until the end of World War II the leadership of the movement was in Europe, and later under Dr. Weizmann in London, especially after Great Britain assumed responsibility for the Palestine Mandate. The dramatic manifestation of American dominance was marked by the conference in May, 1942, in New York which adopted an eight-point plank, the Biltmore Program, which asked that "Palestine be established as a Jewish commonwealth integrated in the structure of the new democratic world."

With this bold new tack, enunciated at the conference by David Ben-Gurion and spearheaded to adoption by Dr. Silver, the Americans became the prime partners with the Palestinians in the leadership of the fight for a Jewish state. The Zionist General Council (Actions Committee) endorsed this action at its conference in Jerusalem later that year, in November. Four years later, following the twenty-second World Zionist Congress, a twenty-man Executive of the Jewish Agency, the operating arm of the World Zionist Organization, was elected with a five-man American Section under the chairmanship of Dr. Silver. The others elected were Rabbi Wolf Gold, Chaim Greenberg, Mrs. Rose L. Halprin, and Dr. Emanuel Neumann. Together with Dr. Nahum Goldmann and Moshe Shertok, then head of the Agency's Political Department, there were generally at least seven members of the Executive in New York.

The purely American program—of education, propaganda, and pressure for a Jewish state—was the responsibility of the American Zionist Emergency Council headed by Dr. Silver. Founded in 1943 and functioning until 1949, its target was American public opinion, Jewish and non-Jewish, for in the early 1940s there was a considerable group of American Jews who in varying degrees opposed the creation of a Jewish state.

Operated nationally, through fourteen committees, the Emergency Council had 200 local emergency councils by January, 1944, 380 the following year, and eventually 400 throughout the nation. Local Zionist emergency councils were influential in securing pro-Zionist resolutions in thirty-nine State Legislatures and hundreds of municipalities representing more than 85 percent of the American population. By October, 1944, the American Zionist Emergency Council said in a report that 411 of the 535 members of the 78th US Congress endorsed the Zionist call for "immediate American action to sanction a Jewish commonwealth."

The Emergency Council operated within the Jewish community to solidify Jewish support and to counteract the American Council for Judaism, a small but militant and vociferous anti-Zionist group under the leadership of Lessing Rosenwald and Rabbi Elmer Berger. The Emergency Council conducted an educational program through the press and radio that sought to justify the Zionist position on Palestine and to open the doors to the hundreds of thousands of survivors of Nazism who had no other haven open to them. It also maintained contacts with American political leaders, primarily the President, the State Department, and members of both the Senate and the House.

President Truman often complained privately—and later publicly, in his *Memoirs*—about the pressure exerted on him by American Jews in behalf of Zionism and the proposed Jewish state. In particular, he complained about Dr. Silver to Dr. Weizmann in the ribald Trumanesque directness that characterized the President. Of Dr. Weizmann's efforts to minimize the extent of these pressures, Mr. Truman wrote in his *Memoirs:* "I do not think that I ever had as much pressure and propaganda aimed at the White House as I had in this instance. The persistence of a few of the extreme Zionist leaders—actuated by political motives and engaging in political threats—disturbed and annoyed me."

Reflecting on President Truman's resentment of the pressures exerted upon him, one of the authors recalls a visit to the White House with a Jewish War Veterans delegation during which David Niles, the very pro-Zionist aide to the President, advised, "Tell the Commander not to be critical about Palestine; to praise the President for his views. Nothing will do more good."

The success of the Silver-led propaganda effort is attested by the hatred of him that it inspired in the White House. Though it was dangerous in that it intensified the mulish streak that sometimes dominated the opinions of the man from Missouri, it also made a profound impression upon the President, who was sympathetic to the Zionist cause and also highly sensitive to political waves. And it also paved the way for, and made necessary, the soft-gloved approach of Dr. Weizmann.

There is no denying the point made by, among others, Rabbi Leon I. Feuer of the Collingwood Avenue Temple of Toledo, Ohio, a close Silver associate and partisan, that American recognition of Israel's independence by President Truman was not a sentimental gesture, either to his onetime haberdashery partner, Eddie Jacobson, or to a blind old man, Dr. Weizmann.

Writing in November, 1967, in the *American Jewish Archives* (Vol. XIX, No. 2), Dr. Feuer said, "Those kinds of political gestures simply do not take place. There was no miracle stemming from the coincidence that a man from Missouri named Truman happened to be President and his erstwhile partner and friend, Jacobson, happened to be a Zionist. What occurred was more prosaic but far more in line with the political realities. Truman was a candidate for President. He knew that the election of 1948 would be, as it was, uncomfortably close. He suspected that the Jewish vote in the populous states would be crucial. He knew all about, and as a politician respected, even if he was often visibly annoyed by, the pressure of the tremendously effective and responsive nationwide organization which Silver had created. He had an opportunity, by recognizing Israel, to make a grab for these votes, State Department or not. He saw his main chance and he took it."

In the May 16, 1948, issue of the *New York Times* Thomas J. Hamilton, then the paper's chief correspondent at the UN, reported three reasons for the sudden Truman de facto recognition of Israel, one of which was the intervention of New York City Democratic leaders, in particular Edward J. Flynn, who "insisted that in an election year it was essential to take some action to propitiate Zionist supporters, who were turning against the Truman administration because of its previous reversal on partition." The other reasons advanced by Hamilton were that the President was disappointed with the failure of the US delegation to the UN "to obtain acceptance of a temporary trusteeship, a truce or any other solution that would have precluded the establishment of a Jewish state" and that the march of events in Palestine made it "necessary to help fill the legal vacuum by promptly giving de facto recognition."

Commenting on the accomplishments of American Jewry in mobilizing public opinion for the Jewish state and its recognition by President Truman, Rabbi Silver, in a self-evaluation, reported to a meeting of the American Zionist Emergency Council on May 25, 1948, that

"The Jewish people of America are a wholesome, politically mature people. We just had to tell them what the situation was, and immediately they went to work. They even pressured us to do things. Throughout these two months their determination was evidenced in meetings, parades, demonstrations, resolutions, writing of letters, telegrams, conferences—it was perfectly amazing. It was because of that amazing strength that the Jewish Agency and the Emergency Council were able to do the things they did, and Washington realized it was facing a powerful popular movement. And that finally broke the back of the conspiracy."

But there is no denying either that Eddie Jacobson played a role by opening the doors of the White House to Dr. Weizmann when the President refused to see American Zionist leaders and that Dr. Weizmann performed a great service in getting the sympathetic ear of the President for the Zionist point of view to counteract the opposition of the State Department; certainly Dr. Weizmann's intervention with the President saved the Negev for the Jewish part of partitioned Palestine.

In some respects the climax of the Silver-Neumann-led American Zionist campaign, certainly its first peak, was the successful fight for partition that gave international recognition to the concept of the creation of a Jewish state in Palestine that was ratified by the United Nations on November 29, 1947. It is doubtful that Great Britain fully realized at the time that the beginning of the end of its control of Palestine occurred on April 2, 1947, when the British UN delegation requested that the Secretary General put the question of Palestine on the agenda of the regular fall session of the General Assembly. This led to the recognition on May 5, a little more than a month later, of the Jewish Agency as the Jewish representative body for consultation with the UN. Seven members of the Agency Executive—Ben-Gurion, Silver, Shertok, Greenberg, Halprin, Goldmann, and Neumann—were designated as its representatives to the United Nations. Three days later, on May 8, Dr. Silver, as the recognized spokesman of the Jewish people, took his seat between Cuba and Czechoslovakia and made his first presentation of the Jewish case before the UN.

Other presentations were by Shertok on May 10 and by Ben-Gurion on May 12, the closing statement by the Jewish delegation. This led to the appointment of an eleven-man United Nations Special Committee on Palestine (UNSCOP), under the chairmanship of Judge Emil Sandstrom of Sweden, that was to visit the displaced persons camps in Europe and Palestine in the course of taking testimony on the Palestine problem. Maj. Aubrey (Abba) Eban and David Horowitz were named Jewish liaison officers to the Committee. After four meetings at Lake Success, UNSCOP went to Palestine for three months where it heard thirty-four witnesses at thirteen public meetings and eighteen closed sessions. The first meetings in Palestine were held June 16–17 in the auditorium of the towered YMCA building in Jerusalem, opposite the King David Hotel. The Arabs boycotted the meetings.

The Jewish Agency testimony demanded the revocation of the 1939 White Paper and the establishment of a Jewish state; it opposed the continuation of the Mandate or the establishment of a trusteeship and rejected the creation of a binational state. Ben-Gurion and Shertok outlined the political aspects of the argument; Eliezer Kaplan, David Horowitz, and Peretz Bernstein made the economic presentation; and Rabbis Yehuda Leib HaCohen Fishman and Isaac Herzog outlined the historic and religious claims of Jews to Palestine. Dr. Weizmann concluded with a moving address that highlighted the tragic plight of a homeless wandering people who had made a great investment in toil, blood, and sweat in the building of a Jewish Palestine.

Speaking as an individual who had no official position in the Zionist movement, Dr. Weizmann advocated partition as the sole constructive solution to the problem, a point of view that was referred to only vaguely by all those who had testified previously for the Jewish cause. Dr. Weizmann's views had, however, been cleared with the Jewish Agency. To reinforce his argument, he read a letter from the respected South African statesman, Jan Christiaan Smuts, endorsing partition as the most acceptable solution.

UNSCOP, the nineteenth commission to grapple with the solution of the Palestine question, signed its final report in Geneva on August 31, 1947. It was unanimous in recommending independence for Palestine without delay, but it disagreed on important details.

A minority plan, signed by representatives of India, Iran, and Yugoslavia, proposed the creation of an independent federated state, the federation to compromise two subordinate states, one Arab and one Jewish. For the first three years the UN would designate the extent of Jewish immigration, which thereafter would be regulated by the proposed federal government.

The majority plan, signed by seven states (Australia signed neither report), proposed an economic union of two states for two years, after which each state would become fully independent if it had adopted a constitution, agreed to guarantee religious and minority rights, and set up safeguards for the Holy Places. This plan called for Jerusalem's becoming a United Nations trusteeship. During the first two years 150,000

Jewish immigrants would be permitted, and 60,000 additional immigrants each year thereafter, if the transitional period lasted longer.

The Zionist General Council meeting in Zurich in September, 1947, rejected the minority report as "wholly unacceptable," while giving a qualified acceptance to the majority report's recommendation for "the early establishment of a sovereign Jewish state." Its attitude was one of resigned acceptance because the plan did not "include areas of the utmost importance."

The American Jewish community received the majority report with approval, although the American Zionist Emergency Council, in a communication on August 29, two days in advance of the issuance of the UNSCOP report, warned its local committees against expressing too wholehearted an approval on the tactical ground that such enthusiasm would bolster the efforts "of our enemies within the UN further to whittle down pro-Jewish recommendations."

The UNSCOP report was referred by the General Assembly to an ad-hoc committee on Palestine under the chairmanship of Herbert V. Evatt of Australia; on October 2 it heard Rabbi Silver define the Jewish Agency's stand on UNSCOP's majority proposal. Making it clear that partition was not the Jewish Agency's proposal, he pointed out that the Jewish national home suggested would now be confined to less than one-eighth of the territory set aside for it in the original Mandate. This was because Palestine had been previously partitioned in 1922, when Transjordan—three-quarters of the area of the original mandated territory—was cut off, later to be set up as an Arab kingdom. Thus acceptance of the UNSCOP partition plan entailed "a heavy sacrifice on the part of the Jewish people," but if this sacrifice was to provide an immediate final solution, the Jewish Agency would reluctantly be prepared to "assume the responsibility of recommending acquiescence to the supreme organs of our [Zionist] movement. . . . We would be prepared to do this because the proposal makes possible the immediate establishment of a Jewish state, an idea for which our people have ceaselessly striven for centuries."

Assuming that acceptance of the plan was "subject to further discussion of the constitution and territorial provisions," Dr. Silver objected specifically to the proposed elimination of western Galilee from the Jewish state and the internationalization of all of Jerusalem. Although recognizing the propriety of placing the Old City, with its Holy Places, under international trusteeship, he objected to taking away the Jewish New City with its 90,000 inhabitants.

Dr. Silver also pointed out that partition was not a new solution for the conflicting Arab-Jewish claims to Palestine, noting that it had been suggested as far back as 1936 by the Peel Commission.

Dr. Goldmann has revealed that Dr. Weizmann, the President of the World Zionist Organization, was unofficially sounded out on a partition plan in 1936 by Professor Reginald Coupland, whom both men respected as the most outstanding man on the Peel Commission. At the time Dr. Weizmann, pledging him to secrecy, asked Dr. Goldmann's opinion, which was that a partition plan should be accepted. Dr. Goldmann said many years later:

"If, at that time, the Zionist movement had reacted spontaneously and unhesitatingly in favor of partition, there might have been a good chance of the British government's putting it into effect . . . but when the Zionist Congress of 1937, after protracted and dramatic debates, and following a twice-repeated roll-call vote, expressed by a small majority, and in a somewhat obscure form, its 'willingness to consider' the partition plan, it was already too late. The Jewish acceptance was too vague and hesitant and, in face of the Arabs' categorical rejection of the plan, the British government began to have second thoughts and shelved the whole project.

"Next to the wholly inadequate reaction of world Jewry to the Nazi danger and the frivolous illusion that Hitler would be unable to make good his threats against the Jews, the attitude of the Zionist movement to the first partition plan was, in my view, the gravest error of this Jewish generation, and one which led directly to the destruction of one-third of our people in the Hitler decade. In fact, the consciousness of our culpability was not only one of the imperative reasons that decided me later to 'take the wrappings off' the partition plan, but it most strongly compelled many of those, like my friend Stephen Wise, who had rejected the proposal, to accept and to fight for it when the plan was revived."

The UN acceptance of the partition plan in 1947 depended upon its approval by both the US and the USSR, a task to which the Jewish Agency representatives—particularly the Russian-speaking Shertok, Horowitz, and Epstein—devoted themselves. By October 13, two days after a similar expression by the American delegate, Herschel V. Johnson, Semyon K. Tsarapkin announced Soviet support for partition. It marked the first time—in fact it is one of the few times in all UN history—that the United States and the Soviet Union agreed on a major international issue.

After considerable debate and much political maneuvering Dr. Silver reported to a joint meeting of the Jewish Agency and representatives of the American Jewish Committee, and other cooperating non-Zionist groups, that victory on the partition issue was in doubt—that the Jewish cause could count on twenty-three sure votes in the General Assembly as against thirteen sure Arab votes, whereas thirty-three votes were necessary for the required two-thirds majority. Dr. Silver reported that some of the Latin American countries were showing a tendency to abstain because they "did not want to become involved" and that the US government "was not giving wholehearted support and firm leadership."

But by the end of October, after the Secretary of State issued strict instructions to the American delegation to make it clear that America was deeply interested in the success of partition and hoped other countries would follow the American lead, there was great concern over the attitude of France, subject to pressures from its Moslem North African colonies. And following the lead of France, it seemed, might be the neighboring states of Belgium, Holland, and Luxemburg. It was encouraging that Canada, South Africa, and New Zealand, much to the annoyance of Great Britain, came out for partition.

The last weeks of October and the first few weeks of November were devoted to interminable though highly significant discussions on the makeup of the territory of the partitioned Palestine, which was divided into six segments—three Arab and three Jewish, plus additional enclaves—by splitting the country in half vertically and into thirds horizontally. The Jewish and Arab areas were interlocked in a checkerboard design by this division, which Pakistan's Zafrullah Khan described as the "craziest and most absurd carpet ever suggested."

Through individual decisions, the Jews were able to come up with historic Safed, the airport at Lydda, and ancient Masada. They lost most of the western Galilee and the important port of Jaffa. But the big issue was the Negev, with its port city, Eilat, an invaluable outlet to the Gulf of Aqaba and the Indian Ocean, which was lost to the Jews until Dr. Weizmann intervened with President Truman. It took a personal phonecall by the President, on November 22, to the US delegation at the UN to bring about a change in the delegation's stand on this issue. The hardest blow the Jews had to accept, as the price of the sovereignty that partition would provide, was the loss of Jerusalem, the nation's historic capital, which was so much the symbol of a Zion reborn. But without this sacrifice the two-thirds majority in the UN General Assembly was impossible.

The partition resolution of November 29 was not to be adopted,
however, without a struggle. Plans were introduced to separate the
problem of Jewish refugees from the Palestine question. A mere one-
vote majority turned back a proposal to refer the entire issue of Palestine to the International Court of Justice at The Hague for an opinion,
a diversionary attempt that would have led to indefinite postponement.
Unexpected speeches of opposition to partition by the delegates of the
Philippines and Haiti raised serious doubt that the necessary vote
would be achieved. When Dr. Oswaldo Aranha, President of the Assembly that month, remarked to Dr. Silver and Dr. Neumann in a corridor meeting that the chances of getting a two-thirds vote "looked
bad," it was decided that a roll-call vote must be postponed while further politicking was done among the delegates by the Agency representatives and its friends.

At first it was thought that a subtle filibuster might provide enough
time. As an additional protection Dr. Neumann approached Gen. John H.
Hildring, the most pro-Zionist member of the American delegation,
with the suggestion that the delegation ask for a cancellation of the
scheduled evening session because the Thanksgiving holiday was to be
celebrated the next day. After consulting with other members of the
delegation, General Hildring came back to the lobby, winked at Dr.
Neumann, and thus told him the session would be called off. It was
also helpful that the Arabs unwittingly joined the filibuster by giving
lengthy answers to each pro-partition speech, thus providing sufficient
time for last-minute Zionist efforts to change votes.

David Horowitz has recalled the helpfulness of the entire American
Jewish community, particularly that of Judge Joseph M. Proskauer who
headed the American Jewish Committee. It was this last-minute effort
by the Zionists and their allies that Secretary of Defense James V. Forrestal referred to in *The Forrestal Diaries* when he wrote that Under
Secretary of State Robert A. Lovett told a Cabinet meeting that "he
had never in his life been subject to as much pressure as he had in the
three days beginning Thursday morning (November 26) and ending
Saturday night (November 29)." The delegations of Haiti, the Philippines, and Liberia, under the impact of various pressures, changed their
minds.

On November 28 Colombia proposed the appointment of a new
committee to effect a reconciliation between the Jews and Arabs that
would have delayed action until the following February. After this was
voted down, France—in an obvious gesture toward her Moslem

colonies—suggested a twenty-four-hour adjournment for the same purpose. With this postponement voted, the decision was delayed until November 29.

Excitement ran high, not only among Jews: UN officials estimated that over 10,000 persons had phoned to request admission passes to the General Assembly meeting; 1000 persons pressed the single entrance gate on that day awaiting admission. Newspaper and radio coverage was widespread.

Camille Chamoun of Lebanon submitted a last-minute compromise adjusting the original Arab plan of a unitary federal state to a formula of cantonization. But the US and the USSR, joined together in the persons of Herschel Johnson and Andrei Gromyko, voted to table this motion and the roll call began after Assembly Chairman Aranha ruled that an Iranian proposal for adjournment to January 15 was out of order.

The vote for partition, officially known as "Resolution 181 (II) on the Future Government of Palestine," was 33 to 13 with 10 abstentions (including Great Britain) and an absence. Thirteen of the thirty-three "Yes" votes were Latin American. Crucial in getting this Latin American support were the efforts of Dr. Jorge Garcia Granados of Guatemala and Dr. Enrique Rodrigues Fabregat of Uruguay, both members of UNSCOP and the most vigorous pro-Jewish spokesmen at the UN, and the backstage work of Samuel Zemurray, the Rumanian-born fruit king of Central America, who headed the powerful United Fruit Company.

After international legal sanction was thus given to the Jewish state, which was to be born less than six months later, Dr. Silver said that "the Jews will be forever grateful to the nations which contributed to the decision." At a joyful celebration held at the St. Nicholas Arena on 66th Street off Columbus Avenue, more than 5000 persons crowded the auditorium, with an overflow of 2500 outside, to hear Dr. Weizmann, speaking in Yiddish, call the partition decision "a practical thing" and state that the most important task ahead was to seek peace with the Arabs.

In Palestine the next day David Ben-Gurion said that the "United Nations decision to reestablish the Jewish people's sovereign state in a part of its ancient homeland is an act of historic justice which compensates at least partly for an unparalleled wrong to which the Jewish people has been subjected for over eighteen hundred years."

BETWEEN PARTITION AND STATEHOOD

THE ALL-IMPORTANT BATTLE on partition had been won, but the war was just beginning. As fighting broke out in Palestine almost immediately, as the British stalled in the Holy Land, and as the Arabs prepared to push the Jews into the Mediterranean, so too did the battle continue at the United Nations, where Great Britain maintained its traditional "divide-and-conquer" tactics, the Arabs never gave up in their attempts to block partition, and America vacillated in her support of partition while seeking to prevent a total war in the Middle East.

The UN resolution for partition called for a five-member United Nations Palestine Commission (Bolivia, Czechoslovakia, Denmark, Panama, and the Philippines), but it didn't provide the means necessary for enforcing the Commission's authority in Palestine. As a matter of fact, the Commission was never admitted into Palestine by the Mandatory government.

Thus the undeclared war in Palestine between the Arabs and the Jews began on November 30, just one day after the UN partition resolution, when eight Jews were killed by the Arabs. Within a few days Jerusalem was split into watertight Jewish and Arab quarters and it became unsafe in various parts of the country for Jews to leave their quarters. In less than a month, by December 20, Jewish and Arab civilian casualties totaled 177 with an additional dozen members of the security forces killed. By January 20 the totals were 720 killed and 1552 wounded.

For the most part this fighting in Palestine was not between native Arabs and Jews. A major role was played by "volunteers," openly recruited by their governments in Egypt, Transjordan, and Syria, who infiltrated across the borders by land and sea. On March 5 even the British conceded in a report by the British Colonial Secretary to the House of Commons that there were 5000 such invaders.

The UN was powerless to stop the fighting. A Security Council resolution on March 5 appealed to "all governments and peoples, particularly in and around Palestine, to take all possible action to prevent or reduce such disorders as are now occurring in Palestine."

A subsequent resolution on March 30, this one introduced by the United States, called upon "Arab and Jewish armed groups in Palestine to cease acts of violence immediately." Shertok, speaking in behalf of the Jews on April 1, objected to this US resolution as giving the impression that the fighting was purely a local outbreak. He insisted that the trouble was caused by "the presence of Arab aggression from outside, sponsored by and organized by Arab states, members of the United Nations, in an effort to alter by force the settlement envisaged by the General Assembly's resolution of November 29, 1947." The Jews could not accept a truce, Shertok said, unless the foreign invaders withdrew. "No people," he pointed out, "will voluntarily sign a truce with invading forces converging upon it and poised to strike. This would not be a truce, it would be capitulation." But the United States brushed aside the objection and pushed through a 9–0 vote, with 2 abstentions.

A third US-sponsored resolution for truce was voted on April 16, but by this time the Shertok point was acknowledged, the resolution referring to "the entry in Palestine of armed bands and fighting personnel, groups and individuals, and weapons and war matériel."

But nothing stopped the fighting in Palestine, particularly as the British frustrated all efforts of the Palestine Commission. Kept out of the embattled country, the Commission was informed that "His Majesty's Government would not regard favorably any proposal that it proceed to Palestine earlier than two weeks before the date of the termination of the Mandate." The Commission reported its failure to the General Assembly on April 10, stating that "the armed hostility of both Palestinian and non-Palestinian Arab elements, the lack of cooperation from the Mandatory power, the disintegrating security situation in Palestine, and the fact that the Security Council did not furnish the Commission with the necessary armed assistance, are the factors which have made it impossible for the Commission to implement the Assembly resolution."

The "disintegrating security situation" in Palestine gave high US officials, traditionally opposed to the idea of Jewish statehood and against partition, the opportunity to work openly against what they believed was the unwise and embarrassing partition decision of November 29.

As early as January 28 Dr. Silver, interviewed in Jerusalem, stated that "certain officials of the Department of State have reverted to the old technique of circumventing the declared American policy on Palestine." He warned that to withhold positive support of the partition decision "at the very moment when Arab violence is directed toward frustrating it would be a betrayal of the United Nations and the Jewish people."

The United States introduced at least three major proposals that would at least have delayed and probably permanently killed the November 29 UN resolution for Jewish statehood through partition.

The first indication of American vacillation occurred on February 24, when Warren Austin made the almost incredible interpretation of the UN partition resolution, saying, "the Charter of the United Nations does not empower the Security Council to enforce a political settlement, whether it is pursuant to a recommendation of the General Assembly or of the Security Council itself."

Generally viewed as an indication of a tendency to "explain away" or even abandon the UN partition plan, the Zionists felt they had to seek again President Truman's intervention. An effort was immediately made by Dr. Weizmann, but the President didn't want to speak to any Zionists and the appointment was made only with great difficulty more than a month later. At that time, March 18, according to the Truman assistant and biographer Jonathan Daniels, the President assured Dr. Weizmann that the position of the United States had not changed. The President is quoted as telling Dr. Weizmann: "You can bank on us, I am for partition."

But less than twenty-four hours later Ambassador Austin announced a complete reversal of US policy in the Security Council. Based on the contention that the General Assembly's partition vote was only a "recommendation" and not a binding decision, he proposed that a "temporary trusteeship for Palestine should be established under the UN Trusteeship Council." He made this recommendation, he said, "because partition cannot be implemented by peaceful means" and because the "maintenance of international peace is at stake." He called for a special session of the General Assembly, but said that pending this, Great Britain should be induced to retain the Palestine Mandate and should "suspend its efforts to implement the proposed partition plan."

The Zionists were not alone in interpreting this as a "sellout." As the Arabs indicated that they thought partition was dead "and the victory theirs," world public opinion generally agreed with Dr. Silver in calling the Austin proposal a "shocking reversal . . . a revision of an international judgment, maturely arrived at after prolonged and objective investigation," a change "extorted by threats and armed defiance."

The lines for Israel's declaration of statehood and the War of Liberation were being drawn. On March 23 a joint meeting of the Jewish Agency and the Va'ad L'umi (National Council) warned that the Jews of Palestine "will oppose any proposal designated to prevent or postpone the establishment of the Jewish state" and that "not later than 16 May next, a provisional Jewish government will commence to function in cooperation with the representatives of the United Nations then in Palestine."

Dr. Silver told the Security Council, after Shertok had spoken on the legal aspects of the partition resolution, that the Jewish Agency did not believe that partition could be implemented only by sending a UN armed force to Palestine. Stating that the Jews were prepared to defend themselves, he warned that the Jews of Palestine "confronted with the threat of annihilation" would be compelled "by the considerations of sheer survival to take all necessary measures which the situation will call for."

The United States plan for trusteeship—a twenty-six-page "Draft Trusteeship Agreement for Palestine" submitted to a special session of the General Assembly convened at American request—found little support from either the member UN states or American public opinion. The notable exception was Great Britain, still hoping against hope that something would develop to continue British control in Palestine. Russia's Gromyko, Sweden's Hagglof, and the representatives of two of Britain's dominions, New Zealand's Berendson and Australia's Hood, demanded that the UN go ahead with the partition plan. Only Nationalist China gave "general support" for the US program.

Ambassador Austin pledged that the US would "undertake its share of responsibility" in providing troops to carry out the trusteeship, but laid down two conditions: a truce between the Jews and the Arabs, and the willingness of other countries to participate in enforcing the trusteeship. (It is highly indicative that American troops were never offered for enforcing the peace after the partition plan was announced.) But the American plan for trusteeship never got off the ground, and Austin had to admit that efforts by the United States to persuade other countries to provide troops "have thus far produced no tangible result."

To dramatize the shift in US policy, the American Zionist Emergency Council mounted an ever increasing series of demonstrations. It was climaxed by the designation of April 8 for daylong prayer, parades, and other forms of public protest. Special services were held in synagogues throughout the country. In New York City 150,000 persons, led by the Jewish War Veterans, paraded down Fifth Avenue to protest the United States reversal on partition. Dr. Neumann, as President of the Zionist Organization of America, in Tel Aviv at a meeting of the Zionist Actions Committee, cabled the parade leaders "assurance that the Jewish state is coming into existence." The parade ended with a mass meeting at Madison Square Park, on lower Fifth Avenue, and a prayer at the Eternal Light memorial. The parade and similar demonstrations symbolized the Silver-Neumann-led American policy of public protests in behalf of statehood as against the earlier Weizmann policy of diplomatic and political bargaining behind closed doors that achieved the important Balfour Declaration.

The second major American effort to forestall the proclamation of statehood, sentiment for which everyone knew was developing in Palestine, was the proposition advanced early in May by Assistant Secretary of State Dean Rusk that the United States fly an Arab-Jewish group to Palestine, or anywhere else, on the President's private airplane, *Sacred Cow,* to effect "an immediate and unconditional cease-fire for ten days beginning May 5." In the discussion or rumor stage for several days, this memo, dated May 3, specifically called for "an extension of the Mandate for ten days," a recess of the Special Session of the General Assembly for ten days, and an immediate movement by air to Jerusalem, or a site mutually agreed upon, of delegated representatives of the Arab Higher Committee and Arab states, designated representatives of the Jewish Agency for Palestine, and designated representatives of those countries holding membership in the Security Council Truce Commission, the United States, France, and Belgium.

Rusk's *Sacred Cow* truce project was the most crucial problem to come before the American Zionists in the days immediately before May 14. It caused a split among the membership of the Jewish Agency's

American Section and the vote taken, certainly when viewed in retrospect, was the ultimate decision taken by the Americans on whether or not Israel should be advised to go ahead with immediate statehood.

The six members of the American Section, which met at 9 P.M. on Monday, May 3, at the Agency's 66th Street office, were joined by ten members of its Political Advisory Committee. They met amidst all sorts of wild rumors—that the United States had threatened economic sanctions if the Jewish state was declared; that there might be an embargo on sending funds to the countries of the Palestine area, which would in effect have nullified the immediate value of the money provided by American Jews through the United Jewish Appeal and other fund-raising efforts.

There was also the advice, and warning, of Secretary of State Marshall, who was a former American military chief of staff, that Haganah and other Jewish military forces couldn't stand up to the British-trained and other Arab militia. It was decided not to make any decisions based upon military capabilities, it being felt that this decision had to be made on the spot in Palestine by the Jewish Agency Executive on the basis of military estimates.

In the political discussion it was generally agreed that the proposals in the form submitted were not acceptable. But led by Dr. Goldmann, a number of those present expressed themselves in favor of the consideration of a three-month truce. Dr. Goldmann strongly cautioned against completely rejecting the American truce proposal. Shertok spoke in a similar vein, feeling that further discussion with the American authorities was in order.

Against this, Dr. Neumann stated that failure to proclaim the Jewish state on the date set for the end of the British Mandate would be forfeiting a great historic opportunity. Mrs. Halprin strongly opposed acceptance of the American proposals. Dr. Silver said that it would be calamitous if a misstep in New York weakened the Yishuv's determination to proclaim a sovereign Jewish state at this propitious moment, and he saw in the Rusk proposal an effort by the anti-Zionist State Department clique to substitute a Trusteeship for the establishment of the Jewish state.

Dr. Goldmann, in urging acceptance of the truce proposal, gave two absolute conditions: the dissociation of the truce from trusteeship and a US guarantee of help in the event of an invasion by the Arab states in view of their freedom to acquire arms during the truce.

It was generally agreed that though there might be valid reasons for considering and discussing the truce aspects with American authorities, there could be no consideration or acceptance of the idea of extending the British Mandate. There was also agreement that the mere acceptance of a truce flight would in large degree be morally binding upon the Jewish leaders in Palestine. There was great fear that acceptance of the Rusk proposal "constituted a provisional political settlement involving the imposition of an international authority."

No vote was taken by the joint meeting, but at a meeting of the American Section, which began at midnight, immediately following the adjournment of the other meeting, the Rusk proposal was turned down by a 4–2 vote, with Dr. Silver, Dr. Neumann, Mrs. Halprin, and Rabbi Gold voting for the turndown and Dr. Goldmann and Shertok voting for acceptance of the American plan.

Even after the vote the American Section and its Political Advisory Committee continued to meet and discuss the truce proposal, giving fuel to the thought that there might still be time for a change. The following morning another session was held, attended by the six members of the American Section, thirteen members of the Political Advisory Committee, and two invited guests, one of whom, Rabbi Levin, was to be a signer of the Proclamation. The group was informed that the *Sacred Cow* flight was voted down by the American Section Executive and that it was agreed that Shertok should soon return to Palestine to report on developments. The group then discussed the advisability of consideration of a proposal for a three-month truce if it involved a deferment of the proclamation of the Jewish state but contained requisite safeguards.

In the discussions that followed four members of the American Section Executive reaffirmed their opposition to any deferment (Dr. Silver, Dr. Neumann, Mrs. Halprin, and Rabbi Gold) and three members of the Advisory Committee (Leon Gellman, Rabbi Israel Goldstein, and Dr. Joseph B. Schechtman) similarly expressed themselves.

Indicating that they were prepared to consider deferment of the proclamation, under variously stated conditions, were two members of the American Section Executive (Dr. Goldmann and Shertok) and seven others (Jacob Greenberg, Jacob Rivtin, Louis Segal, Baruch Zuckerman, Dr. Siegfried Moses, Dr. Otto Wolfsberg, and Rabbi Yitzchak Meir Levin). Their views were cabled to the Executive in Palestine.

The official view of the American Executive was expressed on May 4 in a telegram from Shertok to Rusk that said:

"I have now had an opportunity of consulting my colleagues with reference to the suggestion that Arab and Jewish representatives as well as representatives of the United States and possibly France and Belgium be flown to Palestine immediately in an airplane to be furnished by the President of the United States. We understand that the purpose of this mission is to achieve a truce in Palestine. I do not need to repeat that the Jews were not the aggressors and that we are keenly anxious for the restoration of peace. But we do not consider that the somewhat spectacular proceeding now suggested is warranted. Peace can in present circumstances best be achieved by an unconditional agreement for an immediate 'cease-fire.' The Jewish authorities in Palestine have previously indicated their readiness for such an arrangement and we desire now in the most formal way to state that we are ready forthwith to agree to a 'cease-fire' order provided the Arabs do likewise.

"The procedure now indicated apparently ignores the action already taken by the Security Council in regard to the appointment of a Truce Commission and bases itself on the proposals privately advanced by the American delegation. It would involve us in a moral responsibility in respect of those proposals which we cannot possibly accept. Nor could we lend ourselves to the suggestion that the British Mandate should be prolonged, whether de jure or de facto, beyond the appointed date.

"Permit me to add that insofar as consideration on the spot in Palestine is called for, the Truce Commission appointed by the Security Council could no doubt be relied upon to undertake any consultations with Jewish representatives there; indeed our fully authorized representatives in Palestine are in close contact with that Commission.

"With regard to the Arabs, it must be observed that not a single member of the Arab Higher Committee remains in Palestine, whereas Mr. Jamal Husseini, [Vice-] Chairman of the Arab Higher Committee, and its accredited representative, is of course available in New York, as well as representatives of the other Arab states.

"Permit me again to emphasize our sincere desire to do all that we properly can to restore peace and order in Palestine."

The final American effort to forestall the proclamation was the last-minute attempts on May 14 at the United Nations. The British Mandate over Palestine ended at 6 P.M. (New York time) as the American delegation at the UN was still fighting for the Franco-American trusteeship for Jerusalem and for a general truce. Earlier that day a UN political subcommittee had authorized the appointment of a UN Mediator in Palestine.

That the American delegation did not know that President Truman would recognize Israel within less than two hours, and that they were still seeking to delay the proclamation, is indicated by the fact that when the 135th General Assembly of the UN convened at Flushing Meadow at 4:40

P.M., Francis B. Sayre of the US delegation pointed out that if the Assembly was going to create a trusteeship for the government of Palestine, it had to do so within the hour, before the termination of the British Mandate.

All that happened, though, before the General Assembly adjourned at 8:32 P.M., more than two hours after the Mandate ended, was that it authorized a UN mediator to meet with the Jews and Arabs to do what he could to help them reach a peaceful settlement. But this was a meaningless gesture. When the General Assembly turned down the plan for a temporary trusteeship over Jerusalem, it left the UN partition resolution of November 29, 1947, intact, and there was thus no legal international barrier to Israel's proclamation of independence.

chapter

o o o o o o o o o o o o o |29| o o o o o o o o o o o o o

THE TRUMAN RECOGNITION

IT WAS 6:11 P.M. EDT, Friday, May 14, eleven minutes after the State of Israel had been born at the expiration of Britain's Mandate over Palestine, when Charles G. Ross, President Truman's Press Secretary, summoned the few reporters still on duty at the White House. Only the wire service and radio reporters were on hand, waiting until the news lid was on for the night. The rest had gone home or were at the Massachusetts Avenue office of the Jewish Agency on Embassy Row, covering the wild celebration marking the raising of the Israeli flag.

At 6:20 P.M. Ross broke the news of US recognition of Israel. "As you know," he began, "the Jewish state has been proclaimed in Palestine, at one minute past six our time." Then he read to the astonished reporters the brief historic statement: "This government has been informed that a Jewish state has been proclaimed in Palestine and recognition has been requested by the provisional government thereof. The United States recognizes this provisional government as the de facto authority of the new State of Israel."

The forty-two-word announcement ended three years of doubt and debate over American policy, which had been characterized as "a pretzel-bender's nightmare" because it had twisted and turned so often.

In his book *Years of Trial and Error,* Truman said the announcement was handed to the press "exactly eleven minutes after Israel had been proclaimed a state." What he meant was eleven minutes after independence came into effect at midnight Israel time, May 15.

On the morning of May 14 the President had received a letter from Dr. Chaim Weizmann, personally delivered to the White House by his secretary. The message informed Truman that the state would be proclaimed that day and urged that "the greatest democracy be the first to welcome the newest democracy into the family of nations." Later the White House asked that an official letter of request for recognition be sent to him from Eliahu Epstein, the official representative in Washington of the Jewish Agency and, later, of the provisional government.

Only the day before at his press conference Truman had declined to commit himself on whether recognition would be extended to the new state when it came into being, and he parried all questions by saying he would cross that bridge when he had to. On May 12 Secretary of State Marshall told reporters that it was too early to say if the Jewish state would be recognized in the event the United Nations failed to approve some kind of provisional regime before Friday midnight, Palestine time. He said he wanted to wait and see who did what when the Mandate lapsed.

Coupled with Truman's announcement of recognition was a separate White House statement issued by Ross, reaffirming the United States's continuing desire for an Arab-Jewish truce. "The desire of the United States to obtain a truce in Palestine," the statement explained, "will in no way be lessened by the proclamation of a Jewish state. We hope that the new Jewish state will join with the Security Council Truce Commission in redoubled efforts to bring an end to the fighting—which has been, throughout the United Nations' consideration of Palestine, a principal objective of this government."

The news flash from the White House hit like a bombshell. Consternation and disbelief enveloped the United Nations, where Palestine's fate was being fruitlessly debated. The red-faced United States delegation, still pressing for a different solution, was left holding the bag. The Arabs were shocked and bitter. The Jewish world erupted with joy. Newborn Israel was jubilant when the news became known there three hours later.

The full story of Truman's decision to recognize Israel so quickly is still locked away in classified documents in Washington and Jerusalem. In piecing together the known facts, four main elements emerge. The first was the President's disappointment with the failure of the United States delegation to the United Nations General Assembly to win acceptance of the American proposals for a temporary UN trusteeship, a truce, or any other solution that would have precluded the immediate establishment of the Jewish State. A second was the swift march of events in Palestine, particularly the Jewish military successes, which made it clear that nothing done at Lake Success could alter the partition of the Holy Land. Since the British had refused Washington's last-minute appeal to postpone the termination of the Mandate, Truman felt it essential to fill the legal vacuum by prompt extension of de facto recognition. A third factor was the big city Democratic party leaders who insisted that it was imperative in a Presidential election year to pacify Jewish voters and their supporters who were turning against the Truman Administration because of its previous reversal on partition, a view that was effectively being promulgated by American Zionists under the leadership of Rabbi Silver. A fourth consideration was worry lest the Soviet Union beat the United States to the punch by becoming the first Great Power to recognize Israel.

Added to these political realities were Truman's sharp sense of history and his unwillingness to welch on a private promise he had made to Dr. Weizmann in March and reiterated several times thereafter.

Actually the decision was far from sudden. Press Secretary Ross was not exaggerating when he told his crowded press conference on the morning of May 15 that recognition was "not a matter of snap judgment." The President, he said, "had it in mind for some time," but, he added, it "was impossible to fix a timetable on the approaches to a decision." Final agreement on recognition was not reached until the afternoon of May 14, but preparations for it had started weeks before. Truman's own conditioning for his memorable act had begun almost from the day he became President. (In 1949 Israel's Chief Rabbi Isaac Herzog solemnly assured Truman at the White House that "God put you in your mother's womb so you would be the instrument to bring about the rebirth of Israel.")

A NEW PRESIDENT

On April 19, 1945, a week after he was sworn in, Truman received Rabbi Stephen S. Wise and assured him he would do everything to carry out Roosevelt's policy on Palestine. This didn't mean much, for neither the White House nor the State Department had taken any official notice of the British White Paper of 1939. During the war years the State and War Departments avoided any pronouncement on Jewish claims and interests in Palestine on the ground they did not want to interfere in the affairs of an ally. In fact, in 1943 Secretary of State Cordell Hull and in 1944 Secretary of State Edward R. Stettinius had each submitted to President Roosevelt the draft of a statement to be issued jointly with Britain, asking for the cessation of all discussions on Palestine, but FDR shelved the idea.

In 1944 the 78th Congress was on the verge of adopting a joint resolution that in effect called for American intervention with Britain to help achieve Jewish statehood. The resolution asked that the United States use its good offices to open the doors of Palestine to the free entry of Jews and to take appropriate measures to "provide full opportunity for colonization so that the Jewish people may ultimately reconstitute Palestine as a free and democratic Jewish commonwealth." On March 17, in the midst of hearings on the resolution, Secretary of War Henry L. Stimson sent the House Committee on Foreign Affairs a brief letter saying that further action on the resolution "at this time would be prejudicial to the successful prosecution of the war." On the eve of the landings in Normandy he wanted to avoid any disturbance in the Near East that might require deployment of troops away from the main assault. Army Chief of Staff George C. Marshall simultaneously warned the Senate Foreign Affairs Committee that he would not be responsible for the military effects in the Moslem world if the resolution passed.

The previous day President Roosevelt had seen Rabbis Wise and Silver. On emerging from the White House they told reporters they were authorized to make the following statement in the President's name: "The American government has never given its approval to the White Paper of 1939. The President is happy that the doors of Palestine are open today to Jewish refugees and that when future decisions are reached, full justice will be done to those who seek a Jewish national home, for which our government and the American people have always had the deepest sympathy, and today, more than ever, in view of the tragic plight of hundreds of thousands of homeless Jewish refugees." Some saw these words as a subtle hint to Britain not to carry out the White Paper regulation that would have barred further Jewish immigration after 1944.

In October, 1944, President Roosevelt sent a message to the convention of the Zionist Organization of America, through Senator Robert F. Wagner, pledging himself to effectuate the Jewish commonwealth in Palestine as soon as practicable. "I am convinced that the American people give their support to this aim," he declared, "and if reelected, I will help bring about its realization." Shortly after, the War Department withdrew its objections to the Congressional resolution, but the State Department again stayed Congress' hand.

FDR's correspondence with King Ibn Saud of Saudi Arabia, and his meeting with the desert potentate on the way back from Yalta in February, 1945, indicated that the President had made unknown commitments that conflicted with his promises to the Jews. Bartley Crum, an American member of the Anglo-American Committee of Inquiry on Palestine, said State Department officials had given him a secret file that showed that "since September 15, 1938, each time a promise was made to American Jewry regarding Palestine, the State Department promptly sent messages to the Arab rulers discounting it." Six months after FDR's death Secretary of State James F. Byrnes made public a letter that the President had written to Ibn Saud on April 5, 1945, recalling their recent conversation in which "I assured you I would take no action, in my capacity as chief of the Executive branch of this government, which might prove hostile to the Arab people."

Dr. Joseph B. Schechtman, in *The U.S. and the Jewish State Movement,* concluded that by the spring of 1945 "disappointment with and resentment against the Roosevelt Administration's record on the Palestine question had become bipartisan and widespread among Jews and Gentiles alike." John Marlowe, in *The Seat of Pilate,* a study of the Palestine Mandate, observed that once the 1944 Presidential election was over, and before FDR's death, "it did not appear that American policy toward Palestine would be likely to stand in the way of a resolute implementation of the White Paper policy of His Majesty's Government."

Ben Hecht, in his autobiography, quoted Bernard M. Baruch, a lifelong Democrat, as saying in 1944, "I have had a two-hour talk with President Roosevelt about the Jews and the Jewish problem. I have also spoken to Governor [Thomas E.] Dewey [FDR's opponent in 1944 election] on the same subject. I can only tell you that as a result of these talks . . . I would rather trust my American Jewishness in Mr. Dewey's hands than in Mr. Roosevelt's." David K. Niles, who served as a White House assistant to both FDR and Truman, said later, "There are serious doubts in my mind that Israel would have come into being if Roosevelt had lived."

The gyrating American policy on Palestine was one of FDR's bequests to Truman. Five days after he succeeded Roosevelt, Truman said that Secretary of State Stettinius handed him "a special communication expressing the attitude and thinking of the State Department" on Palestine. The document warned the President that efforts would probably be made shortly by "some Zionist leaders to obtain from you at an early date some commitments in favor of the Zionist program, which is pressing for unlimited Jewish immigration into Palestine and the establishment there of a Jewish state." Truman was cautioned that the Palestine problem involved matters "which go far beyond the plight of the Jews of Europe," and since the United States had vital interests in the Near East, "this whole subject . . . should be handled with the greatest care with a view to the long-range interests of the country."

On the eve of the Potsdam Conference in July, 1945, the State Department worked hard to keep Truman from discussing Palestine with Winston Churchill. "A top-secret briefing book," as Truman called it, was prepared with suggestions for handling the matter with the British Prime Minister. The State Department pleaded with Truman not to press "the Zionist point of view in his talks with Mr. Churchill," even at the risk of incurring sharp criticism from "certain pro-Zionist groups in this country and abroad." He was reminded that a pro-Zionist position "would run the risk of creating hatred for the United States throughout the Arab world."

In his *Memoirs* Truman said "he was skeptical . . . about some of the views and attitudes assumed by the 'striped-pants boys' of the State Department!" He felt they didn't care enough about what happened to the displaced persons and he was confident that it was possible to help the victims of persecution and still be alert to the long-range interests of the United States.

On July 24, 1945, Truman sent Churchill a note voicing the "passionate protests" in America against Britain's White Paper policy and expressing the hope that London would take steps to lift the curbs on immigration. Despite the State Department, Truman raised the question with Churchill. Clement Attlee, who succeeded Churchill as Prime Minister after the unexpected Labour Party victory in the 1945 elections, gave a noncommittal reply. On his return from Potsdam, Truman said he favored letting as many Jews as possible into Palestine without jeopardizing civil peace there. Sincerely concerned with the plights of the Jewish DPs, Truman did not yet connect this with the idea of a Jewish state. In fact, he told Congressman Adolph Sabath of Illinois, he hoped to secure such treatment for the Jews in Europe that they would not have to emigrate to Palestine.

While he was not yet ready to commit himself on the long-range future of Palestine, Truman on humanitarian grounds continued to press the British to open the gates to 100,000 Jewish DPs. On June 22, 1945, he sent Earl G. Harrison, former US Commissioner of Immigration and Naturalization, to investigate the needs and living conditions of the DPs. Harrison's recommendation for the quick evacuation to Palestine of 100,000 Jewish DPs was endorsed by Truman in a letter to Attlee on August 31, 1945.

Instead of acting on Truman's plea, Attlee proposed that an Anglo-American Committee of Inquiry study all facets of the Palestine problem. Truman's reluctant agreement was interpreted by friends of Jewish statehood as an abdication to British imperial interests. On November 29, 1945, exactly two years before the UN voted to approve partition, Truman expressed opposition to a renewed attempt to get a pro-Zionist con-current resolution through Congress. He indicated sympathy with a "free Palestine" and support for making Palestine a haven for Jewish refugees, but he did not favor a Jewish state because he objected in principle to any state established on religious or racial lines. Nevertheless, the resolu-tion passed, in the House on December 17 and in the Senate on Decem-ber 19, 1945, after some modification to accord with Truman's objections.

Shortly before, on December 4, 1945, Truman for the first time re-ceived Dr. Weizmann, who found the President "an encouraging listener." A few days later Weizmann sent Truman a memo, asking his support for a Palestine solution that would lead to "a Jewish democratic common-wealth giving shelter, sustenance and peace to Jews and Arabs alike."

When the Anglo-American Committee on May 1, 1946, recom-mended that 100,000 Jews be allowed into Palestine, Truman was so pleased that he agreed to negotiate on its other proposals, which were un-acceptable to the Zionists. A joint Anglo-American cabinet-level commit-tee then produced the Morrison-Grady plan, which also called for admit-ting 100,000 Jews. Coupled with this, however, were political and territorial conditions that would have doomed Jewish statehood. Jews and Arabs rejected the scheme and Britain insisted that all the recommenda-tions had to be accepted before the immigration proposal could be con-sidered.

On October 4 Truman declared he could not support the Morrison-Grady plan because opposition to it had developed among members of both major political parties in and out of Congress throughout the coun-try. Secretary of Defense Forrestal, the Zionists' bitterest Cabinet foe, later charged that the President's action was tantamount to "a denunciation of the work of his own appointees." He charged, in *The Forrestal Diaries,* that Truman's decision had impelled Secretary of State Byrnes to wash his hands of the whole Palestine issue. Forrestal quoted Byrnes as blaming Truman's action on Niles and Judge Samuel I. Rosenman, the President's former special counsel. According to Byrnes, Niles and Rosenman had warned Truman that Thomas E. Dewey, the probable Republican Presi-dential candidate in 1948, was on the verge of endorsing the Zionist posi-tion, and that unless Truman anticipated this move, the Democrats would lose New York in the 1946 Congressional elections.

In his October 4 statement Truman renewed his plea for "substantial immigration" into Palestine at once without waiting for "a solution to the Palestine problem." More important, however, he also advocated, for the first time, the partition of Palestine along the lines then being advanced unofficially in Washington by the Jewish Agency. "Creation of a viable Jewish state in control of its own immigration and economic policies in an adequate area of Palestine instead of in the whole of Palestine" is a solution to which "our government could give its support," Truman announced.

The nature of such a solution, and the firmness of American backing for it, became the crux of the yearlong struggle that swirled around Truman during the battle over partition in the United Nations. The State and Defense Departments, spurred on by Loy Henderson, chief of the Near Eastern Division, and by Forrestal, bombarded the President with dire warnings against taking any stand that would alienate the Arab world and thus make it amenable to Soviet approaches in the Middle East. The propaganda apparatus of the American Zionist Emergency Council, most American Jewish organizations, and pro-Zionist members of Congress besieged him to support the maximum Zionist position.

These pressures coincided with the heating up of the Cold War. In the same week of May, 1947, in which the UN established UNSCOP, the Truman Doctrine came into play. Earlier that year Britain had notified Washington that she could no longer provide Greece with the help necessary to prevent a takeover by Communist guerrillas backed by Russia and Bulgaria. In response to Truman's request, Congress voted $400 million to extend economic, financial, and military aid to Greece and Turkey. The fear that the fall of Greece and Communist threats to Turkey might trigger serious disorders that could spread to the Middle East made American military and diplomatic strategists hostile to any position that would antagonize the Arab states and further Russian ambitions in the Middle East. Thus Zionist aspirations came into conflict with the views of men in the highest echelons of government that a pro-Zionist stance endangered national security.

During the UN debate on partition between September and November, 1947, Jewish pressure on Truman became so intense that it almost alienated him permanently. "Action of some of our American Zionists," he wrote to Mrs. Eleanor Roosevelt, "will eventually prejudice everyone against what they are trying to do. . . . I regret this situation very much because my sympathy has always been on their side."

By mid-November it became clear that some form of Jewish statehood stood a good chance of being approved by the UN, but no firm decision had yet been reached on the boundaries of the Jewish and Arab states. Foes of Zionism in the US delegation and in the State Department began putting the heat on the Jewish Agency to give up the southern Negev to the Arabs, hinting that if the Zionists remained adamant, the US might withdraw its support of partition. Since this raised the danger that the whole partition plan might be jettisoned, the Jewish Agency's diplomats agreed that only Truman's intervention could save the situation and that only Weizmann could sway the President.

WEIZMANN SAVES THE NEGEV

Eliahu Epstein, director of the Jewish Agency's political office in Washington, had established important contacts in the State Department and had developed close ties with White House aides Clark Clifford and David K. Niles. Through them, an appointment was made for Weizmann to see Truman at noon on November 19, 1947. Too ill to fly, Weizmann left for Washington on November 18 by the overnight train, accompanied by Epstein. On the way he told Epstein that just as the Jews had found a great friend in Lord Balfour on one occasion, so he was confident that Truman would become their champion at an even more crucial moment. According to Epstein, Weizmann credited Truman with setting off the chain of events that decided Britain to surrender the Mandate when he sent Earl G. Harrison to study the DP situation.

At Union Station, Weizmann and Epstein were met by Supreme Court Justice Felix N. Frankfurter, an old friend of Weizmann's. In the judge's limousine they drove to the Shoreham Hotel, where Weizmann rested until a little before noon. At the White House he was received by Niles, Clifford, and Stanley Woodward, Chief of Protocol. The latter escorted Weizmann into the President's oval office. Epstein remained with Niles and Clifford.

Weizmann had with him a short memorandum prepared by Epstein describing the important role Eilat would play in the economy of the Jewish state by providing an outlet to the sea. Attached to the memo was a map of the Negev and the Gulf of Aqaba, graphically depicting how Eilat in the hands of the Arabs would be a constant menace to the Jewish state. Weizmann, who was with Truman for thirty minutes, found the President warm, understanding, and greatly impressed by the argument that without access to the Red Sea the Jewish state would be permanently handicapped. When he left, Weizmann had won Truman's assurance that he would send personal instructions to the US delegation at the UN to support the inclusion of Eilat and the whole of the Negev in the Jewish state.

At the very moment Truman was making this promise the State Department was drafting orders to the US delegation to vote against the incorporation of Eilat within the borders of the Jewish state. The matter was due for a vote in a UN subcommittee at 3 P.M. on November 20. Armed with these instructions, Herschel V. Johnson of the US delegation met with Moshe Shertok and David Horowitz of the Jewish Agency in the lobby at Lake Success a little before 3 P.M. Johnson was about to tell Shertok the news from the State Department when an aide told him he was wanted on the lobby telephone. At first Johnson refused to take the call and sent his deputy, John Hildring. In seconds Hildring was back, reporting that Truman was on the line. Johnson excused himself and, as Abba Eban described it, "leaped to the telephone booth like a startled and portly reindeer." For twenty minutes Shertok and Horowitz sweated out the interruption until Johnson returned. For a moment he was so flustered he forgot that Shertok and Horowitz were waiting, as he was surrounded by aides eager to know what the President wanted.

Flushed with embarrassment, Johnson said apologetically, "What I really wanted to say to you, Mr. Shertok, was that we have no changes to suggest." On November 25 the General Assembly's ad-hoc committee on Palestine adopted the majority report on partition, including the provision to include in the area of the Jewish state the section of the Negev originally proposed in UNSCOP's report. Everyone involved in the episode agreed that the race to preserve the frontiers of the Jewish state was won only because Truman had been persuaded by Weizmann.

THE BATTLE FOR PARTITION

Emboldened by the skin-of-the-teeth pro-partition vote in the UN, the pro-Arab oil lobby and its allies in the State Department and among US military planners instigated a sub-rosa attempt to persuade the Truman Administration to reverse itself.

On January 13, 1948, Secretary of Defense Forrestal told the House Armed Services Committee that the hostile Moslem response to the US-backed partition decision had put the oil pipelines in the Middle East in jeopardy. At a Cabinet meeting two days later he warned that without Middle East oil, the Marshall Plan would fail and the entire US economy would be in danger. Vice-Admiral Robert Carney, deputy chief of naval operations for logistics, backed him up in testimony before the same committee on January 21.

That same day Forrestal suggested to Under Secretary of State Robert

Lovett the possibility that the UN would be unable to implement its decision and that the US might then be pressured into enforcing it unilaterally. Lovett "agreed in general" and then showed Forrestal a document that had just come from the State Department's planning staff. As Forrestal summarized it in *The Forrestal Diaries,* this paper indicated:

1. The UN partition plan was unworkable;
2. The US was under no obligation to support it if it was not workable without force;
3. It was against American interests to supply arms to the Jews while maintaining an embargo against the Arabs, or to accept unilateral obligation for carrying out partition;
4. The US should take steps as soon as possible to secure withdrawal of the partition proposal.

On January 29 Forrestal and some of his aides met with Dean Rusk, director of the State Department's Office of UN Affairs, Loy Henderson, chief of the Near Eastern Division, and others from the State Department. Forrestal reported that Henderson had developed a theory that the General Assembly's partition vote was merely a recommendation, not a final decision of the UN itself. In Henderson's view, American backing for partition was predicated entirely on the assumption that it would prove "just and workable." When Forrestal asked if there was not already sufficient evidence "to support a statement that the unworkability of the proposed solution would justify a reexamination," Henderson agreed. The "evidence" was the worsening situation in Palestine, where the British were deliberately encouraging chaos while the Jews grimly fought Arab irregulars to carry out the UN's decision.

Henderson's ideas were summarized in a paper submitted to Secretary of State Marshall on February 12 and outlined by him that same day to the National Security Council. As Forrestal reported it, the document offered three alternatives as a guide to American policy:

1. Outright abandonment of support for the UN decision;
2. Vigorous support of forcible implementation of partition by the UN Security Council involving the use of substantial American military forces, either unilaterally or jointly with Russia;
3. An effort to refer the question back to the General Assembly and an attempt to reshape the policy without surrendering the principle of partition, but adopting some temporary expedients such as an international trusteeship, a joint Anglo-French-American mandate, or revision of the partition plan along the lines of the cantonal scheme proposed in the defeated UNSCOP minority report.

Dwight D. Eisenhower, then Army Chief of Staff, told Forrestal that effective US participation in a Palestine police force would involve about one division, with appropriate supporting units. According to Gen. Alfred M. Gruenther, Planning Chief of the Joint Chiefs of Staff, employment of more than one US division would necessitate partial mobilization and the reinstitution of the draft. With the Cold War intensifying, the Pentagon was not sympathetic to any policy that would divert American troops to the Near East or precipitate the movement of Russian forces into that area.

The Defense Department's idea of the US stance toward Palestine was outlined in a secret forty-page memorandum that Clark Clifford passed on to Truman on February 17, 1948. The essence of the memo was:

1. The US needs a friendly or neutral attitude on the part of the Arabs which is essential to maintain access to Middle East oil;
2. The US cannot permit the USSR to gain a foothold in the Middle East, which it might do through participation in a UN force involved in implementing the UN partition resolution;
3. The US position on Palestine thus far has bitterly antagonized the Arabs.

The CIA added its opinion that partition could not be implemented. In the Clifford papers there is a copy of a February 20, 1948, CIA report suggesting three alternatives to the UN decision:

1. The UN could set up a Jewish state by force;
2. There could be no action by the UN;
3. The UN could reconsider the whole issue.

The CIA document said that the Jews would probably have to agree to reconsideration and "it is realistic to assume that a new solution would have to be acceptable to the Arabs, who would probably be willing to make some concession on the basis of the UN's minority report."

None of these steps had the approval of either Marshall or Truman, but they indicated what was in the wind. The rumors of an impending US aboutface on partition were vigorously denied by Truman, Marshall, and Warren Austin, US Ambassador to the UN. Nevertheless, the Jewish Agency people and the American Zionist leadership became so alarmed that they once again sought a direct approach to Truman.

In his *Memoirs* Truman spoke of "the Jewish pressure on the White House" that "did not diminish in the days following the partition vote in the UN." Individuals and groups, he recalled, "asked me, usually in rather quarrelsome and emotional ways, to stop the Arabs, to keep the British from supporting the Arabs, to furnish American soldiers, to do this, that and the other. I think I can say that I kept my faith in the rightness of my policy in spite of some of the Jews. . . . As the pressure mounted, I found it necessary to give instructions that I did not want to be approached by any more spokesmen for the extreme Zionist cause. I was even so disturbed that I put off seeing Dr. Chaim Weizmann, who had returned to the United States and had asked for an interview with me."

Weizmann had left for London after the UN vote and was planning to go to Palestine to be on hand when the Jewish state was born. Bowing to the insistence of the Jewish Agency that he was urgently needed in the United States, Weizmann returned on February 4. For the next six weeks desperate efforts were made to get Truman to talk to Weizmann, but official Washington seemed to have drawn a tight curtain between itself and Zionist spokesmen.

Weizmann's letter of February 10 asking for an appointment before Truman left on a Caribbean vacation was answered by Matt Connelly, the President's appointment secretary. It was a "so sorry" note, dated February 12, saying Truman's schedule was completely filled until February 20, when he was leaving Washington. Herbert Bayard Swope was called in to use his high-level political contacts, but he too got the brushoff. To friends and visitors Weizmann said, "Never before in my life have I been on such a fool's errand." On February 16 he wrote to Lovett, requesting an audience, but the best he could get was a tentative date for the last week in February.

Meanwhile, the State Department fired the first shot in the retreat from partition. On February 24 Ambassador Austin told the UN Security Council that the UN Charter did not empower it to enforce a political settlement (partition), whether it grew out of a General Assembly recommendation or originated with the Council itself. While he assured the UN that the US remained committed to partition, his argument that the Security Council could not enforce it made plain the US's waning enthusiasm. Deterred by the agonized appeals from Democratic Party leaders worried over the Jewish vote in the 1948 election, Truman had at first overruled the State Department career officers and many of the admirals and generals. But worsening relations with Russia impelled him to yield.

Three days before Austin spoke out in the UN, Truman's onetime haberdashery partner in Kansas City, Missouri, Eddie Jacobson, entered the picture. Jacobson had never met Weizmann but as a World War I buddy of Truman and still a personal friend, he had easy access to him at the White House.

Jacobson later recalled that on the night of February 20 he was awakened by a telephone call from Frank Goldman, President of B'nai B'rith. Calling from Washington, Goldman said he was acting for the combined Zionist forces who were terribly concerned because Truman had been rebuffing top Democratic Party figures from all parts of the country who had been urging him to see Weizmann. The President had even turned down Ed Flynn, Democratic boss of New York, who only forty-eight hours earlier had tried vainly to get an appointment for Weizmann.

Goldman was so excited that he proposed that Jacobson charter a plane and rush to Washington to see Truman before he left for Key West. As Jacobson tells it, he was assured that he was the last hope of persuading Truman to talk to Weizmann. Jacobson hurried to the Menorah Hospital to consult his lawyer, A. J. Granoff, who was recuperating from a throat operation. At Granoff's bedside the two composed this telegram to Matt Connelly, knowing it was too late to reach Truman before he left on vacation:

"Would appreciate it much if you will place the following message on the President's desk so that he will get it at once: 'Mr. President, I know that you have very excellent reasons for not wanting to see Dr. Chaim Weizmann. No one realizes more than I the amount of pressure that is being thrown on you during these critical days, but, as you once told me, this gentleman is the greatest statesman and finest leader that my people have. He is very sick and heartbroken that he could not get to see you. Mr. President, I have asked for very little in the way of favors during all our years of friendship, but I am begging you to see Dr. Weizmann as soon as possible. I can assure you I would not plead for any other of our leaders. If you wish me to be present, I will fly to Washington at once as I would deem it an honor to be with you gentlemen. I am praying that you will be able to see us. Please wire. Eddie Jacobson.' "

Truman's reply, in a letter dated February 27, came from the submarine base at Key West. It was a virtual "No." Truman told his ex-partner there wasn't anything Weizmann "could say to me that I don't already know." He complained to Jacobson that "the situation has been a headache to me for two and a half years. The Jews are so emotional and the Arabs are so difficult to talk with that it is almost impossible to get anything done. The British, of course, have been exceedingly noncooperative in arriving at a conclusion. The Zionists, of course, have expected a big stick approach on our part, and naturally have been disappointed when we can't do that."

Jacobson refused to accept this as a turndown. When Truman got back from Florida, Jacobson turned up at the White House on March 13. Connelly greeted him effusively as an old friend of the boss, but begged him not to discuss Palestine with the President. In the President's office the two old friends chatted briefly about family matters and Jacobson's business before Jacobson gingerly raised the Palestine question. To his amazement, Truman became tense, grim, abrupt, and angry, and used language that made Jacobson wonder if his old crony had turned into an anti-Semite. Yet Jacobson knew how Truman had suffered under the verbal assaults of Jewish leaders. The meeting appeared to be over, with Truman still adamant.

Then Jacobson changed his approach and began comparing Weizmann to Andrew Jackson, Truman's lifelong hero. Jacobson said Weizman was his hero, that he was ill but had come thousands of miles just to see Truman. He chided the President for refusing to meet with Weizmann just because the President had been insulted by some American Jewish leaders. Jacobson's words slowly seemed to take effect as Truman drummed his desk with his fingers and stared out the window. Suddenly, the President swiveled around, faced his desk, and said, "You win, you baldheaded s.o.b. I will see him. Tell Matt to arrange the meeting as soon as possible after I return from New York on March 17" (Truman was to speak at the St. Patrick's Day dinner at the Hotel Astor).

From the White House, Jacobson walked slowly to the Hotel Statler, where Frank Goldman and Maurice Bisgyer, Executive Vice-President of B'nai B'rith, were anxiously waiting. Also waiting, elsewhere in Washington, was Herman Rosenberg, the forgotten man in the Truman-Weizmann-Jacobson episode. Part of the mythology associated with Eddie Jacobson is the claim that he was ignorant of and unconcerned with Palestine until early 1948, when B'nai B'rith leaders enlisted his aid in opening the White House doors to Weizmann. The facts are somewhat different.

BEFORE JACOBSON

At the end of 1944 the Zionist Organization of America established a Committee on Unity for Palestine whose job it was to counteract the anti-Zionist activities of the American Council for Judaism. The committee's director, Rabbi Arthur J. Lelyveld (now rabbi of the Fairmount Temple, Cleveland, and a former President of the American Jewish Congress), traveled throughout the country addressing parlor meetings arranged by Zionists to which non-Zionist Jews were invited. In April, 1945, shortly after Truman became President, Rabbi Lelyveld went to Kansas City for four such meetings. One was in the home of Mr. and Mrs.

Ernest Peiser because Mrs. Peiser was then a member of the national board of Hadassah.

One of those present was Herman Rosenberg, Peiser's partner in the lithographing business. As a member of Captain Truman's Battery D of the 129th Field Artillery in World War I, Rosenberg had an intimate relationship with the President and with Eddie Jacobson, who also served in Battery D. Rosenberg held identification card no. 2 in the informal Battery D Association. The President's was no. 1, and Ernest Schmidt, the association's secretary-treasurer, held no. 3. After assuming the Presidency, Truman had issued these cards to his fellow members of Battery D. White House aides were instructed to admit cardholders to the President's office whenever they were in Washington. Rosenberg had three of the cards made up in bronze and gave one to Truman.

Peiser and Rosenberg were not only business associates but fast friends. Rosenberg, however, did not work too hard at being Jewish. Nevertheless, the Peisers told Rabbi Lelyveld that it was important to win Rosenberg over to the Zionist cause. When the Peisers asked him to talk to the President about Palestine, Rosenberg pointed out that Eddie Jacobson was even closer to Truman and that Jacobson ought to be exposed to the Zionist story. A member of Congregation B'nai Jehudah (Reform), whose rabbi, the late Samuel Mayerberg, was then flirting with the American Council for Judaism, Jacobson was largely unaware of Jewish or Zionist affairs. When the Peisers contacted him in his store and left Zionist literature with him, they found him polite but not greatly interested. All he would say was that his mentor on Jewish matters was Rabbi Mayerberg. Once the Peisers invited Jacobson to the home of Rabbi Gershon Hadas to hear another prominent Zionist leader, Rabbi Israel Goldstein of New York, but Goldstein's overzealousness left Jacobson unmoved.

At that point Rabbi Lelyveld entered the story. Rosenberg, who had been won over by the Peisers, brought Jacobson to one of Lelyveld's meetings. The haberdasher and the Rabbi hit it off from the start, for Jacobson was impressed with the Rabbi's articulateness and with his look of the "assimilated Jew," with whom Jacobson could identify. Jacobson attended two more of Lelyveld's parlor talks and then had a long private conversation with him in the haberdashery shop. By mail and telephone Rabbi Lelyveld kept in touch with Jacobson. Once Jacobson suggested he might like to take Rabbi Lelyveld to see President Truman.

Rabbi Lelyveld thought this was nothing but talk until he received a message that an appointment had been made for Jacobson and him to see Truman at the White House. As the Rabbi remembers it, the visit occurred on June 26, 1945—he has a newspaper clipping with "1945" penciled on it to prove it—but Rabbi Lelyveld's memory tricked him: the day and the month are correct, but the year was 1946. It could not have been June 26, 1945, because on that day President Truman was in San Francisco, signing the Charter of the United Nations. The official White House appointment records for the Truman years, now in the Harry S Truman Library at Independence, Missouri, show that Jacobson, Lelyveld, and Charles Kaplan (a New York shirt manufacturer) met the President at 11 A.M., June 26, 1946. They also record an earlier White House date for Jacobson and Herman Rosenberg, 12:30 on January 9, 1946; there were no Jacobson or Rosenberg appointments, alone or together, with Truman, at the White House in 1945.

The United Press story about the Lelyveld-Jacobson-Kaplan visit said the trio "entered discussions involving the Palestine situation." Jacobson later told interviewers on the White House lawn that Rabbi Lelyveld wanted "to clear up several things" with the President. Asked what they had talked about, Jacobson cracked, "Kaplan talked about shirts, I spoke of men's furnishings, and the Rabbi about notions." According to Mrs. Peiser, this trip of Jacobson's was underwritten by a group of Kansas Cityans since Jacobson was a man of modest means; the Peisers and the Rosenbergs had contributed.

Until much later Rabbi Lelyveld still believed that he had met Truman in June, 1945, and so he considered his talk with the President to have been "the first full briefing that Harry Truman had on the Jewish state." Lelyveld spent a full hour with Truman and then, at the President's request, met for another hour with David K. Niles. A good part of Lelyveld's conversation with Truman and Niles, he said, "was devoted to moderating their sense of annoyance with the pressures being brought upon them by someone to whom Mr. Truman referred to as 'that New York rabbi,' meaning Rabbi Abba Hillel Silver [he was from Cleveland]. When I reported this to Dr. Silver, he was quite pleased that he had succeeded 'in getting under their skin.' "

The Lelyveld story makes it clear that long before February, 1948, Jacobson was familiar with what the Zionists wanted, thanks to the efforts of the Rosenbergs and the Peisers.

WEIZMANN SEES THE PRESIDENT AGAIN

After Jacobson had won Truman's consent to seeing Weizmann, Jacobson, Rosenberg, and Bisgyer went to New York on March 14 to arrange for the incognito visit. Rosenberg, like Jacobson, had never met

Weizmann, but Bisgyer knew him well. The three were received in the anteroom to Weizmann's suite at the Waldorf-Astoria by Dr. Josef Cohn, Weizmann's secretary, who brought them to Weizmann's bedside. The aging Zionist leader was so ill that he believed he was dying.

On Monday, March 15, Jacobson returned to the Waldorf-Astoria and had tea with Weizmann in his bedroom. From Weizmann's suite Jacobson phoned Matt Connelly and was told the appointment was for 11 A.M., March 18. Because Jacobson was known to the White House press corps, he was told not to accompany Weizmann, whose escorts were thus Rosenberg and Bisgyer. Reservations at the Shoreham Hotel for the entire Weizmann party were made in Bisgyer's name to maintain the secrecy of the visit. A wheelchair was waiting at trackside when Weizmann, accompanied by Mrs. Weizmann, Mr. and Mrs. Bisgyer, and Rosenberg, arrived in Union Station. Also on hand was a delegation from the Washington office of the Jewish Agency whose unexpected presence might have tipped off the press.

After resting for a while at the Shoreham, Weizmann was driven to the White House by Bisgyer, accompanied by Rosenberg. They went in by the infrequently used East Gate. Rosenberg's son, Paul, who has heard his father's version of these events over the years, remembers the elder Rosenberg as saying that just as they entered the White House, the British Ambassador was leaving by the same back door. When they reached Connelly's office, the half-blind Weizmann and Rosenberg were shown into the President's office at once. Bisgyer remained outside.

As they entered the President rose and went to the front of his desk to arrange chairs for his visitors. Truman wanted Rosenberg to stay, but he begged off, saying, "No, Mr. President, you have many things to talk over. I'll be outside and kibbitz with Matt." To Connelly, Rosenberg said, "this man is old and he doesn't talk very fast. Give him a break. Instead of twenty minutes, can't you give him at least half an hour?" Connelly said he'd see what he could do. The interview lasted forty-five minutes. Truman referred to it in these words in his *Memoirs:*

"When Eddie left [on March 13] I gave instructions to have Dr. Weizmann come to the White House as soon as it could be arranged. However, the visit was to be entirely off the record. Dr. Weizmann, by my instructions, was to be brought in through the East Gate. There was to be no press coverage of his visit and no public announcement. . . . I told him, as plainly as I could, why I had at first put off seeing him. He understood. I explained to him what the basis of my interest in the Jewish problem was and that my primary concern was to see justice done without bloodshed. And when he left my office I felt that he had reached a full understanding of my policy and that I knew what it was he wanted."

Rosenberg escorted Weizmann out of the White House. For many years Rosenberg refused to let anyone tell of his role, but in later years he became hurt by the fact that Jacobson's intervention had become part of Jewish history while his efforts remained unknown. In Rosenberg's bedroom hangs a framed citation from Hadassah and the Jewish National Fund, describing Rosenberg as "collaborator and friend of President Harry S Truman, in recognition of his outstanding services to Israel and the American Jewish community." It was presented to him on February 9, 1949, at the same time as an identical plaque was given to Jacobson.

Weizmann left the White House believing he had Truman's promise, not only to stand fast on partition, but to recognize the Jewish state when it was proclaimed. Truman's biographer, Jonathan Daniels, said that the President assured Weizmann, "You can bank on me. I'm for partition." Commenting on this visit fifteen years later, Rabbi Abba Hillel Silver, who was Truman's particular bête noire, scoffed at the belief that "the intervention of someone who was smuggled in one day into the White House through a back door" had "by the magic of his personality won over the President of the United States, and presto, it was all done." Rabbi Silver called this "a naïve and fanciful reconstruction of history," and insisted that it "was American Jewry, rising magnificently to the challenge of the hour, which was responsible for the victories in Washington and Lake Success."

THE US REVERSAL

Less than twenty-four hours after Weizmann walked out of the White House, the US delivered a staggering blow to Zionist hopes by completely reversing itself on partition. On March 19, "Black Friday," Ambassador Austin told the UN Security Council that the US wanted action on partition suspended and the General Assembly recalled to consider a temporary trusteeship over Palestine. (State Department documents published in 1964 contain a memo from Col. Harold B. Hoskins, an FDR emissary to the Middle East, stating that the President leaned toward a trifaith trusteeship for Palestine to make it "a real Holy Land," with a Christian, a Jew, and a Moslem as trustees.) Meanwhile, the US proposed that the British be induced to retain the Mandate. Only five days earlier the US and the USSR had voted together in the Security Council for a resolution committing the Council to "do everything it can under the Charter to give effect" to the Assembly's partition plan.

Anguished and bitter cries of betrayal, sellout, doublecross, and "Munich" came from the stunned Zionists and their supporters in the American Jewish community. The Arabs hailed Austin's blockbuster as the deathknell of partition. Members of Congress, political commentators, and editorial writers saw it not only as an American surrender to Arab violence but also as a heavy blow to the UN itself. In Palestine the Jewish community served notice that only overwhelming military force could deprive them of independence under the guise of trusteeship.

Trygve Lie, UN Secretary General, a firm champion of partition and its implementation, expressed to Austin his "sense of shock and of almost personal grievance." Lie interpreted the American turnabout as impugning the sincerity of Washington's devotion to the UN and a rebuff to himself and the UN. He felt so strongly that he proposed to Austin that they both resign in protest and as a way of arousing public opinion.

Equally outraged was Mrs. Eleanor Roosevelt, who wanted to resign from the US delegation in order to be free to attack its position. Truman and Marshall told her to go ahead and criticize but pleaded with her not to resign. Mrs. Roosevelt had earlier expressed herself on the wavering American policy on Palestine in a letter to Secretary of State George C. Marshall in February, 1948, when she criticized Secretary of Defense Forrestal's opposition to a plan for a UN police force in Palestine to supervise the proposed partition. Forrestal's opposition, based on the opinion that it would place Soviet troops in the Middle East, was called "utter nonsense" by Mrs. Roosevelt.

Her offer to resign her UN post was made on March 22, when it became known that the State Department was leaning toward a British proposal to drop partition and institute a temporary trusteeship for Palestine. She expressed herself in a sharp letter to President Truman, saying: "I feel that even though the Secretary of State takes responsibility for the Administration's position on Palestine, you cannot escape the results of that attitude." In the letter to the President, explaining why she had offered her resignation to Secretary Marshall, she said that although she realized that she was "an entirely unimportant cog in the wheel of our work with the UN," she nevertheless could "quite understand the difficulty of having someone so far down the line openly criticize the Administration's policies."

In a public statement Andrei Gromyko blasted the US for "burying" partition because of its "own oil interests and military strategic position in the Near East."

Truman was beside himself when he read the Saturday-morning newspaper reports of Austin's astonishing proposal. Before breakfast he phoned Clark Clifford and was meeting with him at the White House as early as 7:30 A.M. "I don't understand what happened," the President complained to Clifford, and then ordered him to find out "how this could have happened." Truman was especially embarrassed because "I assured Chaim Weizmann that we were for partition and would stick to it. He must think I am a plain liar."

Later that morning Truman had an appointment with Judge Samuel I. Rosenman. The press corps did not connect this visit with Weizmann or with what had happened at the UN the day before. As a member of a committee mapping Truman's strategy for the upcoming Democratic National Convention and the November election, Rosenman had been seeing Truman weekly. Rosenman was no stranger to the White House, having served as one of FDR's brain-trusters and ghost-writers. He was credited with having inserted into FDR's acceptance speech at the 1932 Democratic National Convention the words, "I pledge you, I pledge myself, to a new deal for the American people." "Sammy the Rose," as FDR called him, had also been Truman's special counsel until his retirement from government on February 1, 1946, but Truman continued to give him private chores to do.

"I have Dr. Weizmann on my conscience," the President said to Rosenman that Saturday morning. Rosenman found Truman greatly agitated lest the "Old Doctor," Truman's affectionate term for Weizmann, might think that the President of the United States had deliberately deceived him. Truman had been much taken with Weizmann, but often caused amusement by the way he pronounced Weizmann's first name: he never learned to pronounce "Chaim" with a guttural "ch," despite Rosenman's patient efforts to teach him; he pronounced "Chaim" as if it rhymed with "game" and the "ch" as in "chance."

While Clifford was trying to reach Marshall on the West Coast and Lovett in Florida, Truman asked Rosenman to get in touch with Weizmann, who was still in Washington. Rosenman was instructed to explain to Weizmann that the policy Truman had discussed with him on March 18 remained unchanged, no matter what Austin had said. Rosenman located Weizmann at the Shoreham Hotel, calmly having coffee with Benjamin V. Cohen and David C. Ginsburg. Cohen, a former FDR brain-truster and onetime counselor to the State Department, was a US alternate representative to the UN. Ginsburg, legal counsel to the Jewish Agency office in Washington, had been an assistant to Supreme Court Justice William O. Douglas and an adviser in 1947 to the US delegation to the

Council of Foreign Ministers in London. Both were part of a small inner circle of government economists, lawyers, and international experts to whom Weizmann turned for guidance and information. Others in this group were Oscar Gass and Robert R. Nathan. All had first met Weizmann when he came to the United States at the end of December, 1939.

Weizmann had already read Austin's statement when Rosenman arrived. Outwardly unruffled, he was nevertheless visibly relieved when Rosenman gave him Truman's reassurance. Rosenman recalled Weizmann's saying that even if the President had changed his mind, he, Weizmann, was so used to reverses in his long struggle on behalf of a Jewish state that he would have been able to bear even this kind of blow.

CLARK CLIFFORD'S ROLE

Rosenman's errand was the first of many behind-the-scenes moves by Truman during the last eight weeks preceding US recognition of Israel. Through Rosenman and Niles, Truman maintained pipelines for conveying information between the Jewish Agency and Weizmann and the White House. Through Clifford, one of the main architects of Truman's Palestine policy, the President was tuned in on the fast-moving events in Palestine, news of which the State Department often tried to keep from him.

A memo in the Clifford papers claims that Truman had not seen the advance text of Austin's speech, but only a draft of its substance. It also asserts that Marshall and Lovett, both of whom were out of Washington on March 19, were equally surprised by Austin's proposal. Nevertheless, after Truman talked to Marshall by telephone, the Secretary of State on March 20 conceded that, with Truman's consent, he had previously approved an agreement to make a trusteeship proposal if it became apparent that partition could not be achieved peaceably, and in order to avoid a vacuum when the Mandate ended. Marshall maintained that trusteeship was a temporary device to maintain peace and to open the way to an agreed settlement, but that it in no way prejudiced an ultimate political solution.

In secret testimony on March 24 before the Senate Foreign Relations Committee, Marshall justified the new American policy strictly on grounds of national security. Use of American troops to enforce partition would bring Russian forces into the Middle East, he emphasized, thus threatening the Western democracies in the Mediterranean.

In an effort to stem the tide of criticism, Truman on March 25 reaffirmed Marshall's statement of March 20. Trusteeship, he said, was not a substitute for partition, but an emergency measure to preserve law and order after the Mandate expired and to prevent the fighting in the Near East from "involving the peace of this nation and of the world." Partition, Truman declared, "cannot be carried out at this time by peaceful means," and he declined "to impose this solution on the people of Palestine by the use of American troops, both on Charter grounds and as a matter of national policy."

David K. Niles has recalled that on the day the State Department was drafting this statement, "we had a big argument about Austin's speech." He was referring to a White House conference attended by Marshall, Truman, Dean Rusk, Loy Henderson, Charles E. ("Chip") Bohlen, Oscar Ewing, J. Howard McGrath, Matt Connelly, Charles G. Ross, Clifford, and Niles. It took place on the day Marshall returned from the West Coast. "This gets us nowhere," a reporter heard Truman mutter as he came out of the meeting.

Truman took comfort in the mistaken impression that Dr. Weizmann "was one of the few prominent Zionists who did not choose this opportunity to castigate American policy" because he knew Truman's real plans. The fact is that on March 25 Weizmann assailed Austin's recommendation "as an act of submission to Arab violence," and ridiculed the argument that partition had to be shelved because it had not won the agreement of all concerned parties. Moreover, he called on the Yishuv to take "those steps which they will deem necessary to assure their survival and national freedom when the Mandate ends."

In retrospect Truman was still of two minds on what had happened. In his *Memoirs* he insisted that Austin's trusteeship proposal was not a rejection of partition, but only an attempt to defer it until proper conditions were achieved. He conceded, however, that it was quite natural for the Jews and Arabs "to read this proposal as a complete abandonment of the partition plan. . . . Anybody in the State Department should have known that it would be so considered. . . . In this sense, the trusteeship idea was at odds with my attitude and the policy I had laid down." But, Truman explained, his policy with regard to Palestine involved "not a commitment to any set of dates or circumstances," but "a dedication to the twin ideal of international obligations and the relieving of human misery." In this sense he felt that the State Department acted "contrary to my proposal."

This confusing explanation in 1956 of what had happened eight years earlier is only part of the story. In April and May, 1948, Truman still hoped for a peaceful solution in Palestine. While he never really swallowed the Forrestal line that partition menaced American security, he was well aware that the State Department was doing everything possible to abort the Jewish state, including pressuring Jewish leaders and even making direct threats. There is no evidence, however, that Truman ever committed himself to more than a temporary delay of partition. The anti-Zionist clique in the State and Defense Departments was confident that deferment of partition would not only postpone but permanently defeat Jewish statehood. Since the ultimate decision rested with Truman, he played for time by operating on two levels.

TRUMAN'S TWO APPROACHES

Through the State Department and the US delegation to the UN he continued to defend trusteeship and the State Department's swiveling from plan to plan. Privately, however, through Clifford, Rosenman, Niles, and their key Jewish contacts, he found ways of sending word to Weizmann that he was still for partition while taking the first steps leading to recognition.

On April 9, 1948, David Ginsburg phoned Weizmann in New York with the ominous news that the State Department was thinking of asking the British to carry on the administration of Palestine beyond the scheduled date of their departure, May 15. That same day Weizmann sent a private letter to Truman, warning that "the clock cannot be put back to the situation which existed before November 29. The choice for our people, Mr. President," he wrote, "is between statehood and extermination. History and Providence have placed this issue in your hands, and I am confident that you will decide it in the spirit of the moral law."

Ginsburg had picked up a hint of a new State Department scheme for a temporary truce in Palestine. Authored by Dean Rusk, it proposed that Arabs and Jews agree to a ten-day cease-fire beginning May 5, a few months of limited Jewish immigration, and British retention of the Mandate for ten days beyond May 15. Included in this last-ditch American effort to delay Jewish statehood was the suggestion that a mixed party of representatives of the Jewish Agency and the Arab Higher Committee be flown to Palestine for on-the-spot negotiations. A typewritten summary of the suggestion forwarded to Truman by Clifford contained an offer to make available the Presidential plane, the *Sacred Cow*. The name of the plane, however, was crossed out and the word "plane" inserted by hand.

Moshe Shertok, the Jewish Agency's chief negotiator, was first shown a draft of Rusk's plan on April 26 after the trusteeship proposal had bogged down in the UN. A few days earlier, however, Truman had told Rosenman that if trusteeship died in the UN before the Mandate ended and if the Jewish state was in fact proclaimed, he would certainly recognize it. The President authorized Rosenman to relay this information, in the strictest confidence, to the "Old Doctor." While the State Department searched for a new way of blocking Jewish statehood, Rosenman gave Truman's message to Weizmann on April 23 in New York. The appointment on April 28 of Gen. John H. Hildring as special assistant to Marshall on Palestine affairs gave rise to rumors of some new shift in the US position, since Hildring was known to be pro-Zionist. But he became ill and never assumed his new post.

Meanwhile, Chicago Democratic boss Jake Arvey and New York's Mayor William O'Dwyer were giving the Democratic National Committee "Eisenhower troubles" by urging Ike as the 1948 Democratic nominee instead of Truman. Their attitude was influenced in part by threats from important Jewish contributors in New York, Illinois, Pennsylvania, and California of withholding financial support because of the Administration's changed stand on partition. Jack Redding, publicity director of the Democratic National Committee, gloomily reported to Truman in April "that we have the Zionist Jews in the office every day, and the pressure is building up a terrific head of steam." Mounting fears of Jewish defections on the Palestine issues coincided with threats on the Left from Henry A. Wallace's Progressive Party and on the Right from J. Strom Thurmond's States' Rights Party.

Truman's instructions to party officials implied that he had already determined to bypass State Department roadblocks to recognition. Anyone who tried to sway him on Palestine through the Democratic National Committee was to be told "it is no use putting pressure on the committee. The Palestine issue will be handled here," meaning the White House, "and there'll be no politics involved."

Nevertheless, politics was not far from his mind. On May 3 he wrote to Eddie Jacobson to thank him for a letter of April 29 in which the eager-beaver Kansas Cityan had referred to the attitude of Jewish voters toward Truman, and had offered to talk it over, "and maybe we can work something out." Truman promised Jacobson that he hoped to have an opportunity to discuss the matter with him, as well as "the course of the developments which took place after you were here"—this was a reference to Jacobson's White House visit of March 18. Truman wrote that "my soul [sic] interest in that problem now is to stop the bloodshed and

see if we can't work the matter out on a peaceful basis" ("soul" was cor-
rected by hand to "sole").

CLIFFORD PLANS FOR RECOGNITION

At about the same time Truman gave Clifford the go-ahead to begin
assembling material for ultimate recognition of the Jewish state. Clifford,
who had joined the White House staff after World War II as liaison officer for naval affairs, became one of Truman's closest advisers and top
speechwriters after Rosenman resigned early in 1946. Impressed with
Clifford's role in the formulation of the Truman Doctrine and the Marshall Plan, Truman made him his chief counselor and source of information on foreign affairs.

Isolated from many key figures in his Administration because of the
belief that he was a sure loser in the 1948 Presidential election, Truman
came to rely heavily on the judgment and advice of his fellow-Missourian.
It was Clifford who in November, 1947, had compiled a forty-page analysis of Truman's 1948 election prospects (now acknowledged to be the
blueprint for the unexpectedly successful Truman campaign), in which he
said "Jews hold the key to New York and the key to the Jewish voters is
what the Administration does about Palestine."

It was Supreme Court Justice Frankfurter who first tipped off Eliahu
Epstein, the Jewish Agency's man in Washington, to Clifford's close ties
with Truman. "Watch Clifford," Frankfurter said. "He's destined to play a
key role in US affairs." Epstein's first contact with the White House was
David K. Niles, Truman's assistant for relations with ethnic groups; he
was not very popular in the State and Defense Departments because of his
unabashed pro-Zionist stand. It was Niles who brought Epstein and Clifford together, thus paving the way for a relationship that proved decisive.

Clifford told the authors that he came to have great respect for Epstein and regarded him as a friend. They often discussed the Palestine situation by phone and in person. According to Epstein, these conversations
enabled Clifford to become intimately familiar with Zionist aims. Clifford
personally confirmed this, and his files reveal how much of his attitude
toward Palestine and recognition of Israel was the result of his frequent
talks with Epstein. A native of Russia who settled in Palestine in 1925,
Epstein headed the Middle East section of the Jewish Agency's Political
Department during World War II and served as the Agency's observer at
the founding of the UN in San Francisco in 1945.

As Truman's aide on foreign affairs Clifford was the clearinghouse through which raw data on Palestine were screened on their way to the President's desk; people eager to give Truman their views on Palestine were seen first by Clifford. Niles and Rosenman, Clifford's pipelines to Jewish leadership, kept him closely informed through a steady flow of news and suggestions that he filtered before passing it on to Truman. Rosenman and Niles also had access to the President, but on Palestine Clifford was the key man.

Shertok's reactions to Rusk's truce plan reached Truman via Clifford to whom Rosenman sent copies of Shertok's letters to Marshall of April 29 and May 7 and of Shertok's telegram to Rusk of May 4. In the first letter to Marshall, Shertok objected strongly to Rusk's proposal because it not only entailed deferment of statehood but rendered its attainment in the future most uncertain as well. He also voiced strong exception to Marshall's intimation at a press conference on April 28 that an agreement on a truce had already been reached between the Jewish Agency and the Arabs. Shertok pointed out that only his colleagues in Palestine, to whom he had cabled the text of the draft and his own views of it, could make a decision. On May 7 he wrote to Marshall again to deny rumors begun by the State Department that Shertok had accepted conditions for a military truce and for a political standstill in Palestine. In his wire to Rusk, Shertok rejected any prolongation of the Mandate beyond May 15, but accepted a cease-fire if the Arabs did likewise.

Rosenman also passed on to Clifford a letter from Nahum Goldmann, of the Jewish Agency's American Section, indicating that he was more amenable to Rusk's suggestion. Clifford's papers note that Truman expressed full agreement with Shertok's May 7 letter to Marshall. The President was quoted as saying that the talks related to a truce were entirely informal and that neither Shertok nor Goldmann had accepted the proposals as submitted.

Shertok's telegram to Rusk followed a stormy all-night session of the American members of the Jewish Agency Executive in New York. A minority was inclined to go along with some arrangement with the State Department, but the majority, led by Rabbi Silver, Dr. Emanuel Neumann, and Mrs. Rose Halprin, turned thumbs down on any last-minute deal that would have meant postponement of independence.

STATE'S DELAYING TACTICS

The truce scheme was one of twenty-six "different expedients" devised by the State Department between April 23 and May 7 to delay or prevent

Jewish independence, Clifford pointed out in a memo to Truman dated
May 7. Another note from Clifford to the President stated that the US
representatives at the UN were "frantically" trying to line up support in
the General Assembly against partition, against Jewish statehood, and for
"anything else" that would cast a cloud of illegality over a proclamation of
independence.

One of the twenty-six "expedients" Clifford cited was the State Department's attempt to exploit the immense prestige of Dr. Judah L.
Magnes, President of the Hebrew University. Clifford's summary of the
"expedients" was Truman's first inkling that the State Department had invited Magnes to the US as a partisan of its truce scheme. The request had
been relayed to him in mid-April via the American Consulate in Jerusalem.

A longtime advocate of an Arab-Jewish state in Palestine, linked to a
Near East Semitic federation, Magnes supported a truce because of fear
for the safety of Jerusalem. When the US tried to scuttle partition in
favor of trusteeship, Magnes' Ihud Society placarded Jerusalem with posters in Arabic, Hebrew, and English, welcoming trusteeship. "Let us save
our common country from the danger of war," the posters said. "Long
live the Jewish-Arab union of peace."

At the end of April and in early May, when Magnes publicly endorsed
the truce plan in New York, he was denounced as a traitor by the supporters of Jewish independence, while in Jerusalem the Hebrew University dissociated itself from his political activities. His private conversations
with American, British, French, and even Egyptian delegates to the UN,
and his talks with Marshall and Truman, all arranged by the State Department, rang alarm bells in the Jewish Agency.

After his meeting with Magnes on May 4, Marshall said it was "the
first talk on Palestine in which I had complete trust." The following day
Magnes saw Truman and, according to Clifford, urged the President to
send a high-ranking American to the Holy Land to negotiate a truce. He
even offered to accompany anyone the President designated and hinted
that he could bring along the head of a well-known but unnamed American rabbinical seminary.

In the ten days before Israel was born Truman sought or received advice on Palestine from virtually every visitor to the White House, but he
disclosed his own plans to no one. One Christian minister told the President that the establishment of a Jewish state would be fulfillment of a
prophecy which no hand, not even that of the President of the United
States, could stay. Another caller retorted to Truman's question of what
would be wrong with a short postponement of statehood by asking

whether American history would have taken the course it did if America's founding fathers had put off signing the Declaration of Independence. Several White House visitors in May claimed they saw the President reading the Bible and the Declaration of Independence.

On May 4 Truman sought the views of former New York Governor Herbert H. Lehman. Interviewed outside the White House, he refused to give any details of his conversation with the President, but vigorously denied a report that he had been offered a post that would have made him the Presidential adviser on Palestine. The next day Representative Sol Bloom of New York, a former chairman of the House Foreign Affairs Committee, pressed Ambassador Austin to tell the Committee what the US position would be on recognition of the Jewish State after May 15. With obvious irritation Austin said, "You don't expect me to answer that question, do you?" He was probably as much in the dark as anyone else. On May 7, the President talked with an old friend from the Missouri Grand Lodge of Masons, Rabbi Samuel Thurman of St. Louis' United Hebrew Temple. Rabbi Thurman told reporters that he did not think the President had changed his mind about partition as the ultimate solution, but he declined to speculate on whether Truman would recognize a Jewish state.

Some time on May 6 Clifford placed on Truman's desk the draft of a proposed statement to be issued by the White House before the Jewish state came into being. The copy in the Clifford papers does not identify the author, but it came from David K. Niles. In a covering note Niles said that the draft had been read and approved by Benjamin Cohen.

Although it never got beyond the draft stage, it reveals something of the struggle in the highest government echelons. In a brief review of the US position since the November 29 UN vote for partition the statement reaffirms American support for partition but stresses that the "disorders" in Palestine had made it impossible to achieve peaceful compliance. It admitted the failure of all US plans to defer partition, including trusteeship and the truce, which had to be abandoned "because events in Palestine had outstripped them."

Then came the surprising disclosure that Marshall and Truman, "after an exhaustive review," had concluded that they should recognize "this practical reality since it conforms to the resolution of the UN, to the security interests of the US, and to the announced and oft-repeated objectives of the US." In the last sentence was the announcement that "we intend therefore to accord formal recognition to the Jewish government when it is established," while continuing to work "for the maintenance of peace, under international guarantees, in the Jerusalem area."

Obviously, this document did not reflect the State Department's position on May 6 since Marshall was not won over to recognition until a week later, but the unsigned author had a pretty good idea of what was in Truman's mind. Clifford's papers give no hint of Truman's reaction to this draft, but the very next day, as Clifford told the authors, the President asked him to put the case for recognition in writing.

THE CASE FOR RECOGNITION

What Clifford prepared, he recalls, was not too different from the many briefs he had submitted to appellate courts during his days in private legal practice. In essence, Clifford argued that recognition was fully consistent with US policy, a separate Jewish state was inevitable and would be set up shortly, the US would have to recognize it ultimately and so it would be wise to do so at once. This position coincided with the views expressed in the unused May 6 draft.

But the State Department and the Pentagon were still of a different mind, as Shertok learned on May 8 when he returned from a quick trip to Palestine to brief Ben-Gurion on the critical situation in Washington and at Lake Success. Washington was a hotbed of rumors of what might happen if the Jews remained obdurate on the truce scheme. One report hinted at an embargo on funds to Palestine from the United Jewish Appeal, which might lose its tax-exempt status. Another intimated that the US would ask the UN Security Council to declare the situation in Palestine a danger to world peace, thus paving the way for sanctions against both Arabs and Jews. This would have cut off the Jewish state from sources of economic support and arms. There was also the suggestion that if the war in Palestine led to a third World War, the Jews would be held responsible.

Neither Marshall nor Lovett made any threats when they met with Shertok for ninety minutes on May 8. Marshall was sympathetic and almost kindly as he made one last attempt to talk Shertok out of independence. Spreading out a map of the Middle East on his desk, the Secretary of State pleaded with Shertok: "Look at that map! How will you 650,000 Jews stand up against five Arab countries? It's not too late. There's still time for you to do the logical thing." Marshall and Lovett hewed firmly to the line that a proclamation of Jewish independence, followed by an Arab invasion, might endanger world peace and that this had to be avoided at all costs.

Marshall cautioned against undue optimism arising from the Jewish victories over the Arab irregulars, pointing out that things would be different when the Jews had to face well-equipped modern forces. He would be happy, he said, if the Jewish state was established and survived invasion. But he still believed that the Jews would be driven into the sea; therefore he pleaded for a delay. Ten days earlier Marshall had told the Associated Press he did not believe that the Arabs would invade Palestine.

Shertok remained unmoved. He said the Yishuv was eager to understand the American position and to maintain friendly relations with the US, but that it would never surrender its fundamental interests. The real problem, Shertok pointed out, was whether the pressure for a truce was a sincere desire to avert war or just another maneuver to postpone statehood with a view to ultimately preventing it from happening.

The atmosphere was quite different in the White House, where Clifford's daily briefings of the President emphasized the growing public sentiment for early recognition of the Jewish state, as well as mounting impatience with the attitude of the State Department. On May 10, Clifford had a crucial meeting with Epstein, undoubtedly with the knowledge and consent of Truman. Epstein had just come back from a ten-day visit to Palestine, armed with a formal denial that the Jewish Agency had already accepted or would ever agree to a truce whose terms jeopardized the establishment of the Jewish state. There was no chance, he said, that the Jews would postpone the proclamation of independence beyond the moment of the British withdrawal.

INDEPENDENCE CERTAIN

Clifford put two questions to Epstein: Was a declaration of independence certain? What were the prospects of the Jews holding off an Arab invasion? Epstein assured him that independence would definitely be announced on May 15 (it was changed to May 14 when the British at the last moment advanced their departure date by twenty-four hours). As for resisting the combined Arab armies, Epstein was blunt: "We have no choice because we know what we are fighting for. There can be no second Auschwitz in Palestine."

Armed with this last word, Clifford again briefed Truman. Thereafter events moved swiftly toward the climactic announcement of May 14.

On May 11 Clifford gave the President a memo entitled "Palestine:

United Press Dispatch in May 11th Morning Papers." It dealt with a United Press story in that morning's *Washington Times-Herald* and *Washington Post* reporting under a Lake Success dateline that "the U.S. has been trying desperately to forestall formation of a Jewish state." The memo asked if the dispatch was correct and suggested, if it was not, that the State Department issue either a formal or informal denial or arrange a calculated leak denying the story.

Clifford also inquired, if the dispatch was accurate, did Marshall know what the State Department was doing at the UN and had he authorized it? Clifford further noted that Marshall "might be interested" in a New York *Herald Tribune* story of May 11 headlined "CUBA DEMANDS FORMAL UN REVOCATION OF PARTITION." He added that at Lake Success, Cuba "is known as the hand of our State Department on Palestine matters." Finally, Clifford cited a *New York Times* report of May 11 stating that Philip K. Jessup of the US delegation to the UN had "again raised the question of the legal basis for any Palestine regime not based on trusteeship."

This memo was obviously intended to alert the President to the last-minute efforts of the State Department to fend off anything the White House might be planning. Shortly after Truman received this memo he called a secret White House conference for May 12. Truman, Marshall, Lovett, Loy Henderson, Clifford, and Niles were present. Truman opened the meeting by saying that the imminent end of the British Mandate and the forthcoming proclamation of Jewish statehood confronted the US with the need for a serious decision. He had called the group together, he explained, to consider the pros and cons of recognition of the Jewish state. Clifford, he said, who had been living with the question for months, would read a brief that the President had asked him to prepare. Marshall became very angry, Clifford later recalled, "in a righteous Goddamned Baptist tone." The Secretary of State not only rejected Clifford's reasoning, but objected as well to his participation in the discussion. When Marshall asked why it was necessary to bring Clifford into the picture, Truman tartly replied, "He's here because I asked him to be here."

MARSHALL STILL OPPOSED

Marshall endorsed the Forrestal view that it was unthinkable to jeopardize American bases in Europe and elsewhere for "the sake of Zionist causes" and thus antagonize the Arab world. Once again Marshall strongly objected to recognition, observing that he did not want to side with a sure loser. Lovett amplified his chief's views, after which what Clifford described as "a general colloquy" ensued. Clifford boldly replied to Marshall's attack by questioning his competence on nonmilitary matters, so enraging Marshall that he threatened to resign if his advice were ignored. Then he slipped out a side door of the White House to find reporters waiting to question him about a report from Tel Aviv, later confirmed, that he had written to Ben-Gurion, urging him to postpone the proclamation of independence. The State Department neither denied nor confirmed the dispatch. A spokesman lamely explained that since the truce terms discussed with the Jewish Agency had proposed that there be "no political change in Palestine" for the time being, this requirement might have given rise to the report of a request for delay.

Clifford says he left the meeting with the feeling that Truman would reluctantly go along with Marshall because he had such high regard for him that he hesitated to act against the wishes of the man he had described as "the greatest living American." When the others had gone, Truman thanked Clifford for his presentation, which had reflected the President's own opinion. Clifford returned to his office, feeling he had lost his biggest case on appeal.

LOVETT SHIFTS

Lovett, who had been the central figure in the trusteeship and truce moves, however, had been swayed by Clifford's brief. On the afternoon of May 12 he went to see Clifford at the White House, where he admitted that he was "so uneasy about the decision made today" that he planned "to get my boys together tomorrow and talk about it." Lovett kept his word. At a meeting with his staff on the morning of May 13 agreement was reached to back recognition. Having changed his own views, Lovett was able to persuade his associates that further opposition to recognition would be heading the US in the wrong direction.

On the strength of this new development, someone prepared the draft of a proposed Truman statement on recognition, a copy of which, dated May 13, is in Clifford's Palestine file. Longer but similar to the May 6 formulation, it had Truman saying that he "looked with favor on the creation of a Jewish state in accordance with the provisions laid down in the UN resolution," and that when the state was set up in accordance with those provisions, he favored its recognition by the US. The document included a suggestion from the President to the Secretary of State that the US representatives at the UN take up early recognition of the Jewish state by other members of the UN. There was also a promise that when the Arab state was created, in keeping with the UN partition plan, it too would be recognized by the US.

Early Friday morning, May 14, Lovett called Clifford to say that Marshall had come around and had already advised the President that he was now agreeable to recognition. Some State Department officers wanted to wait a few days to gain time to consult the British and the French, but Truman saw no reason for postponement. It is probable that Truman himself changed Marshall's mind through an urgent telephone call in which he expressed the conviction that if recognition was the right thing to do, it should not be delayed.

THE GO-AHEAD FOR RECOGNITION

No longer faced with a balky Secretary of State, Truman then gave Clifford the go-ahead to begin preparing a statement of recognition. A first rough draft was composed over lunch at the F Street Club by Clifford and Lovett. Meanwhile, Clifford had requested that the State Department send over a memo on the legal questions involved in recognition. In Clifford's papers is a copy of a memo to the President from C. H. Humelsine entitled "Recognition of Successor States in Palestine." The plural "states" indicated that the document also covered possible action on the Arab state.

Marshall's change of heart occurred shortly after the White House received Dr. Weizmann's letter asking "the greatest democracy" to be the first to welcome "the newest democracy." Truman was impressed with Weizmann's suggestion and asked Clifford and Niles to discuss it with Marshall and Lovett. State Department experts pointed out that since Weizmann held no official position in the Jewish Agency and was still a British subject, something more formal was needed before the White House could act. That was where Eliahu Epstein moved to the center of history's stage, for as the official representative in Washington of the Jewish Agency, he had a certain semiofficial status and Clifford was authorized to contact him.

Earlier that morning Clifford had been handed a note from Epstein, attached to a copy of a cable received during the night from Shertok in Tel Aviv. The cable asked Epstein to seek Truman's personal intervention to stop Emir Abdullah and his Arab Legion from invading Palestine.

Clifford knew where to reach Epstein day or night: in the Clifford papers is a penciled note in his own handwriting listing Epstein's home phone number and the Jewish Agency's number and address. The slip of paper also had two queries jotted down: "At what time will the independence proclamation become effective?" "Was it a provisional government that was formed?"

At a little before 11 A.M. Epstein's phone rang in the Jewish Agency office. Clifford, calling from the White House, wanted to know what the situation was in Tel Aviv and whether the state would be proclaimed that day as press reports had indicated. Epstein had not yet received any official word from Tel Aviv (he didn't get the text of the Proclamation until the next day). But he assured Clifford that the state would be proclaimed, adding that he was reasonably certain that it had already happened, since it was then 5 P.M. in Tel Aviv and the independence ceremonies had been scheduled for 4 P.M.

THE STATE IS BORN

Epstein explained to Clifford that as they talked the state had already been born, although the act of independence would not become effective until the British Mandate expired at midnight Palestine time (6 P.M. EDT in Washington). That being the case, Clifford said, almost matter-of-factly, he was authorized to inform Epstein, personally and confidentially, that the President had decided to recognize the Jewish state from the hour of its legal existence. Clifford then suggested that Epstein submit to him at the White House, "at the earliest possible moment," an official request for such recognition, addressed to the Secretary of State. Thirty minutes later, when news of the Israel proclamation of independence reached the White House, Epstein received another call from the White House. This time it was Niles on the line, reporting that the President had ordered a statement of recognition prepared. Niles remembered that Epstein burst into tears of joy when he heard that the historic decision had at last been made.

A visitor to the White House that morning was Mrs. Herman Rosenberg, who was in Washington as a delegate to the biennial meeting of the National League of American Pen Women. The Battery D Association membership card gained her easy entry through Matt Connelly's office. She had a message for the President from her husband that had nothing to do with Palestine. When Truman said to her, "I think Herman will like what we are doing today," she had no idea what he meant. The next morning Connelly called her at her hotel and said, "Well, I hope you're happy about what we did yesterday."

Excited as he was by Clifford's call, Epstein had some puzzles to solve before he could do what the White House had asked. Before Shertok left for Palestine on May 11 he told Epstein that when the Jewish state came into existence, Epstein would be named its representative in the US, but on May 14 his legal status was in limbo because his only title was Director of the Washington office of the Jewish Agency. There was no time to query Tel Aviv, with which communications were tenuous at best. Epstein had kept in touch with Tel Aviv through what he has described to the authors as "a very primitive method of coded communication." A code had been devised in which key words were used at both ends of the line over which Epstein sent and received messages. David Ginsburg intimated that he had something to do with setting up this communications network when phone and cable links between the US and Palestine began to break down in March, 1948. Although he was not a radio operator, he may have been the key man in the network of Jewish ham operators utilized by the Jewish Agency.

Before he convened his advisers for the drafting of the letter, Epstein made one phonecall. It was to Arthur Lourie, director of the Jewish Agency's New York office, in whom Epstein confided that recognition could be expected that day. Lourie was pledged to secrecy lest the news leak out before the official announcement from the White House. In 1967 Abba Eban, Shertok's deputy at the UN, told the authors that through Weizmann and Epstein he knew that Truman's action was due. This meant that the Jewish Agency people in New York were also counting on it.

In view of the reports Epstein had been forwarding of his meetings with Clifford, the act of recognition itself came as no surprise to the Jewish Agency in New York. What did astonish them, Eban indicated, was its swiftness after the proclamation of independence. The Agency people were aware of the strong opposition Truman faced in his official family, and thus they could not be sure, Eban said, that Truman "would honor his pledge."

Thus Eban indicates that the Jewish Agency knew of a pledge, but he did not amplify whether they knew from Weizmann, to whom the pledge had been made in confidence, or from some other source. Dr. Emanuel Neumann, then a member of the Jewish Agency Executive in New York, remembers that the Zionist leadership was far from surprised by Truman's prompt recognition of Israel. Neumann said they had been tipped off early in May by Bartley Crum, who had close ties with the White House. Crum, says Neumann, informed the Zionists that in mid-April the President had told him, "Should our attempt to delay the proclamation of the Jewish State fail, I will immediately grant recognition." This accords with the timing of Rosenman's message to the same effect to Weizmann on April 23.

THE OFFICIAL REQUEST FOR RECOGNITION

Epstein's most urgent problem in phrasing the letter was the name of the state to be recognized. He knew various names had been under consideration by the people drafting the Declaration of Independence, including "Israel." But he had no advance copies of the Declaration in any of its several versions. The flash that the state had been born was received via a short-wave radio in the Jewish Agency office and confirmed by telephone from the New York office, which had received a cable from Tel Aviv, but there was no definite word of the state's name.

The dilemma was solved by using "Jewish state," the language of the UN resolution of November 29, 1947. Another problem was how to coordinate the fact of independence in Israel with the act of recognition in Washington, since independence would not be legally effective until one minute after midnight in Palestine (6:01 P.M. EDT in Washington). There was also the delicate question of how Epstein should sign himself. The first suggestion was to identify him as representative of the provisional government of Israel, but ultimately it was agreed that "agent" conformed to all legal niceties.

Who actually wrote the letter that bore Epstein's signature is still a question. Ginsburg had a big hand in it, although he says it was a group product. The group was Epstein's "brain trust"—Ginsburg, Robert Nathan, and Oscar Gass, the regulars, and occasionally Benjamin Cohen and Maurice Boukstein, and Niles was always available for advice. Anticipating Clifford's request, on May 12 Epstein had asked Ginsburg to summarize the legal requirements. Sensing that precedent might be important, Ginsburg called attention to the oft-forgotten fact that in 1903 President Theodore Roosevelt had extended recognition to the new Republic of Panama only hours after it seceded from Colombia, and before any request for recognition had been made. As the letter finally shaped up, it was based essentially on the outline prepared by Ginsburg, an expert on international law, as well as on suggestions made by Benjamin Cohen.

While Epstein is still reluctant to concede that he was aware of the
Rosenman-Weizmann meetings in Washington and New York during
the weeks preceding recognition, Ginsburg is positive he knew all about
them. Ginsburg attended one such meeting and was generally familiar
with the plans for winning recognition, but he was not privy to the
events of May 13–14. The first he knew that recognition was imminent
was when Epstein asked him to draft the memo on the international law
of recognition. Ginsburg is also certain that Epstein maintained close liaison with Weizmann. Each knew what the other was doing, and both were
in constant touch with Shertok, Ginsburg says. Ginsburg is also positive
that Epstein knew of the delivery of Weizmann's letter to the White
House on May 14, probably through Niles, if not directly from Weizmann or his secretary, Josef Cohn.

It took nearly three hours to compose the letter asking for recognition,
according to Harry Zinder, chief press officer of the Jewish Agency in
Washington. An American-born newspaperman who had settled in Palestine in 1934, Zinder headed the Middle East Bureau of Time Inc. before
he joined the Agency in March, 1948. Shortly after Clifford's call to Epstein, Zinder was ordered to stand by to deliver the letter. Epstein had set
3 P.M. as the zero hour for sending it on its way so that a reply could be
received by messenger before the onset of the Sabbath.

Zinder recalls that Epstein phoned the White House at 3 P.M. and
read the letter to Clifford, who suggested a few minor changes. It was
then retyped and Zinder went off with it by cab. His taxi had just turned
in to Pennsylvania Avenue and was heading for the White House when a
messenger, driving Epstein's car, overtook him. A few minutes after Zinder had left the Jewish Agency's office Epstein learned by radio that the
Jewish state's name was Israel. One story has it that Zinder returned with
the letter to the office, where the correct name was inserted by hand since
there was no time for retyping. Zinder, however, says that the change was
made in Epstein's car, two blocks from the White House gates. Zinder
handed the letter to Matt Connelly, who was expecting it, and took it at
once to Clifford. Zinder then headed for the State Department, where he
left an identical letter (not a carbon copy), which also had been altered by
hand. An aide to Marshall accepted it from Zinder in the Secretary's outer
office. This is the text of Epstein's letter:

"I have the honor to notify you that the State of Israel has been proclaimed as an independent republic, with frontiers approved by the General Assembly of the United Nations in its resolution of November 29,
1947, and that a Provisional Government has been charged to assume the

rights and duties of government for preserving law and order within the boundaries of Israel, for defending the State against external aggression, and for discharging the obligations of Israel to the other nations of the world in accordance with international law. The Act of Independence will become effective at one minute after six o'clock on the evening of May 14, 1948, Washington time.

"With full knowledge of the deep bond of sympathy which has existed, and has been strengthened over the past thirty years, between the Government of the United States and the Jewish People of Palestine, I have been authorized by the Provisional Government of the new state to tender this message and to express the hope that your Government will recognize and will welcome Israel into the community of nations."

It was signed by Epstein as "Agent of the Provisional Government of the State of Israel."

WAITING ON THE WHITE HOUSE

The White House press room was not aware of the letter, which Clifford handed to Truman shortly after 4 P.M. By 5 P.M. the White House was grinding out copies of Truman's statement of recognition, which was distributed to the press at 6:20 by Charles Ross.

Once the letter had gone to the White House and the State Department, there was nothing more for Epstein to do but wait. Ginsburg recalls that until official word came from the White House, Epstein was pale, worried-looking, and gaunt. He had eaten nothing all day and was terribly jumpy. About 4 P.M. Epstein turned up at the Carlton Hotel suite of David Niles, who greeted him with a *"Mazel Tov"* and the assurance that things were coming to a satisfactory head. Niles too was gratified since he had paved the way for Epstein's contacts with the White House. For half an hour or so Niles filled Epstein in on the details of the immense pressure on Truman in the previous seventy-two hours to get him to resist the demands for recognition and to repudiate partition. Niles also described the reaction in the White House to the receipt that morning of Weizmann's letter. At a little before 5 P.M. Niles phoned his office at the White House to see what was happening. He was told the President's statement was ready and would be released after 6 P.M.

Epstein hurried back to his office, sent off a cable to Shertok, and began phoning the news to Weizmann and the Jewish Agency leaders in New York. The breakdown in communications with Israel delayed Epstein's message to Tel Aviv. The news first reached there through an American ham operator who made contact with Haganah Radio headquarters in the early hours of May 15, Israel time.

The Jewish Agency building and the street in front were already jammed when Epstein returned. The letter from Marshall had not yet arrived, but a high State Department official had phoned to congratulate Epstein and to advise him that a messenger was on the way. The same official invited Epstein to call at the State Department on May 17 to discuss the establishment of "relations between our two governments." It was nearly 7 P.M. when Marshall's letter was delivered into the hands of Isadore Hamlin, assistant press officer of the Jewish Agency. Marshall's note read as follows:

"I have the honor to acknowledge receipt of your letter of May 14, 1948, and to inform you that on May 14, 1948, at 6:11 P.M., Washington time [12:11 A.M., May 15, in Tel Aviv] the President of the United States issued the following statement: 'This Government has been informed that a Jewish State has been proclaimed in Palestine, and recognition has been requested by the Provisional Government thereof. The United States recognizes the Provisional Government as the de facto authority of the new State of Israel.'" It was signed, "G. C. Marshall, Secretary of State."

Thus Israel received the first formal confirmation of its entry into the family of nations.

Epstein had already broken the news to the excited throng toasting Israel's birth. He had slipped away from the celebration to catch the radio reports of Truman's announcement and then returned to read it to the deliriously joyful celebrants. At exactly 6:01 P.M. the blue and white flag of Israel was unfurled from the Jewish Agency's window by eight-year-old Oren Zinder, Harry Zinder's oldest son. The youngster was chosen for the honor because he was the only Palestine-born child in the family of an Agency staffer. Amid shouts of *"Mazel Tov"* and the singing of "Hatikvah" and "The Star-Spangled Banner," the display of the flag marked the conversion of the building into the first Embassy of Israel. Among the crowd, in addition to members of Congress and leaders of the Washington Jewish community, were Mrs. Woodrow Wilson, whose husband had endorsed the Balfour Declaration in 1917, and Sumner Welles, a vigorous champion of Jewish statehood after he left the State Department in 1943. The ceremony ended with Rabbi Zemach Green of the Ohev Sholom Congregation pronouncing the traditional Sheheheyanu prayer, after which boys and girls from Habonim, the Labor Zionist youth organization, danced the hora and sang Hebrew folksongs on the lawn of the building.

The wording of the Truman statement and Marshall's letter initially gave rise to the mistaken notion that the US had extended only de facto recognition. Actually, it was full recognition of Israel as a state, but de facto recognition of the provisional government. Ironically, the man who cleared up this confusion was Philip Jessup, who had been speaking from the UN podium at Lake Success on the evening of May 14 when the UN was stunned by the report from Washington. At that moment Jessup was pushing the UN to adopt his formula for some form of interim Palestine regime under a UN commission.

On December 17, 1948, Jessup explained to the Security Council, while advocating the admission of Israel to the UN, that the "US had extended immediate and full recognition of the State of Israel. . . . There was no qualification. It was not conditional. It was not de facto recognition. It was full recognition. So far as the provisional government of Israel is concerned, the US did extend de facto recognition to that provisional government of Israel."

Nevertheless, for some months after May 14, 1948, Epstein was recognized by the State Department as "Special Representative of Israel," a term completely unknown in international law, instead of by the generally accepted title of "Minister Plenipotentiary and Envoy Extraordinary." Some saw in this the implication of an inferior title, but the identical title was at first held by James G. McDonald, the first US envoy to Israel. Later, Epstein, under his Hebraized name of Elath, became Israel's first Ambassador to the United States.

The suddenness of Truman's announcement, however mixed its motives, upset many important officials who were kept in the dark when they felt they should have been informed in advance. Marshall and Lovett were of course parties to the last-minute decision, but lower-echelon State Department officers were caught entirely unaware. So were the members of the American delegation to the UN, probably in order to avert any leak to the Russians, who were known to be eager to announce recognition first. Immediately after Congress heard of the proclamation in Tel Aviv, Representative Sol Bloom wired Truman, urging prompt recognition of the Tel Aviv regime. In his telegram Bloom said he understood that Russia and many other countries were prepared to accord recognition and that the US should take the lead and "help keep Palestine and the Near East from Soviet influence and domination."

Even Secretary of Defense Forrestal, who remained a foe of the Jewish state to the bitter end, had no idea of what was happening until Lovett phoned him at 6:30 P.M. "to say that at 6:15 P.M. [*sic*] this government had recognized the new State of Israel." As Forrestal reported it in *The Forrestal Diaries*, Lovett said "this position had apparently been reached twenty-four to forty-eight hours ago and had been communicated to Marshall and himself at a meeting which was attended by Clifford and Niles and several others of the White House staff. He said he expected severe fighting would ensue but that the Jewish army was superior in equipment and training to the Arabs and could probably take care of themselves. Repercussions in other parts of the world where United States interests are affected, such as Egypt, Pakistan and North Africa, would probably be felt within the next few days."

Equally unhappy was the anti-Zionist American Council for Judaism. Before they heard that Israel had won US recognition, Alfred M. Lilienthal, then legal adviser to the Council, and Joseph D. Kaufman, Chairman of its Washington chapter, said that "We Americans of Jewish faith wish to declare our complete independence and separation from any state that is, or may be, established." Lessing J. Rosenwald of Philadelphia, then President of the Council, declared that "it must be clearly understood that the provisional government of the Jewish state can only be the government of its inhabitants and citizens; it can have no claim upon the national attachments of those of Jewish faith who are citizens of other lands."

Press Secretary Charles Ross insisted that Truman did not act until after he had received Epstein's letter, but maintained that recognition was "entirely consistent" with the abandoned trusteeship proposal. On May 15 Ross told the press that the time between the decision to recognize and its actual announcement was so brief that there had been no time to inform other governments in advance. But he disclosed that the British had been advised on the afternoon of May 14 that the question was under active consideration and that it would probably be an affirmative decision.

Among those tipped off as to what was coming was Senator Arthur H. Vandenberg, an aspirant for the Republican Presidential nomination and Chairman of the Senate Foreign Relations Committee. Thus recognition was made a matter of bipartisan national policy. Political observers interpreted Truman's swift action as a shrewd move to win back the support of Jewish voters in the big cities, especially in New York, in connection with the upcoming Presidential election. In support of this view they pointed to the rush of such Presidential hopefuls as Vandenberg and Robert A. Taft to endorse Truman's statement. As it turned out, Truman failed to carry New York by 60,000 votes and also lost Illinois and Pennsylvania, with their large blocs of Jewish voters in Chicago, Philadelphia, and Pittsburgh.

TRUMAN EXPLAINS

In his *Memoirs* Truman added a few details about the background of his twelfth-hour decision. "I had often talked with my advisers about the course of action we would take once partition had come about," he wrote, "and it was always understood that eventually we would recognize any responsible government the Jews might set up. Partition was not taking place in exactly the peaceful manner I had hoped, to be sure, but the fact was that the Jews were controlling the area in which their people lived and that they were ready to administer and defend it. On the other hand, I was well aware that some of the State Department 'experts' would want to block recognition of a Jewish State."

Once the Jews were ready to proclaim the State of Israel, the President continued, "I decided to move at once and give American recognition to the new nation. I instructed a member of my staff to communicate my decision to the State Department and prepare it for transmission to Ambassador Austin at the United Nations in New York. About thirty minutes later, exactly eleven minutes after Israel had been proclaimed a state, Charlie Ross, my press secretary, handed the press the announcement of the de facto recognition by the United States of the Provisional Government of Israel. I was told that to some of the career men of the State Department, this announcement came as a surprise. It should not have been if these men had faithfully supported my policy."

Truman blamed only the second- and third-level officers of the State Department and some generals and admirals for trying without authority to make policy in Palestine. He stated categorically that Marshall, Lovett, and Austin all "saw eye to eye" with him on Palestine. Referring to the lower-rank people, Truman quoted Lovett as saying, after May 14, "They almost put it over on you." Truman's assertion that Ambassador Austin was informed in advance of the decision to recognize Israel is at variance with the obvious discomfiture and embarrassment of the US delegation when word of Truman's action reached Lake Success. Austin was not in the UN chamber at the moment, having left for his apartment at the Waldorf-Astoria, five floors above the Weizmann apartment. Rumors that he was contemplating resigning on May 15 were attributed to his resentment at having been bypassed, but the White House ignored the reports and Austin bluntly denied them.

Amid all the pressures of May 14, Truman took the time to write to Mrs. Eleanor Roosevelt that he had honored the pledge he had made to her in March, when he had dissuaded her from resigning as one of the US delegates to the UN. "There was a vacuum in Palestine," the President wrote, "and since the Russians were anxious to be the first to do the recognizing, General Marshall, Secretary Lovett, Dr. Rusk and myself worked the matter out and decided the proper thing was to recognize the Jewish Government."

Within hours after the news of Truman's statement became known, the White House was flooded with a torrent of telegrams of congratulation, followed by 200,000 pieces of mail, most of them supporting Truman's move. Among the wires was one sent from Kansas City at 5:46 P.M. CDT by Eddie Jacobson: "Thanks and God bless you." The message reached the White House at 10 P.M., and Truman acknowledged it on May 18, saying, "It [the wire] is more than appreciated."

The leading actors in the Washington drama of May 14 subsequently had other important roles. Truman, of course, scored an upset victory in the 1948 election without the electoral votes of New York, Pennsylvania, and Illinois. After a successful career as a corporation lawyer, Clifford became Secretary of State in the closing months of the Johnson Administration. Epstein (now Elath), who in 1950 was succeeded as Ambassador to the US by Abba Eban, moved on to London as envoy to the Court of St. James and then served as President of the Hebrew University until 1968. Zinder was promoted to Director of the Israel Government Information office in the US and later held a similar post in Israel. Ginsburg, one of Washington's top lawyers, was secretary of President Johnson's National Advisory Commission on Civil Disorders (the Kerner Commission).

Truman, Epstein, and Zinder were subsequently linked, in a manner of speaking, through the Harry S Truman Center for the Advancement of Peace. Created on Truman's eightieth birthday, the Center was erected on Mount Scopus, adjacent to the original buildings of the Hebrew University, by a foundation whose first executive director was Zinder. The cornerstone of the Hebrew University had been laid in 1925 by Lord Balfour, with whom Truman earned equal rank in the Jewish Pantheon on May 14, 1948.

THE MAN WHO WASN'T THERE

LYING IN BED in a darkened room high above the din of New York's streets, seventy-four-year-old Dr. Chaim Weizmann was entertaining some old Zionist friends at tea as the setting sun ushered in the Sabbath on May 14. They had been coming in a steady stream all day to give the ailing half-blind old man a *"Mazel Tov"* on the miracle that had taken place in Tel Aviv, two continents away, eight hours earlier.

Dr. Joseph Linton, his political aide, was in the next room of the suite on the thirty-seventh floor of the Waldorf-Astoria Towers, working on some correspondence. To shut out the noise from the bedroom, he had turned up his radio. Suddenly, Linton jumped up and burst into Weizmann's bedroom with an excited shout. "Chief," he began, when Weizmann, who could see barely more than the shadowed outlines of his companions from behind his dark glasses, interrupted, "President Truman has recognized our state."

Linton appeared surprised. "How could you know, Chief? You haven't a radio in this room."

"I saw it in your face," Dr. Weizmann answered gently. "And I also had faith in the work we've been doing."

That morning Mrs. Weizmann had written in her diary: "10 A.M. [it was 10:32 A.M. EDT]: Jewish State has been proclaimed. The name 'Israel.' I would have preferred 'Judea.' Arab aggression is threatened on all sides. Ch. [Chaim] is confident. I am anxious."

It was thus that the man who for forty years had been the eloquent pleader for a Jewish state heard that the purpose for which he had come to the United States had ended in a diplomatic triumph. He had neither anticipated nor sought the assignment that he had accepted under the

most unpromising circumstances. It turned out to be the third and final of
his trio of historic achievements, for he was to pass his last years as the
embittered and almost completely powerless first President of the State of
Israel.

This episode in a life that spanned the whole history of political
Zionism—beginning with the Lovers of Zion before Herzl and ending
four years after Israel was born—had begun in London almost six
months earlier. Once the United Nations had adopted partition on November 29, 1947, Weizmann had decided on the inevitable need for the
proclamation of a Jewish state when the British Mandate expired in May,
and he wanted to be in Palestine for this epic occasion. He was confident
that the main responsibility for carrying out partition would rest with the
Yishuv. Soon after he returned to London on December 23, 1947, he
began planning to settle in Palestine permanently. By mid-January the
Weizmanns had disposed of their household effects and terminated the
lease on their apartment in the Dorchester Hotel. They were booked to
fly to Burma on January 25, with an intermediate stop in India, before
going on to Palestine. Only the crisis that developed early in 1948 could
have brought him back into the battle he had fought for so long.

Alarmed by the possibility that Arab violence might necessitate armed
force to implement partition, thus raising the specter of Russian troops in
the Middle East just when the Cold War was heating up, the US State
and Defense Departments panicked. Their insistence on a reversal of the
US position gave rise to the real danger that the UN partition plan might
be jettisoned. The Arabs became convinced that they could gain by force
of arms in Palestine what they had failed to win at the UN. The British
were deliberately sabotaging partition to demonstrate that without British
rule peace in the Holy Land was impossible. The UN Implementation
Commission was barred from Palestine. Arab violence went unchecked as
the British refused to intervene lest they be accused of aiding the fulfillment of partition. Palestine's borders were closed to the UN but left open
to Arab guerrillas. Haganah convoys were searched and Haganah fighters
were arrested in the act of defending Jewish lives.

By January, 1948, Britain had abdicated her role in Palestine, hoping
that the spreading chaos for which she was responsible might yet create a
situation that would enable her to retain the Mandate. In Washington
and at the UN there were well-founded reports that the US was on the
verge of abandoning partition in favor of a new scheme that would defer
Jewish statehood and permit the British to stay on. The miracle of November 29, 1947, appeared to be turning into a tragic mirage.

While "the vastest anticlimax in Jewish history was being prepared,"

Weizmann held no official place in the Zionist movement. At the 1946 World Zionist Congress the American Zionists, backed by Ben-Gurion, had rejected the leadership of the man who since 1917 had been the leading star in the Zionist firmament. Embittered by Britain's White Paper policy, the Zionist Congress took out its anger on Weizmann and his insistence on working with England so long as such an approach was tenable. The split between Ben-Gurion and Weizmann at the end of World War II stemmed from the Englishman's abhorrence of activist resistance to Britain and his bitter opposition to all terrorism, which Ben-Gurion tacitly approved. The rift spilled over into American Zionist circles, where rising anti-British feeling created widespread backing for the maximalist Zionist position advocated by Rabbi Abba Hillel Silver and Dr. Emanuel Neumann. This took the form of aggressive political pressure on both political parties during the first eighteen months of the Truman Administration, and on Truman himself.

Despite his passionate protests against Britain's callous behavior in Palestine in 1939, 1945, and 1946, Weizmann had clung tenaciously to the links with England. But these connections became a handicap rather than an asset because by 1946–47 Zionism no longer played a role in Britain's long-range imperial plans. The coincidence of British and Zionist interests in 1917 had enabled Weizmann to win the Balfour Declaration from the British cabinet after he had captivated Lloyd George, Lord Balfour, and Jan Christiaan Smuts. But after 1945 Britain was liquidating her empire and was well on the way toward becoming a second-class power. Weizmann won only kind words from Churchill, and nothing but heartaches from his successor, Clement Attlee, and the Labourite Secretary for Foreign Affairs, Ernest Bevin. Although he was sympathetic to Jewish aims in Palestine, Churchill in 1946 spoke of the Mandate as "an unfair burden" and "a thankless, painful, costly, laborious, inconvenient task" that Britain should no longer be asked to carry out alone.

Until the final Zionist rupture with Britain in 1947, however, Weizmann continued to hope for some form of partition that would lead to a Jewish state closely tied to England. While Weizmann pressed for a negotiated settlement, Ben-Gurion demanded the immediate creation of a Jewish state. Weizmann had always counseled moderation and patience to his Zionist colleagues while never wavering on the ultimate goal of statehood. However, he wanted to achieve it by compromise and accommodation while Ben-Gurion fought for it through militancy in Palestine and American pressure on Britain.

At the 1946 World Zionist Congress, Weizmann waged an exhausting but losing fight for one last attempt to seek an understanding with

Britain: his plea for participation in a new Arab-Jewish conference the British had convened for January, 1947, was turned down. By a small majority a resolution supporting his position was defeated, and a repudiated Weizmann was not reelected President of the World Zionist Organization, the office being left vacant.

For tactical reasons the Zionists eventually went to the conference, but unofficially. They tried and failed to reach an accommodation on the basis of the 1937 partition plan for which Weizmann had argued. The conference dragged on through February, 1947, after which Bevin told the world that Britain was washing her hands of the whole Palestine business and handing it over to the UN, never suspecting at the time that this would lead to a UN proposal for and endorsement of the establishment of a Jewish state.

The initiative on Palestine had already passed from London to Washington and Tel Aviv. Ben-Gurion had long since taken over the reins in Palestine, and the diplomatic struggle in Washington and New York and at the UN was being directed by Rabbi Silver, together with Moshe Shertok and members of the American Section of the Jewish Agency. Weizmann's star had set, or so it seemed. But when the United Nations Special Commission on Palestine (UNSCOP) arrived in Palestine in 1947 to take testimony, the Zionist leadership that had rejected Weizmann the previous year invited him to testify. His "prestige and power of exposition" were needed to persuade UNSCOP that partition was the only solution. Ironically, the Jewish Agency had also come around to this view for which Weizmann had been pilloried. Officially, though, the Agency was still demanding a Jewish state in the whole of Palestine.

When the struggle shifted to UN headquarters, Weizmann was asked to perform one more urgent task by those who had banished him to private life. He was weary of internal quarrels, severely ill with a chronic respiratory ailment, and already going blind. Yet he came to the US in October, 1947, to help rally the support of UN delegations for the UNSCOP majority report that called for partition and a Jewish state.

The chief Jewish advocates at the UN were the energetic and eloquent Silver and Shertok, but Weizmann's "position in international life conveyed a premonition of Jewish sovereignty." Heads of state received him with courtesy and ministers and high officials "with apprehensive respect," Eban wrote. "They behaved toward him as though he were already president of a sovereign nation, equal in status to their own." He and they knew this was not true—he had once described himself as president of an international federation of *schnorrers*—but, said Eban, "something in his presence and in their own historic imagination forbade them to break the spell. The Jewish people had produced a president before it had achieved a state; and somehow this made the claim to statehood seem less far-fetched in many eyes than it would otherwise have."

Weizmann's address to the UN ad-hoc committee on Palestine on October 16, 1947, was a memorable effort, and the representatives of fifty-seven nations were greatly moved. He had worked on the draft of the speech four hours that day with Eban. "After each sentence was written in huge letters and agreed," Eban noted in his diary, "he would go to the lampstand and bring the text right to his glasses, endeavoring to learn it by heart. By the end of the session his eyes were watering as if in tears. Finally, he said: 'We'll make this do—but how about a *posuk* [biblical verse] for the ending?' We looked for a Bible and eventually found one, supplied by the hotel in the bedside table. Spent half an hour on Isaiah, looking for 'return to Zion' passages. Finally his mind was caught by the prophecy of 'an ensign for the nations.' As I left, he said: 'Well, this is it. Over the top for the last time.'"

Even more crucial was Weizmann's conversation with President Truman at the White House on November 19, on the eve of the final vote on UNSCOP's report. The US delegation to the UN was urging the detachment of the southern Negev from the area assigned to the Jewish state under the partition plan. Weizmann left his sickbed to plead with Truman to prevent this disaster. The President was touched by the aging stateman's magnetism and convinced by his cogent arguments, and the next day the White House countermanded instructions under which the US delegation was about to vote for the elimination of the Negev from the Jewish state's boundaries.

Once the battle for the frontiers was won, Weizmann threw his enormous contacts into the final struggle to win over uncommitted or wavering delegations to the majority UNSCOP recommendations. His long friendship with Léon Blum, former French Premier, was credited with swinging France over at the last minute to support partition. As David Horowitz, a member of the Jewish Agency delegation, put it, Weizmann's "political eminence and personal charm often worked wonders."

The situation in January, 1948, was made to order for another of these "wonders," and pressure began to mount to bring Weizmann back to the US. The suggestion was first made early in January in a transatlantic call from Joseph Linton, who had been political secretary of the Jewish Agency's London office and Weizmann's political aide, and who had just arrived in New York. Because Weizmann and Linton suspected that their telephone lines were being tapped, they spoke enigmatically of the weather. When Weizmann asked about the climate in New York, Linton replied it was "extremely cold, both indoors and outside." Half an hour later Weizmann called Linton in New York to say he would not return unless the Jewish Agency people in New York officially invited him. Lacking such a formal request, he intended to leave for India and Burma in forty-eight hours, as he had planned, before going home to Rehovot.

On January 23 Eban cabled him to reconsider his decision to go to Palestine " in view of the worsening situation there," meaning the Arab rebellion. Eban pointed out that "no conditions exist there [requiring] your constructive political activity," but "everything depending upon outcome negotiations here Lake Success and Washington." Eban's cable revealed that "the most crucial phase of all now approaches here . . . in which we sorely miss your presence advice activity influence."

Similar pleas came from Palestine. But there were also those opposed to bringing Weizmann back into the picture. Some feared he might end up on the side of compromise, while others felt he wasn't needed. It is probable that Weizmann wanted to reenter the fray despite his seeming reluctance. His unwillingness to come on an unofficial basis was motivated by concern that he might be burdened with responsibility for a disaster if his mission failed. When the official invitation arrived, in a cable dated January 27, signed by Arthur Lourie, he accepted.

Weizmann sailed that same day on the *Queen Mary*, arriving in New York on Febuary 4 in the middle of a blizzard. The rough voyage proved too much for him and he had to stay in bed for several days at the Waldorf-Astoria Towers. Linton moved into a room adjoining the Weizmann suite and became Weizmann's political assistant. Eban's diary entry for February 4 says the following: "Dined at Waldorf with Chief and Mrs. Weizmann. He opened belligerently: 'Why in heaven did you drag me to this frozen waste when I might have been in Rehovot?' Told him of our danger at Lake Success and our position in Washington where not a single contact on high level had been possible since November. Truman furious with Zionist leaders and won't even see them. Chief's contact with President our only hope at UN and Washington. Chief decided to seek interview with Truman this month."

Weizmann was no stranger in Washington. Just as his scientific role in the development of acetone during World War I had paved the way for his relations with Lloyd George and the British War Cabinet, so his butyl alcohol process for making artificial rubber in World War II gave him his first access to President Roosevelt and made his name known to

Truman. During the war he had visited the US several times on urgent scientific errands and as the chief Zionist diplomat. In his expanding Washington contacts he had the helpful behind-the-scenes support of Vice-President Henry A. Wallace, Secretary of the Treasury Henry Morgenthau, Jr., Benjamin Cohen of the State Department, Judge Samuel I. Rosenman, Isadore Lubin, Robert Nathan, David Ginsburg, White House aide David K. Niles, and, from a proper judicial distance, Supreme Court Justice Felix N. Frankfurter. Weizmann had first met Truman on December 4, 1945, and a few days later he had sent him a memo, asking his support for a Palestine solution that would lead to "a Jewish commonwealth giving shelter, sustenance and peace to Jews and Arabs alike."

In February, 1947, Weizmann found his channels to the White House and the State Department blocked by the new frigid attitude toward Zionist objectives: not a single one of his contacts could break through to get the appointment he sought. Visitors to Weizmann's apartment brought only bad news: Herbert Bayard Swope reported that Truman had changed his mind on partition and would not be budged; David Ginsburg phoned with the alarming news that the possibility of war with Russia had cooled Washington to a Jewish state.

A letter asking for a White House appointment was carefully framed, in part by Frankfurter and Ginsburg, with Swope and George Backer adding some finishing touches. All it produced was a polite reply from Matt Connelly, the President's appointment secretary, that no date was possible because Truman's schedule was full and he was leaving for a Florida vacation. For nearly six weeks frenzied but futile efforts were made to get Truman to see Weizmann, but Truman was so mad at the unceasing Zionist pressure that he rebuffed every approach. He relented only in response to the insistent request of his wartime buddy and onetime haberdashery partner, Eddie Jacobson of Kansas City, Missouri. The persistent Jacobson succeeded where the most influential figures in the Democratic Party had failed. On March 13 he burst into the White House and talked Truman into agreeing to an off-the-record meeting with Weizmann. Under hush-hush circumstances dictated by Truman, Weizmann accomplished another of his "wonders" at 11 A.M. on March 18, 1948—the promise of the President of the United States to stand fast on partition.

The very next day Ambassador Austin announced to the UN a complete reversal of the US position: instead of partition, the US offered a plan for a temporary UN trusteeship, with the ostensible aim of avoiding further bloodshed in the Middle East.

"Chaim is nonplussed and indignant," Mrs. Weizmann wrote in her diary on March 20. "Dr. Weizmann must think I'm a plain liar," Truman growled to Clark Clifford when he saw the morning papers. American Jewry was outraged and the Zionists hurled thunderbolts of invective at Truman for his seeming doublecross. Weizmann also assailed the trusteeship proposal but carefully avoided blaming Truman personally.

Most heartsick of all was Eddie Jacobson, who was being bombarded in Kansas City with phone calls and wires denouncing his friend in the White House. On Monday morning, March 22, while the storm of protest over the US turnabout was still raging, Weizmann phoned Jacobson at his store and tried to cheer him up. "I don't think that President Truman knew what was going to happen in the United Nations on Friday when he talked to me the day before," Weizmann said. "I am seventy-four years old and all my life I have had one disappointment after another. This is just another letdown for me. Don't forget for a single moment that Harry S Truman is the most powerful single man in the world. You have a job to do to keep the White House doors open."

But Weizmann himself was more depressed by developments than he admitted to Jacobson, as revealed in his correspondence with Justice Frankfurter to whom he confided that he was on the verge of leaving the US. In a letter dated March 26, addressed to "My dear Chaimke," Frankfurter urged him not to go, saying, "I am not whistling in the dark when I say that the new turn of events gives the cause of the Jewish state new opportunities, provided we draw our resources from the strength of our moral position."

In reply Weizmann bewailed the fact that "every day some new hope is being dangled before our eyes and when the sun sets, it is nothing but a mirage. How long, Oh God, how long?" That Weizmann was still bent on leaving is indicated by a wire from Frankfurter dated April 6: "I cannot assure you that staying will not bring frustration and futility any more than I can guarantee that leaving will not result in feelings of what might have been. In the shoes of your dilemma, I would at least postpone going for a week by which time one may see more clearly the situation both here and there."

Despite his despondency, Weizmann knew that his duty was to maintain his ties with Truman, virtually the only man of authority in Washington personally sympathetic to the Zionist cause. On April 9, Weizmann wrote Truman a long private letter, expressing satisfaction with the President's statement of March 25 which indicated that the US was not abandoning partition as the ultimate political settlement in Palestine. Outlining the arguments against trusteeship, Weizmann said he could not

see how the admitted difficulties of partition would be avoided by trusteeship, enforcement of which would be even more difficult since neither the
Jews nor the Arabs had accepted it. He reminded the President that there
was no assurance that the UN would approve trusteeship or that any
effective measures could be improvised by May 15 and that it was dangerous to consider prolongation of British rule. He also drew Truman's attention to the psychological risk of "promising independence in November
and then withdrawing it in March." "The choice of our people, Mr. President, is between statehood and extermination," he wrote. "History and
Providence have placed this issue in your hands and I am confident that
you will yet decide it in the spirit of the moral law."

Weizmann gained some encouragement from an early April meeting
with Col. David ("Mickey") Marcus, the retired American Army officer
who was helping map Haganah strategy. Before his return to Palestine,
Marcus assured Weizmann that once Haganah acquired some heavy artillery,
the whole Arab "war of liberation" would collapse. UN delegates who
trooped into Weizmann's suite in the hope of getting him to modify his
opposition to trusteeship, found him unwavering. To Ambassador Austin
and his deputy, Dr. Philip K. Jessup, he said, "Palestine Jewry would be
off its head if it postponed statehood for anything as foolish as the American trusteeship proposal." To Arthur Creech-Jones, the British Colonial
Secretary, he declared that given half a chance, the Jews of Palestine
would explode the myth of Arab military might. Alexandre Parodi, chief
of the French delegation, lunched with Weizmann at his bedside and
voiced fears that the Jews would be massacred by the Arab armies. Just at
that moment Weizmann's secretary walked in with a copy of the *New
York Post* whose page-one headline reported Haganah's victory at Mishmar Haemek, where an Arab attempt to cut the Haifa-Tel Aviv road had
been beaten back on April 12 after a four-day battle.

As late as April 16, however, Weizmann was still determined to return to Palestine. In a letter of that date to Eddie Jacobson he said "there
is now only a fortnight left before I shall leave this country." He had
booked passage for April 29 so that he would be on hand for the proclamation of independence.

By the third week in April, when it was clear that the American trusteeship plan had no chance of getting through the UN, the US pulled a
new delaying tactic out of the diplomatic hat. It was a suggestion for a
temporary cease-fire in Palestine during which the Jews would be expected to refrain from proclaiming their state pending new negotiations.
The moment of decision on the Jewish state was fast approaching, not

only in Tel Aviv, but in Washington and Lake Success as well. All three top figures in the Zionist movement—Ben-Gurion, Silver, and Weizmann, proud and jealous individualists each—had separately arrived at the same conclusion: a Jewish state must be proclaimed in that area of Palestine set aside for the Jews by the UN as soon as the British Mandate ended. Their relations were tenuous at best, but each had a specific job to do.

In Palestine, Ben-Gurion was erecting the framework of a government and forging the military machine to defend the state-in-the-making. The greatly improved military situation after Haganah's first offensive routed the Arab irregulars in mid-April strengthened Ben-Gurion's confidence that a proclamation of independence would be neither unrealistic nor foolhardy. The prime target of Truman's ire because of the unremitting campaign of pressure on the White House, Rabbi Silver intensified his unswerving efforts to mobilize American public opinion against any US move that would upset the partition plan and put off statehood. Weizmann was busy weaving the thread that would grow into the tapestry of American recognition.

Independently of each other Weizmann and Silver refused to accept the truce plan despite its spurious appeal, believing that any retreat from or delay in independence would be fatal. Ben-Gurion, equally resolute, was not at all clear about the stand of American Jewry and was especially concerned over Weizmann's position. The collapse of the British administration in Palestine made it difficult, and sometimes even impossible, for the shadow Jewish government in Tel Aviv to maintain reliable communication with the Jewish Agency leaders in the US.

Ben-Gurion was apprehensive over reports that some Jewish Agency people in the US were so frightened by State Department pressure and threats that they were counseling acceptance of the truce, with some modifications. Weizmann and Silver, on the other hand, were troubled by rumors that even in Tel Aviv some feared to alienate the US and were ready to go along with a short truce that might buy time to bring in more arms.

Truman, meanwhile, had made up his mind to press forward with partition if no other solution acceptable to all parties was reached by May 15. He still had a bad conscience about Austin's March 19 statement, which he claimed he didn't know was to be made, certainly not on the very day after he had offered Weizmann such great encouragement. Unable to reveal his decision in person to Weizmann, Truman chose as his intermediary his former aide, Judge Rosenman. The day after the Austin bombshell Truman sent Rosenman to reassure Weizmann that nothing had changed since their March 18 conversation.

On Friday evening, April 23, the eve of Passover, Mr and Mrs. Weizmann were due as seder guests at the Central Park West home of Mr. and Mrs. Sigmund Kramarsky. Just before leaving the Waldorf-Towers suite, Weizmann received a telephone call from Rosenman, who had just returned from Washington and was staying at the Essex House on Central Park South. Bedded down with a severe attack of gout, Rosenman was unable to call on Weizmann and asked Weizmann to stop off at the Essex House on the way to the Kramarskys'. Dr. Josef Cohn, Weizmann's secretary, escorted Weizmann to Rosenman's suite and then returned to the Waldorf to fetch Mrs. Weizmann. They waited in the Essex House lobby for nearly an hour while Rosenman disclosed to Weizmann the news for which he had been praying. The President, Rosenman said, had authorized him to inform Weizmann unequivocally but confidentially that the US would recognize the Jewish state immediately after it was declared if before then the UN had not reversed itself on partition. There was only one condition: Truman would deal with no one but Weizmann—which meant that Weizmann had to give up all hope of being in Palestine for the proclamation of independence.

Neither Mrs. Weizmann nor Cohn asked any questions on the way to the Kramarskys', but both sensed that something of the gravest importance had happened. All through the seder the usually voluble Weizmann appeared to be deep in thought and very much aloof. He made his excuses after the meal and left without waiting for the reading of the second half of the *Haggadah*. Back at the Waldorf around 10 P.M. he undressed, put on his colorful pajamas and dressing gown, and unwound for a while in a soft armchair in the sitting room before retiring.

On orders from the White House, Rosenman had sworn Weizmann to absolute secrecy. Eban's account of the Essex House meeting says that Weizmann "discussed the exciting news with his friends" but does not identify them. Dr. Cohn's report of the conversation, written soon after it happened, asserts that the only people in whom Weizmann confided were Mrs. Weizmann, Joseph Linton, and Cohn. Linton does not recall whether Weizmann discussed Rosenman's news afterward, or with whom. He does remember that the gist of Weizmann's two prior talks with Rosenman was passed on confidentially to Shertok and Dr. Nahum Goldmann of the Jewish Agency Executive in New York. Linton, who was present at one of these meetings, drafted the memoranda prepared for Rosenman. Written at the Waldorf Towers and typed by Dr. Cohn, both documents contained detailed analyses of the Palestine situation as Weizmann saw it and were intended for Truman's information.

Thus Rosenman became the middleman between Truman and Weizmann in the effort to gain American recognition. According to David Ginsburg, Weizmann was the link between Epstein in Washington, Shertok in New York, and Silver at Lake Success. Rosenman's decisive role was acknowledged by Weizmann in a letter he wrote to Rosenman on May 17: "This is the first letter which I am writing since the news of last night reached me [Weizmann's election as Provisional President of Israel]. It is only proper that it should be addressed to you who have contributed so much of your effort and wisdom towards bringing about some of the happy results during the past few days." Rosenman turned the letter over to Mrs. Weizmann on one of his visits to Israel after Weizmann's death. It is now in the Weizmann Archives as the first letter of the first President of Israel.

Eliahu Epstein has maintained his silence on whether news of the Rosenman-Weizmann meeting got back to Tel Aviv. Meyer Weisgal, Weizmann's confidant, and Julian Meltzer, Curator of the Weizmann Archives, believe Epstein may have been with Weizmann when he got the Passover-evening call from Rosenman and could have been taken into Weizmann's confidence later. In any event, the circumstances of the Essex House conversation, although not their full import, became known to others in the Jewish Agency circle, but not through Weizmann.

Ben-Gurion was in contact with Weizmann during this period only through intermediaries. On April 14 Weisgal wrote to Weizmann from Tel Aviv to emphasize why it was imperative that he remain in New York. "I know your heart longs for Rehovot and for your home," Weisgal said. "I walked through your grounds yesterday and I prayed that you might . . . be able to return . . . to enjoy the comfort of home and the fragrance of your gardens. But I am afraid it cannot be done. Every responsible person I spoke to—and I spoke to all of them—Ben-Gurion, Kaplan, [Eliezer Kaplan, Jewish Agency treasurer], to the High Command, all . . . are of the opinion that it is unwise and imprudent for you to come back at this time. It is less dangerous for us poor mortals who count for little or naught. You will . . . have to remain as *ya'avor zaam* [until the danger has passed]."

It is still not clear whether Tel Aviv wanted to keep Weizmann away out of concern for his physical safety during the Arab rebellion or because Ben-Gurion had doubts as to his political reliability. Before he sent the letter Weisgal himself had decided to leave Palestine with his family, but was talked out of it by Ben-Gurion. Three days later Ben-Gurion called him to the Red House, Haganah headquarters on the Tel Aviv seashore, and told him, "You must leave the country at once." Ben-Gurion explained his amazing about-face by pointing out that Shertok was held in New York by the critical situation at the UN, communications had broken down, and Ben-Gurion had to know at once what Weizmann's opinion was about declaring independence.

Weisgal, who had been Weizmann's personal political representative in the US and General Secretary of the American Section of the Jewish Agency from 1941 to 1946, held no official Zionist position in 1948. But as Executive Vice-Chairman of the Institute he was on terms of personal intimacy with Weizmann. The only transportation out of Palestine not controlled by the British was an irregular air service to the Mediterranean coast of France. Ben-Gurion got Weisgal and his wife seats on a creaky old Dakota and they flew to Nice. From there Weisgal phoned Weizmann in New York and passed along Ben-Gurion's burning question about an immediate proclamation of independence. Speaking in Yiddish Weizmann replied, *"Vos varten zei?"* ("What are they waiting for?"). Ben-Gurion had his answer but he was unaware that Weizmann was working on another "wonder."

On his way back from Nice to England, Weisgal arrived without visas for himself and his wife for the United Kingdom. He had left Palestine in such a hurry that there had been no time to go to Haifa to get them. When he finally talked his way through passport control at the London airport, a brawny bobby called him over. For a moment Weisgal had visions of the Old Bailey. Instead, the bobby touched his helmet respectfully and said, "You seem to be having a bit of trouble in the country you come from. Don't fear, sir, you will have your Jewish state. It is written in the Book, and whatever is written in the Book will come true."

Like his idol Weizmann, Weisgal never made it back to Palestine in time for the proclamation of independence. May 14 found him in England at the country estate of Henny and Sigmund Gestetner, two prominent Zionists, participating in a pageant staged by Zionist youth.

A similar message from Weizmann reached Ben-Gurion on May 11 via Shertok. Flying back to Tel Aviv with Secretary of State Marshall's warning against precipitate action by the Jews, Shertok let Ben-Gurion know that Weizmann was unalterably opposed to any political standstill. "Moshe, don't let them weaken, don't let them swerve, don't let them spoil the victory," Weizmann pleaded with Shertok before he left New York. In a last-minute telephone call to Shertok at the airport Weizmann again urged him to tell Ben-Gurion to "proclaim the Jewish state—now or never."

Meanwhile, Weizmann, hugging his secret, kept his diplomatic silence when Bartley Crum went to the Waldorf on May 7 with a rumor he had picked up in Washington: the President would recognize the Jewish state within a week! After Crum's visit Mrs. Weizmann wrote in her diary: "President to recognize the Jewish State on 14 May at six o'clock. The President is anxious to do so before the Russians. What a joke! Nevertheless, B. Crum does not wish to be too optimistic. One never knows what influence will be brought to bear on the President by the British, the State Department and the anti-Zionists. Rosenman is being pressed by Chaim to go to see the President today. It is almost zero hour, and the President will have no credit in the Jewish State's birth if his recognition comes too late. Meanwhile, the British go on with their caretakers' proposals. I wish it was all over."

Weizmann was in bed for the next few days, holding the key to a political miracle in his hands. Between bedside conferences and the drafting of letters and memoranda, he was on the telephone constantly to Rosenman, Niles, Ginsburg, and Epstein in Washington, to Eban at Lake Success, and to a long list of Jewish leaders in New York. On May 12 he phoned Niles to pass along the text of Shertok's cabled plea that Truman warn Emir Abdullah of Transjordan against invasion. Crum called in the evening with word that Truman had conferred with Marshall and Under Secretary of State Lovett at the White House on what the US should do on May 14.

On the morning of May 13 Weizmann heard that the American delegation at the UN was proposing the appointment of a mediator for Palestine. On tenterhooks, he phoned Eban at the UN delegates' lounge and asked him to hurry over to the Waldorf. Eban came with assurances that the new scheme would not be incompatible with Jewish statehood. While Eban was in the room, Ginsburg phoned from Washington to suggest that Weizmann send Truman a letter by special messenger that very night. The timetable worked out between Rosenman and Weizmann had called for Weizmann to request recognition at the strategic moment.

The letter Weizmann dictated on May 13 advised the President that the Jewish state would be proclaimed the next day and expressed the hope that "the United States, which under your leadership has done so much to find a just solution, will promptly recognize the provisional government of the new Jewish State." Forgiving Truman for previous reversals, Weizmann said, "The unhappy events of the last few months will not, I hope, obscure the very great contributions that you, Mr. President, have made toward a definitive and just settlement of the long and trouble-some Palestine question. The world, I think, will regard it as especially appropriate that the greatest living democracy should be the first to wel-come the newest into the family of nations."

Dr. Cohn took the letter to Washington by the night train. Early on the morning of May 14 there was an agonizing moment when Cohn called Linton and said he was having trouble in bringing the letter to the immediate attention of the President. The matter was expedited when Weizmann called Niles at the White House. Shortly before noon Cohn was on the line again to report "mission accomplished."

Weizmann's letter raised the curtain on the last act of the White House drama of recognition. Truman would have preferred to move in re-sponse to Weizmann's request, which reached the White House after the ticker had clicked off the news that the Jewish state had been proclaimed at 10:32 A.M. Washington time. But State Department experts consulted by White House aides pointed out that because Weizmann held no offi-cial post in the Zionist movement or in the new state, something more formal was needed. To meet the requirements of protocol, White House aide Clark Clifford was authorized by Truman and Marshall to invite Eliahu Epstein, the unofficial ambassador of the Tel Aviv government, to submit an official letter asking for American recognition. As the Jewish Agency's representative in Washington, Epstein had been in close and frequent touch with Clifford for many months in anticipation of this day. Once Epstein's letter was delivered to the White House at a little after 4 P.M., Truman acted quickly to fulfill his promise to Weizmann. "The 'Old Doctor' will believe me now," the President said as he approved the state-ment of recognition and handed it over for distribution to his Press Secretary, Charles Ross.

All day long Weizmann had been receiving visitors coming to honor the man who had led "Israel through a wilderness of martyrdom and an-guish" into the Promised Land of a nation reborn. One of the callers was his old friend Dr. Judah L. Magnes, who had preferred a binational state to a fully independent Israel.

Another was Bartley Crum, who told Weizmann of an experience Mrs. Crum had had while her husband was in Palestine in 1946 as a member of the Anglo-American Committee of Inquiry. She had hired an Arab guide who carefully showed her only Arab sites in Jerusalem; a Jew-ish guide was equally parochial. Then she went sightseeing alone and came upon the statue of a mother and young child. Mrs. Crum asked a passing Jew what it was, and he replied with a grin, "It's Mrs. Weizmann and the young Chaim." When he heard the story, Weizmann laughed and said, "It could be." Privately he had often voiced to his intimates the feeling that he had been chosen for the role he filled in bringing about an epic change in the status of the Jewish people, starting with the struggle to get the Balfour Declaration in 1917. In the Weizmann Archives there is a letter he wrote as a boy of eleven to his teacher, Shlomo Sokolovsky, in Motol, Poland. Written in 1885 from Pinsk, where Weizmann was then attending high school, it suggested Jewish land settlement in Palestine by the Lovers of Zion Association, formed in 1884, and predicted that of all the great world powers, "England will have mercy on us."

Among the thousands of messages that poured in to Weizmann on May 14 and 15 was a note from Justice Frankfurter to his "Dear Chaim": "Mine eyes hath seen the glory of the coming of the Lord! Happily you can now say that—and can say what Moses could not. I salute you with a full heart . . . full of gladness or, rather, sad gladness. For not only has the road you have climbed been steep and stony but stony and steep it remains. But a commanding height has been reached—and it has been reached decisively because of your faith. Your resourcefulness would not have been enough, through the foulest weather. . . . Long may you inspire them in the ways of righteousness, for these alone are the ways of wisdom."

Frankfurter's "sad gladness" was in tune with Weizmann's own mood on May 14 because his ascent of "the commanding height" was shadowed by bitter disappointment. While the streets of New York rocked with joyful celebrants, Weizmann was brooding over the events in Tel Aviv that had taken place without his presence or participation. While onetime Zionist colleagues with portfolios in the Jewish Agency Executive and the Va'ad L'umi had within hours become Cabinet ministers, Weizmann felt forlorn and forgotten. Depressed and oppressed, he who had dreamed of leading his people to independence in Palestine, and perhaps even of becoming the first Prime Minister of the Jewish state, found himself in enforced exile on the day of its rebirth.

Because of the secrecy imposed upon him by the White House, few people in Palestine knew of Weizmann's crucial behind-the-scenes contribution to the decisions that set the political stage for the final showdown that led to the birth of Israel. His absence from Palestine at the historic moment was criticized by some as a dereliction of duty because of their ignorance of the fact that he had returned to the US and stayed there against his own wishes only at the specific request of the Jewish Agency.

His absence did irreparable damage to his reputation in Israel. By the time he set foot on the Promised Land in the fall of 1948 a crucial period in history had passed him by, and he had been displaced by the new hero, Ben-Gurion.

Weizmann's sense of frustration was intensified on the morning of May 15, when he learned that no place had been left for his signature on the Israel Declaration of Independence. After scanning the New York newspapers of that day, Mrs. Weizmann wrote in her diary: "There was not a word about Chaim in the statement of the Provisional Government [meaning the Declaration], no whisper of the Balfour Declaration. One puzzling note in the general jubilation that swirled around our Waldorf-Astoria apartment the day before had been the absence of any message or cable to Chaim from the Provisional Government."

This may explain why Weizmann's May 15 cable of congratulations to Ben-Gurion does not mention Ben-Gurion by name. The cable twice refers to the "Jewish State" but does not speak of the "State of Israel," apparently because it was dispatched before the official name was known in New York. This was Weizmann's message to the men and women in Israel who had finished what he had done so much to further:

"On this memorable day, when the Jewish State arises after 2000 years, I send my expression of love and admiration to all sections of the Yishuv and my warmest greeting to its government now entering on its grave and inspiring responsibility. I am fully convinced that all who have and will become citizens of the Jewish State will strive their utmost to live up to the new opportunity which history has bestowed upon them. It will be our destiny to create the institutions and values of a free community in the spirit of our great traditions which have contributed so much to the thought and spirit of mankind.

"At this moment, I think with special gratitude and affection of our pioneers and workers who have borne the burden of building Jewish Palestine and who now sustain the brunt and sacrifice of its defense. It is not easy for me to think of the peaceful farmers of Nahalal and Ein Harod, or the youth of our Jewish cities in the role of soldiers on active defense. In the days of Ezra, our forefathers built with one hand while defending themselves with the other. We are called upon today to act in this tradition.

"It is the profound desire of our people to establish relations of harmony and mutual respect with their Arab fellow citizens, with the neighboring Arab states and with all nations in the human family. As the British Mandate ends, we think with gratitude of the vision which inspired its inauguration. We also think of those nations, big and small, who, under the auspices of the United Nations, contributed their share to the international decision which confirmed our right to statehood. My thoughts are with the Yishuv in this fateful hour. May God's blessing rest on you all."

Even to the last, Weizmann had not forgotten the England of Balfour and Lloyd George. Their successors let the birth of Israel pass in official silence, but on May 14 Weizmann remembered the last surviving member of the British Cabinet that had issued the Balfour Declaration, and sent a cable of thanks to Jan Christiaan Smuts, Prime Minister of South Africa.

Weizmann's anger at the lack of any word to him from Tel Aviv on May 14 was not entirely cooled by the receipt of a cable the next day intimating that he would probably be elected Provisional President. "On the occasion of the establishment of the Jewish State," it said, "we send our greetings to you who have done more than any other living man towards its creation. Your stand and help have strengthened all of us. We look forward to the day when we shall see you at the head of the State established in peace." It was a personal message, signed by Ben-Gurion and three other members of the provisional government—Shertok, Golda Myerson, and Eliezer Kaplan—all longtime colleagues of Weizmann.

This communication could have been a response to a strange message of congratulation wired to Weizmann on the evening of May 14 from Washington by four men intimately familiar with his secret activities. Signed by Eliahu Epstein, David Ginsburg, Robert Nathan, and Oscar Gass, the telegram incorporated in a greeting to Weizmann the text of a cable sent to Ben-Gurion. This is how it read:

"In the fullness of our appreciation for your firm and wise leadership we have today ventured to send the following telegram to Palestine: 'David Ben-Gurion, Jewish Agency, Tel Aviv—we feel it our moral responsibility to inform you and the other members of the Provisional Government of the State of Israel how great a role in preparing the way for the prompt recognition of Israel by the United States Government has been played by Doctor Chaim Weizmann. We feel confident that if you had detailed knowledge of his work in this matter you would share our appreciation of his great contribution. Best regards and highest hopes for the new State. Best wishes for your continued health and firm leadership.' "

The language of the cable seems to indicate a concern on the part of its senders that Tel Aviv was not fully aware of Weizmann's role, presumably because he had fully respected Truman's insistence on secrecy. Epstein has declined to discuss the cable. Ginsburg says it was sent, not because of a feeling that Weizmann's activities were unknown to

Ben-Gurion and his associates, but on the contrary, Ginsburg emphasizes, because they were sure that Tel Aviv was well informed. Nevertheless, the senders wanted to remind Ben-Gurion not to forget the man who was not there and already so sorrowful and upset at the fate that had kept him away from Tel Aviv on the day the miracle happened.

Another cable, this one from Tel Aviv, on May 15, added to Weizmann's distress, even though it invited him to accept the Provisional Presidency. This message, from the provisional government, came to Arthur Lourie, director of the New York office of the Jewish Agency, who was asked to convey to Weizmann the government's unanimous resolution that he accept the Presidency. Late that night, after Weizmann had retired, the *New York Times* and *New York Post* telephoned. They had just received dispatches from Tel Aviv, reporting that Weizmann had been elected President (it was already May 16 in Israel), and they wanted to know how he felt about it. Mrs. Weizmann, who was still entertaining guests in the sitting room, took the call and then went into the bedroom. With some bitterness she said to her husband, who was still awake, "Congratulations, Chaimchik, you're now the President." Looking up at her from the bed, Weizmann asked with annoyance, "What nonsense are you talking?"

The official cable from the provisional government arrived on the morning of May 16. That night there was a wild celebration in Madison Square Garden acclaiming the Jewish state, but Weizmann was too ill to attend. Eban, Lourie, and Linton went from the Garden to Weizmann's suite for a champagne nightcap with the President-elect and to extend their personal congratulations.

In Tel Aviv, however, it had been taken for granted that Weizmann would be the first President. *Yom Ha'Medinah (The Day of the State)*, the one-sheet combined publication of all of Israel's newspapers that appeared on May 14, carried an item announcing the abrogation, as of May 14, of the 1939 White Paper laws of the British. The first act of the new government, it was signed for the provisional state council, "Weizmann, President, Ben-Gurion, Prime Minister."

Having been advised that the resident of Suite 37A (the Presidential Suite in the hotel's records) was now the President of Israel, the Waldorf-Astoria hurriedly acquired a large Israeli flag to fly side by side with the American flag, in keeping with protocol that the emblem of his nation flies over the residence of a chief of state wherever he may be. When another resident who occupied a permanent suite complained to the desk that the Israeli flag obscured his view, he was informed that the President of Israel was in the hotel, and that if the guest did not like the flag, he could leave.

Weizmann's first official act as President, and his last on American soil, was to accept President Truman's warm invitation to be the official guest of the US in Washington and to take up residence at Blair House, the government's guest house for distinguished visitors. Pennsylvania Avenue was bedecked with American and Israeli flags when Weizmann arrived by special train on May 24, accompanied by Mrs. Weizmann, Linton, Cohn, George Backer, and Abe Feinberg, an important Zionist figure who was a large contributor to Democratic Party funds. Weizmann's physician, Dr. Stern, and a nurse were also in the party. That night Weizmann was visited at Blair House by Justice Frankfurter, David Niles, Benjamin Cohen, David Ginsburg, Robert Nathan, Oscar Gass, and Eliahu Epstein. On May 25 Weizmann was a luncheon guest at the White House, to which he was escorted by Epstein, who had already been designated as Israel's envoy to Washington. At their last meeting, which was an affectionate reunion, Weizmann presented Truman with a Torah scroll, which is now in the Truman Library at Independence, Missouri.

At that time Weizmann was still a British subject, having carried for more than forty years a British passport that he didn't surrender until September 28, when he mailed it from Switzerland to the British Home Secretary with a covering letter on the eve of his departure for Israel. "I am now . . . on the verge of departing for Israel," he wrote, "and I am sure it will be appreciated that it is appropriate that I should arrive in Israel as a citizen of the country. I am, therefore, taking steps to acquire Israeli citizenship immediately, and assume that as a consequence, I will be automatically relieved of British citizenship, which it has been my privilege and honor to enjoy for the past forty years. In these circumstances, I return herewith the British passport of Mrs. Weizmann and myself, with expressions of the deepest appreciation for all that I was able to do and to become during the time I lived and worked in England. It is still my earnest hope that in my new capacity, I shall be able to work for the reestablishment of the traditional friendly relations between Great Britain and Israel." The letter was never acknowledged. Weizmann landed at Sde Dov airport in Tel Aviv at dawn on September 30, 1948, carrying Israel's diplomatic passport No. 1; No. 2 was held by Mrs. Weizmann.

There was talk later that Weizmann was not invited to sign the Declaration of Independence because he was a British national on May 14, but most authorities regard this as an absurd conjecture since all the other signers were also nationals of Britain or other countries. Weisgal told the

THE MAN WHO WASN'T THERE

authors that he was convinced that the omission of Weizmann from the list of signatories was pure oversight, a tragic error with no deliberate overtones. Someone, in the excitement of the moment, overlooked the man who wasn't there. Weisgal says that Shertok told him this was so, and he repeated it to Julian Meltzer.

Nevertheless, Weizmann and his wife never forgot what they regarded as a deliberate insult and a denigration of his reputation. It continued to prey on their minds during the four years in which Weizmann was "the prisoner of Rehovot," as Mrs. Weizmann described her husband's tenure as President. The government never consulted him and Ben-Gurion used him only as a symbol.

"Chaim had no wish to be embalmed into an empty symbol, a tool of any government or party," Mrs. Weizmann wrote. Weizmann's friends reported to him that Ben-Gurion kept him under constant surveillance, noting the people who visited him at Rehovot. Mrs. Weizmann, in her diary, said that "the conflict between BG and Chaim . . . was not always as great as many people imagined," but their relations remained strained to the day of Weizmann's death, November 9, 1952. Ben-Gurion staged an immense state funeral for Weizmann, but neither Ben-Gurion nor Mrs. Ben-Gurion attended Mrs. Weizmann's funeral in 1966.

Weisgal, who helped edit Weizmann's autobiography, says he persuaded Weizmann to eliminate all but "four insignificant references" to Ben-Gurion because the manuscript "contained reflections on the relations between the two men over the last twenty-five years." The unexpurgated chapter is still in the Weizmann Archives in Rehovot.

Weizmann never publicly mentioned his bitterness at not having been invited to sign the Declaration of Independence, but he often expressed his resentment to his inner circle. Once he remarked, "How could they have forgotten to invite the *chossen* [bridegroom] to the wedding?" He repeatedly pointed out that Dr. Thomas G. Masaryk, the father of Czechoslovakia, had been away from his homeland (he was in the United States, too) when it declared its independence in 1918, yet the first place on the roll of signatures was left blank so that he could sign later.

This was a telling point since twelve of the thirty-seven signers of the Israeli declaration also put their names to the document long after May 14. Only twenty-five of the signers were present when independence was proclaimed in Tel Aviv: eleven were trapped in the siege of Jerusalem and one was in the United States, but space had been left for all twelve to sign in alphabetical order later. On the other hand, it is a fact that the thirty-seven signers were chosen not because of their individual prominence or political eminence, but by virtue of their membership in the National Council. This thirty-seven-man body was comprised of the Palestine members of the Jewish Agency Executive, the Executive of the Va'ad L'umi (the elected Jewish National Council), and additional members drawn from bodies and parties not represented by these two groups. The Revisionists and Communists, for example, who were not represented in the Jewish Agency or Va'ad L'umi Executives, were represented among the signers. Since Weizmann was not on the Agency or Va'ad L'umi Executives, technically he was not eligible for membership in the provisional government council, whose members were designated as signers. Provision was made, however, for a thirty-eighth member, and Weizmann's name was added after his election as Provisional President.

In later years even Ben-Gurion lamented as a tragic oversight the failure to make provision for Weizmann's signature. In 1967 Ben-Gurion, speaking in Los Angeles, rejected the major role attributed to him in bringing about the Jewish state. He gave the credit instead collectively to Weizmann, Herzl, Baron Edmond de Rothschild, Karl Netter, Joshua Stampfer, and Simeon Dubnow.

The faithful Weisgal spent years trying to right the wrong to Weizmann. He raised the matter repeatedly with Ben-Gurion and his successors. They were sympathetic but no one could find a way to amend a historic document: not even the Knesset, Israel's parliament, had the authority to add the signature of a dead man.

Ultimately, Weisgal devised a compromise. During the observance of the fiftieth anniversary of the Balfour Declaration on November 2, 1967, held at the Weizmann Memorial in Rehovot, Zalman Shazar, Israel's President, read "A Declaration by the President of Israel in the Name of the Government and People of Israel." Its keynote was Weizmann's role as "the man who restored the crown of sovereignty to the people of Israel."

Weizmann's name, the Declaration said, "is engraved deep in the chronicles of our nation, for it is that of a leader whose preeminent service to the Zionist cause spanned the years from the very appearance of the seer of Jewish statehood, Dr. Theodor Herzl, through to the realization and fulfillment of the political vision of Zionism. . . . His unique role in the establishment of the State of Israel was gratefully remembered by its people, and on February 17, 1949, the first Knesset, meeting in Jerusalem, elected Chaim, son of Oizer Weizmann, as first President of Israel. Thus is his name linked forever with Israel's independence. By authority of the Government of Israel, this declaration shall be deposited in the Archives of the State [where the Proclamation of Independence without Weizmann's signature also rests], among the documents of primary importance which relate to the history of the Zionist movement and the rebirth of Jewish statehood."

Although the Declaration was read, Weisgal complains in his memoirs that it was never officially published or placed in the official archives.

chapter

∘ ∘ ∘ ∘ ∘ ∘ ∘ ∘ ∘ ∘ ∘ ∘ ∘ ∘ ∘ | 31 | ∘ ∘ ∘ ∘ ∘ ∘ ∘ ∘ ∘ ∘ ∘ ∘ ∘ ∘ ∘

EPILOGUE

MAY 14 WAS the day whose coming had been prayed for by generations of Jews and foretold in centuries-old prophecies. The Biblical portion from the Prophets (Haftorah), which tradition assigned for reading in the synagogue by boys who became Bar Mitzvah on Saturday, May 15 (the sixth of Iyar, in the Hebrew calendar) contained the amazingly prophetic lines from Amos (9:11–15) that end with "And I will plant them upon their land, and they shall no more be pulled up out of their land which I have given them, saith the Lord, thy God."

Because the prophecy was fulfilled on a Friday night, most Jews greeted Jewish statehood with private celebrations or in synagogues filled to capacity for Sabbath-eve services at which prayers of thanksgiving were recited with messianic fervor. The public celebrations began at sundown Saturday, May 15, and continued into May 16 and even later, as non-Jews too hailed the birth of Israel as an event of world importance.

In Rome the community's rabbis, carrying Torah scrolls, led a march toward the ruins of the Colosseum and through the Arch of Titus, which had been erected to commemorate Rome's destruction of the Temple in Jerusalem in 70 C.E. In so doing, the rabbis voided the vow that no Jew would ever walk under this symbol of ancient Israel's conqueror, explaining that the past was now redeemed.

On the outskirts of Rome, in a convalescent home that had been a palatial villa where Herman Goering had been entertained by Benito Mussolini, forty-eight aging survivors of the Nazi Holocaust held a thanksgiving prayer service. And also in Rome the first printed Hebrew visas to Israel were issued to two Americans, Izler Solomon and his wife. Signed by Arie Stern, Jewish Agency representative in Italy, the visas were inserted in the American passport of the celebrated musician who was on his way to Israel as the first guest conductor of the renamed Israel Philharmonic Orchestra.

Not even a steady downpour that drenched the area of the DP camps in Germany and Austria dampened the rejoicing of the 165,000 DPs as they heard the news of Israel's birth. David Trager, one of the leaders of the DP camp organization in Germany, received the word of Israel's independence by short-wave radio on the Voice of Israel in his office on the Sieberstrasse in Munich. Together with Dr. Abrasha Blumovicz and Dr. Samuel Gringauz he had helped organize the illegal immigration from the DP camps to Palestine. By nightfall of May 14 Dr. Chaim Hoffman (Yachil), who in 1946 had come from Palestine as chief of the Jewish Agency workers in the DP camps, in a Flying Fortress provided by General Eisenhower, was named Israel's first Consul in Germany. His first act was to issue an order that all DPs who did not register for military service in Israel would lose their right to emigrate to Israel. The Zionist majority in the camps already regarded themselves as an extension of Israel.

Within hours after President Truman had recognized Israel, Dr. William Haber, Advisor on Jewish Affairs to the US Army of Occupation in Germany and Austria, sat down with Gen. Lucius D. Clay at US military headquarters in the former I.G. Farben Building in Frankfurt to plan for the migration of the DPs. In early April, Dr. Haber had reported that morale among the Jews in the DP camps had plummeted because of the American reversal on partition, but on May 14 he found an incredible change and an intense impatience to get to Israel as swiftly as possible. Haganah recruiting posters in Hebrew, Yiddish, and Polish suddenly appeared in all the camps. At the DP camp in the Mariendorf section of Berlin, refugees who had registered for migration to the US were booed and insulted by the pro-Israeli majority.

The 10,000 Jewish DPs at Bergen-Belsen heard the news of the declaration over their own internal camp radio system at 6 P.M. the hour at which news was broadcast daily by the station's two announcers, Sam Bloch, now an executive of the World Zionist Organization in New York, and Moshe Gershonowitz, now Mayor of Kiryat Motzkin, a small community in Israel. They had heard the news a little earlier on a powerful clandestine receiver, taken from a former German U-boat, that was tuned twenty-four hours a day to Kol Israel. The news was known to the DPs before it was broadcast by the German radio stations and generally known to the German people.

Adjacent to the mass graves of the notorious concentration camp, the excited survivors of the Nazi Holocaust danced with joy, and informally celebrated and prayed throughout the Sabbath. Josef Rosensaft, now a prominent American businessman who was Chairman of the Central Committee of Liberated Jews as well as the leader of the Jewish Committee of Bergen-Belsen, made plans for what was called a "Folk Demonstration" in the Bergen-Belsen Cinema beginning at 9 P.M. on Sunday, May 16. An overflow audience of 2000, who had previously been noisily parading through the DP camp in a procession led by several borrowed Red Cross ambulances, were unrestrained in their joy of the news. A proclamation of congratulation to the new state was issued by Rosensaft and published a few days later in the camp's newspaper.

At the Düppel Center, the largest DP camp in the Berlin sector, news of the establishment of Israel was received at 7 P.M. on May 14, but no formal notice was taken until after sundown on May 15. The festivities began with a special ceremony for children at 10 P.M. On Sunday, May 16, the 5000 homeless Jews paraded with homemade banners and then listened to long emotional speeches. A local German band, conducted by the nephew of the American psychiatrist Dr. A. A. Brill, played "Hatikvah" and a selection of Teutonic marches.

Zionists in Vienna, carrying the blue and white emblem of Israel, made a pilgrimage to the grave of Theodor Herzl in the Döbling Cemetery. Jewish Agency officials in Vienna gasped when a delegation of 200 Austrian war veterans volunteered for service with Haganah.

At the Riedenberg Camp, near Salzburg, US Army Chaplain Oscar M. Lifshutz was involved in one of the most moving celebrations. On Saturday morning, May 15, he was on his way to the former German barracks to conduct Sabbath services for the DPs. There was a joyous bedlam, with the Army MPs who guarded the gates dancing an endless hora with the DPs. Just as the Chaplain was about to open the service, a G-5 officer, Colonel Long, and his staff, climbed out of a jeep and advanced toward the flagpole where the outdoor services were to be held.

"Chaplain," the Colonel said, "this is a great day for you, and we're going to do this the Army way. We're going to have a proper ceremony for an event as important as this. I'm a Protestant, but I feel that I too have given a helping hand in bringing these children of Israel to freedom. I want to be able to tell my children how I once helped a people to find their home."

Colonel Long then motioned to two of the MPs to advance to the base of the flagpole and, at a nod from the Colonel, they lowered the American flag, folded it neatly in regulation fashion, and presented it to Long. Stiffly erect, the Colonel walked over to the camp leader and handed him the flag. "We want you to remember us," he said. "Remember that a lot of my men fought and died to achieve this day. I am proud to have the honor to present you with this flag of my country, which once flew over your camp. It is a symbol of freedom. Keep it as a remembrance of the fighting men of the United States Army and the people they represent."

With tears streaming down his face, the camp leader accepted the flag and then signaled to one of his fellow DPs, who was holding a large bundle. Slowly, he opened it and unfurled the emblem of Israel. Two DPs then replaced the MPs at the base of the flagpole and slowly raised the flag to the halyard. As the wind unfurled it within the shadow of Hitler's Alpine retreat, the soldiers joined the DPs in singing "America" and "Hatikvah."

The official DP celebration of Israel statehood was planned by Dr. Haber and took place, with the cooperation of the US military authorities, in the Prinz Regenten Theater in Munich. At the huge demonstration, attended by representatives from all the DP camps and by high Allied military and diplomatic leaders, Dr. Haber spoke in Yiddish. He apologized to the ambassadors and generals for using a language they didn't understand, but he explained that on such a sacred occasion the DPs would want him to talk in *"mamaloshen"* ("the mother tongue").

In the British internment camps on Cyprus, May 14 was a day of intense excitement among the 28,000 refugees held behind barbed wire. They had been chosen by the Jewish Agency's underground in Europe to brave the hazards and hardships of illegal immigration. Some of them had spent as much as eighteen months in Cyprus in the camps of Caraolos and Dekhelia after having been taken off the illegal ships bound for Palestine. They were the cream of the survivors of the concentration camps, mostly young people who were eager to join Israel's military forces.

On May 15 the Israeli authorities insisted that the British were obligated to return these internees to Palestine since they had been taken to Cyprus forcibly from Palestine's coastal waters or beaches. But the British rejected this argument, and the majority had to stay in the camps another three or four months to await a decision by Count Bernadotte, the UN Mediator, who was conducting truce talks in Rhodes.

EUROPEAN REACTIONS

In Moscow tens of thousands of Jews jammed the streets around the Choral Synagogue in almost messianic frenzy as news of the birth of Israel seeped through on May 14 and 15. A postcard sent by a Russian Jew from Odessa to Israel on May 15 reflects the sentiment of Russian Jews: "Today, with great joy, I heard the tidings about the rise of the State of Israel. With all my heart and soul I send you, the whole Yishuv and the whole Jewish people, my blessings and the greeting, mazel tov, at the commencement of a new epoch in the history of our people. Many thanks to the Soviet Government for the good deeds of kindness for Israel."

Although Russia had supported partition at the UN, and was among the first to recognize Israel, the Soviet press ignored news from Israel after May 14 and prevented Russian Jews from emigrating to Israel. The Soviet satellites, however, permitted Jewish emigration, and in the years from May 15, 1948, to May 15, 1952, a total of 296,813 Jews arrived in Israel from Poland, Rumania, Hungary, Czechoslovakia, and Bulgaria.

In Kiev the Yiddish-language paper of the government-sponsored Jewish Anti-Fascist Committee, "Hinikeit," whose leaders were later liquidated by Stalin, hailed the establishment of "the realm of Israel" and sent congratulatory cables to the city of Tel Aviv and Dr. Weizmann. David Hofstein, a Jew who held high rank in the Communist Party, wired the Vice-Chairman of the Ukrainian Academy of Science to propose the establishment of a chair in Hebrew.

A Jewish prisoner in a Soviet concentration camp in the remote Komi district of northern Russia, where a number of Jews were employed in a factory, wrote, "The evening of the 15th of May was unforgettable. While I was lying on my wooden bunk, I heard the news from Moscow over the loudspeaker. The announcer reported the official statement that the Jewish State had been proclaimed in Tel Aviv. Warm tears of joy streamed from my eyes. All the exiled non-Jews who were there with me became silent with astonishment. Then they rose from their bunks and shook the hands of the Jews and congratulated them. A sweet joy pervaded my whole body. The sadness and bitterness which filled my heart vanished, and I suddenly felt as though reborn. We ran at once to the other Jews in the camp to tell them the news and rejoice with them. . . . In honor of the festive occasion, each of us produced a little food we had hidden and we camp Jews held a feast together. We could not sleep all night. In our hearts and thoughts we were at the front with our brothers and sisters who had begun a bitter war, rifle in hand, against the invading Arabs immediately after the proclamation of the State."

In Warsaw's only synagogue to survive the Nazi occupation, as well as in synagogues in Krakow, Lodz, and Wroclaw (Breslau), Jews of all factions—from ultra-Orthodox to Communist—united in solemn prayers for the future of Israel and in memoriam for the millions of Jews killed in Poland during the Nazi years. Prime Minister Josef Cyrankie-wicz received a delegation from the Jewish Central Committee, headed by Dr. Adolph Berman, a partisan leader, and promised Poland's support to Israel. The Polish national radio devoted a special broadcast to the new state. The Jewish section of the Communist Party called on its branches to explain the significance of Jewish statehood and of the part played by the Soviet bloc in the realization of the "agelong Jewish aspiration."

In Rumania and Bulgaria the Israeli flag decorated hundreds of Jewish homes, and all Jewish-owned shops closed in celebration. The Mayor of Prague cabled congratulations to the Mayor of Tel Aviv. In Bratislava, the capital of Slovakia, blue and white flags bedecked Jewish homes and communal buildings, while the Zionists saluted Israel with a program on the official radio network. In Athens a leader of the Jewish community was summoned by an official of the Greek government and told that the Greek authorities had been asked if Greece would be able to give refuge to thousands of Jews from Palestine when they fled before the Arab invaders.

In Paris one-third of the city's Jewish population staged the world's most massive celebration when they filled the huge Villodrome d'Hiver to its rafters on Saturday night, May 15. Earlier in the day the French National Assembly had sent official greetings to Israel. Among the first emmigrants to embark for Israel after the state was proclaimed were 200 Jews who sailed from Brindisi aboard the Italian liner *Campidoglio* on the night of May 14. In Antwerp, where Jews dominated the diamond market, no one could buy a diamond until May 16 because the Jewish diamond dealers and cutters closed up shop for three days. In Stockholm forty prominent Swedish literary men signed a manifesto pledging solidarity with the Jewish people on the occasion of Israel's independence. In The Hague the General Synod of the Dutch Reformed Church called on its churches to aid Israel.

In Buenos Aires the Jewish stores and businesses were closed and huge throngs of Jews crowded the streets and restaurants on May 14 in enthusiastic celebrations; the next day every synagogue was filled to capacity for thanksgiving services. Mexico City's largest theater was the site of an immense independence celebration on the night of May 15. Uruguay's Parliament, by a vote of 40 to 7, urged the nations of the world to come to the aid of Israel.

THE BRITISH REACTION

There was, quite naturally, a certain amount of ambivalence in England at the news of the birth of Israel. The British Zionists were jubilant and other Jews were, for the most part, pleasurably enthusiastic. The government and the general public, already acceptant of the gradual breakup of the Empire, were glad the matter was finally settled. The public was happy that there would be no more fighting and further English deaths in Palestine, and the government was chagrined and regretful at another colonial failure. The London *Times* of May 15 summed it up by saying that the British "share deeply in the sorrow and regret at this failure of a great mission."

It was the lot of A. V. Alexander, Minister of Defense, to deliver Britain's official obituary in the House of Commons before little more than thirty MPs, none of whom were top officials. Lord Alexander, reporting that another 10,000 square miles, once colored red on the world's maps as was India and Burma, were no longer a part of the British Empire. He said that the British land and sea blockade of Palestine was ended and that no further effort would be made to limit Jewish immigration. Britain's troop withdrawal, he added, would be completed by August 1. The debate, which lasted only an hour, was desultory and did not include any discussion of official British reaction to the new situation created by the establishment of Israel.

A Foreign Office spokesman, indicating that Britain had had no advance notice of Truman's decision to recognize Israel, when asked whether Britain would follow the lead of the United States in granting de facto recognition, quipped, "There's no need to hurry. There is no election in this country until 1950." A week later a government spokesman in Commons declared that "recognition of Israel now would be a positive act of intervening in favor of one side."

England had been well prepared for the fact of independence. Both Palestine correspondents of the Rothmere papers, traditionally anti-Zionist, published dispatches as early as May 11 pointing out that "David Is Beating Goliath." The *Daily Mail* said "The hard fact is that 50,000 Jewish combat troops have used their brains, courage and weapons with great skill and, in fact, the Jews have established a state." The *Evening News* correspondent said, "In Jewish Jerusalem, I saw confidence, dignity, resolution and serenity to which the word 'heroic' does not seem inappropriate. On the Arab side, I saw defeat, withdrawal and a pitiful lack of leadership."

Although the British government had informed the UN on May 12 in utmost secrecy that £50 million sterling of Palestine assets would not be unfrozen until there was assurance that British economic interests— such as the Iraq pipeline and the Haifa oil refineries, among others— would be respected, the Jewish Agency, on the day before the proclamation, opened new financial ties with England by ordering $2 million worth of foodstuffs from Steel Brothers, a non-Jewish London firm that had formerly been food contractor for the British administration in Palestine.

In the face of the immediate Truman recognition of Israel, which stunned both official Britain and the press, Foreign Secretary Bevin urged the dominions not to recognize Israel. London itself, for some time, referred to the new state not as Israel but as the "Jewish National Home."

The Jews made immediate gestures of friendship to Britain. At a London press conference Berl Locker, member of the Jewish Agency Executive, said, "The historic moment which has now arrived is due to historic names in the British Commonwealth, namely, Lord Shaftesbury, Disraeli, and Winston Churchill, and the Holy Land will never forget the good turns that have been done for it by Britain."

A letter to the *Times* signed by many of the country's most eminent Jews—among them Lord Reading, Neville J. Laski, Norman Bentwich, Lord Bearsted, and Anthony and Edmond de Rothschild—voicing the gratitude of British Jewry for Britain's early espousal of the Jewish national home, hoped that when "time has healed the scars of the present lamentable conflict," the Jews of Palestine will again turn to Britain for guidance and counsel. The presidents of both the Board of Jewish Deputies and the Anglo-Jewish Association expressed the official thanks of the Jewish community.

Many Englishmen expected that the Arabs would chase the Israelis into the sea, among them Lord Montgomery, who was recorded as predicting that "the Arabs would knock the Jews for sixes." But in Dublin thirty young Irishmen, many of whom had served in Palestine as police constables, expressed their faith in Israel by offering their services as volunteers.

Although some Jews were uncomfortable about England's "cup of bitter tea," 1600 English youngsters volunteered to serve with Israeli forces, defying Bevin's threat that it would cost them their passports. Older Zionists, who had been confident that there would eventually be a Jewish state, lamented that their pioneer Zionist fathers had not lived to see the happy day.

Many oldtime Zionists were also disturbed that the state hadn't come into being as they had dreamed, with Dr. Weizmann invited to the Colonial Office to take over as Jawaharlal Nehru had been when India became independent.

Prior to the proclamation of independence the office of the Chief Rabbinate of the Empire sent a letter to all synagogues, giving guidance for an Intercession Service for Peace in Eretz Israel that Sabbath. It specified the use of selected Biblical portions, including Psalms 67, 85, and 126 and a reading from Zachariah, to be recited after the traditional prayer for the Royal Family. Psalm 126 was to be sung to the tune of "Hatikvah" and the service was to be concluded with the singing of "Adon Olam," "Hatikvah," and the National Anthem.

The Great Russell Street headquarters of the Jewish Agency and the British Zionist movement heard the news of statehood before sundown on Friday evening from the late edition of the *Evening News* featuring the front-page headline: "STATE OF ISRAEL PROCLAIMED IN PALESTINE TODAY." Worry over rumors of some last-minute difficulty in proclaiming the state had been rampant because of lack of direct communication from Tel Aviv.

A few Zionist officials and newspapermen briefly celebrated the news late Friday afternoon at a favorite hangout, the "White Ladies," a well-known café on Museum Street near the British Museum. But the official celebration was on Sunday, May 16, an overflow mass meeting of the Zionist Federation at the Palace Theatre. Scheduled to have been a guest of honor at the celebration was Blanche Elizabeth Campbell Dugdale (Mrs. Edgar Dugdale), niece of Lord Balfour and herself a longtime staunch friend of Zionism, who died earlier that morning at Maybole, Ayrshire. As though a culmination of the Balfour era, she lived just long enough to learn of the birth of Israel.

In South Africa, one of the most ardently Zionist communities in the world, overflow crowds filled the synagogues in Johannesburg, Capetown, Pretoria, and Durban. On Saturday night, May 15, 5000 people attended a rally in the Johannesburg City Hall Auditorium after marching in a mile-and-a-half torchlight procession from the Great Synagogue. Large numbers of South African Jews were in Haganah, and two South Africans— Abba Eban, Israel's first Ambassador to the UN, and Louis A. Pincus, who is today Chairman of the Jewish Agency for Israel—were among the younger leaders of the new state.

On May 14 South Africa's Prime Minister was Jan Christiaan Smuts, the last survivor of the British War Cabinet of 1917 that had approved the Balfour Declaration. He was so outspoken in support of Israel's claim to statehood that in a speech on May 10 he virtually announced South Africa's forthcoming recognition of the Jewish state. Eight days later South Africa granted official recognition, the first British dominion to do so. Smuts's speech and the swift recognition of Israel are believed to have alienated so many pro-English voters that his United Party went down to defeat in the parliamentary elections on May 22.

In Canada, whose Jewry were proud of the role played by Lester B. Pearson, Minister of External Affairs, in devising the formula for the partition vote at the UN that won the support of both the Soviet and US blocs, and of the profound influence exercised by Justice Ivan C. Rand as the Canadian member of UNSCOP in framing its majority report favoring partition, the birth of Israel by happy chance was linked with the meeting in Winnipeg on May 15 of the Executive Committee of the Zionist Organization of Canada. Thus a number of Zionist leaders learned of the declaration while en route. Justice Harry Batshaw, a Vice-President, heard the news on a portable radio as his plane approached Fort William. Mrs. Harry (Rosa) Singer, President of Canadian Hadassah-WIZO, was among the many delegates on a train bound for Winnipeg who received the news from a Jewish National Fund executive, David Tschertak, who got off at an intermediate station to check on the latest bulletins. When the group reached the Royal Alexandria Hotel, they were greeted by hundreds of youngsters waving Canadian and Zionist flags as they sang "Hatikvah." That night at a private party in the home of Mrs. D. P. (Sally) Gottlieb, a slightly inebriated lady guest did a solo hora atop a piano.

In Montreal the large Jewish community went wild with joy as news circulated throughout the Jewish neighborhoods. Many non-Jews, particularly those of French and Irish extraction, went out of their way to congratulate Jewish friends. As he sat down to breakfast on Saturday morning, Joseph Frank, then President of the Eastern Region of the Zionist Organization, received a visit from an Irish Canadian neighbor dressed in formal attire—striped trousers and frock coat—who said he had seen the Mogen David and the Canadian flags flying from Frank's window. As a man whose father had fought and bled for Irish Independence, he knew what the day meant to Jews, so he had come to bring congratulations and best wishes to Frank and his wife, as well as to all Jewry and Israel.

Frank then left for services at Congregation Shaar Hashomayim, where he and other Zionist leaders were special guests of honor. Although a strictly Orthodox congregation, the services concluded with the singing

of "Hatikvah." Not present was the city's oldest living Zionist, Max
Miller, who was in tears because he was confined as a patient in the Jewish General Hospital; but after the services many Zionist leaders made a
pilgrimage to his bedside.

JOY THROUGHOUT THE US

Because of the time differential, news of the proclamation didn't reach
Australian Jewry until Saturday morning, but a high tea had already been
planned for 8 P.M. at Maccabean Hall in the expectation of the news. So
great was the turnout that the doors had to be closed an hour before their
scheduled opening. In its official statement the Jewish Executive Council
of Australia, expressing its pleasure at the establishment of the Jewish
state, voiced particular gratification that it was Australia's Foreign Minister, Dr. Herbert V. Evatt, who had presided over the historic meeting of
the UN General Assembly that adopted the partition plan for Palestine.

As the city with the world's largest Jewish population, New York reacted to May 14 far more excitedly than Tel Aviv or Haifa. Elevator operators in office buildings and apartment houses wondered why so many of
their passengers greeted each other that evening with loud cries of what
sounded like "Molotov, Molotov." The familiar name of the Russian Foreign Minister had been mistaken for the endless *"Mazel Tovs"* that were
exchanged as one Jew met another.

At the Jewish Agency building Arthur Lourie, the South African who
was director of the Agency's delegation to the US, promptly accepted the
suggestion of I. L. (Si) Kenen, Agency press officer, and invited Chaim
Shertok, teen-age youngest son of Moshe Shertok, to unfurl the Israeli flag
moments after word came from Tel Aviv that independence had been
proclaimed. The grinning youngster, wearing a white sweater emblazoned
with the emblem of Habonim, was accompanied by his mother; his father,
older brother, and sister were all in Israel. Traffic on 66th Street had come
to a complete standstill, blocked by a throng of Zionist youngsters dancing the hora.

The Zionist Organization of America's headquarters on East 42nd
Street was the scene of almost hysterical rejoicing. Dancing, singing, and
drinking were followed by a formal ceremony addressed by the organization's President, Dr. Emanuel Neumann, who called on Americans to observe May 15 as the Sabbath of Liberation. Rabbi Abba Hillel Silver, in
behalf of the American Zionist Emergency Council, declared that the
"Jewish State must translate Jewish precept into action," and urged every
community to mark Israel's birth with local rallies on May 16. The offices

of Hadassah on Broadway were a beehive, with telegrams and cables pouring in and out. Mrs. Rose L. Halprin, Hadassah's President, sent cables of congratulation to Ben-Gurion and Shertok, while chapters throughout the country wired a torrent of pledges of support for Israel.

The American office of Mogen David Adom (Israel's Red Cross) opened a blood bank for Israel on West 39th Street on May 14 and was flooded with volunteers. Hadassah had established blood banks four days earlier at seven New York hospitals, and among the first donors were New York's Mayor, William O'Dwyer, and the novelist Fannie Hurst. All of the Zionist organizations joined forces to set up a temporary air mail service to Israel which opened for business on May 14 at the Jewish Agency office, replacing the regular air mail service, which had been suspended since May 1.

Jorge Garcia Granados of Guatemala and Enricque Rodrigues Fabregat of Uruguay, two UN delegates who had played significant roles in the events leading up to May 14, were among the guests of honor at a happy party attended by young Israeli diplomats in the Arthur Louries' Riverside Drive apartment. The gaiety came to a sudden end when Lourie received a telephone call informing him that Tel Aviv had been bombed.

In virtually every synagogue where the rabbi had scheduled a sermon, he hastily changed the subject to take cognizance of Jewish statehood. A recurrent and particularly appropriate sermonic theme, because the name of the state was Israel, was the Genesis story of Jacob wrestling with the angel. Venerable Jews vied with each other for the privilege of reciting the Kiddush on that historic Sabbath eve.

Without mentioning any names Rabbi Irving Miller revealed to Woodmere's Congregation Sons of Israel the existence of a powerful short-wave radio transmitter aboard a Jewish-owned yacht anchored in Hewlett Harbor. It had been part of the clandestine communications network through which Haganah arms-buyers in the US received instructions from Paris and Tel Aviv.

In Congregation B'nai Jeshurun the veteran Zionist leader Rabbi Israel Goldstein, who later settled in Israel, gave a long review of Zionist history. In Temple Emanu-el, the city's most prestigious Jewish house of worship, many of whose congregation were non-Zionists and not a few anti-Zionist, Rabbi Nathan A. Perilman proposed that the United States send three squadrons of planes to attend the birthday of the State of Israel.

Rabbi Stephen S. Wise, whose name had been synonymous with Zionism for half a century, was absent on the night of May 14 from his Free Synagogue pulpit because of a prior commitment out of the city. His associate, Rabbi Edward E. Klein, led the service of thanksgiving and read from the Israel Declaration of Independence. But on the mind of every worshiper in the Free Synagogue was the oft-repeated story of what Dr. Herzl said to Dr. Wise at the close of the second World Zionist Congress in 1898: "I will not live to see the Jewish State, but you will." Himself the recipient of many messages of congratulation for his fifty years of Zionist leaderhip, Wise sent a letter on May 14 "to the one fellow Zionist in our country" whom he wanted to congratulate. The letter went to Dr. Harry Friedenwald, Baltimore ophthalmologist, who had been President of the Zionist Organization of America from 1904 to 1918, and acting chairman of the Zionist commission that went to Palestine in 1918 after the promulgation of the Balfour Declaration.

Perhaps the feeling of American Jewry was most aptly expressed by the noted religious leader Dr. Mordecai M. Kaplan, who was in Los Angeles on May 14 and made the following notation on page 110 of Volume XIV of his diary at 2:45 P.M. (11:45 P.M. in Israel):

"In fifteen minutes from now the new Jewish State will officially come into being. The physical and mental agonies of its birth are beyond those suffered by any people known to history. May God grant that it be not stillborn." In Hebrew he wrote the following quotation from Ezekiel (16:4–6):

And as for thy nativity, in the day thou wast born, thy navel was not cut, neither wast thou washed in water to cleanse thee, thou wast not salted at all, nor swaddled at all.

No eye pitied thee, to do any of these unto thee, to have compassion upon thee; but thou was cast out in the open field, in the loathsomeness of thy person, in the day that thou was born.

And when I passed by thee, and saw thee wallowing in thine own blood, I said unto thee: When thou wast in thy blood, live; yea, I said unto thee: When thou wast in thy blood, Live.

He then continued in English: "No words of my own could possibly express any better that storm in my heart at this moment. Their full force—it is zero hour at this exact moment—is brought out in Moffat's translation. Even the verse which precedes them has significance for me." In Hebrew he wrote: "Your father the Amorite, and your mother the Hittite." In English he continued: "This new state has been parented by the UN with the US as its father and the Soviet Republic as its mother. It is sent forth by them unto the world as a castaway, but God will say to this state as He said to the one of old [in Hebrew he wrote] 'In thy blood, Live.'"

He then continued in English: "This is 5:30 P.M. Judith and Ira [his daughter and her husband, Rabbi Ira Eisenstein] just phoned telling me

that Truman had issued a statement at 6:01 P.M. [N.Y. time] recognizing the Jewish State. It is simply impossible for me to describe how I feel
at this moment. Again and again [he wrote in Hebrew] 'Blessed be he
who hath kept us alive and sustained us and brought us even to this
time.'"

The New York Stock Exchange on May 14th also joined the celebration by cracking the 1947 highs in the busiest market since May 21,
1940. That night the cast of Habimah, Israel's national theater, in New
York for a six-week engagement, drank a toast before the opening perfor-
mance of *The Golem.* On the Lower East Side a joyful musical *Happy
Wedding,* opened at the Clinton Theater, and the stars, Aaron Lebedeff
and Vera Rosanko, led the audience in toasting the Jewish state.

Mayor O'Dwyer, who as head of the War Refugee Board had helped
in the rescue of Jewish refugees, cabled congratulations to Ben-Gurion as
"premier-designate of Israel." The Mayor's younger brother, Paul
O'Dwyer, was represented in Felony Court on May 14 by an associate,
Mitchell Salem Fischer, in the defense of two young men arrested on
April 27 on charges of attempting to smuggle arms and ammunition to
Haganah. The accused were Joseph Untermeyer, nineteen-year-old son of
the poet Louis Untermeyer, and Isaiah Warshaw, thirty, both members of
a Zionist youth society. Held for violation of the Sullivan Law, the two
men had been paroled in O'Dwyer's custody pending trial. O'Dwyer had
denounced the use of the Sullivan Law "against these defendants . . . as a
shame and a travesty. The Sullivan Law had been enacted to prevent
gangsterism and these two defendants were only doing what every free-
dom-loving person should be doing." The case was adjourned on May 14
by Magistrate Abraham Block, and two weeks later all charges were dismissed.

New York staged not one but three major public celebrations of Israel's birth, including one held before the proclamation, on May 13. The
official celebration was sponsored by the American Zionist Emergency
Council at Madison Square Garden on Eighth Avenue on Sunday, May
16. About 75,000 people were turned away from the Garden when the
Fire Department ordered the doors closed forty minutes before 6 P.M., the
time they were originally scheduled to open. Young and old milled
through the streets adjacent to the Garden on a night of unchecked rain.
Some 6000 braved the downpour to listen to the speeches over loudspeakers set up on 49th Street.

Inside, against the background of a huge banner in blue and white
proclaiming "Long Live the State of Israel," Dr. Emanuel Neumann, the
chairman, set the tone for the evening in his opening remarks: "There are

experiences too rich for expression, emotions too deep for words. None of us can hope to do justice to these events. They are the culmination of two thousand years of exile and anguish for the Jewish people." Speakers at the rally included Senator Robert A. Taft, former Governor Herbert H. Lehman, Mayor O'Dwyer, Henry Morgenthau, Jr., who was National Chairman of the United Jewish Appeal, Dr. Abba Hillel Silver, Mrs. Rose Halprin, Frank Goldman, President of B'nai B'rith, and Brig. Gen. Julius Klein of the Jewish War Veterans.

The biggest ovation went to Dr. Jorge Garcia Granados, the chief of the Guatemalan UN delegation: he was cheered for two minutes before he could speak. Dr. Stephen S. Wise, who was not on the program, received an equally great ovation. He sat next to Dr. Silver, chatting amiably throughout the meeting with the man with whom he had been at odds for some time over Zionist policy. Messages were sent by two distinguished guests who were not present: Dr. Chaim Weizmann, who had just been elected Provisional President of Israel, was ill in bed at the Waldorf Towers; and Mrs. Eleanor Roosevelt, who had a previous engagement.

The May 16 rally had first been announced in paid advertisements in the New York dailies of May 12. It was described as a "salute to the provisional government of the Jewish State." The advertisements in the papers of May 15 called the rally a "salute to the Jewish State."

The left-leaning American Committee of Jewish Writers, Artists and Scientists drew 35,000 people to its rally at the Polo Grounds on Saturday night, May 15. Admission was sixty cents to two dollars. Just as many of the largely left-wing audience booed and hooted as applauded, when the chairman, B. Z. Goldberg, the son-in-law of Sholem Aleichem, said, "We must express our gratitude to President Harry S Truman for giving immediate recognition to Israel." A storm of applause greeted both the mention of Andrei Gromyko's name and the statement that Russia was among the nations that backed the creation of the Jewish state.

After singing a few Palestinian songs in Yiddish, Paul Robeson converted the meeting into an election rally for third party Presidential candidate Henry A. Wallace by singing "Marching on with Wallace" to the tune of "The Battle Hymn of the Republic." Wallace's running mate, Senator Glenn H. Taylor of Idaho, Senator Elbert D. Thomas of Utah, and Congressmen Vito Marcantonio and Leo Isaacson of New York were other speakers. Also on the program were Bartley Crum, Chairman of Americans for Haganah and newly appointed publisher of the newspaper PM; playwright Arthur Miller; and Jacob Riftin, executive member of the Jewish Military Council in Palestine.

The American Zionist Emergency Council disavowed the Polo Grounds rally, pointing out that its sponsoring group had no affiliation with any branch of the Zionist movement in the United States. Rabbis Benjamin Schultz and David S. Savitz of the American Jewish League Against Communism urged that the rally be boycotted as "a Communist-staged affair."

The American League for a Free Palestine, often referred to as "the Ben Hecht Committee," culminated its long and noisy propaganda campaign in behalf of Jewish statehood with a Madison Square Garden meeting on the night before the proclamation of independence. Senator Dennis Chavez of New Mexico was the principal speaker. This rally made no reference to Israel or the Jewish state that was to come into being the next day, but demanded recognition of "the Hebrew state, for all practical purposes already in existence."

Los Angeles' celebration was called "Salute to the Independence of Jewish Palestine" because it was planned before the name of the state was known. Eddie Cantor chaired the rally attended by 25,000 people in the Hollywood Bowl. On May 15 Henry Wallace told a press conference in Los Angeles that the US should cut off all economic aid to Great Britain if London permitted the Arab Legion to move against Israel. By that time the Legion had been in action against Jewish forces for nearly a week.

The Chicago celebration, also planned far in advance, was protected by twenty FBI agents and a Chicago police bomb squad because of telephoned threats that the stadium would be blown up. The biggest cheer at the rally greeted the announcement that forty-nine Chicagoans had endorsed their full week's pay to Israel.

Detroit celebrated Israel's birth on May 16 with a mass rally on the grounds of Central High School, the date having been chosen a week in advance of the actual declaration. Over 20,000 people participated in the meeting, at which Philip Slomovitz, Editor of the *Detroit Jewish News,* presided. It opened with the blowing of the *shofar* by Cantor Hyman Adler.

Thousands of Jews instinctively converged on the Zionist House on Commonwealth Avenue in Boston, a stone's throw from historic Boston Common, for a spontaneous celebration late in the afternoon of May 14. Young and old jammed the building, the mall, and the sidewalk outside to watch as the flag of Israel was unfurled beside the Stars and Stripes. People embraced strangers and wept and sang and shouted *"Mazel Tov."*

On Saturday morning in Boston's Temple Israel, then the pulpit of America's most widely known rabbi, the late Joshua Loth Liebman, the congregation was jolted by a dramatic reference to Israel's birth and fight for survival in the Bar Mitzvah speech of Harold J. Goldfarb. While rehearsing his speech for the last time on Friday night, he had listened to the broadcast of Truman's statement recognizing Israel. Stirred then, he became even more excited on Saturday morning when he heard of the bombing of Tel Aviv. Without a word to the rabbi or to his parents, he inserted a preface in his speech referring to the attack on the Jewish state that was under way even as he spoke. Fourteen years later he was still moved by the recollection of May 14, 1948, and so after his graduation from medical school he went to Israel for graduate study in eye pathology at the Hadassah-Hebrew University Medical Center.

In Atlantic City the boardwalk creaked under dancing feet as hundreds of staid Jewish social workers and educators did the hora on Friday night, May 14. They were gathered for the annual meetings of the National Conference of Jewish Communal Service, the National Association of Jewish Center Workers, and the National Council for Jewish Education, due to convene the following evening. The Center workers cheered a report from Louis Kraft of the National Jewish Welfare Board about plans for Israel's first YMHA. He had just returned from a two-month visit to besieged Jerusalem, where he had gone to lay the groundwork for the YMHA (its new building was dedicated in 1968). The Jewish educators envisioned Israel as giving a great lift to Jewish education in America. And the social workers pledged their full support to Israel. The United Synagogue of America, the lay organization of the Conservative wing of Judaism, voiced similar sentiments at its convention in Chicago on May 14.

Notwithstanding the massive outpouring of enthusiasm on May 14, years later many American Jews confused that historic date with November 29, 1947, when the United Nations partition resolution heralded and paved the way for the Jewish state. The historic UN roll-call vote on partition, heard by millions on radio, had built-in suspense and drama and seems to have made a far greater impact on people's memory than the events of May 14.

In Los Angeles eighteen years later seventy people who were involved in Bar Mitzvahs on May 14, 1948—parents, grandparents, rabbis, and the Bar Mitzvah boys themselves—were interviewed by Julius Bisno. Virtually no one remembered anything special about the day in its relation to the birth of Israel.

Leo B. Ragins, now a public defender for the County of Los Angeles, recalls that he did not change his Bar Mitzvah speech at the Western Jewish Institute, where he shared the Bar Mitzvah spotlight with Jerome Primock. Richard Sanford Cohen, who marked his Bar Mitzvah at Congregation Mogen David, remembers only that he was worried about his speech. Lawrence Jerome Silverstein, who now lives in Chattanooga, Tennessee, recalls May 15 because his father, a World War II veteran, left a hospital to attend his Bar Mitzvah at Congregation Beth Israel, but fainted and had to go back to the hospital. The younger Silverstein's grandmother still resented the fact that the birth of Israel conflicted with her grandson's Bar Mitzvah.

Israel's birth did have a profound impact on the Jewish community's fund-raising effort. The May 14 issue of the *B'nai B'rith Messenger* in Los Angeles headlined that the local United Jewish Appeal had topped the $2 million mark; a week later it reported the campaign had added $1 million, on its way toward $10 million, a sum the community never equaled until the emergency campaign of 1967 following the Six-Day War. On May 14 Leo Gallin, then Executive Director of the Los Angeles Jewish Welfare Fund and Jewish Community Council, convened his entire staff of more than a hundred for a thanksgiving service in the sunken tennis court of the old Pantages estate. Then he spelled out for them what the news from Tel Aviv meant for the fund-raising in Los Angeles.

United Jewish Appeal headquarters in New York was apparently not told that Tel Aviv had advanced the day of independence from May 16 to May 14. On May 14 UJA sent this message to Jewish Welfare Funds throughout the country: "This is the moment we've been waiting for. On May 16th the movement of 25,000 Jews to Palestine [*sic*] from Cyprus will begin." UJA had adopted a record-breaking $25 million quota for 1948, double what it had raised in 1947. Before May 14 the campaign was lagging, but under the inspiration of Israel's birth, $150 million poured into UJA—a sum not topped until 1967 during the Israel Emergency Campaign.

Jewish weeklies that appeared on May 13 and 14 hailed the Jewish state in advance of its actual birth, but many of them referred to it as "New Judea" or "Judea." The Editor of the *Hadassah Newsletter,* Jesse Zel Lurie, reflected the uncertainty as to the exact legal status of the proclamation of independence when he wrote on May 14 to Maurice Boukstein, legal adviser of the Jewish Agency:

"1. Is Israel an actual state under international law which can exchange ambassadors with other countries, or is it simply a national administration which will achieve full independence when the last foreign troops leave its soil?

"2. What is the status of the Jewish Agency and the World Zionist Organization?

"3. Of what value is the present Palestine currency? How much can we expect to get out of the 100,000,000 pounds Great Britain froze in London?"

There was also no unanimity of language used in describing the new state and in explaining who had brought it into being. The eight-column banner headline on the *New York Times* of May 15 read: "ZIONISTS PROCLAIM NEW STATE OF ISRAEL." The Yiddish-language daily, *The Day,* had a unique headline: "JEWISH KINGDOM PROCLAIMS ITS INDEPENDENCE." Unlike the *Times,* which probably avoided the words "Jewish State" on ideological grounds, *The Day*'s language was merely pragmatic. When the UN partition plan was being debated in November, 1947, Moshe Starkman, *The Day*'s City Editor, planned in advance for the final vote and assigned Wolf Yaunin, a rewrite man who was also an artist, to design a banner headline big enough for the occasion. No similar preparations were made in May, 1948, so Starkman used the same headline that had appeared the previous November. The Hebrew word for kingdom is *"Medinah"* and when used in Yiddish the same word also means state. Not a single reader complained.

THE ARAB REACTION

Almost the whole world—non-Jews as well as Jews—hailed the birth of the new Jewish state as an act of atonement for the death of 6 million Jews in the Holocaust. In the Arab countries, however, the proclamation brought immediate violent repercussions, both military and vocal, setting the stage for the War of Liberation and the twenty-five years of subsequent conflict and state of continuing belligerency that has existed between Israel and the Arab states.

The General Secretary of the Arab League, Abdul Rahman Azzam Pasha, lost no time in announcing that a state of war existed between the Arab countries and Palestinian Jewry. The man who a few weeks earlier in Cairo had told *Herald Tribune* correspondent Kenneth Bilby that "there is no chance for the Jews in the long run. . . . Haganah will eventually dissolve like ice," defiantly predicted that US recognition of Israel would not deflect the Arabs from their determination to save "the Arab land of Palestine." He further said that "this will be a war of extermination and a momentous massacre which will be spoken of like the Mongolian massacres and the Crusades."

In Amman, Emir Abdullah visited his troops on the evening of May 14, prior to the formal invasion of Jewish Palestine. Military and political censorship was imposed and ten foreign correspondents—including Americans, British, and Egyptian—were accredited to the Transjordan forces and received uniforms and *kafiyeh* headdresses prior to the trip from Amman to Jericho at dawn.

Taking over after the Arab League Political Committee had withdrawn recognition of the Arab Higher Committee of Palestine, which was dominated by the Mufti of Jerusalem, Emir Abdullah was the titular commander of the Arab invasion. He enunciated a three-point policy: refusal to recognize partition, nonacceptance of the trusteeship idea, and the right of the Palestinians to determine their own form of government.

As Abdullah's troops proceeded in a leisurely motorcade across the salt wastes near the Dead Sea toward Jericho, which the Arab Legion had been guarding for several weeks, they were cheered by Arab civilians. In colorful bright yellow, red and white, and grass-green headdress rather than steel helmets, they paused at the Allenby Bridge at a quick-lunch stand that sold them hardboiled eggs and bread. After the long convoys of truck-borne artillery and light armored vehicles crossed the muddy Jordan, the Arabs took military control of a large area of the Judean Hills, twenty miles northeast of Jerusalem. The Arab Legion also smashed at Ein Gev, on the eastern shore of Lake Tiberias, and Ashdot Yaacov, Shaar Hagolan, and Gesger, all in the area assigned to Israel under the UN partition proposal.

In Cairo, Premier Fahmy Nokrashy Pasha proclaimed martial law beginning at midnight when the Mandate ended. Assuming the role of military governor, he announced that "Egyptian armed forces will begin moving across the Palestine frontier at one minute past midnight." By the evening of May 15 the Egyptian troops reached the Gaza Strip, occupying the hills of Ali Mintar.

Censorship was immediately invoked on mail, newspapers, photographs, and parcels entering or leaving Egypt, as well as on broadcasts, phonograph records, and plays. Captains of merchant vessels were warned that their vessels would be liable to search in Egyptian ports. A regime of terror began against Egypt's Jews, and hundreds were thrown into concentration camps as Jewish offices, shops, and dwellings were looted by police and roving gangs.

As four hundred Communists and Zionists were rounded up in Cairo, Alexandria, and Port Said by the Ministry of Interior prior to being placed in detention camps, one of which was set up in Abbassia, a Cairo suburb, Sheikh Mamoun al Shinawi, rector of the thousand-year-old Al Azhar University, said in an official radio broadcast that "The hour for jihad has struck." He stated prophetically that "Unless you fight your enemy and are ready to die for Allah and your countries, humiliation will be your lot."

As bombs exploded in the Jewish quarter and some Jews were denounced to the police as "spies," two Jewish members of the Egyptian Parliament, seeking to emphasize their loyalty, telegraphed Chief Rabbi Nahoum Effendi declaring that "our Fatherland is Egypt." The message, signed by Senator Aslan Bey Cattaoui and Deputy Rene Bey, said, "Following the proclamation of the Jewish State by the Jewish Agency and its claim that this was done with the support of world Jewry, we challenge the possibility that Jewry is at the same time a religion and a nation. Please note that our nationality is Egyptian, our religion Judaism and our Fatherland Egypt."

Former Chief Rabbi Ventura, a French subject who had resigned three months earlier, received a call from the Egyptian police, acting on instructions of the Ministry of Interior, asking him to leave the country within twenty-four hours. No reason for the expulsion was given, but it was recalled that the Rabbi, who defied the expulsion order, had expressed strong pro-Zionist views in the years between his assumption of the Chief Rabbinate of Alexandria and his resignation.

Daniel Schorr, a radio reporter and commentator then with the ABC network, recalls a stopover in Cairo in the early evening of May 15 on a KLM flight from Amsterdam to Indonesia. When the plane landed at Farouk Airport, he learned that the Arabs had invaded Israel.

The passengers, who were to stop overnight at an airport hotel, were warned by the KLM passenger agent, if they were Jews, not to admit it when questioned by the Egyptian immigration officers, unless they wanted to spend the night in jail. Schorr, a Jew, refused to state his religion and got away with it.

When he sought to cable ABC with details of the Egyptian mobilization, which he read in the local French newspaper, Schorr couldn't get his story transmitted because, although censorship had been invoked, no censor had as yet been appointed. Schorr gave his story the next morning to a pilot bound for Amsterdam for delivery to a news agency bureau chief, who then relayed it to New York, where ABC broadcast it as the first word from Cairo following the outbreak of the war.

In Beirut the Lebanese government adopted a protective policy for its Jews, as it joined its Moslem allies in prosecuting the war. The Jewish quarters were heavily patroled by the police to prevent "irresponsible" attack and Jews were permitted to continue business activities. But they were not allowed to leave the country and were compelled to contribute large sums to aid Arab refugees from Palestine. The Lebanese troops immediately crossed the border and captured Malikay, a town about a mile inside the Israeli border on the northern frontier.

In Baghdad, Jews were immediately treated as enemies within the gates—as spies, agents, and provocateurs—and were forbidden to leave the country. The government announced that its army immediately entered Palestine. Stunned by US recognition of Israel, Iraq regarded it as a hostile act. Ali Jawdat Ayubi, Iraqi Ambassador to the US, home on a visit, pooh-poohed the recognition as of no great importance. He confidently predicted that the Arab governments would continue their anti-Zionist policies until the "liberation of Palestine" was achieved.

In Damascus the government immediately launched a boycott and other discriminatory practices against its Jewish population that was quickly to bring economic ruin to the French-oriented community. The Syrian Army began an invasion of Israeli territory, crossing the Jordan into the area south of Lake Tiberias.

As Syria went on a war footing its Parliament proclaimed martial law for a period not to exceed six months. Premier Jamil Mardam was named Military Governor and £10 million ($4.2 million) was appropriated for expenses for "operations outside of Syria." The Defense Ministry was also empowered to use proceeds from persons buying their way out of compulsory military services, estimated at £6 million (Syrian) to recruit an additional 5000 men.

Despite a government promise to protect the lives and property of Syrian Jews, demonstrations were staged against Zionists and one Jew was killed on May 15 by a student mob. There were also attacks against the United States and its legation.

It was thus that the battlelines were immediately and, as it seems almost twenty-five years later, irrevocably and tragically drawn. Though conceived in the diplomatic compromise of an agency of peace as the first-born of the United Nations, Israel was to have to fight for its life from the very day it came into being. The new state not only had the normal birth pangs of political organization and economic maturation; it also accepted about 1.5 million impoverished immigrants in fulfillment of its unprecedented pledge to give refuge to the remnants of world Jewry that had survived and were suffering in the aftermath of the Nazi Holocaust.

The Sinai engagement of 1956 and the Six-Day War of 1967 were the active flareups during the almost quarter-century of a technical state of war between the Arab states and Israel that exists to this day. Even the occasional moments of peace enjoyed by Israel's more than three million people have been and are still clouded with the ever present specter of war. A western democracy has been born in the land of the Prophets, but the backlash of a feudal past still seeks to block recognition of the forces of progress that Israel has brought to the Middle East.

APPENDIX I: THE SIGNERS
OF THE PROCLAMATION *

THE THIRTY-SEVEN SIGNERS of the Scroll of Independence represent a cross-section of Israel's population and include three of its four Prime Ministers—Ben-Gurion, Sharett, and Meir—as well as several individuals so forgotten that biographical material on them is not readily available. Of Israel's three Presidents, one—Itzhak Ben Zvi—signed the Proclamation.

Sixteen of the thirty-seven signers have been members of the Cabinet at one time or another, and three are presently Cabinet members—Meir, Warhaftig, and Kol. Twenty-five have been members of the Knesset, including one Speaker—Nahum Nir-Rafalkes—and three are presently members.

Only one signer was a native Palestinian, Behar Shitrit, a Sephardic Jew born in Tiberias whose ancestors left Morocco in the eighteenth century. Another, Saadia Kovashi, was born in Yemen. The others were born in Europe, mainly in what is now Russia, Poland, Rumania, Czechoslovakia, and Austria. Two of the signers were Americans, though not born in the United States—Golda Meir and Rabbi Wolf Gold. And two were women—Mrs. Meir and Rachel Cohen (now Kagan).

Of the signers the oldest was eighty-two-year-old Eliahu Berligne, who was born in 1866, and the youngest thirty-year-old Meir Wilner. Two of the signers settled in Israel as far back as 1906—Ben-Gurion and Sharett; Warhaftig had settled in Israel less than a year before independence.

Fewer than half of the signers, fourteen, are still alive in 1972. Of the twenty-three who have died, the first was David Remez, who died in 1951, only three years after statehood. The most recent deaths were those

* Listed in the order in which their signatures appear on the Scroll of Independence.

of Nir-Rafalkes and Lurie in 1968, Gruenbaum and Shapira in 1970, and
Bernstein and Levin in 1971.

1. DAVID BEN-GURION

David Ben-Gurion, who was responsible for the wording of the final
version of Israel's Proclamation of Independence, was appropriately the
first man to sign it after presenting it officially at the Proclamation Ceremony at the Tel Aviv Museum. Born David Green in Plonsk, Poland, on
October 16, 1886, he settled in Palestine in September, 1906.

Acknowledged to be the chief exponent of immediate statehood,
David Ben-Gurion, born to a Zionist family, was a youthful co-founder of
the Poale Zion Party in Poland in 1903. On his arrival in Palestine a few
years later he worked as a laborer in Petach Tikvah and Rishon le Zion,
during which period he was elected chairman of the Poale Zion Party at
its first convention in Palestine.

In 1910, in accordance with a party decision, he moved to Jerusalem
as a member of the editorial staff of the party's newspaper, Ha'Achdut. To
acquire a knowledge of the language and law of Turkey, the country of
which Palestine was then a part, Ben-Gurion went to Salonika and then
the Ottoman University in Constantinople. It was as a delegate from Constantinople in 1913 that he attended the eleventh World Zionist Congress
in Vienna, his first.

Following his exile from Palestine in 1915 by the Turkish authorities,
he went with his friend Itzhak Ben Zvi to the United States, where he
lived until 1918. In 1916 he married his late wife, Paula Munweis, a nurse.
While in New York he was a founder of the Jewish Legion, in which he
served as a part of the British armed forces. A disciple of the Zionist-
socialist editor Berl Katznelson, he was a founder of Histadrut shortly
after his return to Palestine and he emerged as a power in the Labor
Zionist forces when he became General Secretary in 1921, a post he
held until 1933.

Ben-Gurion was elected to the Jewish Agency Executive in 1933, became its Chairman in 1935, and from this post in 1948 became Chairman
of the National Administration, which in turn became the provisional
government, of which he became Prime Minister and Defense Minister.
Following Israel's first elections, in 1949, he was elected Prime Minister
and Defense Minister, posts he held until he retired to Sde Boker in
1953; he returned to these posts in 1955, and was head of government
until he retired again in 1963, serving as Israel's Prime Minister for thirteen years in all. Although in retirement, he has continued to be an im-

portant voice in Israel. He maintained his seat in the Knesset until May 18, 1970, twenty-two years and four days after having proclaimed the State of Israel. In 1971 his eighty-fifth birthday was celebrated in a ten-week series of events during which he was eulogized by Prime Minister Golda Meir. He refused her invitation, however, to rejoin the Labor Party (Mapai), from which he had earlier resigned in a party split that created the Rafi group, since dissolved.

2. DANIEL AUSTER

Daniel Auster was born in Galicia in 1893 and died in Jerusalem in 1963. First settling in 1914 in Palestine, where he became a teacher, Auster had been active in student Zionist circles in his hometown and later at the University of Vienna, where he completed his law studies. In 1948 he was asked by the Mandatory Governor to take over leadership of the Jewish part of Jerusalem. Following statehood, he became the first Mayor of Jerusalem, a post he held until 1951. A General Zionist, he was a member of the Va'ad L'umi. Auster was in Jerusalem on May 14 and signed the Proclamation when he traveled to Tel Aviv by a small plane in the latter part of June, following the break in the siege of Jerusalem. He felt honored that a space had been reserved for his signature right under that of Ben-Gurion, but he never knew whether this was because he was Mayor of Jerusalem or because his name began with the letter "A."

3. MORDECAI BENTOV

Mordecai Bentov, the first actual signer after Ben-Gurion, was born in Warsaw on March 28, 1900. He settled in Palestine in 1920, after having been a student at the University of Technology in Warsaw. Bentov was in New York as an advisor to the Jewish Agency representatives at the United Nations when the partition resolution was adopted in November, 1947. A member of the National Administration, he served in the Cabinet of the provisional government as Minister of Labor and Reconstruction. He later served in two Cabinet posts: Minister of Development and Minister of Housing, and he was a Mapam member of the first five Knessets (1949–65). For many years he was editor of the daily newspaper *Al Hamishmar*. He now resides in Kibbutz Mishmar Haemek.

4. ITZHAK BEN ZVI

Itzhak Ben Zvi was the second President of Israel. Elected to succeed Dr. Chaim Weizmann in December, 1952, he was twice reelected and served until his death in 1961. He settled in Palestine in 1907 after having visited the country in 1904. The son of Zvi Shimshelevitz, an ardent member of the early Zionist group Hovev Zion who visited Palestine as early as 1891, Ben Zvi was born in Poltava, Ukraine, in 1884. A well-known journalist and early intimate associate of Ben-Gurion, Ben Zvi founded the first Hebrew-language Socialist journal in Palestine in 1910.

To prepare themselves for eventual Jewish statehood, Ben Zvi and Ben-Gurion studied law at the Ottoman University of Constantinople, from which they returned at the outbreak of World War I. After their imprisonment in 1915 by Jamal Pasha, they went to New York by way of Egypt, and devoted themselves to recruiting for the Jewish Legion, which reached Palestine for the fighting in 1918. A leader of the Labor movement in Palestine, he was elected Chairman and later President of the Va'ad L'umi, in which capacity he helped pave the way for the transition of the Yishuv to the State of Israel. Ben Zvi was in besieged Jerusalem on May 14 and later signed the Proclamation in Tel Aviv.

5. ELIAHU BERLIGNE

Eliahu Berligne, born in Mogilev, Russia, in 1866, was at eighty-two the oldest signer. He died eleven years later in Jerusalem at the age of ninety-three, having lived in Palestine for fifty-two years since settling there in 1907. A pioneer Zionist who was associated with Theodor Herzl at the first World Zionist Congress, he organized the committee to build Achuzat, a suburb of Jaffa, where he resided and which was the beginning of the development of Tel Aviv. A member of Va'ad L'umi and at one time its Treasurer, he participated in the proclamation ceremonies.

6. PERETZ BERNSTEIN

Peretz Bernstein was born in 1890 in Meiningen, Germany, and died in Jerusalem on March 21, 1971, at the age of eighty-one. He settled in Palestine in 1936 after having lived in The Netherlands since 1908. Following the proclamation, he served as Minister of Commerce and Industry in the Cabinet of the provisional government, a post to which he returned in the coalition government during the years 1952–55. At the time of his death he was President of the Liberal Party, which he represented in the first five Knessets. He stood out as a champion of free enterprise in a socialistically oriented regime, and although greatly respected, was often at odds with his Cabinet and Knesset colleagues. From 1937 to 1946 he was editor of *Haboker,* after which he became President of the General Zionists and was elected to the Jewish Agency Executive as head of its Economic Department. He was in Tel Aviv for the signing of the Proclamation.

7. RABBI WOLF GOLD

Rabbi Wolf Gold was born in Szczecin (Stettin), Poland, in 1889 and died in Jerusalem in 1956. He settled in Palestine in 1924 after having lived in the United States since 1907, when he arrived as a youthful rabbi. He again lived in the United States from 1931 to 1934 as President of American Mizrachi and during World War II. In 1946 he became a member of the Jewish Agency Executive and was a member of the Jewish delegation to the United Nations. In the last year of his life he served as President of the World Mizrachi Organization. In 1938 he established an agricultural yeshiva at K'far HaRo'e.

8. MEIR GRABOVSKY

Meir Grabovsky (Argov) was born in Zabrnica, Russia, January, 1905, and died November 29, 1963. Settling in Palestine in 1926 as an agricultural worker, Grabovsky was active in labor circles, and as a member of the Executive of the Va'ad L'umi he served on the National Council. He was a member of the first five Knessets, until his death, serving from the second Knesset on as Chairman of the important Foreign and Security Affairs Committee.

9. ITZHAK GRUENBAUM

Itzhak Gruenbaum was born in Warsaw on November 24, 1879, and died in his ninetieth year on September 7, 1970. An active Zionist since his high-school days in Plonsk in 1898, he settled in Palestine in 1932 after a long career as a journalist and lawyer in Russia and Poland. In 1908 he became Secretary General of the Central Organization of Russian Zionists in Vilna; following Polish independence at the end of World War I, he presided over the club of Jewish members of the Polish Parliament and became an important political figure in Poland as one of the top leaders of the Jewish community.

Immediately after his settlement in Palestine, he was elected to the

Jewish Agency Executive. In Jerusalem on May 14, Gruenbaum could not participate in the proclamation ceremonies, but signed when he reached Tel Aviv after the end of the siege of Jerusalem and assumed his duties as Minister of Interior in the Cabinet of the provisional government. In this capacity in 1949 he organized Israel's first general election to the Knesset, but he personally failed to be elected.

10. ABRAHAM GRANOVSKY

Abraham Granovsky (Granott), who was in Jerusalem at the time of the signing, was born in Bessarabia on June 19, 1890, and died in Jerusalem, July 21, 1962. After settling in Palestine in 1907, he became one of the country's leading economists, holding the post of Professor of Agrarian Economy at the Hebrew University. A member of the National Council, he served on its Finance Committee and assisted in the preparation of Israel's first state budget and the creation of its fiscal system. He was a General Zionist member of the first two Knessets, and first Chairman of its Finance Committee. Granott was first Managing Director and then for many years President of the Jewish National Fund. The author of many books on agriculture and economics, he was also a member of the Board of Governors of both the Hebrew University and the Weizmann Institute and Chairman of the Board of Directors of the Jerusalem Economic Corporation.

11. ELIAHU DOBKIN

Eliahu Dobkin was born in Bobruysk, Russia, in 1898. A graduate of the University of Kharkov, he settled in Palestine in 1932 after years of leadership in the Zionist movement in Poland. He was a member of the Jewish Agency Executive from 1935 to 1968, serving at various times as head of its Immigration, Information, and Youth Departments. He was in Jerusalem on May 14 and signed the Proclamation in Tel Aviv a month later, following the truce that was the first break in the siege of Jerusalem. An expert in *aliyah,* he was active in the leadership of the rescue of Holocaust survivors and the illegal immigration to Palestine. He wrote a book on the subject in 1946: *Aliyah and Rescue During the Holocaust.*

12. MEIR WILNER

Meir Wilner (Kovner), who was born in Poland in 1918 and settled in Palestine in 1938, was the only Communist signer of the Proclamation and also the youngest. The Secretary of the Politbureau of the Communist Party of Israel, he has been a member of all seven Knessets. He signed the Proclamation in Tel Aviv in his capacity as a substitute for Samuel Mikunis, then General Secretary of the Party, who was the official representative on the National Council.

13. ZERAH WARHAFTIG

Zerah Warhaftig was born in Warsaw on February 2, 1906. In Jerusalem at the time of the Proclamation, he was a recent immigrant, having arrived in the middle of 1947 after living for four years in New York, where he was Deputy Director of the Institute for Jewish Affairs of the World Jewish Congress. A member of all seven Knessets, he has been Israel's Minister of Religious Affairs since 1961, after having previously served eight years as Deputy Minister. A law graduate of the University of Warsaw, with a Doctorate in Law from the Hebrew University, he is a member of the Law Faculty of the Hebrew University. Of the signers of the Proclamation, he was the last to settle in Palestine.

14. HERZL VARDI

Herzl Vardi signed the Proclamation with the Hebrew pseudonym he used as a member of the editorial board (1936–50) of the daily newspaper *Haboker*. Better known by his real name, Dr. Herzl Rosenblum, he has been editor of another Hebrew daily, *Yediot Aharonot*, since 1950. Vardi, who settled in Palestine in 1935, represented the small Jewish State Party section of the United Revisionists when he signed the Proclamation.

15. RACHEL COHEN

Rachel Cohen (now Kagan) was born in Russia in 1888. Settling in Palestine in 1919, she was Director of the Social Welfare Department of the Va'ad L'umi and Chairman of the Women's International Zionist Organization (WIZO) at the time of statehood. She is now Honorary President of WIZO. A member of the first and fifth Knessets, she is an ardent feminist and one of the two women signers of the Proclamation, a representation she felt was not adequate.

16. RABBI KALMAN KAHANA

Rabbi Kalman Kahana was born in Brody, Poland, in 1910. After attending the Rabbinical Seminary in Berlin and receiving his doctorate from the University of Berlin, he settled in Palestine in 1938, the year in which he co-founded Kibbutz Chafetz Chaim. The Sabbath that followed the signing of the Proclamation was the first in his twenty years in Palestine that he spent in Tel Aviv. He has been a member of all seven Knessets, representing the orthodox Poale Agudat. He has also served several terms as Deputy Minister of Education and Culture.

17. SAADIA KOVASHI

Saadia Kovashi was born in 1902 in Shahil, Yemen, where his family had lived for over six hundred years. Settling in Palestine as a child in 1909, he was later ordained as a rabbi and became a teacher and director of religious schools. At the time of independence he was the Principal of the Torah Or Talmud Torah and Assistant Director of the Department of Communities of the Union of Yemenite Jews, which he represented on the Executive of the Va'ad L'umi. He was in Jerusalem on May 14, but illness kept him from the office of the Jewish Agency that day. Until his retirement in August, 1967, he was a supervisor and principal of religious schools in Jerusalem and Tel Aviv. In 1972 he was living in Brooklyn, where he has been serving for the past few years as the rabbi of a small congregation.

18. RABBI YITZHAK MEIR LEVIN

Rabbi Yitzhak Meir Levin, born in 1893 in Gur, Poland, settled in Palestine in 1940. He died in Jerusalem on August 8, 1971, and was buried on the Mount of Olives after an almost unprecedented three-mile-long funeral procession, on foot, along the entire route from his home. Rabbi Levin was related to the Gur Hassidic dynasty. His father-in-law, the Rabbi of Gur, founded the Agudat Israel Movement to serve as an anti-Zionist counterbalance to the increasing influence of the mainly secular Zionists. He was a strong political leader of Polish Jewry when he fled the German takeover in Poland and went to Palestine in 1940. He led the Movement in Palestine in non-Zionist rather than anti-Zionist directions and was a strong influence in leading his Party to the acceptance of the State of Israel when it was established. As one of the founders and longtime president of the World Agudat Israel, he served as a member of the National Administration as Minister of Social Welfare in the provisional government. With statehood, he became the Minister of Social Welfare in the Cabinet until 1952, when his Party left the government coalition. A member of the first Knesset, he maintained his membership until his death. He was in the United States on May 14, the only signer who was actually outside of the country at the time of the Declaration. He was actually the last of the thirty-seven signatories.

19. MEIR DAVID LEVINSTEIN

Meir David Levinstein, nineteenth signature on the Proclamation, was born in Denmark in 1905 and settled in Palestine in 1934. In charge of the Agudat Israel office in Tel Aviv, he was a member of the National Council representing the Religious Bloc. After signing the Proclamation, he availed himself of Ben-Gurion's offer to make a statement on his reservations on the secular nature of the Proclamation at the first meeting of the National Council on Sunday, May 16. He was a member of the first Knesset, and then withdrew from party politics.

20. ZVI LURIE

Zvi Lurie, born in Lodz, Poland, on June 1, 1906, died in Tel Aviv on May 21, 1968. He settled on a kibbutz in Palestine in 1925 after having been an early member in Poland of the Hashomer Hatzair movement, which later became the Mapai Party of which he was a top leader. Elected to the Jewish Agency for Israel Executive in 1949, and serving as head of its Aliyah and Youth Departments until 1955, he became one of the world's best-known Zionist leaders as the head of the Jewish Agency-World Zionist Organization's Organization Department, 1956–68. For a number of years he made his headquarters in New York. At the time of the Proclamation he was in Tel Aviv, setting up the facilities for the broadcast of the ceremonies. He was a dedicated exponent of better Arab-Jewish relationships.

21. GOLDA MYERSON (MEIR)

Golda Myerson (Meir), born Golda Mabovitch in Kiev in 1898, was brought to the United States by her parents at the age of eight. A Milwaukee schoolteacher who was graduated from the Teachers' Training

College of Milwaukee in 1917, she married Morris Myerson that year and settled in Palestine four years later. As Golda Meir (the Hebraization of her name), she was appointed successor to Levi Eshkol as Israel's fourth Prime Minister in March, 1969. She was subsequently elected to this post the following October.

An active worker in the Poale Zion movement in the United States, she immediately entered Labor Zionist politics in Palestine, where she and her husband settled in Kibbutz Merhavia in the Jezreel Valley, where she specialized in poultry raising. Within a year she was the kibbutz delegate to the Council of Histadrut. Her husband couldn't stand kibbutz life, and after two years the family moved first to Tel Aviv, and then in 1924 to Jerusalem, where her two children were born.

Four years later she became Secretary of Moetzet HaPoalot, the Women's Labor Council, and later was one of the founders of Mapai, the Israel Labor Party. By 1936 she was put in charge of Kupat Holim, the Histadrut's welfare program. In 1946 she gave evidence in behalf of the Histadrut at the hearings of the Anglo-American Committee of Inquiry.

When Moshe Shertok, together with other leaders of the community and the Zionist Movement, was detained by the British in June, 1946, she took his place as acting head of the Jewish Agency's Political Department in Jerusalem, and remained in charge when he went back to Lake Success to plead the Jewish cause at the United Nations.

In November, 1947, she negotiated with Emir Abdullah of Transjordan who promised not to join in an attack on the Jews. In January, 1948, when the Jews were urgently in need of arms for defense, she left for the United States to collect funds for the purpose and made an extraordinary impression on the leaders of American Jewry, raising an unprecedented $50 million in two and a half months. When she went back to Palestine as the time of the British withdrawal was approaching, the Jews knew that they would face an invasion by the neighboring Arab States when they proclaimed their independence in accordance with the UN resolution. Dressed as an Arab woman, with only one companion, Mrs. Myerson went to Amman to meet Emir Abdullah and try to persuade him to keep his promise.

This dangerous mission did not succeed and she came back to Tel Aviv in time to play her part in the fateful decision to declare a Jewish state on the eve of the British withdrawal. Again she had to go to the United States, this time as a delegate for the infant State of Israel. While there she was told that the government had decided to appoint her Israel's first Ambassador to the Soviet Union.

A member of the Knesset since its inception, she was appointed Minister of Labor in April, 1949. Since she was in great demand as a speaker to Jews overseas, she had to make frequent and tiring journeys, especially to America. In 1951, while she was campaigning, her husband died.

In June 1956, when Moshe (Shertok) Sharett resigned as Prime Minister, she was appointed Foreign Minister and loyally supported Prime Minister Ben-Gurion during the difficult years that followed, playing a vital role in the diplomatic struggle that followed the Sinai Campaign.

During the bitter controversy between David Ben-Gurion and Levi Eshkol, she felt that she could not support Ben-Gurion's attitude despite their lifelong friendship. When Eshkol became Prime Minister in 1963, she retained her post and stood by him until his death in February, 1969.

After the 1965 elections she decided to rest from the cares of office and resigned her post at the Foreign Ministry. Reluctantly she responded to the call of her colleagues and took up the position of Secretary-General of Mapai. On the death of Eshkol the great majority of the Party's leaders pressed her to accept nomination for the post of Prime Minister.

22. NAHUM NIR-RAFALKES

Nahum Nir-Rafalkes was born in Warsaw on March 17, 1884, and died in Israel on July 10, 1968. An attorney who received his Doctorate in Law from the University of Taru-Dorpat, he settled in Palestine in 1925. A member of the first four Knessets, he was the second Speaker of the Knesset from 1955 to 1959, after having previously served as Deputy Speaker. A member of the Va'ad L'umi Executive, he was Deputy Chairman of the National Administration, which after statehood became the provisional government.

23. ZVI SEGAL

Zvi Segal (Hermann) was born in Plock, Poland, November 13, 1901, and died in Tel Aviv, September 23, 1965. After having organized the illegal immigration from Danzig, he settled in 1938 in Palestine, where from 1940 to 1948 he was president of the Revisionist movement. After serving on the National Council until it was superceded by Israel's first elected government, he retired from political life to found and become Managing Director of Barnea Ltd., the sponsor of Barnea, the tourist and film town.

24. RABBI YEHUDA LEIB HACOHEN FISHMAN

Rabbi Yehuda Leib HaCohen Fishman (Maiman) was born in Marcu-
lesti, Rumania, in 1875, and died in Tel Aviv, July 10, 1962. Already a
rabbi when he settled in Israel in 1913, Rabbi Maiman was one of Israel's
greatest Talmudic scholars and the owner of the largest private collection
of scholarly books in the country. He was a co-founder of Mizrachi in
1904 and one of the leaders of the Religious Bloc during his long lifetime.

A member of the National Administration, he became Minister of Religious Affairs in the provisional government, and continued in that post
until 1951. He was a member of the first Knesset. On his eightieth birthday he was named an Honorary Citizen of Tel Aviv. Rabbi Maiman was
founder of the Rabbi Kook Institute and the author of many scholarly volumes. Condemned to death by Turkish authorities during World War II,
he was saved only through the intercession of American Jewish leaders.

25. DAVID ZVI PINKUS

David Zvi Pinkus was born in Sopron, Hungary, December, 1895,
and died August 14, 1952. Settling in Palestine in 1925, he became active
in Mizrachi, was a member of its Executive, and Chairman of the Board
of the Mizrachi Bank of Tel Aviv. A member of the Tel Aviv City Council, beginning in 1932, and the Va'ad L'umi, he was a member of the National Council. Elected to the first two Knessets, he served as Deputy
Speaker, and was a member of the Knesset at the time of his death.

26. AHARON ZISLING

Aharon Zisling was born in Baravovichi, Russia, in 1901 and died in
Kibbutz Ein Harod, January 16, 1964. After settling in Palestine as a
thirteen-year-old, he became engaged in Labor Party affairs as a youth and
was one of the founders of the Histadrut in 1920. By 1925 he was secretary of the Jerusalem Labor Council and later was one of the founders of
the Palmach. A member of the National Administration, he was Minister
of Agriculture of the provisional government and a member of the first
two Knessets. During the last four years of his life, he was a member of
the Jewish Agency Executive, heading its Absorption Department.

27. MOSHE KOLODNY

Moshe Kolodny (Kol), who was born in Pinsk, Russia, on May 28, 1911, settled in Israel in 1932. In Jerusalem at the time of the signing of the Proclamation, at the age of thirty-seven he was one of its youngest signers. Chairman of the Independent Liberal Party since 1959, Kol has been a member of four Knessets and Minister of Development and Tourism since 1966. He was a member of the Jewish Agency Executive from 1946 to 1966, and for many years head of its Youth Aliyah Department during which time he supervised the immigration to Israel of over 100,-000 children from Europe, Asia, Africa, and Latin America.

28. ELIEZER KAPLAN

Eliezer Kaplan was born in Minsk, Russia, in 1891 and died in Genoa, Italy, in 1952. Born into a prominent Zionist family, he visited Palestine in 1920 and settled there in 1923. An engineer by profession, he was associated with various economic and building institutions until he took charge of the economic and financial activities of the Jewish Agency in 1933, on whose behalf he floated the first large international loan for the Yishuv. He was Israel's first Minister of Finance, after having held the same post in the provisional government. At the time of his death he was Deputy Prime Minister. A close confidant of Ben-Gurion, he played a major role in financing the establishment of the Jewish state.

29. ABRAHAM KATZNELSON (NISSAN)

Abraham Katznelson (Nissan), born in Bobruysk, Russia, in 1888, died in Israel in 1956. A physician who had studied at the Universities of St. Petersburg and Moscow, he settled in Palestine in 1924, where he became director of the Health Department of the Zionist Executive and later the Va'ad L'umi. With the establishment of the provisional government, he became director of the Ministry of Health. He entered the diplomatic service in 1949, first as a member of the Israel delegation to the United Nations, and then, from 1950 until shortly before his death, as Minister to the Scandinavian countries.

30. PINHAS ROSENBLUETH

Pinhas F. Rosenblueth (Rosen) was born in Berlin May 1, 1887. A lawyer in Germany, he went into the private practice of law after settling in

1931 in Tel Aviv, where he also served on the City Council from 1935 to 1946. He was a member of the National Administration and became Minister of Justice in the Provisional government after having had a hand in the drafting of the Proclamation. He later served as Minister of Justice for ten years, 1949–51 and 1953–61, and until his resignation in 1968 he was a member of the first six Knessets, representing the Liberal Party of which he was for many years President. He played an important role in the construction of Israel's legal system.

31. DAVID REMEZ

David Remez was born in White Russia in 1886 and died in Jerusalem in 1951, the first signer of the Proclamation to die. After having gone to the University of Constantinople in 1911 with David Ben-Gurion and Yitzhak Ben Zvi to study law, he settled in 1913 in Palestine, where he became a leader of the Socialist Party. For thirteen years he was Secretary-General of Histadrut, and from 1944 to 1949 he was Chairman of the Va'ad L'umi. On March 1, 1948, at a plenary session of Va'ad L'umi, he proposed the establishment of the provisional government and on February 13, 1949, the eve of the first meeting of the Knesset, Remez adjourned the final session of Va'ad L'umi, marking the end of the provisional government, the final step in the transition toward an independent Jewish state. With Ben-Gurion he was one of the leaders of the move toward statehood. He was Minister of Communications of the provisional government and a member of the Israel Cabinet from 1949 to 1951, first as Minister of Communications and later as Minister of Education and Culture. He was a member of the first two Knessets.

32. BERL REPETUR

Berl Repetur was born in Rosin, Ukraine, August 7, 1902. After settling in Palestine in 1920, he was active on the Executive of the Histadrut and the management of the Histadrut-controlled Solel Boneh. In Tel Aviv for the signing ceremonies, he was active in the coordination of Haganah—for which he had been an organizer during the previous ten years—with the other underground defense groups. He was a member of the first Knesset.

33. MORDECAI SHOTTNER

Mordecai Shottner was born in 1904 in Sniatyn, Eastern Galicia, then a part of the Austrian Empire, and died in Jerusalem, April 18, 1964. He settled in Palestine in 1925 in Kibbutz Ein Charod. In the pre-state years he was an emissary abroad on many missions in behalf of *aliyah,* among them as Director of Youth Aliyah in London. Head of the Economic Department of the Va'ad L'umi at the time of the Proclamation, he worked closely with Finance Minister Eliezer Kaplan and was responsible for providing and storing food, fuel, construction material, and transportation vehicles, particularly in Jerusalem, a work he continued in the provisional government of the new state. Retiring from politics in 1949, he became a civil servant and served in the Finance Ministry as Custodian of Abandoned [Arab] Property, as head of the Development Authority and as Supervisor of Savings. He was also Chairman of the Jerusalem Economic Corporation.

34. BEN ZION (BENO) STERNBERG

Ben Zion (Beno) Sternberg was born in Kadivisti, Bukhovina (now Rumania) on May 26, 1894, and died in Tel Aviv, May 31, 1962. An officer in the Austrian Army, he was wounded four times and decorated with five medals for valor, and named a top Austrian war hero by the Emperor. President of the Revisionist Party in Rumania from 1925 to 1940, when he settled in Israel, he became a member of the Revisionist Central Committee. A lawyer and a banker, he was for many years a member of the boards of the banking firm, Jacob Japhet and Co. Ltd. and the Association of Foreign Investors in Israel. Following his membership on the National Council, in which capacity he signed the Proclamation, he served from 1949 to 1952 as head of the Department of Investments, Ministry of Commerce and Industry, and from 1952 on as Director of the Investment Center.

35. BEHOR SHALOM SHITRIT

Behor Shalom Shitrit was the only native Palestinian among the signers. Born in Tiberias in 1895, the son of a Sephardic family whose ancestors left Morocco for Palestine in the eighteenth century, he joined the police force of the Mandatory government in 1919 after the completion of his education (he was graduated as a rabbi). He became Police Chief of Tel Aviv in 1927, a Magistrate in 1935 after completing his legal studies at the Jerusalem Law School, and Chief Magistrate for the Tel Aviv area in 1945. The only representative of the Sephardic community in the provisional government, he was appointed Minister of Police and Minorities after independence. He was in the Cabinet as Minister of Police until his death in 1967, and had been a member of the Knesset since 1949.

36. CHAIM MOSHE SHAPIRA

Chaim Moshe Shapira was born in Grodno, Poland, on March 26, 1902, and died on July 10, 1970. A graduate of the Hildesheimer Rabbinical Seminary in Berlin, he settled in Palestine in 1925 after serving as a delegate to the World Zionist Congress. Undisputed leader of the National Religious Party, he was President of the World Movement of Mizrachi Hapoel Hamizrachi. In 1948 he was a member of the Jewish Agency Executive, having headed its Department of Immigration from 1934 to 1948. He was Minister of Immigration and Health in the provisional government in 1948, and was a member of every Cabinet until his death, at various times heading the Ministries of Immigration, Health, Social Welfare, Religious Affairs, and Interior. A member of the Knesset from its inception in 1949, he was the initiator of the United Religious Front at Israel's first election. In 1957 he was gravely injured when a deranged man threw a grenade at the Cabinet table in the Knesset.

37. MOSHE SHERTOK

Moshe Shertok, better known as Moshe Sharett, was actually the last of the twenty-five signers at the May 14 ceremonies, twelve of the signers not being present. Born in Kherson, Russia, on October 15, 1894, he died in Jerusalem on July 8, 1965. Settling in Palestine in 1906 at the age of twelve, Sharett studied law at the Ottoman University in Constantinople from 1913 until it was closed at the outbreak of World War I, after which he enlisted in the Turkish Army. He earned his B.S. at the London School of Economics.

Sharett—the literal meaning of his chosen Hebraic name is "service"—started his public career after World War I as Secretary of the Department for Land and Arab Affairs; he then served for six years on the staff of the newspaper *Davar*. The man who was to create Israel's Foreign Service first entered diplomacy in 1931 as Secretary of the Jewish Agency's Political Department under Chaim Arlosoroff, whom he succeeded two years later as head of the department following Arlosoroff's assassination.

A linguist and stylist of note—he was proficient not only in Hebrew, Yiddish, and Russian but in English, Arabic, Turkish, German, and French as well—Sharett was in large part responsible for the final text of the Proclamation. In the fifteen years preceding independence he was one of Israel's top spokesmen before various British Royal Commissions, the League of Nations, the British Colonial Office, the Anglo-American Committee of Inquiry, and the United Nations. One of Ben-Gurion's most intimate associates, he was also close to Dr. Chaim Weizmann, and often served as a liaison and conciliator between them. A member of the National Administration, Sharett became Foreign Minister of the provisional government and served as Israel's Foreign Minister until 1956, when he resigned after a fundamental split with Ben-Gurion. He was Israel's second Prime Minister, during the interval (1953–55) between Ben-Gurion's first retirement and return.

He remained a member of the Knesset until his death, but he never returned to active government leadership although he was always a powerful voice and a beloved figure in Zionism. For years he headed the Am'Oved Publishing Company, and in 1960 was elected Chairman of the Jewish Agency Executive, a post he held until his death.

ZEEV SHAREF

Zeev Sharef, though not a signer of the Proclamation, must nonetheless be included in any biographical listing of the signers. As the Secretary of the Political Department of the pre-State Jewish Agency, he became the Secretary of the National Administration and the Secretary of the provisional government when it came into being. As such it was he who, more than any other man, created the structure of Israel's first government and set the stage for the ceremonies at which the State of Israel officially came into being.

Sharef, who settled in Israel in 1925, was born in Isvor-Szeletin, Rumania, on April 21, 1906. In 1968 he assumed two major posts in the Cabinet of Prime Minister Levi Eshkol—Minister of Finance, a post he assumed on August 6, 1968, and Minister of Commerce and Industry, a post he had actually held since 1966. In 1969, in Mrs. Meir's Cabinet, Sharef became Minister for Housing. He was the first Secretary of the government, a position he filled with distinction until 1957. He has since been Civil Service Commissioner, Director General of the Prime Minister's office, and head of the Revenue Department of the Ministry of Finance. He was elected to the Knesset in 1965.

APPENDIX II: THE PROCLAMATION OF INDEPENDENCE *

IN THE LAND OF ISRAEL the Jewish people came into being. In this Land was shaped their spiritual, religious, and national character. Here they lived in sovereign independence. Here they created a culture of national and universal import, and gave to the world the eternal Book of Books.

Exiled by force, still the Jewish people kept faith with their Land in all the countries of their dispersion, steadfast in their prayer and hope to return and here revive their political freedom.

Fired by this attachment of history and tradition, the Jews in every generation strove to renew their roots in the ancient homeland, and in recent generations they came home in their multitudes.

Veteran pioneers and defenders, and newcomers braving blockade, they made the wilderness bloom, revived their Hebrew tongue, and built villages and towns. They founded a thriving society, master of its own economy and culture, pursuing peace but able to defend itself, bringing the blessing of progress to all the inhabitants of the Land, dedicated to the attainment of sovereign independence.

In 1897 the First Zionist Congress met at the call of Theodor Herzl, seer of the vision of the Jewish State, and gave public voice to the right of the Jewish people to national restoration in their Land.

This right was acknowledged in the Balfour Declaration on 2 November 1917, and confirmed in the Mandate of the League of Nations, which accorded international validity to the historical connection between the

---

* This is the text of the official English translation of the Israel Proclamation of Independence as it appears in the 1972 *Facts About Israel* published by Keter Books for the Information Division of the Israel Ministry for Foreign Affairs.

Jewish people and the Land of Israel, and to their right to re-establish their National Home.

The holocaust that in our time destroyed millions of Jews in Europe again proved beyond doubt the compelling need to solve the problem of Jewish homelessness and dependence by the renewal of the Jewish State in the Land of Israel, which would open wide the gates of the Homeland to every Jew and endow the Jewish people with the status of a nation with equality of rights within the family of nations.

Despite every hardship, hindrance and peril, the remnant that survived the grim Nazi slaughter in Europe, together with Jews from other countries, pressed on with their exodus to the Land of Israel and continued to assert their right to a life of dignity, freedom and honest toil in the Homeland of their people.

In the Second World War, the Jewish community in the Land of Israel played its full part in the struggle of the nations championing freedom and peace against the Nazi forces of evil. Its war effort and the lives of its soldiers won it the right to be numbered among the founding peoples of the United Nations.

On 29 November 1947, the General Assembly of the United Nations adopted a resolution calling for the establishment of a Jewish State in the Land of Israel, and required the inhabitants themselves to take all measures necessary on their part to carry out the resolution. This recognition by the United Nations of the right of the Jewish people to establish their own State is irrevocable.

It is the natural right of the Jewish people, like any other people, to control their own destiny in their sovereign State.

ACCORDINGLY WE, the members of the National Council, representing the Jewish people in the Land of Israel and the Zionist Movement, have assembled on the day of the termination of the British Mandate for Palestine, and, by virtue of our natural and historic right and of the resolution of the General Assembly of the United Nations, do hereby proclaim the establishment of a Jewish State in the Land of Israel—the State of Israel.

WE RESOLVE that, from the moment the Mandate ends, at midnight on the Sabbath, the sixth of Iyar 5708, the fifteenth day of May 1948, until the establishment of the duly elected authorities of the State in accordance with a Constitution to be adopted by the Elected Constituent Assembly not later than 1 October 1948, the National Council shall act as the Provisional Council of State, and its executive arm, the National Administration, shall constitute the Provisional Government of the Jewish State, and the name of that State shall be Israel.

THE STATE OF ISRAEL will be open to Jewish immigration and the ingathering of exiles. It will devote itself to developing the Land for the good of all its inhabitants.

It will rest upon foundations of liberty, justice and peace as envisioned by the Prophets of Israel. It will maintain complete equality of social and political rights for all its citizens, without distinction of creed, race or sex. It will guarantee freedom of religion and conscience, of language, education and culture. It will safeguard the Holy Places of all religions. It will be loyal to the principles of the United Nations Charter.

THE STATE OF ISRAEL will be prepared to cooperate with the organs and representatives of the United Nations in carrying out the General Assembly resolution of 29 November 1947, and will work for the establishment of the economic union of the whole Land of Israel.

WE APPEAL to the United Nations to assist the Jewish people in the building of their State, and to admit the State of Israel into the family of nations.

EVEN AMIDST the violent attacks launched against us for months past, we call upon the sons of the Arab people dwelling in Israel to keep the peace and to play their part in building the State on the basis of full and equal citizenship and due representation in all its institutions, provisional and permanent.

WE EXTEND the hand of peace and good-neighbourliness to all the States around us and to their peoples, and we call upon them to cooperate in mutual helpfulness with the independent Jewish nation in its Land. The State of Israel is prepared to make its contribution in a concerted effort for the advancement of the entire Middle East.

WE CALL upon the Jewish people throughout the Diaspora to join forces with us in immigration and construction, and to be at our right hand in the great endeavour to fulfil the age-old longing for the redemption of Israel.

WITH TRUST IN THE ROCK OF ISRAEL, we set our hands in witness to this Proclamation, at this session of the Provisional Council of State, on the soil of the Homeland, in the city of Tel Aviv, this Sabbath eve, the fifth day of Iyar, 5708, the fourteenth day of May, nineteen hundred and forty-eight.

APPENDIX III: DECLARATION OF
THE ESTABLISHMENT OF
THE STATE OF ISRAEL *

ERETZ ISRAEL was the birthplace of the Jewish people. Here their spiritual, religious and political identity was shaped. Here they first attained to statehood, created cultural values of national and universal significance and gave to the world the eternal Book of Books.

After being forcibly exiled from their land, the people kept faith with it throughout their Dispersion and never ceased to pray and hope for their return to it and for the restoration in it of their political freedom.

Impelled by this historic and traditional attachment, Jews strove in every successive generation to re-establish themselves in their ancient homeland. In recent decades they returned in their masses. Pioneers, *ma'pilim* [illegal immigrants] and defenders, they made deserts bloom, revived the Hebrew language, built villages and towns, and created a thriving community, controlling its own economy and culture, loving peace but knowing how to defend itself, bringing the blessings of progress to all the country's inhabitants, and aspiring towards independent nationhood.

In the year 5657 (1897), at the summons of the spiritual father of the Jewish State, Theodor Herzl, the First Zionist Congress convened and proclaimed the right of the Jewish people to national rebirth in its own country.

This right was recognized in the Balfour Declaration of the 2nd November, 1917, and re-affirmed in the Mandate of the League of Nations which, in particular, gave international sanction to the historic connection

* This English translation of the Proclamation or Declaration differs in a number of significant instances from the English translation as published in the *Official Gazette,* No. 1, of the fifth year of Iyar, 5708 (May 14, 1948).

between the Jewish people and Eretz-Israel and to the right of the Jewish people to rebuild its National Home.

The catastrophe which recently befell the Jewish people—the massacre of millions of Jews in Europe—was another clear demonstration of the urgency of solving the problem of its homelessness by re-establishing in Eretz-Israel the Jewish State, which would open the gates of the homeland wide to every Jew and confer upon the Jewish people the status of a fully-privileged member of the comity of nations.

Survivors of the Nazi holocaust in Europe, as well as Jews from other parts of the world, continued to migrate to Eretz-Israel, undaunted by difficulties, restrictions and dangers, and never ceased to assert their right to a life of dignity, freedom and honest toil in their national homeland.

In the Second World War, the Jewish community of this country contributed its full share to the struggle of the freedom- and peace-loving nations against the forces of Nazi wickedness and, by the blood of its soldiers and its war effort, gained the right to be reckoned among the peoples who founded the United Nations.

On the 29th November, 1947, the United Nations General Assembly passed a resolution calling for the establishment of a Jewish State in Eretz Israel; the General Assembly required the inhabitants of Eretz-Israel to take such steps as were necessary on their part for the implementation of that resolution. This recognition by the United Nations of the right of the Jewish people to establish their State is irrevocable.

This right is the natural right of the Jewish people to be masters of their own fate, like all other nations, in their own sovereign State.

ACCORDINGLY WE, MEMBERS OF THE PEOPLE'S COUNCIL, REPRESENTATIVES OF THE JEWISH COMMUNITY OF ERETZ-ISRAEL AND OF THE ZIONIST MOVEMENT, ARE HERE ASSEMBLED ON THE DAY OF THE TERMINATION OF THE BRITISH MANDATE OVER ERETZ-ISRAEL AND, BY VIRTUE OF OUR NATURAL AND HISTORIC RIGHT AND ON THE STRENGTH OF THE RESOLUTION OF THE UNITED NATIONS GENERAL AS-SEMBLY, HEREBY DECLARE THE ESTABLISHMENT OF A JEW-ISH STATE IN ERETZ-ISRAEL, TO BE KNOWN AS THE STATE OF ISRAEL.

WE DECLARE that, with effect from the moment of the termination of the Mandate, being tonight, the eve of Sabbath, the 6th Iyar, 5708 (15th May, 1948), until the establishment of the elected, regular authorities of the State in accordance with the Constitution which shall be adopted by the Elected Constituent Assembly not later than the 1st October, 1948, the People's Council shall act as a Provisional Council of State, and its executive organ, the People's Administration, shall be the Provisional Government of the Jewish State, to be called "Israel".

THE STATE OF ISRAEL will be open for Jewish immigration and for the Ingathering of the Exiles; it will foster the development of the country for the benefit of all inhabitants; it will be based on freedom, justice and peace as envisaged by the prophets of Israel; it will ensure complete equality of social and political rights to all its inhabitants irrespective of religion, race or sex; it will guarantee freedom of religion, conscience, language, education and culture; it will safeguard the Holy Places of all religions; and it will be faithful to the principles of the Charter of the United Nations.

THE STATE OF ISRAEL is prepared to cooperate with the agencies and representatives of the United Nations in implementing the resolution of the General Assembly of the 29th November, 1947, and will take steps to bring about the economic union of the whole of Eretz-Israel.

WE APPEAL to the United Nations to assist the Jewish people in the building-up of its State and to receive the State of Israel into the comity of nations.

WE APPEAL—in the very midst of the onslaught launched against us now for months—to the Arab inhabitants of the State of Israel to preserve peace and participate in the upbuilding of the State on the basis of full and equal citizenship and due representation in all its provisional and permanent institutions.

WE EXTEND our hand to all neighbouring states and their peoples in an offer of peace and good neighbourliness, and appeal to them to establish bonds of cooperation and mutual help with the sovereign Jewish people settled in its own land. The State of Israel is prepared to do its share in common effort for the advancement of the entire Middle East.

WE APPEAL to the Jewish people throughout the Diaspora to rally round the Jews of Eretz-Israel in the tasks of immigration and upbuilding and to stand by them in the great struggle for the realization of the age-old dream—the redemption of Israel.

PLACING OUR TRUST IN THE ALMIGHTY, WE AFFIX OUR SIGNATURES TO THIS PROCLAMATION AT THIS SESSION OF THE PROVISIONAL COUNCIL OF STATE, ON THE SOIL OF THE HOMELAND, IN THE CITY OF TEL-AVIV, ON THIS SABBATH EVE, THE 5th DAY OF IYAR, 5708 (14th MAY, 1948).

APPENDIX IV: THE SHERTOK DRAFT OF THE PROCLAMATION *

WHEREAS THE JEWISH PEOPLE, exiled by force from its land, the land of Israel, kept forth in all the generations of its exile, and in all the lands of its dispersion, and never bartered it for any other land, and never ceased from prayer and hope for ingathering its scattered ones, and for renewing its national independence;

And whereas, in every generation, the sons of the Jewish people strove to return to and possess their historic birthright until the pioneers of Israel in recent generations were privileged to go up to the land in masses, to occupy its soil, and to make its waste places blossom, to revive on it their Hebrew language and to establish a substantial settlement controlling its own economy and culture, dedicated to self-sufficiency, political independence and national growth;

And whereas the Jewish people succeeded in having its renewed independent life in the land of Israel recognized by a proclamation of the British government on November 2, 1917, which established the basis for the British Mandate over the land of Israel;

And whereas the Mandate, which was guaranteed by forty-two member nations of the League of Nations, recognized the historic tie between the Jewish people and the land and recognized the right of the Jewish nation to establish anew in the land of Israel its national homeland, to emigrate to it and to settle on its soil;

And whereas the persecutions which since then were inflicted upon the Jewish masses in various lands, and with the special cruelty of the

---

* A translation of the original handwritten version of the Proclamation in Hebrew as written by Moshe Shertok which was the basis for the document finally adopted. The handwritten version is in the possession of Moshe Guerary.

Holocaust which broke over their heads in Europe, in which millions of men, women and children were slaughtered, proved once again the necessity for a solution to the problem of the Jewish people by the renewal of independent nationhood in its own land in order that its gates should always be open to every Jew who had been persecuted and exiled, and in order that the Jewish people should begin to enjoy equal status as a national entity in the family of nations;

And whereas the Assembly of the United Nations, at its annual session, after diligent investigation and deep deliberation, affirmed the decision by a two-thirds majority on the 29th day of November, 1947, to establish a Jewish nation in the land of Israel;

And whereas the British government, which had been governing the land of Israel on behalf of the United Nations, relinquished its Mandate this day, and gave up the responsibility for administering the land;

And whereas the Jewish community in the land of Israel contributed a full share in the struggles of free and peace-loving nations against the forces of evil and slavery in the Second World War, and with the deeds of its strength and the blood of its soldiers, won for itself the right to establish a place for itself among the nations which were joined together in the United Nations charter;

And whereas the few European Jews who were saved, the people of the saving remnant, did not cease to strive for the land despite the Holocaust, danger, exile and imprisonment, and did not cease, demanding of the world their right to a life of honor, freedom and national uprightness in their national homeland;

Therefore, we, members of the National Council, representatives of the Zionist movement and the Jewish community in Palestine, gathered this day on a momentous occasion, and on the basis of the decision of the United Nations Assembly, do hereby proclaim to the Jewish people of the Diaspora and the entire world the establishment of a Jewish State in the land of Israel, to be named Medinat Yisrael.

We pledge that our country, Israel, will be established on the foundations of liberty, justice, and peace; open to Jewish immigration; granting complete equal social and political rights to all its citizens without regard to race or religion; dedicated to the development of the land for the benefit of all its inhabitants; guaranteeing freedom of religion, conscience, education and culture; protecting the Holy Places and the peoples of all faiths; and adhering to the principles of the United Nations Charter.

We accept the responsibility of dealing with all the members of the United Nations to help realize the Assembly decision and we call upon them to give aid to the Hebrew people in the building of its state and its defense. Despite the savage attack launched against us, and in the midst of the whirlwind of hate which encircles us, we call upon the Arab inhabitants of Israel to maintain peace and to take their part in the building of the land which offers them full citizenship. In the very midst of conflict, and even while we are repulsing evil aggression, we stretch out the hand of peace and friendship to the people of all neighboring countries and call upon them to end their conflict against the Hebrew people which aspires, as they do, for a life of freedom and independence in its land and is prepared to share in the progress of the entire Middle East.

We call upon the Hebrew Yishuv for supreme efforts and for the dedication of all their powers of soul and property, so that we may stand firm in the building of a community to replace the losses in Europe. To the Jewish people in all parts of the world, we issue a call to rally around the Yishuv, which is at war, and to come to its aid in its difficult time.

To the youth of our nation we raise our voice in a call to stand with us in this great moment of pride.

We determine that from this day forth, until it is possible to create instrumentalities of government and have regular elections, that the legal vacuum resulting from the end of the machinery of the Mandate will be temporarily filled by the National Council and the National Administration; that it will serve the needs of the people as the temporary government of the Jewish State, Israel.

This proclamation is attested by the signatures of the members of the Provisional Council, in the temporary capital, here in the city of Tel Aviv on this day, the 7th of Iyar, 5708, May 15, 1948.

BIBLIOGRAPHY OF
SUPPLEMENTARY READING

AGAR, HERBERT, *The Saving Remnant* (New York: Viking, 1960).

AMERY, LEOPOLD S., *My Political Life* (London: Hutchinson, 1953).

AVINOAM, REUVEN, *Such Were Our Fighters* (New York: Herzl Press, 1965).

BAR-DAVID, MOLLY LYONS, *My Promised Land* (New York: G. P. Putnam's Sons, 1953).

BAR-ZOHAR, MICHAEL, *Ben-Gurion, The Armed Prophet* (New York: Prentice-Hall, 1968).

BEIGIN, MENACHEM W., *The Revolt* (New York: Abelard-Schuman, 1951).

BELL, J. BOWER, *Besieged* (Philadelphia: The Chilton Co., 1966).

BEN-GURION, DAVID, *From the Vision of Statehood to War of Independence* (Jerusalem: Israeli Ministry of Defense, 1964).

——, *Israel: A Personal History* (New York: Funk & Wagnalls, 1971).

——, *Israel, Years of Challenge* (New York: Holt, Rinehart & Winston, 1963).

——, *Memoirs,* Compiled by Thomas R. Bransten (New York: World, 1970).

——, *Rebirth and Destiny of Israel* (New York: Philosophical Library, 1954).

BENTWICH, NORMAN, *For Zion's Sake* (Philadelphia: Jewish Publication Society of America, 1954).

——, *Israel Resurgent* (New York: Frederick A. Praeger, 1960).

——, *My 77 Years* (Philadelphia: Jewish Publication Society of America, 1961).

BENTWICH, NORMAN AND HELEN, *Mandate Memories, 1918–1948* (New York: Schocken, 1965).

BERGER, EARL, *The Covenant and the Sword* (Toronto: University of Toronto Press, 1965).

BERKMAN, TED, *Cast a Giant Shadow* (New York: Doubleday, 1962).

BERNSTEIN, MARVER H., *The Politics of Israel* (Princeton, N.J.: Princeton University Press, 1957).

BILBY, KENNETH W., *New Star in the Near East* (New York: Doubleday, 1950).

BISGYER, MAURICE, *Challenge and Encounter* (New York: Crown, 1968).

BLOOMFIELD, BERNARD M., *Israel Diary* (New York: Crown, 1950).

CARNEGIE ENDOWMENT FOR INTERNATIONAL PEACE, *Israel and the United Nations* (New York: Manhattan Publishing Co., 1956).

COHEN, GEULA, *Woman of Violence* (New York: Holt, Rinehart & Winston, 1966).

COHEN, ISRAEL, *The Rebirth of Israel* (London: E. Goldston Ltd., 1952).

COOKE, HEDLEY V., *Challenge and Response in the Middle East* (New York: Harper & Row, 1952).

CROSSMAN, RICHARD H. S., *A Nation Reborn* (New York: Atheneum, 1960).

CRUM, BARTLEY C., *Behind the Silken Curtain* (New York: Simon & Schuster, 1947).

DANIELS, JONATHAN, *Man from Independence* (Philadelphia: J. B. Lippincott, 1950).

DEKEL, EFRAIM, *Shai* (New York: Thomas Yoseloff, 1959).

DUGDALE, BLANCHE, *Arthur James Balfour* (London: Hutchinson, 1936).

DUNNER, JOSEPH, *The Republic of Israel* (New York: Whittlesey House, 1950).

EBAN, ABBA, *The Voice of Israel* (New York: Horizon Press, 1947).

ELIOT, GEORGE FIELDING, *Hate, Hope and High Explosive* (New York: Bobbs, Merrill, 1948).

ELSTON, D. R., *Israel* (London: Oxford University Press, 1963).

ESCO FOUNDATION FOR PALESTINE, *A Study of Jewish, Arab and British Policies* (New Haven, 1947).

ETHRIDGE, WILLIE, *Going to Jerusalem* (New York: Vanguard, 1950).

EYTAN, WALTER, *The First Ten Years* (New York: Simon & Schuster, 1958).

FEUER, LEON I., *Abba Hillel Silver: A Personal Memoir* (Cincinnati: American Jewish Archives, Vol. XIX, No. 2, November, 1967).

FINE, MORRIS, and SCHNEIDERMAN, HARRY, *American Jewish Year Book*, Vols. 49 and 50 (Philadelphia: Jewish Publication Society of America, 1949 and 1950).

FINK, REUBEN, *America and Palestine* (New York: American Zionist Emergency Council, 1944).

FRANKFURTER, FELIX N., *Felix Frankfurter Reminiscences* (New York: Reynal, 1960).

FUCHS, LAWRENCE, *The Political Behavior of American Jews* (Glencoe, Ill.: The Free Press, 1956).

GARCIA GRANADOS, JORGE, *The Birth of Israel* (New York: Alfred A. Knopf, 1948).

GLICK, EDWARD B., *Latin America and the Palestine Problem* (New York: Herzl Press, 1958).

GOLDMANN, NAHUM, *The Autobiography* (New York: Holt, Rinehart & Winston, 1969).

GOLDSTEIN, BERNARD, *The Stars Bear Witness* (New York: Viking, 1949).

GRAVES, RICHARD M., *Experiment in Anarchy* (London: Gollancz, 1949).

GREENSPUN, HANK, WITH ALEX PELLE, *Where I Stand* (New York: David McKay, 1966).

GRUBER, RUTH, *Destination Palestine* (New York: A.A. Wyn, 1948).

HABAS, BRACHA, *The Gate Breakers* (New York: Herzl Press, 1963).

HABER, JULIUS, *Odyssey of an American Zionist* (New York: Twayne, 1956).

HALPERIN, SAMUEL, *The Political World of American Zionism* (Detroit: Wayne State University Press, 1961).

HALPERN, BEN, *The Idea of the Jewish State* (Cambridge, Mass.: Harvard University Press, 1961).

HECHT, BEN, *Perfidy* (New York: Julian Messner, 1961).

HELLER, ABRAHAM M., *Israel's Odyssey* (New York: Farrar, Straus & Giroux, 1959).

HERTZBERG, ARTHUR, *The Zionist Idea* (New York: Doubleday, 1959).

HIRSCHMAN, IRA A., *Life Line to a Promised Land* (New York: Vanguard, 1946).

HIRSZOWICZ, LUKASZ, *The Third Reich and the Arab East* (Toronto: University of Toronto Press, 1966).

HOLLY, DAVID C., *Exodus 1947* (Boston: Little, Brown, 1969).

HOROWITZ, DAVID, *State in the Making* (New York: Alfred A. Knopf, 1953).

HULL, CORDELL, *The Memoirs* (New York: Macmillan, 1948).

HULL, WILLIAM L., *The Fall and Rise of Israel* (Grand Rapids, Mich.: Zondervan, 1954).

HUREWITZ, J. C., *The Struggle for Palestine* (New York: Norton, 1950).

HYAMSON, ALBERT, *Under the Mandate* (New York: British Book Centre, 1951).

ISRAEL OFFICE OF INFORMATION, *Israel's Struggle for Peace* (New York, 1960).

JABOTINSKY, VLADIMIR, *The Story of the Jewish Legion* (New York: Bernard Ackerman, 1945).

JACOBS, MONTY, *The Birth of the Israel Air Force* (New York: Shulsinger, 1965).

JANOWSKY, OSCAR I., *Foundations of Israel* (Princeton, N.J.: Van Nostrand, 1959).

JOSEPH, BERNARD, *British Rule in Palestine* (Washington, D.C.: Public Affairs Press, 1949).

JOSEPH, DOV, *The Faithful City* (New York: Simon & Schuster, 1960).

KAGAN, BENJAMIN, *The Secret Battle for Israel* (New York: World, 1966).

KATZ, SAMUEL, *Days of Fire* (New York: Doubleday, 1968).

KIMCHE, JON, *Seven Fallen Pillars* (New York: British Book Centre, 1951).

KIMCHE, JON AND DAVID, *Clash of Destinies* (New York: Frederick A. Praeger, 1960).

————, *The Secret Roads* (New York: Farrar, Straus & Giroux, 1955).

KOBLER, FRANZ, *The Vision Was There* (London: Lincolns-Prager, 1956).

KOESTLER, ARTHUR, *Promise and Fulfillment* (New York: Macmillan, 1949).

KURZMAN, DAN, *Genesis 1948* (New York: World, 1970).

LAPIDE, P.E., *A Century of U.S. Aliyah* (Jerusalem: Association of Americans and Canadians in Israel, 1961).

LEVENSOHN, LOTTA, *Vision and Fulfillment* (New York: Greystone, 1950).

LEVIN, HARRY, *Jerusalem Embattled* (London, 1950).

LITVINOFF, BARNETT, *Ben-Gurion of Israel* (New York: Frederick A. Praeger, 1954).

————, *To the House of Their Fathers* (New York: Frederick A. Praeger, 1965).

LLOYD GEORGE, DAVID, *War Memoirs* (London: Nicolson & Watson, 1933–36).

LORCH, NETANEL, *The Edge of the Sword* (New York: Putnam's, 1961).

MANUEL, FRANK E., *The Realities of American-Palestine Relations* (Washington, D.C.: Public Affairs Press, 1949).

MARDOR, MUNYA, *Haganah* (New York: New American Library, 1966).

MARLOWE, JOHN, *The Seat of Pilate* (London: Cresset, 1959).

MCDONALD, JAMES G., *My Mission to Israel* (New York: Simon & Schuster, 1951).

MEINERTZHAGEN, RICHARD, *Middle East Diary, 1917–1956* (New York: Thomas Yoseloff, 1960).

MELTZER, JULIAN, *Chaim Weizmann* (London: Weidenfeld & Nicholson, 1962).

MERIDOR, YA'ACOV, *Long Is the Road to Freedom* (New York: Barak Publications, 1961).

MILLIS, WALTER, Ed., *The Forrestal Diaries* (New York: Viking, 1951).

NADICH, JUDAH, *Eisenhower and the Jews* (New York: Twayne, 1953).

NAOR, MORDECAI, *History of Israeli Air Force* (Tel Aviv: Israel Ministry of Defense, 1965).

O'BALLANCE, EDGAR, *The Arab-Israeli War 1948* (New York: Frederick S. Praeger, 1957).

PARKES, JAMES, *End of an Exile* (New York: Library Publishers, 1954).

PARZEN, HERBERT, *A Short History of Zionism* (New York: Herzl Press, 1962).

PATAI, RAPHAEL, Ed., *Encyclopedia of Zionism and Israel* (New York: Herzl Press and McGraw-Hill, 1971).

PEARLMAN, MOSHE, *Ben-Gurion Looks Back* (New York: Simon & Schuster, 1965).

———, *The Army of Israel* (New York: Philosophical Library, 1950).

PERETZ, DON, *Israel and the Palestine Arabs* (Washington, D.C.: Middle East Institute, 1959).

PEROWNE, STEWART HENRY, *The One Remains* (New York: Dutton, 1955).

POLIER, JUSTINE W., and WISE, JAMES W., *The Personal Letters of Stephen Wise* (Boston: Beacon Press, 1956).

POLK, WILLIAM R., *The United States and the Arab World* (Cambridge, Mass.: Harvard University Press, 1965).

POLK, WILLIAM R., STAMLER, DAVID, and AFOUR, EDMUND, *Backdrop to Tragedy* (Boston: Beacon Press, 1957).

PROSKAUER, JOSEPH, *A Segment of My Times* (New York: Farrar, Straus & Giroux, 1950).

RACKMAN, EMANUEL, *Israel's Emerging Constitution* (New York: Columbia University Press, 1954).

REDDING, JOHN M., *Inside the Democratic Party* (New York, 1950).

REYNOLDS, QUENTIN, *Leave It to The People* (New York: Random House, 1948).

ROBINSON, JACOB, *Palestine and the United Nations* (Washington: Public Affairs Press, 1947).

ROSENBLATT, BERNARD A., *Two Generations of Zionism* (New York: Shengold, 1967).

ROSS, IRWIN, *The Loneliest Campaign* (New York: New American Library, 1968).

ROYAL INSTITUTE OF INTERNATIONAL AFFAIRS, *Great Britain and Palestine, 1915–1945* (London, 1947).

RUBIN, JACOB A., *Partners in State Building: American Jewry and Israel* (New York: Diplomatic Press, 1969).

RUSHBROOK, WILLIAM, *The State of Israel* (London: Faber, 1958).

SACHAR, HARRY, *Israel, the Establishment of a State* (New York: British Book Centre, 1952).

SACHAR, HOWARD M., *From the Ends of the Earth* (New York: World, 1964).

SAFRAN, NADAV, *The United States and Israel* (Cambridge, Mass.: Harvard University Press, 1963).

ST. JOHN, ROBERT, *Ben-Gurion* (New York: Doubleday, 1959).

———, *Shalom Means Peace* (New York: Doubleday, 1949).

SAMUEL, HERBERT L., *Groves of Change* (New York: Bobbs-Merrill, 1946).

SCHECHTMAN, JOSEPH B., *Rebel Statesman; The Jabotinsky Story* (New York: Thomas Yoseloff, 1956).

———, *The United States and the Jewish State Movement* (New York: Herzl Press, 1966).

————, *Zionism and Zionists in Soviet Russia* (New York: Zionist Organization of America, 1966).

SCHWARZ, LEO, *The Redeemers* (New York: Farrar, Straus & Giroux, 1953).

SHAREF, ZEEV, trans. by Julian Meltzer, *Three Days* (New York: Doubleday, 1962).

SHIHOR, SAMUEL, trans. by Julian Meltzer, *Hollow Glory* (New York: Thomas Yoseloff, 1960).

SILVERBERG, ROBERT, *If I Forget Thee, O Jerusalem* (New York: William Morrow, 1970).

SLATER, LEONARD, *The Pledge* (New York: Simon & Schuster, 1970).

SPICEHANDLER, DANIEL, *Let My Right Hand Wither* (New York: Beechurst, 1950).

STEIN, LEONARD, *The Balfour Declaration* (New York: Simon & Schuster, 1961).

————, *Weizmann and England* (London: W. H. Allen, 1964).

STEINBERG, ALFRED, *The Man From Missouri* (New York: Macmillan, 1962).

STEMBER, CHARLES HERBERT, ET AL, *Jews In the Mind of America* (New York: Basic Books, 1966).

STONE, I.F., *This Is Palestine* (New York: Boni & Gaer, 1948).

SUGRUE, THOMAS, *Watch for the Morning* (New York: Harper & Row, 1950).

SYKES, CHRISTOPHER, *Crossroads to Israel* (New York: World, 1965).

————, *Orde Wingate* (New York: World, 1959).

SYRKIN, MARIE, *Golda Meir* (New York: Putnam's, 1963).

TELLER, JUDD L., *The Kremlin, the Jews and the Middle East* (New York: Thomas Yoseloff, 1957).

TRUMAN, HARRY S., *Years of Trial and Hope,* Vol. II (New York: Doubleday, 1958).

TUCHMAN, BARBARA W., *Bible and Sword* (New York: New York University Press, 1956).

UDIN, SOPHIE A., *Palestine Year Book and Israeli Annual,* Vol. IV (New York: Zionist Organization of America, 1949).

UNIVERSAL JEWISH ENCYCLOPEDIA (New York: Universal Jewish Encyclopedia, Inc., ten volumes, 1939–43).

VASA, PINHAS, *Assignment Weapons* (Jerusalem: Israel Ministry of Defense, 1966).

VESTER, BERTHA H., *Our Jerusalem* (New York: Doubleday, 1951).

VICTOR, EDWARD, *Meyer Weisgal at Seventy* (London: Weidenfeld & Nicolson, 1966).

VILNAY, ZEV, *The Guide to Israel* (New York: World, 1960).

WEBSTER, CHARLES, *The Art and Practice of Diplomacy* (New York: Barnes & Noble, 1962).

WEISGAL, MEYER W., *Chaim Weizmann, a Biography by Several Hands* (New York: Atheneum Publishers, 1963).

————, . . . *So Far* (New York: Random House, 1972).

WEIZMANN, CHAIM, *Trial and Error* (Philadelphia: Jewish Publication Society of America, 1949).

WEIZMANN, VERA, *The Impossible Takes Longer* (New York: Harper & Row, 1968).

WILLIAMS, L.F.R., *The State of Israel* (New York: Macmillan, 1957).

ZAAR, ISAAC, *Rescue and Liberation* (New York: Bloch, 1954).

ZIDON, ASHER, *Knesset* (New York: Herzl Press, 1967).

INDEX

① ... 1897 ...

② ...

① ... 1897 ...